T0339541

'With a wealth of empirical evidence, this book exposes a fundamental choice underlying infrastructure development in Africa and elsewhere. Western development agencies emphasize institution-building, good governance and transparency with the result that investment is slow. In contrast, Chinese agencies seek to get it done so that investment is quick, but possibly unsustainable. Foreshadows a new era of geopolitics on the African continent.'

Carliss Y. Baldwin, Harvard Business School

'Africa's capacity for prosperity – which depends on the development of its infrastructure – is central to our way of life for a slate of reasons that are laid out in this terrific book. Gil explains what it will take to assure Africa's stability and security. This is essential reading for scholars interested in the construction of institutions, and for anyone interested in international political economy.'

Anita McGahan, University of Toronto

'*Duality by Design: The Global Race to Build Africa's Infrastructure* is a rich and thought-provoking work, whose data and conclusions illuminate the Latin American reflection on the challenges in the development of infrastructure projects.'

Rafael Valim, President of the Brazilian Institute of Legal Studies in Infrastructure (2014–16) and editor of the Brazilian Journal of Infrastructure

'Africa has a rapidly growing population, which is projected to reach forty percent of the world's population by 2100. This rapid growth in population highlights the challenges presented by an infrastructure which is already woefully inadequate. Drawing on an extensive body of research, this book focusses on the incompatibility between building institutions and capital investment, a fundamental question that will become ever more pressing as the growth in population demands better infrastructure to serve it. The Western approach of institutional building as a necessary precursor to investment contrasts sharply with the Chinese focus on speed of investment, a contrast which will become more sharply drawn and debated in the future. This book makes a valuable contribution to that debate and is essential reading for all those interested in the provision of infrastructure to meet the needs of the growing population of Africa.'

John Roberts, Former CEO of United Utilities

'This book presents a new, probing and insightful slant on the well-trodden discussion of the duality involved in promoting infrastructure development in emerging market countries with weak institutions. Rather than treating this as a dilemma with dichotomous alternatives, each with its pros and cons, this book delivers hard-hitting arguments and multiple case studies to support the idea of looking for hybrid organizational solutions that can maximize the benefits and minimize the risks of both approaches. It poses questions that can help to launch a new set of research and experimentation in support of the aspirations and goals of both the local populations and the grantee countries and multilateral institutions that support infrastructure development. It is well worth a read!'

Raymond E. Levitt, Kumagai Professor of Engineering Emeritus and Director of the Global Projects Center, Stanford University

'*Duality by Design* is critical reading for anyone wanting to understand the dynamics of global development and the options we have for constructing a world that serves us all. It provokes us to think differently, to see alternative paths to progress, to more deeply understand challenges in developing economies, to open a more expansive conversation and to engage in a constructive debate about our collective future.'

Sara Beckman, University of California, Berkeley

'*Duality by Design* lays out two development models that are implemented in a vast number of countries across Africa … One model puts emphasis on investments and enhanced capacity while the other follows an approach of aligning infrastructure investments with much-needed institutional capacity building and governance. Perhaps the two models will need to come together to make a real development impact for the continent. A great start for a much-needed discussion on effectiveness of infrastructure development in Africa.'

Benedict L. J. Eijbergen, The World Bank

'This book has brought together some of the finest minds within the academic and research fields, who have real knowledge and understanding of the complex challenges faced by governments and their international agencies, and global private sector enterprises in responding, at a relevant scale, to the infrastructure needs of Africa. They have articulated the risks of not meeting this urgent challenge, while clearly acknowledging the risks of doing so. They have dared to confront these challenges, and to think very radically; nothing less will suffice.'

Ian Reeves, Chairman, The Estates and Infrastructure Exchange, eix.global

Duality by Design

Africa's rapid population growth and urbanisation has made its socio-economic development a global priority. But as China ramps up its assistance in filling Africa's gap in very basic infrastructure, to the detriment of building institutions, warnings of a debt trap have followed. Building upon an extensive body of evidence, the editors argue that developing institutions and basic infrastructure when there is a shortfall of institutions in the environment are two equally desirable but organisationally incompatible objectives. In conceptualising this duality by design, a new theoretical framework proposes better understanding of the differing approaches to development espoused by traditional agencies, such as the World Bank, and emergent Chinese agencies. This new framing moves the debate away from the fruitless search for a 'superior' form of organising, and instead suggests looking for complementarities in competing forms of organising for development. For students and researchers in international business, strategic and public management, and complex systems, as well as practitioners in international development and business in emergent markets.

Nuno Gil is a professor of New Infrastructure Development at the Alliance Manchester Business School (AMBS), University of Manchester, where he is also the director of the AMBS Infrastructure Development Research Group. Gil's research focuses on the design of structures and processes to achieve collective ends. He teaches organisation design and megaproject leadership. He has worked or carried out research with various organisations, including CH2M HILL and Intel (USA); Rolls-Royce, BAA (now Heathrow Ltd), BP, Network Rail and London 2012 (UK); India's DDFCIL; Nigeria's LAMATA; Egypt's Ministry of Housing; Uganda's KCCA; and Brasil's IBEJI amongst many others.

Anne Stafford is Professor of Accounting and Finance at the Alliance Manchester Business School (AMBS), University of Manchester. Her research focuses on financial analysis and evaluation of public policy, particularly in relation to infrastructure governance and accountability. She has researched public- and private-sector organisations in the UK, Europe, North America and Africa and contributed to submissions to governments, the OECD, the World Bank and other global organisations.

Innocent Musonda is a professor of construction management at the University of Johannesburg in South Africa. He has worked for the public and private sectors in Botswana, South Africa and Zambia. He is founder and director of the Centre for Applied Research and Innovation in the Built Environment (CARINBE) at the University of Johannesburg, South Africa, and chairperson of the DII conference series on infrastructure development and investment in Africa.

Duality by Design

The Global Race to Build Africa's Infrastructure

Edited by

Nuno Gil
University of Manchester

Anne Stafford
University of Manchester

Innocent Musonda
University of Johannesburg

CAMBRIDGE
UNIVERSITY PRESS

University Printing House, Cambridge CB2 8BS, United Kingdom

One Liberty Plaza, 20th Floor, New York, NY 10006, USA

477 Williamstown Road, Port Melbourne, VIC 3207, Australia

314-321, 3rd Floor, Plot 3, Splendor Forum, Jasola District Centre, New Delhi - 110025, India

103 Penang Road, #05-06/07, Visioncrest Commercial, Singapore 238467

Cambridge University Press is part of the University of Cambridge.

It furthers the University's mission by disseminating knowledge in the pursuit of education, learning and research at the highest international levels of excellence.

www.cambridge.org
Information on this title: www.cambridge.org/9781108461030
DOI: 10.1017/9781108562492

© Cambridge University Press 2019

First published 2019
First paperback edition 2022

A catalogue record for this publication is available from the British Library

Library of Congress Cataloging in Publication data
Names: Gil, Nuno, editor. | Stafford, Anne, 1963– editor. | Musonda, Innocent, 1971– editor.
Title: Duality by design : the global race to build Africa's infrastructure / edited by Nuno Gil, University of Manchester, Anne Stafford, University of Manchester, Innocent Musonda, University of Johannesburg.
Description: Cambridge, United Kingdom ; New York, NY : Cambridge University Press, 2019. | Includes bibliographical references and index.
Identifiers: LCCN 2018060969 | ISBN 9781108473163 (alk. paper)
Subjects: LCSH: Infrastructure (Economics) – Africa. | Public works – Africa.
Classification: LCC HC800.Z9 C343 2019 | DDC 363.6096–dc23
LC record available at https://lccn.loc.gov/2018060969

ISBN 978-1-108-47316-3 Hardback
ISBN 978-1-108-46103-0 Paperback

Contents

Figures

Tables

Contributors

CLETUS AGYEMIN-BOATENG, University of Ghana Business School

BONIFACE BWANYIRE, Ethiopian Civil Service University

ANTON EBERHARD, University of Cape Town

NUNO GIL, University of Manchester

TRYNOS GUMBO, University of Johannesburg

NCHIMUNYA HAMUKOMA, Brenthurst Foundation Johannesburg

MARK HELLOWELL, University of Edinburgh

MALIK ISMAIL, University of Toronto

MUNDIA KABINGA, University of Cape Town

VALERIE J. KARPLUS, Massachusetts Institute of Technology

DONALD R. LESSARD, Massachusetts Institute of Technology

BRIAN LEVY, Johns Hopkins University and University of Cape Town

SAMUEL C. MACAULAY, University of Technology Sydney

JOCHEN MARKARD, Swiss Federal Institute of Technology Zurich

MADELEINE MCPHERSON, University of Toronto

MURRAY METCALFE, University of Toronto

REHEMA MSULWA, University of Manchester

WALTER MUSAKWA, University of Johannesburg

INNOCENT MUSONDA, University of Johannesburg

WAFAA NADIM, German University in Cairo

RICHARD DE NEUFVILLE, Massachusetts Institute of Technology

CHIOMA OKORO, University of Johannesburg

IGNACIO PÉREZ-ARRIAGA, Massachusetts Institute of Technology

JEFF PINTO, Penn State Erie

NINAD RAJPURKAR, Massachusetts Institute of Technology

AMY ROSE, Massachusetts Institute of Technology

ARUN SINGH, Massachusetts Institute of Technology

ANNE STAFFORD, University of Manchester

PAMELA STAPLETON, The University of Manchester

ROBERT STONER, Massachusetts Institute of Technology

BERNHARD TRUFFER, Swiss Federal Institute of Aquatic Science & Technology and Utrecht University

UWE WISSENBACH, European External Action Service

HAGEN WORCH, Swiss Distance University of Applied Sciences

Foreword

Most academics, if they are honest, will admit to living with a constant worry about the usefulness of the theoretical exercises that they engage in. Worse, there is the creeping guilt that what we enjoy doing may be contributing too little to the solution of really important problems in the world. The current volume goes a long way to reassure researchers and practitioners that what sound theory and careful research have something to say that is of value to those engaged in trying to solve important real-world problems.

The creation of infrastructure in Africa is arguably one of the top global concerns for this decade. 'Failure to act, and make Africa a better place to live and work, will saddle future generations with a major bottleneck to global sustainable development. Africa's struggle is our struggle', as the editors of the introduction to this volume eloquently put it.

The central organising idea that the editors use for this volume is that of duality – of the tension between jointly valuable but organisationally incompatible objectives. At the level of organisations, the typical poles of a duality are efficiency and effectiveness, revenue enhancement and cost efficiency, innovation and stability. At the level of national and regional policy, the duality this volume refers to is that between developing institutions and attracting capital.

Rules, procedures and norms for transparent and stable governance take time to build and require hard choices; attracting capital today creates pressures towards expediency. It is a very important tension and one that the organisation designers in many developing economies (i.e. their policy makers) will recognise, beginning as they often do from a situation of significant 'institutional voids'. The tension in this duality seems pronounced in the African context because of the role of China as a source of investment, a role which, at best, is agnostic to the development of local institutions and at worst, is suspected of aiming to keep them stunted. 'If the water is too clear, you don't catch any fish', as a senior Chinese administrator is reported to have said (p. 25). Shrill rhetoric from interested parties arrayed at the two poles of this duality has for too long seemed to have substituted for carefully collected evidence, creating an 'evidentiary void' of its own.

The authors contributing to this volume help fill this 'evidentiary void'. This does not mean they agree on everything. We learn of cases in which the prioritisation of institution building over capital investment has led to outcomes that can be classified as 'politics beats economics'. We also learn of situations in which rapid infrastructure development has occurred, but at the risk of jeopardising the long-term viability of institutions.

The most practically relevant insights to emerge from this book may be around strategies for dealing with this duality. Organisation science has pointed to three broad approaches to dealing with organisational dualities: structural separation (different parts of an organisation pursue different poles of the duality), temporal separation (the organisation pursues different poles at different times) and what is known as 'contextual ambidexterity' – finding ways to allow every organisational member to internalise the trade-offs and optimise them in a manner that benefits the organisation. It is interesting to speculate whether these different strategies, in the context of the current problem, are best adopted in the case of each different stakeholder (e.g. investors, multilateral funding agencies and national policy makers).

The evidence and concepts that Gil, Stafford and Musonda have curated here can serve as a very useful platform to improve the quality of discussion and decision making around what is clearly one of the grand challenges for the world today. I congratulate them for putting this work together, and thank them for this valuable contribution to public discourse.

PHANISH PURANAM

Acknowledgements

The development of an edited book is a collaborative work. When we set off on this journey, we did not know where we would end up. But we had friends and colleagues who endorsed our ideas and sustained us through this project. And so we started by relying on them, and the friends and colleagues of our friends and colleagues who were also doing good empirical work grounded in Africa's challenge to pursue socioeconomic development by filling critical gaps in basic infrastructure. Many of these scholars went on to become coauthors of chapters in this book, and reviewers of chapters from other authors. We are immensely grateful to them all for having taken up the challenge.

Other colleagues chose, for different reasons, to be bystanders, but often agreed to review submissions and offer the teams of authors detailed developmental reviews with actionable feedback. Syd Howell helped review papers related to energy issues; Jeff Pinto collaborated on papers with a strong emphasis on projects as the unit of analysis; Rehema Msulwa added domain knowledge of Africa to reviews; Deborah Bräutigam helped us with her expertise on the presence of Chinese organisations in Africa. And this list is not exhaustive: we would also like to mention Lavagnon Ika, Ashwin Mahalingam, Amira Osman, Owen Zinaman, Catrina Godinho, Colm Lundrigan, Matti Siemiatycki, Mathias Beck and any others who, if we've omitted to name you, we sincerely apologise for doing so. Many thanks go to all of you.

And also to Mark Kureishy, who painstakingly edited all our chapters for consistency of style and grammar. Ray Levitt, who struggled to find the time to join the editorial team, but strongly encouraged us all the way to pursue this project. At Cambridge University Press, our publisher, our sincere thanks go to Paula Parish, Stephen Acerra, Tobias Ginsberg, Grace Morris, James Gregory, Sunantha Ramamoorthy and Frances Tye who were part of our editing team and were both sympathetic to and understanding of the delays that we experienced. We are also grateful to the Alliance Manchester Business School for financial support. And send our thanks, too, to the three anonymous reviewers who endorsed our original proposal for this project.

Last, but certainly not least, we thank our families for also making this journey with us and, moreover, putting up with long hours of work that kept us away from them: Maria, Francisca, Joaquim, Luis, Simão, Patricia, Nkatya, Nkumbu, Santi, Chris and Catherine – all of you, in your own ways, are part of the team too. We could not have done this without you.

Thank you.

1   Duality by Design: The Global Race to Build Africa's Infrastructure

Nuno Gil, Anne Stafford and Innocent Musonda

Mahhamba Ndopfu

('The new dawn')

This book starts from the idea that much can be learned about the design of new forms of organising, theoretically and empirically, by examining a phenomenon central to the global order: Africa's struggle to bridge a growing gap between supply and demand for basic infrastructure. A gap linked, amongst other factors, to the rapid growth of the continent's population, projected to reach 40 per cent of the world's population by 2100.[1] Infrastructure is a vast class of capital-intensive technologies that input into a wide range of productive processes that generate positive externalities and social surplus. Whether it is about transport (airports, railways and roads); utilities (power, water, sanitation and telecoms); or social assets (social housing, schools and hospitals), most forms of infrastructure are durable public goods, shared in use by many people and organisations. This is the fundamental attribute that makes infrastructure technology a source of broad value creation and appropriation.[2] This attribute also explains the role of infrastructure technology in enabling economic growth and social development and in equipping societies for climate change. So it is incumbent on those who provide assistance to development, and on the African policy makers themselves, to fill the gap in basic infrastructure. Failure to act, and failure to make Africa a better place to live and work, will saddle future generations with a major bottleneck to global, sustainable development. Africa's struggle is our struggle.

In this book, we argue that there is a fundamental duality in the design of the inter-organisational contexts set up to tackle this grand societal challenge of our times. Design dualities exist when organisations wish to

---

[1] Africa's 2017 population was around 1.3 billion, 16.6 per cent of the world's population. The UN (2017) projects it will double into a quarter of the world's population by 2050, and by 2100 it will reach 4.5 billion; together with Asia's population, projected to reach 4.8 billion by 2100, the two regions are projected to represent around 82 per cent of the world's population by 2100.

[2] Frischman (2012).

pursue two objectives that are jointly desirable, but they struggle to reconcile the two because the organisational design attributes that underlie one objective tend to be incompatible with the attributes of the other,[3] for example, whether to exploit or to explore; to integrate or to differentiate? Faced with difficulties in designing organisations in such a way as to pursue dualities, organisational architects choose to focus on one of the poles, as opposed to aiming for both; so, they end up choosing 'gains from focus' at the expense of 'gains from ambidexterity'.

The empirical studies curated for this book on global efforts to bridge Africa's gap between supply and demand for basic infrastructure reveal a duality between *building institutions* and *building technology* – two equally desirable objectives that turn out to be organisationally incompatible. Both institutions (the prescriptions created and used by humans to orga- nise all forms of interaction[4]) and basic infrastructure (the technology needed for the functioning of a modern society) are key enablers of socio- economic development.[5] But building robust institutions is time- consuming and costly, and requires orderliness and transparency. In contrast, adaptability and opacity rule organisational design and evolu- tion in order to enable quick development of new capital-intensive tech- nology. Faced with difficulties in reconciling these two attributes, the organisations set up to promote development choose to focus on either pole of the duality.

To make sense of this duality *by design* we need to attend to the newly emerging global order. China is rising to become the world's biggest economy, whilst the share of the global economy of the advanced economies, hobbled by fiscal pressures and populism, shrinks. This shift has given African policy makers agency to choose between two groups of intermediaries – the development agencies that broker resource exchanges between the recipient country governments, and primary donors (taxpayers) and contractors.[6] 'Traditional' intermedi- aries include multilateral organisations such as the World Bank and the development agencies that are fully owned by the advanced econo- mies; the 'emergent' intermediaries are mainly associated with the eco- nomic rise of China (Bräutigam 2009, 2011). Chinese assistance to the

---

[3] Lawrence and Lorsch (1967); Evans and Doz (1989); Birkinshaw and Gibson (2004); Smith and Tushman (2005); Gulati and Puranam (2009).
[4] Ostrom (1990), North (1990).
[5] To the extent that the Global Competitiveness Index framework of the World Economic Forum (2017) lists institutions and infrastructure as the first two pillars of basic requirements.
[6] Martens (2005); McDermott, Corredoira and Kruse (2009); Mair, Marti and Ventresca (2012).

development of Africa already equals that disbursed by the World Bank and dwarfs the assistance disbursed by the advanced economies. Irrespective of the intermediary, the higher-order goal is the same – socio-economic development. Yet, the priorities for action differ immensely. In the organisational contexts enabled by traditional credit, the emphasis is on building institutions, but this emphasis shifts to technology building when the Chinese credit is involved. And since the design attributes underlying the two objectives are incompatible, the leading participants choose to focus coordinated collective action on one objective or the other.

The choice of focus is rooted in the differing preferences of the intermediaries and in the self-interests of the recipients. Traditional assistance to development is conditional on two factors: First, on Western ideals of 'good' governance – transparency, accountability, inclusiveness, equity and the rule of law; and second, on the idea that development projects, the typical form whereby assistance is disbursed as this gives the intermediary leverage over inputs and activities, need to be delivered on time and within budget. But disbursing assistance under these institutional constraints is protracted because it requires mitigating many institutional voids. These voids correspond to the absence, or under-development, of the institutions of capitalism that support economic activity in advanced economies, e.g. efficient markets, strong regulation, independent judiciary, property rights and contractual enforcement mechanisms.[7] So, under this approach, organisational design choice is guided by the principles of orderliness and transparency; that is, building the institutions first, and the infrastructure second. In contrast, Chinese assistance is not tied to governance and project-management ideals, and so comes with limited conditionality.[8] The Chinese approach takes the local environment as a given and does not seek to change it.[9] Instead, the aim is to fast track new infrastructure development by exploiting those institutional voids, or artfully manoeuvring around them. With this model, the principles of adaptability and opaqueness rule choice in organisational design, and that results in the choice to build infrastructure first and build institutions second.

---

[7] Khanna and Palepu (1997; 2010). Of course, customary rules and traditions are also 'institutions' that play an important role in structuring human interactions; how they complement the institutions of capitalism is a debate for another place.

[8] Henderson (2008); Henderson, Appelbaum and Ho (2013).

[9] Bräutigam (2009, 2011).

By foregrounding this duality by design, we are not suggesting moral equivalence or the abandonment of principles entwined with the traditional approach. And neither are we suggesting that one approach is 'superior' to another, far from it. Indeed, we find equifinality, in that we argue both forms of organising are pursuing a similar superordinate goal – socio-economic development. Furthermore, we need to appreciate that the rise of a 'new' approach reflects the failure of the 'old' one to deliver. In fact, we still know little about how to organise for the tackling of grand challenges when there is a shortfall of institutions. What we are doing here is uncovering a duality that explains empirical regularities. We believe this duality offers a conceptual foundation for building a novel theory of organisational design with which to navigate institutional shortcomings.

But we are getting ahead of our story. We turn first to summarise the infrastructure gap facing Africa, and introduce our cognitive lens with which we propose to further our understanding of how to tackle this grand societal challenge. We then offer an overview of our empirical findings and the book's structure. Finally, we sketch the rudiments of a theory of (meta-)organising in environments with weak institutions, in light of the design duality revealed by this volume of studies on efforts to build basic infrastructure in Africa, a critical part of our global commons.

1.1   Africa's Infrastructure Gap: A Grand Challenge of Our Times

Africa is the last frontier in management research.[10] So it is not surprising, then, that the continent's struggle to bridge its infrastructure gap, whilst long a topic of interest to development economists, remains a largely untapped problem in management scholarship. Yet Africa's infrastructure gap is a useful setting in which to produce fresh evidence and insight into new forms of organising to tackle the grand societal challenges of our time – seemingly intractable problems that, in the way they intertwine technical and socio-economic elements, cannot effectively be addressed without coordinated and sustained effort from multiple actors.[11] Management literature suggests that tackling grand challenges requires unconventional approaches and novel ideas. But we still know little about how to design these actionable organisational solutions, even less so when there is a shortfall of institutions in the environment.

---

[10] Klingebiel and Stadler (2015); George et al. (2016).

[11] Some grand challenges are discrete, with a clear endpoint, like developing an HIV vaccine; others are broad and open-ended like building Africa's infrastructure, curing cancer or eliminating poverty; Colquitt and George (2011); Ferraro, Etzion and Gehman (2015).

The root causes of Africa's growing gap in basic infrastructure are well understood: a conflation of rapid population growth, fast urbanisation, climate change and a complicated colonial legacy. Assessments of this gap, estimated in monetary terms at \$130–170bn per year, with a related financing gap of \$68–108bn, are plentiful in the technocratic literature.[12] We find it useful to share some illustrative figures before introducing our core argument on tackling this grand challenge. For example:

- The International Energy Agency estimates that nearly half of Africa's population lack access to grid-connected electricity, and that the frequency of power outages experienced by industrial users costs about 2 per cent of the continent's GDP every year.[13]

- According to the UN, economic water scarcity is a widespread problem in sub-Saharan Africa, whilst physical water scarcity is problematic in northern Africa.[14]

- The proliferation of slums is a cause for global concern – 60 per cent of sub-Saharan Africa's urban population live in slums, lacking property rights and access to very basic public infrastructure and services.[15] With 90 per cent of urban growth happening in the developing world, particularly in Africa, the UN projects that by 2023 the number of slum dwellers will reach 2 billion (a quarter of the world's population). If the world fails to act, this will fuel poverty, social exclusion, radicalisation, hunger, gender inequality and mass migratory pressures; all of which threaten the global order.

- Equally worryingly, by 2100, Africa will host many of the largest megacities in the world. Metropolises such as Lagos, Kinshasa, Dar es Salaam, Khartoum and Niamey are all projected to exceed 55 million people.[16]

So it is not surprising that the UN asserts that investment in basic infrastructure is the most important requirement that must be fulfilled in order to meet its Sustainable Development Goals (SDGs). These goals include ending all forms of poverty, fighting inequalities, protecting the planet, tackling climate change and ensuring prosperity. The ninth SDG, in particular, spells out the need to build resilient, reliable and sustainable infrastructure, with a focus on affordable and equitable access for all. Importantly, a 1 per cent increase in the stock of basic infrastructure is estimated to correspond to a 1 per cent increase in GDP.[17]

With this backdrop, we turn now to examine this challenge through an organisational lens.

[12] African Development Bank (2018).   [13] IEA (2016); IRENA (2014).
[14] UNEP, 2010. Africa Water Atlas. United Nations Environment Programme (UNEP)
[15] UN-Habitat (2016); UN (2018).   [16] Hoorweg and Pope (2017).
[17] UN (2013); World Bank (1994); Esfahani and Ramirez (2003).

1.2   Institutional Voids, Intermediaries and Organising for Development

At the crux of the challenge of tackling Africa's infrastructure gap is the problem of navigating institutional voids. Institutional voids relate to the lack of developed prescriptions with which to organise interaction between humans and economic agents; institutions are interdependent with norms, but the two concepts are distinct. Norms are the cultural prescriptions that are part of the generally accepted moral fabric of societies. In contrast, the best way to think of institutions is in terms of the 'rules of the game' that individuals and organisations design, both formally and informally, to enable and constrain collective and individual action. Broadly, these rules encompass three dimensions. They clarify:

- who the participants are in a set of interactions, their distinctive roles and how to achieve the superordinate goals that unify the participants.
- the arrangements that monitor interactions between participants within an organisational system and with external stakeholders, as well as the arrangements that are used to assess the performance of the system in relation to the identifiable system-level goals; and
- the arrangements by which the consequences of non-compliance are established, how conflicts between participants and between participants and external stakeholders are adjudicated, and how penalties for non-compliance are enforced.

In developing countries, the under-development or absence of the institutions of capitalism, which enable and support economic activity in advanced economies, creates institutional voids.[18] Institutional voids hinder the mechanisms that allow resource exchanges, increasing the transaction costs for businesses and the state. These voids include:

- Inefficient markets for capital, skilled labour and products.
- Poor and under-developed regulation.
- Ill-defined property rights.
- Weak systems of checks and balances; the so-called non-executive institutions of accountability, capable of constraining arbitrary action by the political leadership and the public bureaucracy.
- Weak rule of law and independent judiciary, which are needed to act as impartial third-party structures in the arbitration of conflict, enforcement of legal contracts and resolution of disputes.
- Absence of competitive, free and fair elections.

---

[18] Khanna and Palepu (1997, 2010).

- Limited openness in the way civil society operates and information flows, due to institutional constraints imposed on the media and on freedom of information.
- Emphasis on the conferral of patronage in the way political parties are organised.

Gaps in basic infrastructure are in themselves a class of physical or 'hard' institutional void that are challenging to navigate. A lack of transport infrastructure complicates the flow of goods and people, making it harder for individuals and organisations to coordinate action, cooperate and trade; an unreliable power supply deters private investment and undermines productivity; lack of basic social infrastructure makes it harder to develop and retain talent, tackle gender inequality and poverty, and so build local capabilities. And yet, basic infrastructure voids also hold opportunities for multiple public and private actors to work together to create and appropriate value. In the short-term, new infrastructure development projects are a boost to the local economy and create lucrative opportunities for private firms, as either suppliers or development partners. Further, in the long-term, new infrastructure are common goods that can be leveraged to promote societal prosperity at large. But regrettably, corrupt actors also see in new infrastructure development projects opportunities for rent-seeking by breaking the law and pursuing informal private gains at the expenses of the common good.

The lack of infrastructure and other institutional voids remain a feature of most African states. Of course, Africa is not a homogeneous continent. Around half of African states have already achieved middle-income status, and in many others, a democratic central government has devolved power to local authorities.[19] Still, most African states are settings where deep-seated aspects of neo-patrimonial governance enable the local elites to concentrate vast amounts of political, economic and, even, juridical and military power.[20] Helping African states and private firms build infrastructure and navigate the institutional voids are the intermediaries. In the infrastructure sector, development agencies play this role by brokering the resource exchanges necessary for the local authorities to build capital-intensive public goods. This occurs to the extent that assistance to development as a source of revenue (including official aid but also export credits and loans) is roughly 10 per cent of the GDP for many emerging economies. These intermediaries fall into two categories.

The 'traditional' intermediaries provide about two thirds of development assistance; these include development agencies owned by the advanced economies, and multilateral agencies such as the World Bank.

---

[19] African Development Bank (2014).
[20] Chabal and Daloz (1999); Erdmann and Engel (2006).

These traditional intermediaries make assistance conditional on the recipients conforming to Western standards of 'good' governance and project management.[21] If the recipients fail to meet these conditions they cannot qualify for assistance, or the development agencies apply pressure, i.e. by threatening to terminate assistance, actually terminating it or reducing it. In other words, traditional agencies act as open-system intermediaries that seek to both create benefits for parties beyond a restricted set of system participants, and to improve the general institutional environment.[22]

The other third of assistance to development comes from the 'emerging' intermediaries – the countries that lie outside the OECD Development Assistance Committee. China bears by far the greatest weight in this group. Assessing assistance disbursed by China (mostly in the form of buyer's credits and concessional loans) – as opposed to pledges of assistance yet to be committed – is difficult, as the Chinese authorities are very secretive. However, reliable figures suggest that assistance from China in Africa will soon exceed assistance disbursed by the World Bank; Chinese assistance also dwarfs that from Western agencies.[23] Assistance provided by intermediaries such as the China Eximbank and the China Development Bank comes with limited conditionality.[24] This is not to say, though, that the Chinese intermediaries act as closed-system intermediaries, only seeking benefits for the participants in the organisational contexts enabled by Chinese credit. This is not the case. Instead, Chinese assistance seeks to replicate the successful model of Japanese assistance used to develop China decades earlier, and so the Chinese loans tend to be tied only to purchasing and importing from China as much technology and as many services as possible.[25]

Much has been written in the economic development literature of the last decade about how, with the economic rise of China, African governments have gained agency to choose between two competing forms of intermediation.[26] Before we develop our argument from an organisational

---

[21] Good governance is one of a broader set of prescriptions on how to engineer development that became known as the 'Washington Consensus' in the early 1980s. Other prescriptions include a neo-liberal agenda of economic reform, promoting less government, the benefits of markets and the importance of avoiding excessive inflation, excessive budget deficits and overvalued exchange rates. The Washington Consensus has since lost its allure, but assistance to development by traditional donors remains conditional on good governance; UN (1995); Burnside and Dollar (2000); Hermes and Lensink (2001); Rodrick (2006).

[22] Mair and Marti (2009); Dutt et al. (2016).

[23] From 2000 to 2015, US$63 billion were disbursed by the Export-Import Bank of China (China Eximbank) against US$1.7 billion by the USA Eximbank; in 2015, the World Bank provided US$14.3 billion of loans to Africa, a figure similar to the finance committed by China; Eom et al. (2017).

[24] Henderson (2008); Henderson, Appelbaum and Ho (2013).

[25] Bräutigam (2009, 2011).

[26] Hernandez (2017); van Dijk (2009); Woods (2008); Tan-Mullins, Mohan and Power (2010).

perspective, we summarise here the gist of this unresolved debate: On one side are scholars who see Chinese assistance as allowing profligate African states to build up unsustainable levels of debt, retain weak financial, economic and political governance, and occasionally infringe human and civil rights. For harsher critics, Chinese assistance is nothing more than a 'narrow elite business dialogue' and 'rogue aid', serving an opaque clique of interests dominated by informal and personal relationships.[27] China's true motives for cooperation with Africa are also questioned, particularly around the use of natural resources as collateral in return for credit, the so-called 'resource for infrastructure deals'.

Yet other scholars argue that China-bashing is hypocritical and only serves to bolster Western interests. They claim that Western assistance to development is dogmatic and inflexible, that good governance requirements increase transaction costs too greatly and that Western assistance's impact on socio-economic development has been negligible. And so, in their view, China provides much-needed investment in critical infrastructure; brings technical and commercial know-how and widens market access; and quickly completes the new infrastructure necessary for development without any tiresome strings attached. Disagreements notwithstanding, there is agreement that the availability of alternative sources of credit has strengthened the bargaining power of African states in their negotiations for assistance to development. This gained agency raises the question of whether a 'race to the bottom' will ensue in terms of the conditions offered to borrowers who are of strategic importance to both groups of intermediaries.[28]

1.3   Using Organisational Design to Navigate Institutional Voids

The debate amongst development scholars on the new global order is instructive, but leaves out issues that are important from an organisational design perspective. Broadly speaking, intermediaries enable public agencies and private firms to come together in actor-networks unified by an identifiable system-level goal. But environments with poor institutions are a boundary condition that lies outside most extant organisational design studies. Hence, our understanding remains incipient on the choices that organisational designers need to make to navigate institutional voids. To further our understanding of this issue, we first need to amass evidence in the tradition of inductive research. Armed with data assembled through

---

[27] Naim (2007).   [28] Mohan and Lampert (2013); McLean and Schneider (2014).

painstaking fieldwork, we can cycle between more data and theory to identify relevant constructs, propose relationships that link those constructs and develop new underlying theoretical arguments on how those logical relationships illuminate general phenomena.[29] So, empirical studies about Africa's struggle to build basic infrastructure are useful to help us develop the rudiments of a theory on designing organisations to navigate institutional voids.

This volume of empirical studies reveals efforts to mobilise a diversity of organisational structures in order to fill Africa's infrastructure gap, such as: markets, to address the lack of power-generation capacity; authority hierarchies, to develop new railway lines; alliances, to build new hospitals; self-organising structures, to upgrade informal settlements; and other hybrid forms of organising. This diversity is not surprising. Indeed, it mirrors the diversity of the designed structures by which advanced economies pursue similar goals. Given that the focal problems have differing attributes, it is predictable to find differing structures designed to help economise on transaction costs and leverage local capabilities.[30] Furthermore, African states are not alike from an institutional perspective, another factor contributing to organisational diversity. Changing institutions is also costly and time-consuming and those transaction costs are a source of organisational diversity.[31] Grand-challenge task environments also require both a high degree of differentiation to attend to the different facets of the tasks and a high degree of integration amongst the participants in order to achieve desirable outcomes – two attributes that also contribute to organisational heterogeneity.[32]

Our goal here, then, is not to explain this diversity of forms of organizing to tackle Africa's infrastructure gap. Rather, we were driven by the question as to whether we could identify any general underlying patterns in the way these differing structures sought to tackle this grand challenge. Could we, then, dig below this diversity to identify patterns in the way these structures were designed to adapt to their environment? As we probed deeper into the evidence amassed for this book, a pattern did emerge. All the studies illuminate organisational contexts set up to ultimately promote socio-economic development by way of tackling basic infrastructure. Yet the evidence leveraged to explain the extent to which these organisations succeeded or failed to achieve their objectives suggest the existence of two fundamentally different approaches to navigating institutional voids. One group of studies focuses the analysis of

---

[29] Eisenhardt, Graebner and Sonenshein (2016).
[30] Williamson (1985); Ostrom (1990).   [31] Libecap (1989).
[32] Knudsen and Srikanth (2014).

organisational success or failure on the extent to which the participants managed or did not manage to fill the institutional voids in the environment before building the infrastructure. Another group of studies advances explanations for organisational success or failure that are rooted in the way those very same institutional voids were exploited in order to build the infrastructure.

But before we turn to our argument, and in the tradition of inductive research, we offer an overview of the evidence collated across the next twelve chapters. The studies differ in that some touch more on technological aspects, whereas others focus on the institutional issues. Irrespective, though, of the cognitive lens deployed to guide data collection and analysis, all the studies offer fresh evidence on organising to build basic infrastructure, from transport and energy, to hospitals and social housing. As we worked to make sense of the findings, it dawned on us that we should organise this book according to whether the focus was on building institutions or building infrastructure – a duality to which we return after presenting the findings.

1.3.1 Building Institutions before Building Infrastructure (Part I)

Part I offers a set of empirical studies focused on inter-organisational contexts enabled by traditional intermediaries. Symptomatic of the issues with an organisational focus on building institutions, the emphasis of most studies is on the struggle in these contexts to fill the infrastructure gap that they are targeting. The delays are rooted in difficulties to build first institutions and capabilities, and, thus, difficulties in building markets, polycentric structures and strengthening regulation.

Specifically, Chapter 2, by Worch et al., adopts a 'capability perspective' to explain the failure to change and develop institutions. The authors ground their insights on South Africa's electricity crisis between 2005 and 2008, when institutional difficulties with reforming the state's monopolistic national electric utility, Eskom, led to multiple power outages. The institutional reform aimed to create a competitive market to attract private investment in order to develop power-generation capacity, expand the distribution and transmission network, and ameliorate the coal-supply chains. But the analysis reveals the unintended consequences of the reform, such as a substantial loss of critical competences, skills and experience within Eskom, which merely exacerbated the energy crisis. The main insight is that institutional changes come with an added risk of letting an existing capability gap grow further, and, once lost, local capabilities are hard to regain because the gaps take time to identify and resolve.

Chapter 3, by Hamukoma and Levy, also focuses on institutional reforms as a prerequisite to filling infrastructure gaps. They, too, ground their insights on the South Africa energy crisis. They trace a six-year delay in the implementation of the new energy policy to a conflict between powerful political stakeholders with diverging visions – an unresolved conflict exacerbated by the lack of dispute-resolution mechanisms in the environment. The study reveals difficulties with reconciling competing political interests, between letting the market set energy prices to attract private investment and keeping energy affordable to reduce poverty. The authors note that, in the end, 'politics trumped economics', leaving South Africa's power industry overwhelmingly vertically integrated and controlled by Eskom, the state-owned utility – and so, after all these years, the much-sought institutional reform is yet to happen.

Karplus et al. yield a similar insight in Chapter 4, on the institutional enablers of energy system transition. Their research is grounded on the expansion of solar photovoltaic power capacity in eight African countries. The analysis reveals that institutional voids, if successfully navigated with the help of intermediaries, are not always impediments to technological progress. For example, development agencies can substitute for lack of capital markets, or a market reform can overcome vested interests in the organisational status quo. But the authors also note that seizing technological opportunities in sustainable ways requires institutional reform in order to enable efficient markets and competitive procurement – and, as their evidence shows, these institutional reforms take a long, long time to implement.

Chapter 5, by Rose et al., picks up on the problem of ameliorating existing institutions to make them effective. The authors ground their argument on the Southern African Power Pool (SAPP) – the oldest and most advanced electricity market in Africa. Their research shows the SAPP has the potential to enable resource-rich countries to export power to countries with limited resources, and so improve security of supply for participants and reduce the cost of providing reserves. But, twenty years after its inception, the SAPP still struggles to encourage capital investment and reform of national policies because the participants cannot agree the design of contracts, and the transaction costs remain too high. Difficulties in reconciling the efforts of the states to resolve their power issues are traced to the lack of a cross-border body with the authority to harmonise national regulations and policies, whilst deferring implementation to the states. The authors conclude by suggesting that a more polycentric structure could encourage cooperation in the agreement of decisions on investment priorities, but its creation is hampered by a gap in local capabilities.

Adopting a technological perspective, Chapter 6, by Ismail, Metcalfe and McPherson, argues that innovation is creating new opportunities to fill infrastructure gaps. But the authors also recognise that institutional reform is a prerequisite to seizing those opportunities. Their study focuses on Zambia's growing gap in power-generation capacity, due to population growth and climate change. The analysis points to hybrid technological paths, which combine capital-intensive technology, e.g. large-scale solar and wind generation, with decentralised solutions, e.g. off-grid solar. But implementing this idea requires setting up a hybrid organisational system capable of concomitantly navigating different sets of institutional voids. The authors suggest working both with traditional intermediaries to promote decentralised solutions and with emergent intermediaries geared to capital-intensive developments – an idea, therefore, that overcomes the organisational incompatibility that underlies the two poles of the duality.

Chapter 7, by Hellowell, looks into a different organisational structure – alliances between the public and private sectors, or so-called public–private partnerships (PPPs). The author grounds his study on a PPP contract for a new hospital and a range of core clinical services in Lesotho; PPP is a form of organising much promoted by the Western intermediaries. But the analysis illuminates how capability gaps got in the way of equitable distribution of value. Specifically, the study reveals how a PPP once labelled 'the future of healthcare delivery on the African continent' became a major source of budgetary uncertainty and a demanding pull on the government's scarce resources. Hellowell traces difficulties in ensuring an equitable distribution in value appropriation back to a failure to first build the state's contractual capabilities.

Along the same lines, Chapter 8, by Stafford, Stapleton and Agyemin-Boateng, reveals the urgency of improving PPP governance. The study looks at five PPPs in Ghana, a country that ranks in the top half on measures of good governance in Africa. Yet the study reveals that in order to accelerate much-needed infrastructure developments, some PPPs have exploited institutional voids to avoid transparency in the processes of project choice and public procurement, or to negotiate contracts in dubious ways. Their findings leave it unclear whether the long-term value of the public goods will outweigh the short-term public bads. But, as the authors claim, without improvements aiming to increase accountability, e.g. the creation of independent agencies staffed with a small group of well-paid technocrats, the situation is unsustainable.

The focal problem informing the last two chapters in Part I is the growth of informal settlements. Here, the beneficiaries of aid are the poorest of the poor, and because investments are non-revenue-generating, solutions cannot be found in market forces. In Chapter 9, by Nadim, the effectiveness of self-governance is contrasted with failed centralised approaches. The study is grounded on efforts to fill gaps in affordable housing in Greater Cairo, Africa's largest city by population. The analysis shows that centralised approaches undertaken by an authoritarian state produced many 'ghost cities' as a result of ignoring the needs and interests of the poor. In contrast, self-governance enabled the poor to build informal mixed-use buildings, combining residential and work uses – a sustainable, flexible model of zero-commuting housing. But the study does not suggest that self-governance is *the* solution: informal settlements remain a cause of extreme poverty and social inequality.

This part concludes with Chapter 10, by Gil and MacAulay, in which the authors introduce the idea of collective action under the shadow of contractual governance. The research is grounded on a participatory approach to upgrading informal settlements in Greater Cairo. The analysis reveals how multiple resourceful actors – state, donors, intermediaries, suppliers and NGOs – forged a set of legal contracts to upgrade informal settlements. Contractual governance was then leveraged to grant the poor decision rights in resource allocation. The study shows this hybrid structure succeeds in encouraging mutual trust and norms of cooperation to flourish, a prerequisite for the poor to volunteer their knowledge, time and effort – informal resources much needed to identify real problems and co-produce sustainable solutions. Another advantage of this structure is that it economises on the transaction costs that would otherwise be necessary to resolve the ill-defined property rights of the poor. But questions remain as to whether this hybrid structure can be scaled up and remain effective.

We turn now to summarise the findings at the other pole of the duality.

1.3.2   *Building Infrastructure before Building Institutions (Part II)*

The second part of this book offers a collection of empirical studies on inter-organisational contexts formed to tackle Africa's infrastructure gap, as enabled by Chinese credit. Some studies document the rapid development of new railways, whilst others illuminate organisational struggles and failures in attempts to fast-track new infrastructure developments. In all cases, though, there have been limited efforts to change the institutions in the environment and there is no certainty of the sustainability of the technological outcomes.

Specifically, Chapter 11, by Wissenbach, argues that designing a powerful, centralised organisational structure to fill an infrastructure gap is a double-edged sword. Wissenbach grounds his insights on the

475-km-long railway line linking the port of Mombasa to Nairobi – an infrastructure built by the Kenyan state with Chinese assistance, initially designed as part of a broader railway network to boost transport capacity in the East Africa region. The analysis traces the development of the railway line, which took place in a record four years, to a hierarchical authority controlled by the president of Kenya. This centralised structure had the capability to unilaterally resolve disputes, adapt to uncertainty, mobilise state resources quickly and circumvent problems caused by ill-defined property rights. But the high speed in getting things done was achieved at the expense of transparency, accountability, probity and equitability in value allocation. It also remains unclear whether the railway will ever catalyse broader benefits, since the centralised approach failed to encourage collaboration and coordination with the neighbouring countries and other stakeholders.

Chapter 12, by Musonda et al., offers a more optimistic tone on the concomitant risks and opportunities that derive from 'looking east'. The authors ground their claims on a comparative study between two cases: the Gautrain rapid rail in South Africa, the continent's first rapid rail system, and the Addis Ababa light rail in Ethiopia. The first case illustrates a structure by which a democratic state leveraged an emerging market to form an alliance with a private firm – in line with Western standards of good governance. The second case illuminates how an authoritarian state entered into an alliance with Chinese state-owned companies under opaque conditions. It is too early to tell if the public goods produced by both contexts will be sources of long-term value creation, but evidence so far suggests that both partnerships are creating broad societal value. Clearly, though, the state–state approach enabled by Chinese credit is only available to authoritarian states. But if this approach does succeed in boosting economic growth and social development, then, conceivably, the option is open for the recipient state to adopt more transparent Western-style approaches when they seek to tackle other gaps in basic infrastructure in the future.

Chapter 13, by Gil, Pinto and Msulwa, concludes Part II by anticipating the thesis advanced in this book. The authors ground their research on a sample of four inter-organisational contexts formed to fill gaps in very basic transport infrastructure in Nigeria and Uganda; two contexts are enabled by traditional intermediaries and two by Chinese intermediaries. Their research shows that in the contexts enabled by the World Bank, building institutions is prioritised to the detriment of new infrastructure development. When the intermediary is a Chinese actor, the priorities are reversed. Underlying this choice are design attributes that are organisationally incompatible: transparency and orderliness rule as guiding principles when the focus is on building institutions; adaptability and opaqueness rule when the focus is on new infrastructure development. Crucially, the four cases show that gains from whichever focus may be insufficient to achieve the ultimate goal, socio-economic development.

1.4   Duality by Design: Between Building Institutions and Building Infrastructure

The idea that institutional voids can be navigated in different ways is not new. We know that institutions are more than just background conditions; institutions directly influence the choices available to an organisation, and organisations are known to achieve and sustain competitive advantage through strategies that overcome, shape and capitalise on the nature of their institutional environments.[33] Furthermore, studies of firms entering in emergent markets show some organisations see institutional voids as 'opportunity spaces', which they choose to strategically either exploit or overcome.[34] Other organisations see the very same institutional voids as constraints that need to be mitigated first, before taking any further action.[35]

Yet we still know little about how the choice between differing approaches to navigation of institutional voids affects the organisational design choices made in order to navigate those voids. We can expect, though, the two sets of choices to be interdependent, since organisation design is contingent on the environment to which the organisation must relate.[36] So a choice between intermediaries that espouse differing principles in order to navigate institutional voids is, necessarily, a choice between differing organisational designs used to relate the intermediated systems to their intermediaries. In other words, a choice between competing systems of intermediation is a choice between organisational contexts with differing architectures in terms of their system components, their relationships to each other and to the environment, and the underlying principles that guide organisation design and evolution.[37]

In agreement with these precepts of organisation theory, the body of evidence curated for this book is suggestive of an organisational duality.

---

[33] Khanna and Palepu (1997, 2010); Henisz, Dorobantu and Nartey (2014); Khanna and Rivkin (2001).

[34] Mair, Martı and Ventresca (2012).

[35] Doh et al. (2017); Luo and Chung (2013); Pinkham and Peng (2016).

[36] Lawrence and Lorsch (1967); Thompson (1967); Scott (1981).

[37] Simon (1981); Fjeldstad et al. (2012).

In the group of organisational contexts enabled by traditional credit, the system should evolve step by step and engage openly with government at different levels and within the legislative environment. These principles also offer a basis on which to evaluate organisational performance. That is, the difficulties with implementing these principles explain delays, cost over-runs, and other forms of organisational failure. In marked contrast, underlying the design and growth of the organisational contexts enabled by Chinese credit are the principles of opaqueness and adaptability. Engagement with stakeholders is seen as an unnecessary source of confusion and delays, and adaptability is regarded as desirable to enable quick capital investment. For the participants in the contexts enabled by Chinese credit, high performance hinges on getting the new infrastructure put in place quickly. And this focus on quick technology development restricts the efforts to build institutions to building only those institutions that are necessary to ensure that the technology can function and is sustainable. This therefore excludes efforts to build institutions with a view of meeting the Western good governance ideals during the infrastructure development process.

If we accept that these two forms of organising are pursuing objectives that are jointly desirable – and, we argue, they are – the empirical studies here show that these two objectives are organisationally incompatible. The two objectives are hard to reconcile because the design attributes that underlie one pole of the duality cannot be reconciled with those of the other pole. And consistent with predictions of organisational theorists, the organisational designers choose to focus on only one or other of the poles of the duality.[38]

We turn now to examine in more detail the choices at each pole of this duality.

1.5   Organizational Design for Building Institutions before Building Infrastructure

The choice to focus on building institutions in the pursuit of development is rooted, in Western scholarship, on the contribution of institutions to economic growth and market development. This large body of literature traces economic growth to the way evolution in institutions has allowed states to credibly commit to upholding property rights, to the quality of the rules governing economic exchange, and to governing how these rules are enforced and may be changed. From this perspective, other key

---

[38] Gulati and Puranam (2009); Birkinshaw and Gibson (2004); Smith and Tushman (2005).

markers of modern societies are the separation of policy interests from the personal economic interests of the elites, and the quality of regulation.[39] These ideas as a whole apply pressure to traditional inter-mediaries and recipients of assistance to extensively carry out tasks associated with planning and cost–benefit analysis before allocating capital, procuring suppliers and transforming designs (the instructions by which we can get things done) into usable technological artefacts. Furthermore, the organisational participants must ensure that value creation goes beyond the value that is created and appropriated by the restricted set of participants in the focal interorganisational context.

An organisational system that fails to meet these principles compro-mises its ability to claim positive performance and legitimacy because it fails external validation relative to the norms that Western actors deem appropriate. Hence, if the recipient state lacks regulation to acquire private resources, e.g. land and supplier capabilities, this void needs filling first, in a fair and transparent way, before the system can grow further. If the state lacks local capabilities to write and administer contracts to govern buyer–supplier relationships and PPPs, organisational evolution becomes contingent on building these local capabilities first. Engaging with stakeholders is also a prerequisite to encourage norms of cooperation to flourish; setting up efficient markets pre-empts illegal activity, and projects are expected to keep the scope stable, and be delivered on time and within budget.[40] So, under this approach, filling the institutional voids has priority over infrastructure building.

Implicit here is the acceptance, socially constructed, that socio-economic development is a *slow* process. And so, accordingly, the time that elapses between identifying an infrastructure gap and allocating capital to fill that gap is ruled out of performance evaluation. What matters here is that organisational growth is orderly and transparent. A substantive delay in allocating capital – to the extent that the focal infrastructure gap widens rather than shortens before the capital is invested – is not a failure per se. Rather, this outcome is attributed to exogenous factors that prevent the adoption of forms of organising that have been tried and tested in advanced economies to develop similar

---

[39] North and Weingast (1989); North, Wallis and Weingast (2009).
[40] Professional project-management norms are still rooted in classic scholarship that associ-ates high performance with stable scope, budget and schedule (Morris 1994; Flyvbjerg, Bruzelius and Rothengatter 2003). But these ideas have been refuted on the basis that they underestimate interdependencies between projects and the environment (Miller and Lessard 2000; Lenfle and Loch 2010). More recently, scholars have suggested that performance assessments need to account explicitly for whether slippages in targets do or do not allow for social value creation (Gil and Pinto 2018; Love and Ahiaga-Dagbui 2018; Lavagnon, 2018).

technologies. In other words, a failure to build infrastructure is attributed to a failure to build local institutions and capabilities in the context, not to a failure of this form of organising to navigate the institutional voids in the environment.

1.6   Organisational Design for Building Infrastructure before Building Institutions

The sense that the organisational choices espoused by the traditional intermediaries are at odds with the urgency of filling Africa's infrastructure gap has encouraged African governments to 'look East' in their search for other actionable solutions. With the economic rise of China and its novel approach to foreign policy, epitomised by its Belt and Road Initiative, African states gained the agency to choose between alternatives. The fact this edited collection offers a smaller number of empirical studies on organisational contexts enabled by Chinese credit is irrelevant from a theoretical perspective. Our purpose here is not to test the statistical significance of our insights, but instead illuminate a duality in designing organisations to navigate institutional voids. Furthermore, the lack of transparency in the decision making that guides organisational choice in contexts enabled by Chinese credit is a real obstacle to negotiating access to these sites.

When the focus is on exploiting institutional voids – or overcoming them by avoidance through artful manoeuvring – organisational growth is opaque and adaptable. By rejecting Western governance ideals, or any sense of a moral mission to change the ways Africans live, the Chinese intermediaries win the political favour of the sovereign-conscious states.[41] And by limiting the engagement with external stakeholders, the Chinese intermediaries opt for narrow searches for solutions to focal problems, trading off less exploration for quick stability in the solution of the focal problem. Bluntly stated, the idea here is not to tackle a grand challenge in innovative and cooperative ways; Chinese-enabled organisational contexts are not designed to cope with turbulence and complexity in the stakeholder environment, but rather discount the importance of stakeholder acceptance and of enlisting stakeholder support for any proposed solution. Instead, the objective here is to quickly mobilise resources in order to build a new infrastructure. And, of course, it would be disingenuous not to recognise the opportunities that such an approach creates for informal private gains to the political leadership and public bureaucracy – on both sides of the bilateral arrangements.

---

[41] Tull (2006); Brewer (2008).

This organisational choice centralises decision-making authority in a tight-knit coalition of actors involving the state, the intermediary and private firms chosen by the intermediary. Such centralised structures exploit weak institutions that govern the acquisition of resources in order to fast-track organisational growth. Price setting happens, not through the market, but through opaque decision-making processes. Enfranchisement of primary stakeholders is ruled out to accelerate the decision-making process. Improvisation and ingenuity are then employed to eliminate any bottlenecks that may emerge along the way. These contexts are not, then, constrained by accountability pressures: budgets and timescales are negotiated and renegotiated behind closed doors; participants act without pressure to justify slippages in cost and schedule targets; and the lack of local capabilities is circumvented by importing these from outside markets. Performance is tied to the speed at which the infrastructure gets built and to the building of the institutions that are strictly necessary to operate the new infrastructure.

Importantly, though, the evidence here suggests that there is no guarantee that an organisational context designed to exploit institutional voids to quickly build a durable and shareable technology can meet this objective. For example, institutions protecting property rights and customary rights may be fragile, but they can still get in the way and stall organisational growth. This is often the case with efforts to compulsorily acquire land. Often, the land is protected by customary tenure regimes structured around tribal, clan or village entities, as well as by an incipient legal framework and judiciary system left behind by the colonialist.[42] And landowners will not, therefore, part ways with their land without first putting up a major fight. Organisational growth may also be stalled by difficulties to pay back the loans due to poor planning. So this approach to organising may fall foul of the very same institutional voids that it seeks to exploit.

Complicating matters further, even when a centralised and authoritarian approach succeeds in quickly building an infrastructure, it remains unclear whether it has created value beyond the private value that was appropriated by its participants. There is a risk that the infrastructure, once ready to be used, will fail to meet the local needs because key stakeholders were disenfranchised in the development process. Which does not mean this design choice cannot create shareable public goods that add value for end-users and other beneficiaries. It can. But because

---

[42] Less than 10 per cent of the African land estate is subject to formal entitlement; Wily (2011).

stakeholder enfranchisement is limited and decision making is opaque, it is harder for third parties to see if the outcomes are a source of broad value creation or not. Exacerbating the difficulties in evaluating performance is an attribute of the main objective itself: infrastructures are durable assets that operate enmeshed within the environment. If demand for a new infrastructure does not materialise straight away, it does not mean that demand will not pick up later on. Furthermore, a new infrastructure may not be financially self-sustainable, but it can still be a source of social value creation if it catalyses economic growth and social development. More theoretically, any capital investment in a new basic infrastructure works like a real option in that it creates the right, but not an obligation, to take an action at a price – the exercising cost – in the future.[43] New transport infrastructure creates the opportunity to access and build new markets; new power plants create an environment for accommodating economic growth; water desalination plants safeguard against climate change, and so on. There is, of course, uncertainty about when and if these scenarios will be realised, and about the cost of exercising the option, which loads uncertainty on whether the capital investment will ever pay off. But if the infrastructure is not there, no option is open to create social value should the uncertainties resolve favourably in the future.

However, there is a catch. Building and maintaining infrastructure is not free. It is an investment that uses capital resources that could otherwise be mobilised to tackling competing needs. When the needs are many, a question arises about priorities. If strategic planning is rushed, if information flows are hidden and decision making is opaque, the leaders who sanction investments are asking third parties to put their faith in the good judgement of those same leaders – assuming that the leaders care about third parties. Third parties may be willing to give the leaders the benefit of the doubt, even amid rumours of corruption and bribes, if the state is not too fragile; that is, if the state remains fundamentally able and willing to operate in the public interest, albeit with weak institutions.[44] Such environments, for example, are not dissimilar to those that surrounded infrastructure development in the nineteenth century in the United States.[45] But trusting leaders is hard if state fragility is very high, for example in settings with high levels of conflict and

---

[43] Trigeorgis (1996); Gil (2007, 2009).

[44] State fragility research comes from efforts in the development literature to understand how the world's least developed countries, such as Somalia and Sudan, differ from developing countries that seem to be advancing much more rapidly, such as Mexico and China; Collier (2009); Marshall and Cole (2008).

[45] Levy (2014); Chandler (1977).

instability in political and economic life, and where the lack of basic bureaucratic capacities leads to a fundamental disregard for the rule of law and a lack of public services. In these conditions, policy decisions and the personal interests of local elites closely intertwine. Under these circumstances, expecting third parties to give the leaders the benefit of the doubt is asking too much.

1.7   Towards a Theory of Designing Organisations for Development

Taken together, our insights reveal an important duality in designing organisations to pursue development by means of building basic infrastructure. On one pole of the duality are the organisational contexts that choose to focus on building institutions before building the technology. The degree to which these contexts succeed in building the infrastructure varies, and progress is invariably slow. Yet the delays are attributed to difficulties in building the institutions and not to the choice of focus. In other words, it is not the organizational design choices that are inadequate, but rather that it takes time to build institutions. And at the other pole is an organisational choice that takes the institutional environment as it is, and, indeed, takes advantage of weak institutions in order to pursue quick infrastructure building. Our findings also suggest substantive variation in the extent to which these contexts succeed to achieve their main objective.

Strikingly, this duality invigorates a debate that is central to the development literature, and that has been unresolved for decades: Albert Hirschman's seminal idea that assistance to development should put less emphasis on planning activities so as to undercut the propensity of the borrowers to underestimate their own ability to tackle all the difficulties and troubles that future events may bring.[46] Hirschman claimed that had it not been for a lack of awareness of the difficulties encountered in the course of many development projects – the 'hiding hand' principle – people would not have embarked on those projects, as they would not have been viewed as feasible. In other words, Hirschman suggested a 'bias for hope' could be advantageous to induce action through error in institutionally under-developed settings. As he put it, 'the hiding hand does its work essentially through ignorance of ignorance, of uncertainties, and of difficulties'.[47] Furthermore, he challenged the value of conditionality tied to assistance disbursed by the traditional intermediaries, claiming that a 'failure complex' was a socio-psychological obstacle to the effectiveness of development policy and assistance.

---

[46] Hirschman (1967, 1975).   [47] Hirschman (1967, p. 35).

Hirschman's ideas were dismissed, however, by the institutional pre-scriptions of the multilateral lenders and Western development agencies, based on the argument that he ignored the difficulties on the ground. So it is striking that, to a degree, the choices of the Chinese intermediaries conform to Hirschman's ideas. When the focus is on quick infrastructure building, organisational choice escapes from the straitjacket of precondi-tions for receiving Western assistance.[48] Instead, organisations are encour-aged to take risks and be pragmatic, and organisational choices rely on the participants' capacity for improvisation, ingenuity, creativity and flexibility in solving problems. In alignment with Hirschman's prescriptions, these organisational contexts evolve by trial and error, and rely on learning-by-doing to eliminate bottlenecks to their evolution and growth.

Our collection of studies reveals mixed results about organisational contexts wholly focused on infrastructure building. Whilst the surround-ing institutions may be weak and under-developed, these organisational contexts rarely operate in a vacuum. And when creativity, improvisation and flexibility fail to eliminate emerging bottlenecks, these contexts unra-vel and fail. Still, faced with the certainty that a focus on building institu-tions cannot offer quick solutions to urgent problems, many African policy makers are happy to take the potential bargain offered by Chinese actors. This suggests a duality, in that both objectives are desir-able. The challenge remains that organising for one pole of the duality is incompatible with organising for the other. However, there is equifinality in that the higher-order goal unifying the participants in both forms of organising is the same – socio-economic development. And neither approach is superior to the other. The traditional approach struggles to tackle basic infrastructure gaps; as for the emergent approach, it is too soon to know how its outcomes will play out in the long term. But the evidence assembled here is suggestive of mixed results.

More certain seems the fact that this duality is here to stay, as China emerges as the world's biggest economy, and its more transactional-based, mercantilist order gains traction. Amplifying this duality are the fiscal pressures on advanced economies, and the doubts about their own models of liberal democracy, individual freedom, rules-based order and market economies in the context of successfully managing their own affairs in the aftermath of the financial crisis and the rise of populism.[49] For certain, this new global order takes us beyond traditional boundary conditions in organisational studies. It also suggests a trove of new

---

[48] Hirschman (1971).

[49] We leave it to historians to strike potential parallels with the way in which the rise of Japan also challenged the global uniformities in the state, political ideologies and economic life imposed on the world by Western domination centuries before; Bayly (2004).

research questions to enable us to further our understanding of designing organisations for development and to navigate institutional voids more generally. These might include:

- When does stakeholder enfranchisement cause more harm than good?
- Can too much transparency and accountability become hindrances to value creation?
- Is orderly and transparent growth worth the added transaction costs and delays?
- Is fast-tracking and opaque growth worth the risk of disarray and value destruction?
- Can ambidextrous systems be designed to address both poles of the duality?
- Can informal activities be leveraged to compensate for the less desirable effects of formal activities?
- How does the quality of the institutions influence the choice to focus on one pole of the duality to the detriment of the other?
- Are there merits in the co-existence of the two forms of organising?

It is not the purpose of this book to provide the answers to these, and other, emerging complex questions. But, by illuminating this design duality, we hope more research will ensue on designing organisations to tackle grand challenges albeit institutional shortcomings.

1.8   Final Considerations

Our focus on how intermediaries directly influence choice in organisational design should not be interpreted to mean that we feel this is the crux of tackling grand societal challenges in institutionally under-developed environments. Choices in organisational design are not only determined by institutions, and institutions are not the single cause that determines how actors behave.[50] For example, some studies here make clear that modular technologies that require less cooperation and coordination, e.g. off-grid solar power, change the structure of the focal problem. And though we do not have a case on telecom infrastructure development, the rapid expansion of mobile phone use in Africa can be attributed in part to its more decomposable architecture. Modular technologies may thus hold one key for effective alternative organisational solutions. Nonetheless, institutions are an element that directly affects organisational design, and we still know little on designing effective organisations when there is a need to overcome institutional shortcomings.

---

[50] Ostrom (2005).

Our choice to focus on logic linking intermediation and organisation design choices also reflects our sense that, with China's economic rise and the advanced economies hobbled by populism and fiscal pressures, a new global order is setting in. And this raises new questions that require major attention. The Chinese involvement in Africa is historically unprecedented and likely to remain opaque – as the China Eximbank president said, 'If the water is too clear, you don't catch any fish'.[51] This sentiment could not contrast more with the Western approach, which is also unlikely to change if we go by the words of the World Bank's 2017 World Development Report (p. 27) – 'Development assistance can be more effective when donor engagement supports the emergence of more accountable and equitable governing arrangements that become embedded in the domestic context'. By foregrounding this duality, we are not suggesting the abandonment of the principles entwined within the traditional approach. But neither does it mean we do not see value in the emergent approach. It may well be the case that superior solutions lie in organisational designs that combine the two approaches. It may also be the case that different approaches are better suited for differing infrastructure developments, according to the attributes of the focal problem. We can also expect the quality of the institutions to determine whether organisational designers have agency at all. To sum up, we leave this book with a new set of research questions for which we do not yet have answers. But we do claim that there is a fundamental duality in designing organisations to navigate institutional voids, which presents new opportunities to reset the debate. A new dawn awaits; it is up to us to find ways to make the best of it, and prepare for it today.

References

African Development Bank (2014). African Development Bank Group strategy for addressing fragility and building resilience in Africa. Abidjan, Cote d'Ivoire: African Development Bank.

African Development Bank (2018). African economic outlook. African Development Bank Group, Abidjan, Côte d'Ivoire: African Development Bank.

Bayly, C. (2004). *The birth of the modern world 1780–1914: Global connections and comparisons*. Oxford: Blackwell.

Birkinshaw, J. and Gibson, C. (2004). Building ambidexterity into an organisation. *MIT Sloan Management Review*, 45(4): 47–55.

Bräutigam, D. (2009). *The dragon's gift: The real story of China in Africa*. Oxford: Oxford University Press.

---

[51] Bräutigam (2009, p. 296).

Bräutigam, D. (2011). Aid 'with Chinese characteristics': Chinese foreign aid and development finance meet the OECD-DAC aid regime. *Journal of International Development*, 23: 752–764.

Brewer, N. (2008). *The new Great Walls: A guide to China's overseas dam industry.* Berkeley, CA: International Rivers.

Burnside, C. and Dollar, D. (2000). Aid, policies, and growth. *American Economic Review*, 90(4): 847–868.

Chabal, P. and Daloz J.-P. (1999). *Africa works: Disorder as political instrument.* Oxford: James Currey; Bloomington and Indianapolis, IN: Indiana University Press, in association with the International Institute.

Chen, S. and Ravallion, M. (2008). The developing world is poorer than thought but no less successful in the fight against poverty. Policy Research Working Paper 4703. Washington, DC: World Bank.

Collier, P. (2009). The political economy of state failure. *Oxford Review of Economic Policy*, 25(2): 219–240.

Colquitt, J. A. and George, G. (2011). Publishing in AMJ: Topic choice. *Academy of Management Journal*, 54: 432–435.

Doh, J., Rodrigues, S., Saka-Helhout, A. and Makhija, M. (2017). International business responses to institutional voids. *Journal of International Business Studies*, 48: 293–307.

Dutt, N., Hawn, O., Vidal, E., Chatterji, A., McGahan, A. and Mitchell, W. (2016). How open system intermediaries address institutional failures: The case of business incubators in emerging-market countries. *Academy of Management Journal*, June 59: 818–840.

Eisenhardt, K. M., Graebner, M. E. and Sonenshein, S. (2016). Grand challenges and inductive methods: Rigor without rigor mortis. *Academy of Management Journal* (August 2016) 59: 1103–1112.

Eom, J., Hwang, J., Atkins, L., Chen Y. and Zhou, S. (2017). China Africa Research Initiative. School of Advanced International Studies Policy Brief No. 18. Johns Hopkins University.

Erdmann, G. and Engel U. (2006). Neo-patrimonialism revisited: Beyond a catch-all concept. GIGA Research Paper No. 16. Hamburg: German Institute of Global and Area Studies.

Esfahani, H. and Ramirez M. (2003). Institutions, infrastructure and economic growth. *Journal of Development Economics* 70: 443–477.

Evans, P. and Doz., Y. (1989). The dualistic organisation. In A. Laurent (Ed.) *Human resource management in international firms*. Basingstoke, UK: Macmillan.

Ferraro, F., Etzion, D. and Gehman, J. (2015). Tackling grand challenges pragmatically: Robust action revisited. *Organisation Studies*, 36: 363–390.

Fjeldstad, Ø. D., Snow, C. C., Miles, R. E. and Lettl, C. (2012). The architecture of collaboration. *Strategic Management Journal*, 33: 734–750.

Flyvbjerg, B., Bruzelius, N. and Rothengatter, W. (2003). *Megaprojects and risk: An anatomy of ambition.* Cambridge, UK: Cambridge University Press.

Frischman, B. M. (2012). *Infrastructure: The social value of shared resources.* Oxford: Oxford University Press.

George, G., Corbishley, C., Khayesi, J. N. O., Haas, M. R. and Laszlo Tihanyi, L. (2016). Bringing Africa in: Promising directions for management research. *Academy of Management Journal*, 59: 377–393.

Gil, N. (2007). On the value of project safeguards: Embedding real options in complex product and systems. *Research Policy* 36(7): 980–999.

Gil, N. (2009). Project safeguards: Operationalizing option-like strategic thinking in infrastructure development. *IEEE Transactions on Engineering Management*, 56 (2) May: 257–270.

Gil, N. and Pinto, J. (2018). Polycentric organising and performance: A contingency model and evidence from megaproject planning in the UK. *Research Policy*, 47: 717–734.

Gulati, R. and Puranam, P. (2009). Renewal through reorganisation. *Organisation Science*, 20(2): 422–440.

Gulati, R., Puranam, P. and Tushman, M. (2012). Meta-organisation design: Rethinking design in interorganisational and community contexts. *Strategic Management Journal*, 33: 571–586.

Henderson, J. (2008). China and global development: Towards a global-Asian era? *Contemporary Politics*, 14(4): 375–392.

Henderson, J., Appelbaum, R. P. and Ho, S. Y. (2013). Globalization with Chinese characteristics: Externalization, dynamics and transformations. *Development and Change* 44: 1221–1253.

Henisz, W. J., Dorobantu, S. and Nartey, L. J. (2014). Spinning gold: The financial returns to stakeholder engagement. *Strategic Management Journal*, 35 (12): 1727–1748.

Hermes, N. and Lensink, R. (2001). *Changing the conditions for development aid: A new paradigm.* London: Frank Cass.

Hernandez, D. (2017). Are 'new' donors challenging World Bank conditionality? *World Development*, 96 (August): 529–549.

Hirschman, A. O. (1967). *Development projects observed.* Washington, DC: Brookings Institution.

Hirschman, A. O. (1971). Introduction: Political economics and possibilism. In A. O. Hirschman (Ed.), *A bias for hope: Essays on development and Latin America*, 1–37. New Haven, CT: Yale University Press.

Hirschman, A. O. (1975). Policymaking and policy analysis in Latin America: A return journey. *Policy Sciences* 6:385–402.

Hoorweg, D. and Pope, K. (2017). Population predictions for the world's largest cities in the 21st century. *Environment and Urbanization*, 29(1): 195–216.

IEA. (2016). *World energy outlook 2016.* Paris: International Energy Agency.

IRENA. (2014). *REmap 2030: A renewable energy roadmap. Summary of findings.* International Renewable Energy Agency, June, Abu Dhabi.

Khanna, T. and Palepu, K. G. (1997). Why focused strategies may be wrong for emerging markets. *Harvard Business Review* 75: 41–51.

Khanna, T. and Palepu, K. G. (2010). *Winning in emerging markets: A road map for strategy and execution.* Boston, MA: Harvard Business Press.

Khanna, T. and Rivkin, J. (2001). Estimating the performance effects of business groups in emerging markets. *Strategic Management Journal* 22(1): 45–74.

Klingebiel, R. and Stadler, C. (2015). Opportunities and challenges for empirical strategy research in Africa. *Africa Journal of Management*, 1(2): 194–200.

Knudsen, T. and Srikanth, K. (2014). Coordinated exploration: Organising joint search by multiple specialists to overcome mutual confusion and joint myopia. *Administrative Science Quarterly* 59: 409–441.

Lavagnon, A. I. (2018). Beneficial or detrimental ignorance: The straw man fallacy of Flyvbjerg's test of Hirschman's hiding hand. *World Development*, 103: 369–382.

Lawrence, P. R. and Lorsch, J. W. (1967). Differentiation and integration in complex organisations. *Administrative Science Quarterly*, 12: 1–47.

Lenfle, S. and Loch, C. (2010). Lost roots: How project management came to emphasize control over flexibility and novelty. *California Management Review*, 53(1): 32–55.

Levy, B. (2014). *Working with the grain: Integrating governance and growth in development strategies*. New York, NY: Oxford University Press.

Libecap, G. D. (1989). *Contracting for property rights: Political economy of institutions and decisions*. Cambridge, UK: Cambridge University Press.

Love, P. E. D. and Ahiaga-Dagbui, D. D. (2018). Debunking fake news in a post-truth era: The plausible untruths of cost underestimation in transport infrastructure projects. *Transportation Research Part A* 113: 357–368.

Luo, X. and Chung, C. (2013). Filling or abusing the institutional void? *Organisation Science*, 24: 591–613.

Mair J., and Marti, I. (2009). Entrepreneurship in and around institutional voids: A case study from Bangladesh. *Journal of Business Venturing*, 24: 419–435.

Mair, J., Marti, I. and Ventresca, M. (2012). Building inclusive markets in rural Bangladesh: How intermediaries work institutional voids. *Academy of Management Journal*, 55: 819–850.

Marshall, M. G. and Cole, B. R. (2008). Global report on conflict, governance, and state fragility 2008. *Foreign Policy Bulletin* 18(1): 3–21.

Martens, B. (2005). Why do agencies exist? *Development Policy Review*, 23(6): 643–663.

McDermott, G., Corredoira, R. and Kruse, G. (2009). Public–private institutions as catalysts of upgrading in emerging market societies. *Academy of Management Journal*, 52: 1270–1296.

McLean, E. V., and Schneider, C. J. (2014). Limits of informal governance? The scope of conditionality in the World Bank. Proc. 7th Annual Conference of the Political Economy of International Organizations, 16–18 January, Princeton University.

Miller, R. and Lessard, D. (2000). Public goods and private strategies: Making sense of project performance. In Roger Miller and Donald Lessard (Eds.), *The strategic management of large engineering projects*. Cambridge, MA: MIT Press.

Mohan, G., and Lampert, B. (2013). Negotiating China: Reinserting African agency into China–Africa relations. *African Affairs*, 112(446): 92–110.

Morris, P. W. (1994). *The management of projects*. London: Thomas Telford.

Naim, M. 2007. Rogue aid. *Foreign Policy*, 159: 95–96.

North, D. (1990). *Institutions, institutional change, and economic performance*. Cambridge, UK: Cambridge University Press.

North, D. C., Wallis, J. and Weingast, B. (2009). *Violence and social order: A conceptual framework for interpreting recorded human history*. Cambridge, UK: Cambridge University Press.

North, D. C., Weingast, B. R. (1989). Constitutions and commitment: The evolution of institutions governing public choice in seventeenth-century England. *The Journal of Economic History* 49(4): 803–832.

Ostrom, E. (1990). *Governing the commons: The evolution of institutions of collective action*. New York, NY: Cambridge University Press.

Ostrom, E. (2005). *Understanding institutional diversity*. Princeton, NJ: Princeton University Press.

Pinkham, B. C. and Peng, M. W. (2016). Overcoming institutional voids via arbitration. *Journal of International Business Studies*, 48 (3): 344–359.

Rodrick, D. (2006). Goodbye Washington consensus, hello Washington confusion. *Journal of Economic Literature*, 44(4): 973–987.

Scott, W. R. (1981). *Organisations: Rational, natural, and open systems*. Englewood Cliffs, NJ: Prentice Hall Inc.

Simon, H. A. (1981). *The sciences of the artificial*. 2nd ed. Cambridge, MA: MIT Press.

Smith, W. K. and Tushman, M. L. (2005). Managing strategic contradictions: A top management model for managing innovation streams. *Organisation Science* 16(5): 522–536.

Tan-Mullins, M., Mohan, G. and Power, M. (2010). Redefining 'aid' in the China–Africa context. *Development and Change*, 41: 857–881.

Thompson, J. D. (1967). *Organisations in action: Social science bases of administrative theory*. New York: McGraw-Hill.

Trigeorgis, L. (1996). *Real options: Managerial flexibility and strategy in resource allocation*. Cambridge, MA: MIT Press.

Tull, D. (2006). China's engagement in Africa: Scope, significance and consequences. *Journal of Modern African Studies*, 44(3): 459–79.

UN. (1995, January). *Public sector management, governance, and sustainable human development: A discussion paper*. Management Development and Governance Division. New York: Bureau for Policy and Programme Support, United Nations Development Programme.

UN. (2013). *Financing for sustainable development: UN task team on the post-2015 UN Development Agenda, executive summary*. New York: United Nations.

UN. (2017). *World population prospects: The 2017 revision*. Department of Economic and Social Affairs, Population Division. New York: United Nations.

UN. (2018). *The United Nations world water development report: Nature-based solutions for water*. France: United Nations World Water Assessment Programme, United Nations Educational, Scientific and Cultural Organization.

UN-Habitat. (2011). *Infrastructure for economic development and poverty reduction in Africa*. Nairobi: UN-Habitat.

UN-Habitat. (2016). *World cities report 2016: Urbanization and development. Emerging futures: Key findings and messages*. Nairobi: UN Habitat.

van Dijk, M. P. (2009). *The new presence of China in Africa*. Amsterdam: Amsterdam University Press.

Williamson, O. E. (1985). *The Economic institutions of capitalism.* Free Press: New York.

Wily, L. A. (2011). 'The law is to blame': The vulnerable status of common property rights in sub-Saharan Africa. *Development and Change* 42: 733–757.

Woods, N. (2008). Whose aid? Whose influence? China, emerging donors and the silent revolution in development assistance. *International Affairs* 84(6): 1205–1221.

World Bank (1994). *World development report: Infrastructure for development.* New York: Oxford University Press.

World Economic Forum. (2017). *The global competitiveness report 2018–2018.* Edited by Klaus Schwab. Geneva: World Economic Forum.

Part I

Mitigating Institutional Voids by Design

2 Why the Lights Went Out: A Capability Perspective on the Unintended Consequences of Sector Reform Processes

*Hagen Worch, Mundia Kabinga, Anton Eberhard,
Jochen Markard and Bernhard Truffer*

Abstract

In this chapter we advance the argument that regulatory policies can have a far-reaching impact on the organizational capabilities and, ultimately, on the performance of public utilities. Once capabilities are lost, it may be hard to regain them in the short term. Our insights are based on a qualitative-comparative analysis of capability-losing processes at Eskom, South Africa's national electric utility. South Africa experienced severe power outages between 2005 and 2008, which are commonly explained as having been caused by inadequate generation capacity, badly maintained power plants and insufficient coal supply. In this chapter, we go a step further and examine the underlying reasons at the organizational level. We show that a variety of new regulations led to a substantial loss of critical competences and skills at Eskom. This caused a deterioration of planning, operation and maintenance procedures, and made swift reactions to the crisis difficult. The 'capability perspective' presented in this chapter complements traditional theoretical explanations of utility and sector performance.

2.1 Introduction

Between 2005 and 2008, South Africa experienced a series of major electricity blackouts, with serious implications for residential and industrial electricity customers, and the economy as a whole. Eskom, the national electricity supplier, launched emergency measures, such as scheduled load shedding, and the government set up a task force, new regulations and ad hoc energy-saving programmes. Despite these

33

interventions, the country still suffers from a poorly performing power sector, with the grid and power plants working at their limits and a high risk of power outages due to a critically tight reserve margin.

Reliable, secure and cost-efficient electricity supply is a central challenge, not only in South Africa (Marquard 2006; National Planning Commission 2011) but also in many other countries (OECD 2006, 2007; UN-HABITAT 2011; Eberhard and Shkaratan 2012; Karplus et al. 2019; Rose et al. 2019). Electricity sector reform processes, including liberalization and privatization, have been initiated in many cases to tackle these challenges. However, numerous infrastructure sector reform processes worldwide are incomplete, were implemented much slower than expected, experienced resistance from sector players, or were even reversed (OECD 2006; Joskow 2008; Gratwick and Eberhard 2008). The underlying reasons for these drawbacks are not entirely clear. Also, sector reforms tend to be confronted with unintended consequences. These developments require a more detailed look into the underlying processes, and a potential revision of the conceptual frameworks energy policy scholars are working with (Gil and Beckman 2009; Künneke, Groenewegen and Ménard 2010; Worch et al. 2013).

In South Africa, the electricity crisis is commonly explained as being caused by insufficient generation capacity, badly maintained power plants, insufficient coal quality and a weak electricity grid (Eberhard 2007a; NERSA 2006, 2008; Hamukoma and Levy 2019). But how did such a situation occur? How could a 40 per cent reserve margin for power generation in 1991 (Eberhard 2007b: 219) turn into an estimated capacity shortfall of 10 per cent in 2008? Why were existing power plants in such bad shape? How could a supposedly experienced company like Eskom buy below-specification coal and allow coal stocks to fall to unacceptable levels? And why is it taking years to ameliorate the situation, despite early interventions by government and management?

The reasons for the power outages and the residual tense situation in the South African power sector are complex and multi-dimensional. Conventional explanations of failures in electricity supply focus on the sector's regulatory framework, and whether it provides sufficient incentives for investments into power plants and the network (Joskow 2002; Gómez-Ibáñez 2003; Armstrong and Sappington 2006; Guthrie 2006). Consistent with these explanations, our analysis shows that the impact of regulatory changes on investments has also played a key role in the South African electricity crisis. However, this only explains one part of the story. In particular, it leaves open why Eskom failed in domains like capacity planning, power-plant maintenance and coal contracting, where we would normally expect it to succeed thanks to its long-term professional experience.

By focusing on capabilities, we show that electricity sector reforms and the sociopolitical transformation in South Africa led to a loss of critical competences at the firm level, which not only worsened planning, operation and maintenance procedures, but also made swift reactions to the crisis difficult. More generally, we argue that regulatory changes and other external factors can have a far-reaching impact on the organizational capabilities of utilities. Once these capabilities are lost, they may be very hard to regain. With this 'capability perspective', we complement traditional theoretical explanations of utility and sector performance.

In our study, we apply a capability-based framework, which enables us to identify, examine and explain the emergence of capability gaps and the corresponding performance deficiencies in utility firms that occur as a result of policy and regulatory changes (Worch et al. 2013). The term 'capability gap' is defined as an inadequate availability of competences, skills and experiences. In the management literature, capability gaps are an important conceptualization (Lavie 2006; Capron and Mitchell 2009; Dominguez et al. 2009; Worch et al. 2012). Recent research has extended this concept further to include the study of capability erosion dynamics (Rahmandad and Repenning 2016). Our own research has conceptually linked capability-based explanations with the literature on infrastructure sector performance (Dominguez et al. 2009; Worch et al. 2013). The role of organizational capabilities for utility performance is an emerging but still under-researched area (see e.g. Dyner and Larsen 2001; Delmas and Tokat 2005; Delmas et al. 2009; Gebauer, Worch and Truffer 2012; Worch et al. 2012).

The case of Eskom and the South African electricity sector is an ideal, natural experiment–type of setting in which to study causes of incomplete sector reform processes and crisis situations, which go beyond traditional incentive-based explanations; and in which to examine the performance outcomes at the organizational level that result from sociopolitical and regulatory changes. Since Eskom is a dominant national utility, its organizational performance is directly reflected in the quality of power supply in the whole country. This specific situation enables us to examine the impact of changes in the regulatory environment on organizational capabilities, and how this, in turn, affects the performance of the utility and the national electricity sector as whole.

The chapter proceeds as follows:

> **Section 2.2** presents conventional theoretical approaches that are used to explain performance deficiencies in utility sectors. We also review how the crisis in South Africa has been

explained so far. Finally, the capability perspective is introduced as a complementary conceptual framework with which to study the performance of utilities.

Section 2.3 describes the research design, data collection and data analysis carried out in this study.

Section 2.4 provides a brief historical overview of Eskom and of the development of the South African electricity sector.

Section 2.5 presents our empirical findings on how changes in the policy and regulatory environment changed Eskom's capability structure (related to power-plant operation).

Section 2.6 discusses our results, interprets them in the context of South Africa's power crisis and draws more general conclusions about the unintended consequences of reform processes in infrastructure sectors.

Section 2.7 concludes our chapter.

2.2   Theoretical Framework

2.2.1   *Conventional Explanations*

Principal–agent approaches and transaction–cost economics have a long tradition of use in the analysis of infrastructure sectors and explanation of performance deficiencies (see Armstrong and Sappington 2006). The two approaches emphasize asymmetric information and the opportunistic behaviour of utility firms as reasons for poor service delivery.

For example, principal–agent approaches argue that an inadequate regulatory framework generates asymmetric information and, therefore, may result in insufficient levels of investment (e.g. Guthrie 2006). Transaction–cost economics maintains that uncertainty and high asset specificity are typical features of infrastructure sectors, which induce hold-up problems (see e.g. Joskow 2002; Spiller and Tommasi 2005). Such hold-up problems occur as different players interact – generators and coal suppliers, utilities and the regulator, and/or the regulator and policy makers, etc. – and lead to sub-optimal performance outcomes from infrastructure services. So, traditional approaches have identified inadequate regulation and contractual issues as the main causes for inefficiencies, and have suggested changes in the incentive structures and institutional frameworks in order to improve performance (see e.g. Joskow 2002; Gómez-Ibáñez 2003, 2007; Irwin and Yamamoto 2004; Armstrong and Sappington 2006; Guthrie 2006; von Hirschhausen, Beckers and Brenck 2011).

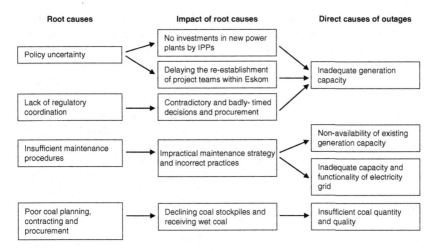

Figure 2.1 Conventional explanation of South Africa's power outages

South Africa's electricity crisis has been analysed in a number of reports and studies (NERSA 2006, 2008; Eberhard 2007a; Public Protector South Africa 2009; Hamukoma and Levy 2019), mainly through the lens of traditional approaches. These reports highlight four direct causes for the crisis:

1) Lack of generation capacity due to under-investment in new power plants
2) Non-availability of existing generation capacity due to insufficient maintenance
3) Insufficient coal quantity and quality
4) Inadequate capacity and functionality of the electricity grid.

The prevailing explanations link these four direct causes to another four underlying root causes:

 i) Policy uncertainty
 ii) Lack of regulatory co-ordination
 iii) Insufficient maintenance procedures
 iv) Poor coal planning and contracting.

The first two root causes are located at the policy level, whilst the latter are located at the organizational level at Eskom. Figure 2.1 illustrates the link between the direct and root causes.

Policy uncertainty, as first root cause, is related to the fact that electricity sector reforms in South Africa were not fully implemented. Whilst Eskom was prohibited from building new generation capacity, mechanisms were not put in place to contract independent power producers

(IPPs). When the construction ban on Eskom was finally removed in 2004, capacity scale-up was already far behind schedule. Policy uncertainty also delayed the re-establishment of dedicated project teams and departments within Eskom in order to manage generation capacity expansion. The two impacts of policy uncertainty led to an inadequate generation capacity.

A second root cause was the lack of co-ordination and integration of the different electricity planning, investment decision making, approval and procurement processes between Eskom, the National Energy Regulator (NERSA), the Department of Minerals and Energy (DME) and the Department of Public Enterprises (DPE). This led to contradictory and badly timed decisions and procurement processes, and ultimately resulted in a further setback of the investments in new generation plants.

As a third root cause, the existing studies identify a 'negligence of maintenance procedures' at Eskom for both power plants and the electricity grid (NERSA 2006: 3, 2008: 21). Furthermore, remedial actions were inadequate, protection systems had been operated incorrectly, licence conditions were breached and the maintenance strategy was not practical. As a result, existing generation capacity was unavailable and transmission capacities limited.

Finally, poor coal planning, contracting and procurement led to low coal stockpile levels and poor coal quality (NERSA 2008: 38), which, again, reduced the actual generation capacity of the power plants. This combination led to load losses and to unplanned power-plant outages.

Whilst these explanations seem to be comprehensive and convincing at first sight, they leave a series of questions open. The maintenance deficiencies, for example, were not just a problem in one or a few locations, but emerged as a general issue across most power plants. So why did a systematic lack of adequate maintenance procedures emerge, despite maintenance being one of Eskom's core competences? Why did Eskom suddenly fail in key tasks such as coal contracting, in which the firm could reasonably be expected to have long-term experience? Why did it take Eskom so long to set up teams for new generation capacity expansion programmes after the government reversed an earlier decision that had stopped Eskom building new power plants?

One explanation could be that Eskom was just a case of bad management. Such a view, though, presumes that management and performance problems were unrelated to the sector reform processes, which was not the case, as we will show.

It seems that conventional explanations do not fully account for the processes that unfold at the organizational level and their accompanying challenges. They implicitly assume that changes and adaptations at the organizational level occur easily and quickly, i.e. that the organizational resources and capabilities necessary to accommodate regulatory changes are readily available. Insights from the management literature, though, suggest that resource and capability development at the organizational level might be complex, ambiguous and time-consuming processes (see e.g. Dierickx and Cool 1989; Barney 1991; Zollo and Winter 2002; Kraaijenbrink, Spender and Groen 2010).

So, conventional explanations for performance deficits in infrastructure sectors have to be complemented by approaches that take processes at the organizational level explicitly into account. The capability perspective we introduce and apply below is a step towards this goal.

2.2.2   *A Capability Perspective to Explain Utility Performance*

Organizational capabilities have been widely studied in the management literature to better understand the performance of firms, especially in situations where tasks are highly complex or market environments are changing rapidly (Barney 1991; Barney, Ketchen and Wright 2011; Teece, Pisano and Shuen 1997; Eisenhardt and Martin 2000; Winter 2003; Newbert 2007). Organizational capabilities enable a firm to execute tasks such as production, marketing and product development. In the case of electric power producers, key tasks include planning, building, operating and maintaining power plants. Organizational capabilities develop over time and depend on, amongst other things, the competences, skills and experiences of the employees of a firm. Ideally, the organizational capabilities of a firm are well adapted to the key tasks it has to perform.

When tasks change, e.g. due to changes in the market environment, or the capability structure changes, e.g. due to well-functioning teams leaving the firm, a capability gap might occur and negatively affect firm performance (Lavie 2006; Capron and Mitchell 2009; Dominguez et al. 2009; Worch et al. 2012; Rahmandad and Repenning 2016). A major challenge in such a situation is that capability gaps are not always easy to identify, and often take quite some time to be resolved, if at all. This is particularly the case, if the lost capabilities comprise long-term experiences or tacit knowledge.

In this chapter we apply a recently developed capability perspective that explicitly links changes in the regulatory environment to the emergence of capability gaps in utility firms (see Worch et al. 2013). A capability gap is an insufficient availability of competences, skills and experiences for a specific organizational task. The framework suggests that regulatory interventions can directly affect the capabilities of utility firms. A capability gap occurs if

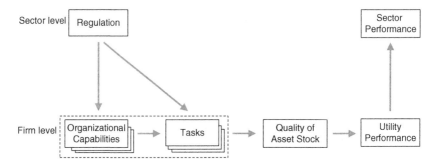

Figure 2.2 Capability perspective on utility and sector performance

existing capabilities are weakened whilst tasks remain the same, or if new tasks emerge for which the capabilities are not yet available (Worch et al. 2013: 5). The two effects can occur simultaneously or independently. Capability gaps tend to be particularly persistent in situations where the adaptation of existing capabilities or the development of new capabilities is time-consuming, complex and poorly understood.

In electricity supply, unbundling is an example in which regulation directly affects the organizational structures of electric utilities with potentially negative consequences for the existing capabilities of the affected organizational units (Pollitt 2008). Market liberalization is an example whereby regulatory changes lead to the emergence of new tasks, such as marketing, power trading or balance group management, for which new organizational capabilities are required.

The result of a capability gap is a performance decline in, or even complete failure of specific organizational tasks, and eventually of the organization as such. If *existing capabilities* are weakened or get lost because of regulatory changes, this may result in a decline of organizational performance. Regulatory interventions can also change the tasks utilities have to fulfil. If tasks change, *new capabilities* will be required, which means that they have to be developed in order to fulfil the tasks. A decline in organizational performance may have repercussions at the sector level, especially if all utility firms are affected in a similar way, or if very critical firms, such as single suppliers, are affected. Figure 2.2 depicts the applied framework.

With this study we provide empirical evidence for the relevance of a capability perspective. We will show how regulatory changes unintentionally affected the capabilities and tasks of a utility company, so that performance deficits occurred at the organizational and sectoral level. The broader purpose of the chapter is to demonstrate the benefits of a capability perspective as an important complement to conventional approaches in terms of explaining the impact of regulation and other sector developments on organizational performance.

2.3   Research Method

Given the limited understanding of the impact of regulatory changes on capability structures in utilities, we use an inductive case study methodology (Eisenhardt 1989; Miles and Huberman 1994) to understand how capability gaps emerged at Eskom, and what factors caused these gaps.

As a first step, we identified all factors that played a role in changes in the capability structure of Eskom's generation division. We derived a set of six broader context factors that caused capability gaps in generation operations, which resulted in power plants being poorly operated and existing generation capacity being insufficiently available. These factors (see Table 2.1, first column) and the unfolding processes of loss in capability formed the six cases that we then examined in a comparative setting.

In the second step, we analysed and compared the underlying capability change processes for each of these factors. Here we report our findings from the six cases (related to the six factors) of capability change processes within Eskom's power-generation division. The comparative research design enabled us to derive specific insights on the influence of these factors on Eskom's capability structure. It also allowed us to infer some more general conclusions about the emergence of capability gaps in utility firms, and, therefore, to contribute to theory-building in this area.

We conducted twenty semi-structured interviews in 2009 and 2010. Former CEOs, board members and executive managers, and former and current senior-level managers served as key informants for the case study. The interviewees were closely involved at different levels in Eskom when changes in the business environment affected the generation division. They were asked to give a detailed account of the capability processes in generation, with a specific focus on the factors causing capability gaps to emerge and the implications of these for capability structures and performance. They also provided illustrations of how competences and skills changed. Insights into the processes leading to capability losses emerged inductively from the fieldwork. All the interviews were recorded and transcribed; transcriptions of around 500 pages were analysed using standard qualitative data analysis software (MaxQDA 10).

Table 2.1 *Factors impacting on Eskom's generation-capability structure*

External factors	Emerging capability gap as a result of:	Reasons for emerging capability gap (i.e. change in the capability structure)	Factors lacking as a result of the capability gap
Sector reform processes	Loss of existing capabilities	Encouraging early retirements Resignations	Long-term experience
	Newly required capabilities	Running power plants at higher load levels with less maintenance	More experience of how system components interact was required
Sociopolitical transformation	Loss of existing capabilities	Encouraging early retirements Resignations	Long-term experience
Large technological systems with long life-cycles	Loss of existing capabilities	Retirements through cohort effect	Long-term experience
Technological change	Loss of existing capabilities	Encouraging early retirement	Long-term experience
Economic growth and development	Loss of existing capabilities	Highly qualified staff left to start a new job elsewhere (most of these were staff with long-term experience)	Highly qualified engineering, technical and managerial competences and skills
		Reinforcing drain of capabilities, as those who left encouraged other staff members to follow once they were established in the new job	Bias towards those with long-term experience
Changing weather conditions	Newly required capabilities	Running power plants with coal of lower quality	More experience of how system components interact was required
		Running power plants at higher load levels with less maintenance	

In addition, extensive archival material, such as annual reports, internal documents, monographs and company reports, were included in our analysis to enrich our database, triangulate the interview information and so increase the validity of our research.

The data analysis started with a within-case analysis, in which we became familiar with each case – i.e. each identified factor and its unfolding influence on Eskom's capability structure – as a stand-alone entity

(Eisenhardt 1989). The within-case analyses were conducted in three steps. Firstly, we reviewed the data so as to create a basic understanding of each capability-losing process. Secondly, we described the impact of the external factors and established how the unfolding chain of events affected the capability structure in Eskom's generation operation. And thirdly, we characterized the types of competences and experiences that were lost. Once all the within-case analyses were completed, we continued with the cross-case (comparative) analysis (Eisenhardt 1989). Comparing the six processes in an iterative process, we identified similarities and differences across the capability-losing processes. Inferring from this analysis, we identified two distinct mechanisms of emerging capability gaps. We therefore derived a better understanding of the capability gaps' nature and their implications from our data.

Identifying capability gaps was a key aspect of our analysis. The following quote is an example of how we inferred from an informant's description that Eskom's generation division lost capabilities, and that the critical dimension of this loss was a long-term experience:

People that have not been around long enough, they don't fully understand . . . that if this part of a plant I'm looking at behaves in a certain way, it's going to have a certain knock-on effect on another part of the plant. And it's purely an issue of experience.

In the following section, we briefly describe Eskom's history to provide some context of the empirical case we analyse. After this overview, we present our results.

2.4   Eskom – A Brief Historical Overview

Eskom, founded in 1923, is one of the largest electric utilities worldwide today. It has around 48,000 employees (2018); an installed generation capacity of more than 48,000 MW (2018), predominantly from coal-fired power plants; and generates approximately 95 per cent of the electricity used in South Africa. Eskom has been a limited liability company since 2002, and is owned by the national government.

In the 1970s and early 1980s, Eskom expanded its generation capacity substantially (Conradie and Messerschmidt 2000: 217). As a result of the capacity expansion, Eskom had a need for qualified technical and engineering staff to run its new power stations, and recruited many of those who had been involved in constructing the plants. In the early 1980s, economic growth rates slowed down, as did the need for new generation capacities. However, Eskom's programme to build new power stations could not easily be stopped: orders had been placed and contracts concluded. This led to a growing reserve margin, reaching almost 40 per cent in 1991 (Eberhard 2007b: 219). In order to facilitate financing of capacity expansion, electricity tariffs increased by as much as 48 per cent in 1977 and by 22 per cent in 1982.

Following customer complaints, the government intervened. The central motivation was to implement an adequate control and management system that aimed to transform Eskom into a more efficient organization. A new organizational structure was introduced in 1985; this was the beginning of a phase commonly referred to as Eskom's commercialization process. Eskom changed over time from being an engineering-dominated organization to becoming a commercially thinking firm. The new strategy highlighted terms such as customer needs, cost-effectiveness, running Eskom as a business and value maximization. Balancing the trade-off between engineering excellence and organizational efficiency had not been part of Eskom's prior thinking and common identity. Similarly, laying off a substantial number of employees was a fundamental deviation from the 'old' Eskom. Between 1985 and 1990, Eskom reduced its staff from 66,000 employees to 50,000, whilst, at the same time, electricity supply rose by 20 per cent. Eskom also introduced a performance management system. The combined result of cutting the number of employees and improving the performance of personnel in the firm significantly increased Eskom's productivity.

With the sociopolitical transformation in South Africa in the 1990s, new policy frameworks were implemented, including employment equity legislation. At about the same time, a reform of the electricity sector was initiated, which included the opening up of the market to IPPs and the establishment of a national regulator. Both the sociopolitical transformation and the electricity sector reform had a major impact on Eskom and the energy sector as a whole.

At the organizational level, Eskom extended its so-called 'space creation' programme to respond to the government's new employment equity policy, which made it mandatory for companies to consist representatively of employees from previously disadvantaged groups. The space creation programme was initially launched in 1988 as part of the efforts in the commercialization process. Starting in the latter half of the 1990s, the programme aimed to hire more qualified black professionals for engineering, management and leadership roles in the organization, whilst employees from more privileged groupings retired. In this sense, the latter created space for a new cohort of employees at Eskom. The number of Eskom's employees declined further still to about 29,000 in 2004.

As part of the sector reform process, the South African government corporatized Eskom in 2001, which meant that the utility became a company fully owned by the DPE. Furthermore, the government envisaged the introduction of IPPs as a way of increasing investment (Marquard 2006: 187). To facilitate this sector reform, and to ensure that Eskom would not have an unfair advantage over new entries, the government also prohibited Eskom from building new generation capacity. When electricity demand grew remarkably, but not unexpectedly, in the early 2000s, Eskom's reserve margin started to decrease to an extent that supply shortages became more and more likely.

Responding to the looming shortages, Eskom was again allowed to construct new power stations in 2004. However, it became increasingly difficult for Eskom to balance demand and supply. Between 2005 and 2008, South Africa experienced several blackouts and significant load shedding. Moreover, Eskom was unable to keep its existing power plants working adequately. In January 2007, for example, almost 5,000 MW of capacity were not working due to technical breakdowns and equipment failures, in addition to another 5,000 MW of generation capacity out for planned maintenance. The electricity crisis caused costly damage to the economy and a substantial loss of welfare to electricity consumers (Eberhard 2007a). For example, there was an extensive period of power rationing, and even mines were forced to close for certain periods. Although the situation has stabilized since 2008, the status of South Africa's electricity system is still critical, with electricity supply substantially strained in peak hours and an ongoing risk of power outages.

2.5   Results: The Emergence of Capability Gaps

Six sets of factors were identified as having an impact on Eskom's capability structure in electricity generation, and as finally contributing to power outages. These are:
1) Electricity sector reforms
2) Sociopolitical transformation
3) Substantial cohorts of employees close to retirement
4) Technological change
5) Economic growth and an increased demand for qualified labour in the economy
6) Extreme weather conditions

Our analysis shows that there were two distinct mechanisms by which capability gaps were conditioned. Some factors affected the existing capability structure, for instance, by incentivizing experienced staff to leave the utility. Other factors altered the required capability structure by changing the nature of tasks. Table 2.1 summarizes the impact of these factors.

The first two sets of factors, namely electricity sector reforms and sociopolitical transformation after the end of apartheid, will be the focus of the subsequent analysis because they are of prime importance for our conceptual argument, and had a major effect on the capability structure at Eskom. The two factors are related to major public-policy-reform programmes, which were political efforts to improve economic efficiency and implement other public-policy goals in South Africa's electricity sector. More precisely, the electricity sector reforms included the commercialization of Eskom in order to improve the efficiency of power generation in South Africa, and the opening of the electricity supply market for private investment and IPPs. The sociopolitical reform programme included policies to ensure and enforce the implementation of equal-opportunity employment practices in South Africa. The impact of these two public-policy programmes will be elaborated on in Subsections 2.5.1 and 2.5.2.

The remaining four factors are either related to specific technical and natural conditions that characterize the electricity sector, or to general changes in the environment of the firm, e.g. economic growth, and are reported in Subsection 2.5.3. As they do not reflect the impact of regulatory changes on capabilities they receive somewhat less attention in the following.

2.5.1   *The Impact of Electricity Sector Reforms*

Two major reform processes of South Africa's electricity sector were initiated to ensure a broadly available, secure and efficient power supply. The first was the commercialization of Eskom in the mid-1980s. The second process was the government's reform of the regulatory framework. Begun in the late 1990s, it was intended for this reform to open the wholesale market for more private investment, and was linked to the corresponding cabinet decision that prohibited Eskom from building new generation capacity. The latter move can be characterized as an attempt to partly liberalize the electricity sector. As emerged from our data, the two processes had a substantial effect on Eskom's capability structure and contributed to the aggravation of capability gaps. However, the channels through which the sector reform processes affected the capabilities differed. Whilst the commercialization process decreased Eskom's existing capability structure, the changes of the regulatory framework, and specifically the government decision to stop Eskom from building new capacity, changed the nature of operating power plants considerably. This contributed to the capability gap by generating additional requirements for competences and skills that were already scarce. Table 2.2 summarizes the results and presents representative quotes.

2.5.1.1   Commercialization

Starting in 1985, Eskom went through a major organizational transition with long-lasting implications (Eberhard 2007b).The aim was to establish a more commercially professionalized organization with adequate management and control structures.

Our analysis showed that the commercialization process diminished Eskom's capability to operate power plants substantially. The emerging capability gaps were persistent and had long-lasting implications, which decisively contributed to Eskom's supply failures between 2005 and 2008. Six factors influenced Eskom's capabilities in the area of generation operation.

First, Eskom introduced an early retirement programme in 1986, to contain medium- to long-term operating costs. The scheme not only allowed operations staff to retire before the age of 65, but also paid out lucrative packages. By setting the early retirement age at 55, Eskom lost cohorts of highly experienced operators and operations managers between 1986 and 2004. And so, existing capabilities that comprised a substantial part of the company's long-term experience were lost.

Second, the commercialization process fostered the appointment of managers with business and financial skills to administer Eskom's business units. As a result, power-station managers with many years of engineering experience (thirty years on average) were replaced by relatively young power-station managers with degrees in business or finance. Similarly, the highly experienced (in engineering) operations managers were progressively replaced by cohorts of less experienced operations managers, most of whom possessed both a business and engineering degree. Over time, a strong financial focus was established at the expense of the engineering mindset. This change broadened the available capabilities within operations, but at the cost of a substantial decrease of the company's access to long-term experience in the engineering and technical aspects of operating power plants.

Third, as a result of this commercialization process, the identification of employees with Eskom as a long-term employer faded away, especially amongst engineers. As a mindset shift was required towards more commercial thinking, many engineers decided to leave the company. Furthermore, those engineers who were better qualified and who performed better tended to leave the company in larger numbers, because it was easier for them to find other positions

Table 2.2 *The impact of sector reform processes on the capability structure*

Impact of sector reform programmes	Description of the impact	Impact on the capability structure	Skills lacking as a result of the capability gap	Representative quotes
		Commercialization of Eskom starting in 1985		
Introducing early retirement programmes	Lucrative early retirement packages for staff between 55 and 65 years in order to contain operation costs	Loss of existing capabilities through retirement	Long-term experience in operating power plants	'.. we allowed a lot of experience [operators and operations managers] to move out of the organization … you know, with early retirement packages, etc.' '… the lack of skilled operators is a problem … I have operators that have put in water too fast in the boiler, or have dropped temperature too fast in a boiler or have fired the boiler too fast. Those [operating errors] affect … the generating plant'
Increasing managerial competences	Appointment of managers with business and financial skills	Loss of existing capabilities through the replacement of managers with extensive engineering and operation experience	Long-term experience in operating power plants	'[We] introduced a lot more business competence. We started to employ chartered accountants; we started to get exposure in management to financial people and commercial people other than engineers'

Resignations	Commercialization required mindset shift amongst engineers from engineering excellence to commercial thinking, i.e. focus on cost minimization and strict performance criteria	Loss of existing capabilities as a result of engineering personnel leaving	Long-term experience in operating power plants	'I think the level of rigour with which people appreciate the importance of running those systems in a certain manner; I think that must have changed' 'From 2005 onwards we reinforced the need to maintain ... the systems, thinking in terms of maintenance and so forth, because we saw it going downhill'
Implementing a leaner organizational structure	Reduction of personnel to save costs, e.g. spare shifts that operated power plants when regular operators underwent training	Loss of existing capabilities as a result of reducing number of personnel in operations	Long-term experience and possibilities for younger personnel to gain experience decreased	'It was John Maree [Eskom's Board Chairman between 1984 and 1998] who said: "There are too many people working here! Our job isn't to supply jobs. Our job is to supply cheap electricity and then, other industries will supply jobs." And so ... some power stations were closed and all the staff moved on' '... on the operating side of the plant, we used to have, what we call the spare shift. I don't think there's many stations these days which have got a spare shift anymore' '..with cost-cutting the [power] station would not be able to afford to have [an] additional shift [and] ... to make sure that the people [operators] are being retrained continually'

Table 2.2 (cont.)

Impact of sector reform programmes	Description of the impact	Impact on the capability structure	Skills lacking as a result of the capability gap	Representative quotes
		Commercialization of Eskom starting in 1985		
Decreasing training budgets	Number of instructors and operators in training progressively reduced as Eskom considered outsourcing power-plant operations	Loss of existing capabilities through reducing training personnel and personnel in training	Long-term experience and possibilities for younger personnel to gain experience decreased	'… the money [training budget] … allowed a limited number of experienced instructors to sit [remain in the organization]. So, even if we wanted to do training, maybe we did not have enough instructors available for that'
		Changes of the policy and regulatory framework starting in 1998		
Running power plants harder	Operating the power plants at higher load levels in response to the diminished reserve margin	Additional capabilities required	Disproportionately high inputs for managing, operating and controlling at the operator and operations management level was required	'… [The operation regime is] not the same animal that we had ten years ago … it's a different animal. It was a lazy donkey then, this is a wild horse now' '[To] move from 65 per cent to 70 per cent load factor means I probably don't work 5 per cent harder, I am actually working 15 per cent harder to achieve the same thing … ' 'As you get closer to the maximum [levels] of driving the plant … and also, trying to overcome other limitations …

			'within that, poor coal quality, increased emissions ... those type of things ... by trying to operate your plant [at higher load levels], you [the operations manager] are actually putting it under more stress than what you would think'
Re-commissioning power plants	Operating previously decommissioned power plants as response to the diminished reserve margin	Additional capabilities required	Experience in operating the old power-plant technologies was required	'... if you have older people [operators] with newer technology, that, that in itself is a mismatch ...' '... in terms of technology ... that environment is changing ... because now most things are monitored [computerized monitoring] ... most of our plants [are] now condition monitored'
Running plants with less maintenance	Operating power plants with limited maintenance as response to the diminished reserve margin	Additional capabilities required	Broader knowledge about the interactions of the different parts of a power station was required	'I [as an operator] cannot operate the plant as I was taught to do, because the plant is no longer the same'

in the job market. The implication was not only the loss of competences and skills, but also that the average qualifications and experience of the remaining engineering staff declined.

Fourth, in an attempt to improve financial viability, Eskom adopted a leaner organizational structure. One example of re-organization was to phase out the cohort of experienced – and more costly – operators that made up the spare shift in the power stations. The purpose of the spare shift was to keep the power stations operational when the less experienced operators were undergoing training. Usually, operator training in Eskom's power stations takes a long time, and requires the combination of training during plant operations with training through simulations at the Eskom College in Johannesburg. Phasing out the spare shift of experienced operators substantially diminished the training opportunities available for the next generation of operators. Both experience and the possibility to gain experience decreased, with the consequence of inadequate plant operation.

Fifth, Eskom's new management decreased the power stations' training budgets. As a result, the number of operators in training decreased progressively. Some of Eskom's more experienced operator instructors were forced to retire as a number of training facilities were dismantled and replaced with a more centralized operator training structure (the Eskom College and Academy of Learning). The diminished number of instructors resulted in insufficient training opportunities for less experienced plant operators.

Sixth, and finally, in an attempt to further reduce operating costs due to low electricity demand and an increasingly idle generation capacity, Eskom's management started to decommission some of its older and more labour-intensive plants in the mid-1980s. This also resulted in many experienced operators and operations managers retiring early.

2.5.1.2   *Changes in the Policy and Regulatory Framework*

Part of South Africa's democratic transformation in the 1990s was a new energy policy. A key element of this new policy was to establish a competitive wholesale electricity market (see Energy Policy White Paper of 1998). To foster this process, South Africa's government enacted a moratorium, in 2000, forbidding Eskom from building any power stations in the future, whilst a Nordpool-style power exchange and market was being designed. The thinking amongst policy makers at the time was that this was an essential prerequisite for creating a competitive wholesale electricity market. It was assumed the moratorium would stimulate the private sector to enter the electricity supply market and undertake a substantial part of the required generation capacity expansions in a more cost-effective manner. However, the proposed power pool was not implemented and the moratorium failed to attract significant private-sector investment in the four years that it was in effect. No procurement or contractual arrangements were put in place to attract IPPs. Consequently, South Africa's electricity generation capacity remained stagnant.

The robust growth in electricity demand, and a fixed supply of electricity, severely depleted Eskom's generation reserve margin from 27.1 per cent in 1999 to 5.1 per cent in 2007. In an attempt to meet the escalating demand, Eskom responded in three ways. Firstly, it ran its power plants at higher capacity factors. Secondly, the utility recommissioned and ran some of its very old, and previously mothballed, thermal plant fleet. And thirdly, Eskom had to operate its power plants whilst carrying out less maintenance work on them because of the tight reserve margins, which made scheduled maintenance more difficult. As we will demonstrate in this section, and as presented in Table 2.2, all three responses changed the nature of operating power plants and affected their required capability structure, and also contributed to the emerging capability gap. In effect, changes in power-plant operation would have required a different – or at least adjusted – capability structure.

Regarding running its power plants harder, Eskom had historically run its thermal plant at load levels below 60 per cent. In fact, it was only in the years of severe crises in the mid-1950s and early 1980s that Eskom's thermal plants ran at maximum load levels in excess of 60 per cent. In all other years until 1995, the thermal plants ran at load factors of 53 to 58 per cent. After 2003, the load profile of the thermal power stations changed considerably. Whilst the load factors were about 61 per cent in 1999, they were between 74 and 78 per cent in 2008. The increased stress from operating the thermal plant at such high load levels not only altered the reliability of the plant by making it more vulnerable to failure, but also increased the level of capability required in order to perform operational tasks at the managerial and operator levels. One interviewee illustrated the changed nature of performing generation operations in this way: ' ... [the operation regime is] not the same animal that we had ten years ago ... it's a different animal. It was a lazy donkey then, this is a wild horse now.'

Running the plant harder required a disproportionately great increase in human and material input. For example, one interviewee explained that a 5 per cent increase in the load factor required about 15 per cent more work input to manage, operate and control the process. In addition to the changed requirements at the operator level, an increase of capabilities was also required at the operations manager level. Managers had to facilitate more cautious operation of the highly stressed plant. They also had to adapt its operating systems to the increasing complexities. This entailed re-assessing and redesigning various aspects of the thermal plant operating regime; in fact, no one at Eskom had experience of running the plants at these higher load factors.

The second internal Eskom process that was initiated in order to respond to the crisis was the re-commissioning of power plants that Eskom had decommissioned when it had excess generation capacity, and as a result of the commercialization process. Running a fleet of aged and re-commissioned thermal plants represented a new and complicated task for Eskom. Between 1980 and 2000, Eskom procured and commissioned six new, technologically advanced, coal-powered plants. The utility also modernized its thermal fleet's operating regimes and staff complement as a precursor to computerizing its plant operations process. Simultaneously, it phased out its older and more labour-intensive fleet of thermal plants, along with a large section of the plant staff (Conradie and Messerschmidt 2000).

By 2005, this situation had changed considerably, as Eskom's excess capacity had expired. Eskom attempted to modernize its previously decommissioned thermal plants, but it proved difficult to completely overhaul all of the old plant's operating systems because they were premised on old engineering designs and technologies. As a consequence, only older operators and operations managers were able to operate these old plants. The younger, and better formally educated operators, found themselves at variance with the old plant technologies and systems. According to one interviewee, the cohort of operators and operations managers around the mid-2000s were not familiar with operating a thermal plant without 'bells and whistles', which is a reference to the ability to run a power plant without adequate IT operational controls.

A third implication of the diminished reserve margins was that Eskom had to run its plants with less maintenance. This was a significant change, because operating a power plant that is regularly maintained according to a schedule is a different process from operating one that is not maintained. The maintenance staff would have needed broader knowledge about the interactions of the different parts of a power station in order to understand which parts required priority observation and treatment when not maintained according to schedule. Given the tightened windows of opportunity to take the power stations off the grid for planned maintenance, project management know-how was required to ensure project procedures carried out the necessary maintenance strictly within the defined timelines.

In sum, the commercialization process and changes in the policy and regulatory framework ultimately resulted in tightened reserve margins. This had a substantial impact on Eskom's generation capabilities, as highly experienced personnel left the organization. The personnel's long-term experience in operating power plants diminished. As a result, operators and operations managers were not able to operate the plant adequately. This already critical situation was further exacerbated when sector reform processes led to a moratorium on Eskom investments in new generation capacity, and declining reserve margins. As an unintended consequence of this policy, the plants had to be run harder, which in turn required additional capabilities. This widened the capability gap even further.

2.5.2 The Impact of South Africa's Sociopolitical Transformation

Sociopolitical transformation further amplified the high employee turnover caused by the sector reform processes. Accelerated retirement and resignation of key staff affected Eskom's generation capabilities critically. Power-generation-related capabilities diminished. The transformation in South Africa impacted on Eskom's capability structure in generation through three underlying specific factors. Table 2.3 summarizes the results and presents representative quotes.

One crucial factor was the government's employment equity policy and Eskom's response to it, which it described as the 'space creation' programme. In the early 1990s, Eskom started to promote a few selected individuals from previously disadvantaged backgrounds into the previously all-white middle and higher echelons of power-station management as part of the space creation programme. Although it was implemented in a piecemeal manner in the beginning, the programme focused on filling operator and operations-manager positions that had become vacant as a result of retirements and resignations.

This initial response to political and social change, e.g. to the release of Nelson Mandela in 1990 and the commencement of constitutional negotiations, was followed up in the late 1990s with the acceleration of the early retirement programme. Following the democratic elections in 1994, the ANC-led administration enacted the Reconstruction and Development Programme (RDP) of 1995 and Employment Equity Act of 1997, which set very stringent targets for companies in South Africa to achieve demographically representative staffing profiles. In an attempt to

Table 2.3 *The impact of sociopolitical reform programmes on the capability structure*

Impact of sociopolitical reform programmes	Description of the impact	Impact on the capability structure	Skills lacking as a result of the capability gap	Representative quotes
Government policy on employment equity and Eskom's response of implementing space creation				
Extending the early retirement programmes	Retirement age was further decreased, with lucrative early retirement packages offered to staff aged between 45 and 65 years to create space for a new cohort of engineers and managers	Loss of existing capabilities through retirement	Long-term experience in operating power plants	'The young engineers [operations managers], they are probably technically qualified and they [are] trying their best to be there [operate the plants], but there are certain aspects that they can't inherit from me [older operations manager] or, from you or, from anybody else, they've got to learn it themselves. And with the power stations being in a more stressful operating environment they don't have the time to learn. They are expected to understand immediately and probably to know better than the old engineers [operations managers] knew because the conditions are now tougher [diminished reserve margins]'
Resignations	Following the sociopolitical change in South Africa, a substantial number left Eskom as a state-owned enterprise or even the country	Loss of existing capabilities as a result of the loss of personnel	Long-term experience in operating power plants	'. . . a lot of people have gone to Australia. I know good people [operators and operations managers] that have gone to Australia. The demand there is huge.'

Pursuing multiple goals	Managers lost focus by pursuing demographic transformation in addition to engineering excellence in power-station operation	Loss of existing capabilities as a result of loss of engineering personnel	'... overseas companies, targeted specific skills like plant operators. ... It just meant that we [Eskom] had less spare capacity [on the operating side of the plant] ...'
			'... the organization had a more focused engineering mindset prior to 1994. After 1994 it became more politically conscious. When it became more politically conscious it started driving the transformation agenda [tackling the demographic imbalance within Eskom's organizational structures] more than the engineering agenda .... which was fine, but it didn't ... let's say, it didn't sufficiently in my mind ... at least, recognize the importance of the engineering agenda. So, we sort of changed priorities along the way'
		Long-term experience in operating power plants	'I would say the next generation of management [operations managers] wasn't as forceful [in enforcing engineering excellence], they were more transformational leaders [focused on demographic transformation within Eskom]'
			'... we had these chaps operating [the thermal power stations] here, that really made bad mistakes, and we could not understand. Then, they [the power-station operators] had supervisors working who really were not experienced. They [the power stations] had inexperienced supervisors supervising inexperienced operators ...'

achieve approximately 60 per cent representation for black individuals from previously disadvantaged backgrounds in middle to top management levels between 1996 and 2000, Eskom scaled up its space creation programme. Eskom reduced the retirement age for experienced white operators and operations managers from 55 to 45 years in an attempt to create space for affirmative action appointees, and achieve national affirmative action targets. At the same time, a larger number of operators and operations managers from previously disadvantaged backgrounds were appointed or promoted into these positions, based mainly on potential (as opposed to years of specialist engineering experience) and within a context of limited succession planning.

A second factor was that a wave of resignations affected the cohort of experienced operations staff that were well below the retirement age. There were various reasons for this; within this cohort, one stream of (mainly white) operators and operations managers resigned from Eskom because they did not want to work under black management (supervisors, managers or executives). Another stream of experienced operators and operations managers resigned from Eskom and left South Africa on account of perceived uncertainties of life in the post-apartheid political dispensation.

Finally, managers lost focus whilst pursuing multiple goals, thus further aggravating capability gaps. The primary focus shifted from managing the attainment of engineering excellence in operations to administering organizational-level demographic transformations. As a result of the progressive decline of experience in Eskom, subsequent cohorts of less experienced technical supervisors and operations managers failed to adequately supervise their subordinates in plant operations, and thereby caused operator errors.

In sum, transformational factors such as the adoption of employment equity policy and pursuit of affirmative action as an additional organizational goal impacted on the existing capability structure of power stations by resulting in the loss of experienced labour at the operator and operations-manager levels. In making this observation, the authors do not wish to convey the impression that these policies were not necessary. Indeed, they most certainly were; apartheid had systematically blocked opportunities for black South Africans. We merely note that the way these employment equity and affirmative action policies were implemented exacerbated an already perilous problem within Eskom around operational experience. As the power stations had an already limited cadre of experienced operators and operations managers due to high employee loss as a result of the commercialization process, the remaining staff were partly replaced with less experienced operating staff from previously disadvantaged backgrounds. Consequently, the level of available experience for the performance of operations tasks diminished further in this second wave of lost critical competences and skills. The subsequent promotion of young and relatively inexperienced operators and operations managers further eroded the level of experience available, and ensured that the operation performance remained persistently low over time. It is important to highlight that it was less the engineering qualifications that were lost, more the engineering experience. Regarding qualifications, the incoming young cohort of engineers were highly qualified and brought modern engineering knowledge into Eskom.

Summing up, the policy-induced reform programmes created persistent capability gaps within the utility, which ultimately resulted in severe performance deficiencies. Certain positions within the power-station operations departments could no longer be filled and as a consequence, the operations managers were increasingly unable to understand the technical complexities across the integrated generation processes. Therefore, operators failed to strictly adhere to the plants' specific operating procedures.

2.5.3   *Further Factors Contributing to the Loss of Capabilities in Electricity Generation*

In addition to the two public-policy programmes presented above, technical, general economic and natural conditions affected the capability structure of Eskom in a negative way. We identified four additional factors that contributed to a loss of capabilities in electricity generation (see Table 2.1 for a summary).

Firstly, electricity sectors represent large technical systems with long lifetimes (Markard 2011). As a consequence of Eskom's power-generation capacity expansion in the 1970s and 1980s, a large number of engineers and technicians involved in the construction of power stations were hired to operate the plants. A considerable part of this cohort faced retirement in the late 1990s and 2000s. In these years, Eskom lost a highly experienced group of staff with intimate knowledge of the specificities of the various power plants. This caused a significant gap in the company's existing capability structure.

Secondly, new technologies in electricity generation contributed to the emergence of capability gaps. In order to reduce over-capacity, older power plants were decommissioned and mothballed, i.e. shut down and put into long-term storage, and power-plant staff were offered jobs at other, newer Eskom plants. Many of these newer plants were operated with technologies that were much more IT-based than the older power stations; staff members close to retirement, in particular, showed little enthusiasm for learning about new generation technologies. Therefore, they accepted early retirement offers or decided to leave Eskom. This development generated a capability gap with a loss of long-term experience in generation, which became relevant later on when formerly decommissioned power plants had to be put back into operation due to dwindling reserve margins.

Thirdly, strong economic growth after the fall of the apartheid regime in 1994 resulted in an increasingly competitive labour market, with a high demand for skilled professionals – particularly in the engineering and technical area. This created pressure and a novel situation for Eskom, which had been one of the top employers for engineers for a long time. The favourable situation in the labour market led to many employees leaving Eskom. Once established in new private companies, they encouraged former Eskom colleagues to join them. Moreover, the loss of capabilities had a bias in the sense that the better-performing employees, who often also had more experience, left because their chances of finding attractive positions outside Eskom were higher. At the same time, there was an increasing exodus of experienced professionals out of South Africa to utilities in Europe, North America and Australia.

Finally, exceptional weather conditions during the years of the major blackouts, coupled with increased demand, contributed further to the loss of capabilities. Unusually heavy rainfall in January and February 2008 decreased the quality of coal. Handling and processing the wet coal at power stations altered the nature of the task. Wet coal had lower net calorific values per unit mass and power plants had to be run harder; i.e. with higher load factors and fewer opportunities for maintenance. Because of the uncertainty of operating these plants under unexpected and largely unknown conditions, more experience was required; i.e. there was a need for more engineers and technicians with an intimate understanding of the affected power plants, and of how their various components interacted under a tight operating regime.

2.6   Discussion

Our empirical findings suggest that a central underlying reason for the inadequate operation of Eskom's power plants was a dramatic lack of operation-related competences and skills. We identified six factors that either caused the loss of highly experienced engineering, technical and managerial capabilities, or significantly changed the nature of the tasks Eskom had to perform in generation operations. Two public-policy-reform programmes had particularly severe unintended effects on

Eskom's capability structure. They caused a loss of capabilities due to experienced personnel leaving the utility, and due to changes in the various tasks that required staff to have new capabilities that were not readily available. This explains why power plants were not operated to an adequate standard, which contributed to the power outages. Other factors, such as technological change, economic growth and extreme weather conditions, reinforced this effect and therefore aggravated the power crisis.

In addition to the immediate impact on the capability structure, the loss of experienced staff had long-lasting consequences. Many positions remained vacant because the acquisition and build-up of professional experience takes time in this sector. Succession programmes have to be planned and implemented over considerable time spans. Thus, the long-term experience of operating power plants, which the ex-staff had accumulated, could be replaced neither by young professionals nor by externally hired experts in the short term. Furthermore, little emphasis was placed on programmes to ensure capabilities were maintained at the beginning of the reform processes. This was because policy makers did not expect the changes in the policy and regulatory environment to have a relevant and negative influence on Eskom's capability structure and performance.

Surprisingly, during the electricity crisis, many actors with an intimate knowledge of South Africa's electricity sector acknowledged the relevance of capabilities and the significance of losing them. But they failed to develop a collective perception of the cumulative effect that the public-policy programmes had had on the capability structure, and of how that had affected organization and, ultimately, sector performance. More generally, the trade-off between the necessity of sector reforms and transformational policies on the one hand, and the impact on organizational capabilities on the other, has received hardly any attention.

Inferring from these insights, we draw two conclusions. First, the capability dimension is an important, but neglected and little-understood, dimension of infrastructure sector regulation in both research and practice. Second, and as a consequence, there is little knowledge of the specific challenges that emerge at the organizational level due to sector reforms and regulations, and how these affect the performance of utilities and other firms in the sector. Our results are, therefore, a strong call for more research to gain a better and more detailed understanding of the causes, mechanisms and implications of infrastructure sector reform processes as they relate to capabilities, and to examine more thoroughly the specificities and time lags of these processes.

Moreover, our analysis adds a further root cause to the existing list of causes (see Figure 2.1) for South Africa's power outages between 2005 and 2008. Power plants were not only maintained to an insufficient level (NERSA 2006, 2008), but also inadequately operated, which was an additional reason why the existing generation capacity was unavailable. This is an important finding, because it reveals that sector reforms influenced Eskom's operational capabilities critically. Even if sufficient generation capacity had been built and maintained, inadequate capabilities in operations, due to unintended consequences of the sector reform process, would have jeopardized secure electricity supply. Thus, our findings show, more generally, that policy and regulatory changes not only influence the level of investment in a sector but have – through their impact on capabilities – a substantial effect on organizational-level processes such as operations and maintenance.

This argument is corroborated by the examination of other causes commonly listed as explanations for the power failures in South Africa in 2005–2008. Our in-depth analysis of Eskom's capacity expansion, maintenance and coal-contracting processes suggests that similar mechanisms could be identified across power-plant operations. In other words, the different public-policy reforms caused a substantial loss of competences and skills across all organizational functions within Eskom. And these were important factors explaining why the blackouts occurred, and why they could not be remedied within an acceptable time span.

However, whilst our study looked into the consequences of changes in policy and regulation, other factors may also have negatively affected organizational capabilities. For example, there is evidence of significant attempts at political capture of Eskom's corporate governance, which may have led to management decisions that undermined necessary organizational transformation and restructuring efforts. Politically driven governance dynamics may also have resulted in management decision making that gave limited attention to cost and efficiency implications, and therefore contributed to performance deficiencies. Finally, the findings do not recommend slowing down or even reversing the efforts to reform South Africa's electricity sector. On the contrary, they suggest that policy, regulatory and management decision makers take the crucial role of capabilities in these reform processes more carefully into account.

To what extent can these results be generalized beyond the specific context of the selected case study? An obvious specificity of our case is the sociopolitical transformation process that South Africa accomplished after the end of the apartheid regime. However, South Africa's transformation can be understood as a particularly broad case of a changing policy and regulatory environment. Examples of less far-reaching policy changes may still show similar impacts on capabilities. For instance, if a government's energy policy aims at promoting new electricity generation technologies, there is a need to take into consideration the emerging trade-off between the achievement of an intended policy goal and its unintended effect on the capability structure, and to actively manage this trade-off. In this sense, the broad transformational and regulatory changes in this study reflect and illustrate policy-induced situations, in which utilities might be confronted with the loss of qualified personnel and struggle to attract employees with the required experience.

South Africa also represents a special case in the sense that Eskom dominates its national electricity supply. This situation is by no means unique. But it has been a key advantage for us in that it has allowed us to track the immediate consequences of capability gaps at the sectoral level, and comprehensively study the impact of public-policy reform programmes on the nationwide failure of the electricity supply. It might be argued that a sector with more power generators would have been able to adjust faster to the challenges posed by regulatory and transformational changes. This is because a greater number of firms would have enabled the initiation of different trial-and-error processes to cope with, and respond to, those challenges. Ideally, other utilities could have imitated the best practices. Conversely, one might also argue that several small utilities, which were very similar and relatively homogeneous in their structure and function, would not have been able to develop an adequate response to the emerging complex challenges in the way that a large organization such as Eskom could. Therefore, further research is needed to understand the role that sector structure plays in the response processes of utilities to policy and regulatory reforms.

2.7   Conclusions

In this chapter, we applied a capability perspective to the analysis of the performance of utilities and other strongly regulated firms in order to better understand the unintended consequences of sector reforms. Analysing South Africa's electricity sector and the causes that led to Eskom's poor performance between 2005 and 2008, the findings exemplify how the complex interaction of various factors influences a firm's capability structure and, in turn, determines its performance. Electricity sector reforms and other public policies may, in fact, affect the capability structure of utility firms in a fundamental and sometimes even irreversible way.

On the one hand, regulation can have a direct impact on the structure of organizational capabilities. This is the case when capabilities are split into different organizational entities or when organizations lose know-how. A typical example of the first case is the unbundling of generation, network operation and sales in the electricity sector. An example of the second case from this study is Eskom's space creation programme, which was triggered by electricity sector and sociopolitical reforms in South Africa, and as a result of which Eskom experienced a substantial loss of experienced staff.

On the other hand, regulation can have an indirect effect on organizational capabilities due to changes in the tasks and requirements an organization has to fulfil. Changing tasks and requirements necessitate new capabilities that may not be readily available. An example from this study is the decision to re-commission previously decommissioned power plants. This required know-how in operating old power-plant technologies, which was not sufficiently available. The capability effect of this decision became even more problematic as power plants operated under limited reserve margins.

More generally, we can expect that many electricity utilities will have difficulties in adapting to a more competitive market environment, or to technological changes related to decentralized renewable power generation, which are mostly stimulated and accompanied by new regulations. The direct and indirect effects of these factors on organizational capabilities may lead to severe and persistent capability gaps. The impact of regulation on organizational capabilities is certainly an under-researched topic, both in the literature on regulation and in the field of management studies.

Traditional explanations of utility sector reforms have neglected the role of capabilities and have, instead, primarily focused on incentive structures and contractual concerns. The prevalence of these explanations may have contributed to our finding that there was hardly any perception at the sectoral and organizational levels of the relevance and importance of capability losses. We showed that the capability perspective provides a complementary explanation for the unfolding of an electricity supply crisis. Our findings suggest that, in addition to establishing adequate incentives and contracts, the impact of policy reforms on organizational capabilities decisively determines the success of the reforms themselves. In other words, even if the incentive structures are sufficiently established, the loss of substantial capabilities may undermine the intended outcome of such programmes. Thus, reform programmes need to implement adequate measures to track and mitigate any negative influence they might have on organizational capabilities.

Summing up, we have laid out the basic argument that reform processes have a fundamental impact on the capability structure of utility firms and, therefore, influence the performance of public service delivery. It is critical to recognize the importance of organizational capabilities, especially when there is a runoff of experience due to ageing out, processes of organizational restructuring and changes in the political, regulatory and economic environment. Furthermore, if a technical or organizational system goes into stress, the required capabilities tend to be higher and so require even more careful attention. With these results, we add the capability dimension to the literature on regulation, sector reform and the governance of utilities. The findings from applying this perspective suggest that capability-related processes, and their impacts, need to be taken much more seriously in order to achieve successful utility sector reforms.

Acknowledgement

The authors gratefully acknowledge financial support from the Swiss–South African Joint Research Programme (SSAJRP), Project No.7.

References

Armstrong, M. and Sappington, D. E. M. (2006). Regulation, competition, and liberalization. *Journal of Economic Literature*, 44(2): 325–366.

Barney, J. (1991). Firm resources and sustained competitive advantage. *Journal of Management*, 17(1): 99–120.

Barney, J. B., Ketchen Jr., D. J. and Wright, M. (2011). The future of resource-based theory: Revitalization or decline? *Journal of Management*, 37 (5): 1299–1315.

Capron, L. and Mitchell, W. (2009). Selection capability: How capability gaps and internal social frictions affect internal and external strategic renewal. *Organization Science*, 20(2): 294–312.

Conradie, S. R. and Messerschmidt, L. J. M. (2000). *A symphony of power: The Eskom story*. Johannesburg: Chris van Rensburg Publications.

Delmas, M. and Tokat, Y. (2005). Deregulation, governance structures, and efficiency: The U.S. electric utility sector. *Strategic Management Journal*, 26 (5): 441–460.

Delmas, M. A., Russo, M. V., Montes-Sancho, M. J. and Tokat, Y. (2009). Deregulation, efficiency and environmental performance: Evidence from the electric utility industry. In C. Ménard and M. Ghertman (Eds.), *Regulation, deregulation, reregulation: Institutional perspectives*. Cheltenham and Northampton, MA: Edward Elgar, pp. 170–195.

Dierickx, I. and Cool, K. (1989). Asset stock accumulation and sustainability of competitive advantage. *Management Science*, 35(12): 1504–1511.

Dominguez, D., Worch, H., Markard, J., Truffer, B. and Gujer, W. (2009). Closing the capability gap: Strategic planning for the infrastructure sector. *California Management Review*, 51(2): 30–50.

Dyner, I. and Larsen, E. R. (2001). From planning to strategy in the electricity industry. *Energy Policy*, 29(13): 1145–1154.

Eberhard, A. (2007a). Plugging into source of the failures. *Business Day*, p. 13.

Eberhard, A. (2007b). The political economy of power sector reform in South Africa. In D. Victor and T. C. Heller (Eds.), *The political economy of power sector reform: The experiences of five major developing countries*. Cambridge: Cambridge University Press, pp. 215–253.

Eberhard, A. and Shkaratan, M. (2012). Powering Africa: Meeting the financing and reform challenges. *Energy Policy*, 42(1): 9–18.

Eisenhardt, K. M. (1989). Building theories from case study research. *Academy of Management Review*, 14(4): 532–550.

Eisenhardt, K. M. and Martin, J. A. (2000). Dynamic capabilities: What are they? *Strategic Management Journal*, 21(10–11): 1105–1121.

Gebauer, H., Worch, H. and Truffer, B. (2012). Absorptive capacity, learning processes and combinative capabilities as determinants of strategic innovation. *European Management Journal*, 30(1): 57–73.

Gil, N. and Beckman, S. L. (2009). Infrastructure meets business: Building new bridges, mending old ones. *California Management Review*, 51(2): 6–29.

Gómez-Ibáñez, J. A. (2003). *Regulating infrastructure: Monopoly, contracts, and discretion.* Cambridge, Massachusetts, and London: Harvard University Press.

Gómez-Ibáñez, J. A. (2007). Alternatives to infrastructure privatization revisited: Public enterprise reform from the 1960s to the 1980s. Policy Research Working Paper No. 4391, World Bank, November 2007.

Gratwick, K. N. and Eberhard, A. (2008). Demise of the standard model for power sector reform and the emergence of hybrid power markets. *Energy Policy*, 36(10): 3948–3960.

Guthrie, G. (2006). Regulating infrastructure: The impact on risk and investment. *Journal of Economic Literature*, 44(4): 925–972.

Hamukoma, B. and Levy, B. (2019). When the quest for electricity reform and the need for investment collide: South Africa, 1998–2004. In N. Gil, A. Stafford and I. Musonda (Eds.), *Duality by design: The global race to build Africa's infrastructure*. Cambridge: Cambridge University Press, pp. 69–96.

Irwin, T. and Yamamoto, C. (2004). Some options for improving the governance of state-owned electricity utilities. Energy and Mining Sector Board Discussion Paper No. 11, World Bank, February 2004. www.energytoolbox.org/library/w ater_utility_corporatization/references/Some_Options_for_Improving_Electri city_Utility_Governance.pdf.

Joskow, P. L. (2002). Electricity sector restructuring and competition: A transaction-cost perspective. In E. Brousseau and J.-M. Glachant (Eds.), *The economics of contracts: Theories and applications*. Cambridge: Cambridge University Press, pp. 503–530.

Joskow, P. L. (2008). Lessons learned from electricity market liberalization. *Energy Journal*, 29 (Special Issue 2): 9–42.

Karplus, V. J., Lessard, D. R., Rajpurkar, N., and Singh, A. (2019). Institutional enablers of energy system transition: Lessons from solar photovoltaic in eight African countries. In N. Gil, A. Stafford and I. Musonda (Eds.), *Duality by design: The global race to build Africa's infrastructure*. Cambridge: Cambridge University Press, pp. 97–129.

Kraaijenbrink, J., Spender, J.-C. and Groen, A. J. (2010). The resource-based view: A review and assessment of its critiques. *Journal of Management*, 36(1): 349–372.

Künneke, R., Groenewegen, J. and Ménard, C. (2010). Aligning modes of organization with technology: Critical transactions in the reform of infrastructures. *Journal of Economic Behavior and Organization*, 75(3): 494–505.

Lavie, D. (2006). Capability reconfiguration: An analysis of incumbent responses to technological change. *Academy of Management Review*, 31(1): 153–174.

Markard, J. (2011). Transformation of infrastructures: Sector characteristics and implications for fundamental change. *Journal of Infrastructure Systems*, 17(3): 95–136.

Marquard, A. (2006). The origins and development of South African energy policy. Phd thesis. University of Cape Town, January 2006. www .erc.uct.ac.za/sites/default/files/image_tool/images/119/Papers-2006/06Marqu ard-PhD_Thesis.pdf

Miles, M. B. and Huberman, A. M. (1994). *Qualitative data analysis: An expanded sourcebook* (2nd ed.). Thousand Oaks, London, New Delhi: Sage.

National Planning Commission (2011). Diagnostic overview. The Presidency, Republic of South Africa.

NERSA (2006). *Investigation into the electricity outages in the Western Cape for the period November 2005 to March 2006*. Pretoria: National Energy Regulator of South Africa.

NERSA (2008, 12 May). *Inquiry into the national electricity supply shortage and load shedding*. Pretoria: National Energy Regulator of South Africa.

Newbert, S. L. (2007). Empirical research on the resource-based view of the firm: An assessment and suggestions for future research. *Strategic Management Journal*, 28(2): 121–146.

OECD (2006). *Infrastructure to 2030: Telecom, land transport, water and electricity*. Paris: OECD Publishing.

OECD (2007). *Infrastructure to 2030 (Volume 2): Mapping policy for electricity, water and transport*. Paris: OECD Publishing.

Pollitt, M. (2008). The arguments for and against ownership unbundling of energy transmission networks. *Energy Policy*, 36(2): 704–713.

Public Protector South Africa (2009, February 18). Report on a preliminary investigation relating to electricity load shedding implemented by Eskom Holdings Limited. Report No. 31 of 2008/9.

Rahmandad, H. and Repenning, N. (2016). Capability erosion dynamics. *Strategic Management Journal*, 37(4): 649–672.

Rose, A., Pérez-Arriaga, I., Stoner, R. and de Neufville, R. (2019). Harnessing Africa's energy resources through regional infrastructure projects. In N. Gil, A. Stafford and I. Musonda (Eds.), *Duality by design: The global race to build Africa's infrastructure*. Cambridge: Cambridge University Press, pp. 130–160.

Spiller, P. T. and Tommasi, M. (2005). The institutions of regulation: An application to public utilities. In C. Menard and M. M. Shirley (Eds.), *Handbook of new institutional economics*. Dordrecht: Springer.

Teece, D. J., Pisano, G. and Shuen, A. (1997). Dynamic capabilities and strategic management. *Strategic Management Journal*, 18(7): 509–533.

UN (2007). UN global compact annual review: 2007 Leaders Summit. United Nations Global Compact Office. New York: United Nations. www .unglobalcompact.org/docs/news_events/8.1/GCAnnualReview2007.pdf

UN-HABITAT (2011). *Infrastructure for economic development* and *poverty reduction in Africa*. Nairobi: UN-HABITAT.

von Hirschhausen, C., Beckers, T. and Brenck, A. (2011). Infrastructure regulation and investment for the long-term – An introduction. *Utilities Policy*, 12(4): 203–210.

Winter, S. G. (2003). Understanding dynamic capabilities. *Strategic Management Journal*, 24(10): 991–995.

Worch, H., Kabinga, M., Eberhard, A. and Truffer, B. (2012). Strategic renewal and the change of capabilities in utility firms. *European Business Review*, 24(5), 444–464.

Worch, H., Truffer, B., Kabinga, M., Eberhard, A. and Markard, J. (2013). A capability perspective on performance deficiencies in utility firms. *Utilities Policy*, 25 (June): 1–9.

Worch, H., Truffer, B., Kabinga, M., Markard, J. and Eberhard, A. (2012, January). Tackling the capability gap in utility firms: Applying management research to infrastructure sectors. CID Research Fellow and Graduate Student Working Paper No. 55. Harvard: Center for International Development at Harvard University.

Zollo, M., and Winter, S. G. (2002). Deliberate learning and the evolution of dynamic capabilities. *Organization Science*, 13(3): 339–351.

3   When the Quest for Electricity Reform
     and the Need for Investment Collide:
     South Africa, 1998–2004

Nchimunya Hamukoma and Brian Levy

Abstract

In 1998 South Africa signalled its intent to pursue a far-reaching agenda of electricity-sector reform. This chapter explores the political challenges of moving from vision to action – with a focus on decision-making vis-à-vis reforming the market structure for electricity generation, and setting prices for purchases from electricity generation providers. Whilst on the surface the reforms were supported by government, beneath that surface were many unresolved conflicts amongst stakeholders. The result was six years of reform churning – at a time when forward progress with investment in new electricity generation capacity was required. The analysis offers a cautionary tale as to the unintended consequences of embracing far-reaching policy reform proposals without any clarity as to how they might be implemented.

3.1   Introduction

In 1998, the South African government released its White Paper on the Energy Policy of the Republic of South Africa (DME 1998: 1). The paper noted that:

Eskom's present generation capacity surplus will be fully utilized by about 2007 ... The next decision on supply-side investments will probably have to be taken by the end of 1999 to ensure that the electricity needs of the next decade are met. (DME 1998: 53)

A decade later, as predicted, the lights went out:

Cities were paralysed by traffic gridlocks. Food processing enterprises and supermarkets lost their stock. At least one person died on an operating table. On 25 January – a date known as Black Friday in the mining industry – gold and platinum mines were forced to stop all production for five days. (PARI 2013: 1)

The 1998 warning that additional electricity generation capacity would be needed within a decade did not set in motion an immediate process of planning for new investment. Within the White Paper's overarching vision was the intent that private providers would take the lead in supplying the new generation capacity. However, the six years after the paper's issue were characterized by what we call 'churning': ongoing political contestation, and multiple and inconsistent policy proposals from a diverse array of state actors – with limited, if any, actual gains made in terms of restructuring the 'rules of the game' of South Africa's electricity sector in ways that could credibly attract private investment. Only in 2004 did the South African government make the commitments necessary to put in place the requisite (public-sector-driven) investments. What accounts for the lost years?

South Africa's 1998 White Paper laid out an ambitious vision of reform along the lines of the so-called 'standard model' (Gratwick and Eberhard 2008: 3952), to transform monopolized, state-owned electricity sectors by unbundling generation, transmission and distribution, rebalancing prices to cover the full cost of new investment, creating competition in electricity generation – and attracting private investors to meet the demand for new generation capacity. In South Africa's political context, each of these tasks involved distinctive and difficult political challenges. Indeed, from a political perspective, the most immediately urgent of these challenges was a proposed radical restructuring of electricity distribution, which would shift control from municipalities to new regional electricity distributors; however, this reform was at most tangentially related to the aim of increasing generation capacity.

A comprehensive analysis of the overall electricity-reform package laid out in the White Paper is a task which goes well beyond the scope of the present effort. Instead, the focus here is on the political challenges associated with moving forward vis-à-vis two aspects of the reform which are of central, direct relevance to the vision of addressing generation-supply constraints via private investment: clarifying what the market structure for electricity generation should be; and clarifying how electricity purchased from electricity generation providers should be priced. Our hope is that the insights which emerge from this narrow focus can help create a broader understanding of the politics of electricity-sector reform – in South Africa and beyond.

This chapter details what happened, vis-à-vis the above aspects, over the six-year period between 1998 and 2004 – and explores the reasons why things unfolded as they did. Using analytic-narrative and process-tracing methodologies, it will examine the following hypothesis:[1]

Hypothesis The inability to attract private investment into new electricity generation was a result of an inability to move beyond general principles and put in place a credible regulatory framework capable of attracting such investment. This failure was, in turn, a result of a failure to address contradictory perspectives on the reform principles of politically influential stakeholders, both within and outside government.

Process tracing is an approach to conducting case study analysis that focuses on sequential processes with the aim of 'tracing the links between possible causes and observed outcomes ... to see whether the causal process a theory hypothesizes is, in fact, evident' (George and Bennet 2005: 4, 6). In this case, research was focused on the actions of key stakeholders from the period of the White Paper's publication in 1998, up until 2004, when the policy was unofficially shelved. Newspaper and journal articles over the period were used to recreate a telling representation of the political economic climate at the time. As detailed below, this 'process-tracing' methodology provides an empirical basis with which to document the absence of a shared vision amongst the multiple stakeholders, the consequent unresolved conflicts and the absence of a collective mechanism for resolving these conflicts in ways which were capable of moving the reform process forward.

Over the past dozen or so years, a rapidly expanding literature has highlighted the limits of narrowly technocratic approaches to reform in which development policy-making is perceived as an 'expert' task of identifying the 'optimal' policy, promulgating and then implementing it (Andrews 2013; Carothers and de Gramont 2013; Levy 2014; Green 2016; Yanguas 2018). The intent of this paper is to contribute to this literature with a focused case study of what can happen when technocracy and politics collide in the electricity sector. The analysis offers a cautionary tale of the unintended consequences of embracing far-reaching policy reform proposals without any clarity as to how they might be implemented. The South African experience is hardly unique; in 2008, building on the difficult reform experiences of many countries, Gratwick and Eberhard (2008) pronounced the 'demise of the standard model of power sector reform'.

---

[1] The primary source of data for this analysis was Nchimunya Hamukoma's 2014 dissertation, 'Investing in New Electricity Generation in South Africa: What Short-Circuited Decision-Making, 1998–2014?'

The chapter proceeds as follows. Section 3.2 provides additional detail on the White Paper, its background and its proposals. Section 3.3 steps back, to describe the broader political economy context within which the White Paper was written. Section 3.4 details the course of policy-making vis-à-vis the reform of the market structure for electricity generation. Section 3.5 describes the evolution of the discourse on electricity pricing. Section 3.6 concludes.

List of Abbreviations

ANC – African National Congress
BEE – Black economic empowerment
COSATU – Congress of South African Trade Unions
DME – Department of Minerals and Energy
DPE – Department of Public Enterprises
ESI – Electricity supply industry
GEAR – Growth, employment and redistribution
IPP – Independent power producers
NER – National Electricity Regulator
NERSA – National Energy Regulator of South Africa
NUM – National Union of Mineworkers
WEPS – Wholesale Electricity Pricing System

3.2   The 1998 White Paper

The 1998 White Paper was South Africa's first attempt at large-scale electricity reform in the post-apartheid era. At that time, the South African electricity supply industry (ESI) was dominated by the state-owned utility, Eskom. The organization had an entrenched monopoly in the ESI, with almost total control over generation and transmission, and control over distribution in some localities, though not the major munici-palities. Eskom owned twenty-four power stations with a nominal capacity of 39,872 MW, and was highly ranked as one of the top five power utilities globally in terms of size and sales, producing approximately 50 per cent of the electricity consumed in Africa (Eskom 1998: 1; International Energy Agency 1998: 380). The introduction of a reform process to introduce a more competitive market seemed, at least to some, to be a logical next step in achieving international best practice.

The White Paper initiated a series of varied policy directives, including a broad attempt to secure the future success of the ESI through:

- Giving customers the right to choose their electricity supplier
- Introducing competition into the industry, especially the generation sector
- Permitting open, non-discriminatory access to the transmission system
- Encouraging private sector participation in the industry.

(DME 1998: 42)

The above-mentioned vision essentially meant restructuring the ESI, shifting it from a vertically integrated model to a more competitive market model. This vision, though, was neither the product of careful political engagement and coalition-building, nor part of a plan to signal a stable market to investors, but was, rather, 'the result of the convictions of a small group of analysts and government officials that were observing international trends in power sector reform, and were beginning to be concerned with the potential problems of monopoly power' (Eberhard 2005: 5314).

The reform of the distribution sector was seen as the initial focus; reform in the transmission and generation sectors was seen as necessary but not urgent (DME 1998: 41). As such, distribution was the focus of much of the detailed discussion in the policy document, and the paper remained intentionally open-ended when it came to considering models that might be used to attract private sector investment into the system, as seen in the following excerpt:

Government will initiate a comprehensive study on future market structures for the South African electricity supply industry . . . and fundamental market restructuring is likely to be delayed for a number of years while the distribution sector is restructuring and the bulk of the electrification programme is undertaken. (DME 1998: 55).

The White Paper made clear the government's willingness to restructure the ESI and include independent power producers (IPPs) in the capacity generation process, thereby removing Eskom's de facto monopoly in generation; it stated that 'the introduction of Independent Power Producers (IPPs) will be allowed in the South African electricity market' (DME 1998: 53, 55) and that:

It is government's intention to ensure greater public participation in future decisions on public expenditures of this magnitude. Government also intends to steadily increase competitive pressures in the generation sector in order to improve efficiencies and reduce electricity prices. (DME 1998: 53).

Whilst the paper did not offer a detailed blueprint of what the South African ESI would look like, it did begin to explore how the country's major energy utility, Eskom, could be transformed into an organization capable of functioning within a more competitive market environment (DME 1998: 55). It proposed that Eskom be split into separate transmission and generation companies in order to create more investment opportunities to support black economic empowerment (BEE) and other private sector investment. This separation would be coupled with an organizational separation of some of Eskom's existing technological support and research capacities, primarily housed in the Technology Research and Investigations Division, so these capacities could be harnessed by other actors in the ESI (DME 1998: 55). The policy proposals did not make any overarching prescriptions against Eskom participating in new generation-capacity projects. It did state, though, that future capacity investments would have to be anchored in 'integrated resource planning' methodologies (DME 1998: 53).

So, though the intent of the White Paper was to open the way to far-reaching reform of the electricity sector, this is not what happened. Instead, subsequent efforts to put the White Paper's vision into practice opened a Pandora's box of conflicts amongst powerful political stakeholders – both within and outside government, and in terms of both interests and ideologies – which had been papered over amidst the euphoria of South Africa's seemingly miraculous democratic transition away from apartheid.

3.3   The Political Context

This section has two tasks. Firstly, to lay out the overarching political context within which the 'play' of the electricity-sector reform 'game' unfolded. And secondly, to provide a more detailed mapping of the stakeholders with explicit roles in electricity-sector reform, and their relationships with one another.

3.3.1   *The Overarching Context*[2]

The championing in the White Paper of a more market-friendly and private-sector-friendly approach to the electricity sector was part of a broader embrace of market-based policies by the new African National Congress (ANC) government. This embrace, in turn, can only be understood within the broader context of the profound political changes of the early 1990s: the ending of apartheid; the commencement of negotiations between the white minority National Party government

---

[2] Parts of this section are extracted directly from a related paper, coauthored by one of this paper's two authors; see Hirsch and Levy (2017).

and its opponents; the democratic elections of 1994, won by the ANC; and the consolidation of authority by the ANC.

During the transition period of the early 1990s, South Africa's business community was very proactive in the exercise of its 'soft power' influence on policy-making. Forward-looking business leaders helped to unlock deadlocks in the negotiations. They also actively engaged in working to shape economic thinking in post-apartheid South Africa away from state ownership and control towards more market-friendly solutions. The broader global and regional context supported these efforts. Globally, statist economic development paths became discredited in the 1980s, underlined by the capitulation of the Soviet Union after the Cold War. Regionally, the reputation of many African governments for poor economic policies added to a sense of caution in the ANC, as did the threat of capital flight. The result was the adoption of market-opening reforms.

The commitment to market-oriented economic policies continued to deepen under the first elected ANC government. One aspect of this is evident in the embrace of more private involvement in sectors which had long been dominated by state-owned enterprises. Alongside those in the electricity sector, far-reaching reforms to foster greater private involvement were initiated successfully, at least for a while, in the telecommunications sector, and, less successfully, in plans to contract the operation of at least some ports to private participants.

In addition to the reforms noted above, key policy initiatives, explored in detail in Hirsch and Levy (2017), included:

- A far-reaching commitment to tariff reduction and trade liberalization, as part of the Marrakesh Round of global trade policy reforms
- A broader embrace of Washington Consensus economic policy prescriptions (including conservative fiscal and monetary policies), as part of a home-grown Growth, Employment and Redistribution (GEAR) strategy, announced in 1996
- Abolition, in March 1995, of the dual exchange rate, and liberalization of the foreign exchange market – following an incremental path, favouring capital exports to Africa and culminating in a relatively liberal exchange rate regime by 2003
- A ramping-up of domestic competition policy, including the promulgation, in 1998, of a Competition Act, and the establishment of an independent Competition Commission with both investigative and prosecutorial powers
- A constitutional mandate to the central bank to protect the internal and external value of the currency, and pursue money supply-driven monetary policies.

The decision to embrace Washington Consensus-style reforms was driven in large part by the desire of the country's new political leadership – notably including the University of Sussex-trained Thabo Mbeki, as Deputy President and then President – to signal to the international community that the country was 'open for business' – and, in a post-Soviet world, had embraced the global pro-market consensus. Indeed, the 1996 GEAR programme was not underpinned by a consultative process, but was announced without significant prior signalling as a 'confidence-building' measure by Deputy President Mbeki and the then-new Minister of Finance, Trevor Manuel.

Yet beneath this bold embrace of reforms was a much more complex political reality. In 1994, the ANC had won a sweeping electoral mandate – but this was more an affirmation of its leadership role in winning freedom for the majority of the country's citizens from apartheid oppression, than support for an economic reform agenda along the lines laid out above. Indeed, with its long history, dating back to 1913, as a broad-based, nationalist political movement, the ANC was, in practice, a multi-polar umbrella organization, with a broad social foundation. Upon taking hold of the reins of power in 1994, it confronted the challenge of mediating amongst diverse stakeholders:

- As a mass political movement with a long history of political struggle against oppression, it had a deeply rooted commitment to address South Africa's profound challenges of poverty, and racial and class inequality
- It formally incorporated as members of the 'ruling alliance' both the South African Communist Party and the Congress of South African Trade Unions (COSATU), both formally members of the 'ruling alliance'
- Since the earliest days of its founding in 1913, it had also voiced the aspirations of African, other black, 'petty bourgeois' and other groups seeking economic empowerment.

These varied interests had had a long and uneasy co-existence within the ANC – with the resulting contradictions evident in ongoing conflicts amongst stakeholders vis-à-vis electricity-sector reform.

3.3.2 *The Electricity Stakeholders*

Figure 3.1 maps out the primary relationships amongst the key stakeholders active in the electricity-sector reform process over the period 1998–2004 – legislative relations (solid lines), policy relations (dashed lines) and informal relations of influence (dotted lines). The following

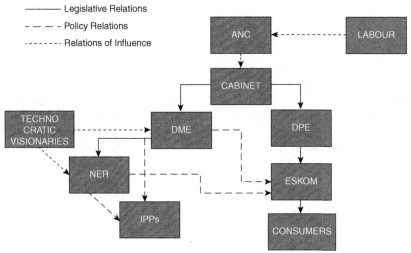

Figure 3.1 Governing South Africa's electricity sector – A web of interconnectedness
Note: Legislative relations are defined as those with a clear legal mandate under South African law. Policy relations are those where the overhanging department has a legal mandate to develop policy for the various institutions but no direct authority over the organizations. Relations of influence are those where there is no clear legal or policy mandate; however, the various organizations have significant influence on which policies are adopted and how they are implemented

paragraphs provide detail on the roles in the reform process of each of the stakeholders included in the figure.

3.3.2.1   The Department of Minerals and Energy (DME)[3]

The DME was the arm of government with a legal mandate to oversee the governance of the minerals and energy industries (DME 2005: 2). Resources within the department were disproportionately focused on the minerals portion of the portfolio. Its policy-making capacity with respect to energy was widely dispersed across its branches (EGI-SA 2010: 16). With respect to energy, the department's main function was

---

[3] In 2009, the Department of Minerals and Energy was split into the Department of Mineral Resources and the Department of Energy (DOE 2014).

to provide the policy and legislative framework to ensure a functional industry.

3.3.2.2   *The Department of Public Enterprises (DPE)*

The DPE was the arm of government responsible for overseeing the country's state-owned enterprises. As a government organization, Eskom fell under the legislative mandate of the DPE. Whilst energy policy was created within the DME, the DPE acted as the main shareholder representing government in Eskom, and took a keen interest in electricity planning (DPE 2014; EGI-SA 2010: 15).

3.3.2.3   *The National Electricity Regulator (NER)*

Founded as an independent regulatory authority in 1995, the NER was established to provide a means of external governance and oversight over the electricity industry (Morgan 2002: 19; 21). One aim was to ensure the protection of consumer interests from 'the monopoly power of their suppliers' (DME 1998: 10; South Africa, the Presidency 2006: 2). With regard to the IPP process, the NER had three main functions: to determine the price at which electricity would be supplied, to provide licences and to develop the regulatory framework for IPP participation (Belinska 2003: 18; Morgan 2002: 22, 23).

3.3.2.4   *Eskom*

Eskom, established in 1923 as South Africa's national electricity supply commission, was the key supplier of South Africa's electricity. A state-owned enterprise, the company had an almost total monopoly over the South African ESI for the majority of the twentieth century. Eskom was a vertically integrated utility, with total control over generation and transmission. The utility shared control of distribution networks with municipalities across the country.

3.3.2.5   *Organized Labour*

Though not part of the governmental executive structures, the inclusion of organized labour in Figure 3.1 signifies the close relationship between the ANC and unions as part of the tripartite alliance: a long-standing coalition between the ANC, South African Communist Party and COSATU (COSATU 2014).

3.3.2.6   Independent Power Producers (IPPs)

In terms of the 'global standard model', IPPs are a key component in the process of achieving more competition in generation and the benefits thereof, as well as reducing the pressure of the ESI's investment and operations on the national fiscus. However, in the South African context, they had a very limited role in orchestrating determining events in the period under study (i.e. 1998–2004).

3.3.2.7   Technocratic Visionaries

The inclusion of this category in Figure 3.1 is intended to signify the influence of a number of policy advisers in the sector, including some academics, who were responsive to the then-prevailing global conceptions of 'best practice' reforms in the power sector.

As Sections 3.3 and 3.4 will detail, the unfolding of the reform effort between 1998 and 2004 revealed radical differences in the visions, strategies and policy positions vis-à-vis the electricity sector of each of these stakeholders – including those who formally were within government and/or incorporated under the broad political umbrella of the ANC governing alliance.

3.4   How the Discourse on Market Structure Evolved

The general proposition that the private sector should play a role in electricity generation leaves some fundamental questions unaddressed as to the market structure within which that private sector would be embedded: should all new generation investment be made by the private sector, or only some portion, and if the latter, how much? Should the status quo, whereby existing generation capacity is virtually entirely in the hands of the dominant state enterprise, Eskom, continue – or should there be some unbundling, and perhaps partial privatization? Either way, what should the balance be between domestic and foreign participation in generation? And are black investors to be included in the process, as part of the broader effort nationally to further BEE?

The process-tracing analysis in this section details how efforts to wrestle with these questions unfolded between 1998 and 2004, and focuses on the evolution of the policy discourse in two domains: proposals as to how Eskom might be transformed, and efforts to put in place a governance framework for IPPs. As will become evident, and as is consistent with our hypothesis, both domains were characterized by ongoing conflicts amongst stakeholders with divergent visions as to the way forward, and by the absence of a collective mechanism for resolving these conflicts. The result was 'churning' – as of 2004, the details as to how the general vision of greater private participation in generation would be translated into practical arrangements vis-à-vis the market structure for electricity generation still had not been clarified.

3.4.1   *Restructure Eskom?*

In 1999, the Minister of the DPE, Jeff Radebe, presented new policy initiatives to restructure Eskom into separate generation, transmission and distribution businesses (Lunsche 1999: 4). The DPE was adamant that it was not implementing a privatization strategy. Rather, the proposed changes in policy were aimed at making the ESI more competitive, and to signal strongly to international investors that the market would soon be opening. The rhetoric of Eskom officials seemed to indicate support for the proposed policy initiatives (Chalmers 1998: 10).[4]

Other stakeholders, though, were more dubious. Shortly after the release of the White Paper, the DME took pains to iterate its intention to drive a reform process that would not 'break Eskom up' (Chalmers and Vermuelen 1998: 1). Unsurprisingly, organized labour, which had a strongly statist ideology, did not support the proposed reform trajectory. The National Union of Mineworkers (NUM) accused government of pursuing a privatization agenda through the 1998 White Paper and the Eskom Amendment Act. The NUM was of the opinion that government was committed to the 'piecemeal privatization of Eskom' (Chalmers 1999a: 3).

The NER was a surprising additional ally of organized labour, standing against the immediate privatization of Eskom's assets. In 2000, the regulator made a report to Parliament's Minerals and Energy Committee with the aim of dissuading the government from selling any stakes in Eskom until the organization had been restructured. Their stance was based on the view that premature privatization would merely entrench the monopoly within the South African ESI. The NER presented an alternative model, whereby a holding company would be created 'under which, would fall four or five subsidiaries housing Eskom's independent generation entities, which could be sold' (Ensor 2000: 5).

In September 2000, the DPE proposed a bill, the Eskom Conversion Act, for the corporatization of Eskom; the department maintained that

---

[4] As an initial tentative step in the direction of reform, in 1999 Eskom also established Eskom Enterprises, as an arm of the business designed specifically to focus on Eskom's non-regulated business nationally and to expand the company's reach to the rest of Africa through work in energy and energy-related services (Eskom, 1999).

the bill had 'nothing to do with privatization' (Ensor 2000: 4). This was followed by an announcement that the government had plans to sell off 30 per cent of Eskom's generation capacity to private (domestic and/or foreign) players, opening up the market for competition and potentially raising more than R30 bn (IC Publications 2000).

These announcements led to protests by the umbrella trade union organization, COSATU, outside of Parliament. The DME also contributed to the backlash, re-affirming its insistence that Eskom would retain its dominant position in power generation, that, as an organization, it was not 'desperate to raise money' and that the main drive for reform was to explore the role the provision of electricity could play in poverty alleviation, and to contain upward pressures on pricing (Chalmers 2001c: 1).

By April 2001, Eskom's internal re-organization had proceeded to the point where, to better prepare for future market competition, it had grouped its power stations into five entities. However, as the following statement from the group CEO Thulani Gcbashe signal, Eskom itself had also begun to explicitly challenge the proposed reforms: 'Eskom has the lowest electricity price in the world, and excellent technical performance when benchmarked against the rest of the world. We need clear objectives as to why we are going this route' (Chalmers 2001a: 17).

3.4.2   Attracting IPPs

Shortly after the release of the White Paper, the NER began talks with various IPPs to discuss future investment options, as well as the potential structure of a regulatory framework that included IPPs (PARI 2013: 13). In short order, a number of international power-producing firms began setting up offices in South Africa in response to what seemed like a favourable investment climate (Chalmers 2001b: 15; Marrs 2001: 2). But nascent discussions with IPPs were somewhat frustrated when the 1999/2000 NER Annual Report was released, and stated that the NER would not grant licences with inflexible pricing schedules (PARI 2013: 13). This was an unusual decision in the context of a developing country.

In developing countries, the approach to attracting IPPs generally centred around long-term power-purchase agreements of fifteen to twenty years, with fixed-price 'take-or-pay' contracts, in order to attract and secure long-term investments (Kessides 2004; Eberhard and Gratwick 2008). In this pattern, competition is for the market. The NER report, by contrast, seemed to signal a commitment to a flexible wholesale market, with spot pricing – competition 'in the market' – which is much more challenging to operate. From a political perspective, the flexible market option had the virtue of not requiring a signal as to what price adjustments might be needed to attract private investment.

In early 2000, the World Bank sponsored a seminar to address the lack of a coherent government narrative, and to help align the various departmental actors. Whilst no single reform model was championed at the meeting, implicit in the discussion was some form of private participation. The Minister of Minerals and Energy, Phumzile Mlambo-Ncguka, expressed the following as the government's main objectives for reform:

1) Increase economic efficiency and reduce operational costs so that costs and prices are as low as possible.
2) Maximize financial and economic returns to government from ESI.
3) Increase the opportunity for black economic empowerment.
4) To protect public benefits such as widened access to the poor, energy efficiency, ongoing R&D and environmental sustainability.

(Eberhard 2005: 5314, 5315)

After the workshop, senior leaders from the various agencies, including Eskom and the NER, decided to draft a paper on the restructuring of the ESI. One of the main recommendations that arose from the conference was that Eskom reduce its share of generation capacity to 35 per cent (Eberhard 2005: 5315).

The NER continued to interact with IPPs, and the general expectation was that the first licences for new IPPs would be granted by 2001. The organization attempted to create a vision for a reformed ESI with a medium-term plan to 'establish an internal power pool for electricity trading fed by imported electricity and independent producers ... The vision in the longer term was the creation of a power exchange, fed by Eskom's competing generating companies, imports and independent power producers. The state-owned transmission company would be independent and feed power through to the regional electricity distributors' (Chalmers 2000: 4). But no specific modalities for contracting, competitive bidding or for licensing were laid out.

A private sector IPP player, Peter Leaver, Cape Power Project Manager, signalled the limits of ongoing efforts to elaborate a vision of the future without spelling out the details:

Nobody in their right minds is going to invest billions of Rands in a power station and then ask if they can have a license to run it. I don't think there has been any change in the government's licensing of IPPs. (Marrs 2001: 2)

In 2002, the postponement of the licensing deal with a second national telecommunications operator sent clear signals of the potential for significant delays in ESI reform (Chalmers 2002c: 11).

3.4.3   *2001–2004: Roads to Nowhere*

In May 2001, the Cabinet acted in a way that was intended to bring clarity, announcing a new set of policy guidelines on ESI reform. These included the following:

- Eskom retains no more than 70% of existing generation capacity
- Private sector participation in the electricity generation market of up to 70% of the existing generation capacity
- Black Economic Empowerment (BEE) of about 10% of the generating capacity to be achieved by no later than 2003
- In order to ensure meaningful participation of the private sector in the medium term, Eskom will not be allowed to invest in new generation capacity in the domestic market.

(Belinska 2003: 89, 90)

Aiming to maintain its dominant position in the ESI, Eskom proposed a plan to introduce competition without privatization by allowing BEE partners to operate some of its mothballed stations, thereby making up the 10% BEE capacity requirements. This was to be supplemented by bringing in private actors in the medium term to provide 20 per cent of capacity, thus introducing 30 per cent private ownership of generation resources (Chalmers 2001d: 3).

The NER then proposed an alternative three-phase restructuring policy. This would build on establishing Eskom as an independent company through the Eskom Conversion Act, en route (as per the seeming intent) to the separation of the transmission, distribution and generation sectors. The proposed policy envisaged IPPs coming into the market by 2004, either through the purchase of some of Eskom's generation assets or through the development of a new capacity-building programme (Chalmers 2002a: 1).

In early 2002, the Minister of Public Enterprises, Jeff Radebe, announced a reform that mirrored Eskom's October 2001 proposal of a 10 per cent asset dispersal to BEE partners and a 20 per cent stake to a private equity partner by 2003 (Thompson 2002: 15). He affirmed that the DPE was 'clearly committed to introducing competition into the domestic market'. At the time, though, no clear legislative proposal had been made as to what shape the market structure and regulation would take. This may have been part of the reason why Eskom's policy suggestions were being favoured over those of the national regulator (Chalmers 2002b: 21).

In July 2003, Eskom provided a public warning of the impending electricity crisis, and of the need to begin building new power stations

(Phasiwe 2003a: 2). Major blackouts in the United States added to an atmosphere of urgency, and Eskom began to upgrade its transmission grids and look to alternative energy sources such as wind, solar and nuclear (Phasiwe 2003b: 2). A September 2003 Cabinet meeting instructed Eskom to ensure the security of supply until 2007. This included the building of new stations, with a caveat that Eskom would be commissioned for 70 per cent of new capacity post-2008, with 30 per cent commissioned from IPPs (Sonjica 2008: 3, 4).

In August 2004, Eskom CEO Thulani Gcbashe asked for clarity as to the DME's electricity generation policy. Though the department had committed to involving IPPs in the capacity-development process, six years on it lacked any clear policy on how that would occur. The long lead times in power plant construction meant that investment decisions needed to be made in a short time frame if there was to be a chance of avoiding blackouts in 2007. Gcbashe stated: 'we cannot allow a lack of clarity to impede development so that there is a lack of capacity when we need it ... we need to make investment decisions' (Ensor 2004: 2).

In October 2004, the Cabinet completely reversed its 2001 decision to prevent Eskom from engaging in any new-build projects and approved a five-year investment for infrastructure development. The project would cover generation, transmission and distribution to the cost of R93 bn, with R84 bn going to Eskom and the remainder to IPPs (PARI 2013: 17). The then-Minister of Public Enterprises, Alec Erwin, announced that as a result of a Cabinet decision, Eskom would be the main champion of South African capacity development (Chalmers 2004: 13).

3.5   How the Pricing Discourse Evolved

Paralleling the discourse on market structure and regulation was a similarly haphazard discourse on pricing. Globally, a move towards cost-reflective pricing was central to the new 'standard model' for electricity-sector reform. However, as of 1998, South Africa's price structure for electricity was disconnected from costs. Indeed, the very high levels of poverty within the South African context – and major efforts over the preceding decade to expand access to electricity across the country[5] – meant that there had been a strong drive to move towards a pricing mechanism that 'moderately subsidized tariffs for poor domestic consumers' (DME 1998: 51).

---

[5] In January 1991, only 36 per cent of households had electricity connections; by 2000, this was estimated at 70.6 per cent, and in 2012, 85.3 per cent of households were connected to the grid (Messerschmidt 2014a; Messerschmidt 2014b: 23).

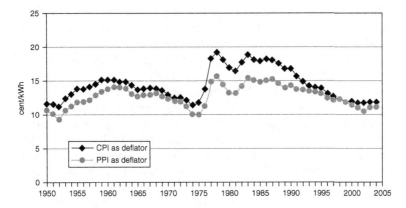

Figure 3.2 Trends in South African electricity pricing, 1950–2005 (Steyn 2006: 28)

Historically, trends in South Africa's electricity prices had largely been shaped by the timing of investment. Eskom had a history of pushing up prices in order to finance large-scale investments, whereby tariffs were initially used to cover the cost of capital expenditure. Over time, though, as the assets were paid off, tariffs became representative of operating costs, as opposed to the replacement cost. Established as a self-financing organization, set to operate 'neither at profit nor at loss', Eskom's prices were set according to the estimates of the following year's electricity sales. The revenue generated from sales was to be no more than necessary to 'cover production costs, contributions to the Interest Fund (to cover expected annual interest charges), contributions to the Loan Redemption Fund (to provide for loan amortization), and small contributions to the Reserve Fund (used to finance the eventual replacement of existing plant)' (Steyn 2006: 23, 24).

Figure 3.2 displays the trends in electricity pricing over the period 1950–2005, in constant 1998 prices. The 1970s were a period of very substantial investment for Eskom. Correspondingly, as the figure shows, to help cover the costs of investment, real prices almost doubled between 1974 and 1978. As it turned out, the new investments in electricity generation capacity were based on vast overestimates of future demand. The result was huge excess capacity in electricity, mothballed generation plants and (given the pricing regime) declining electricity prices. Indeed, as Figure 3.2 shows, as of 1998, South Africa had experienced thirteen consecutive years of decreasing electricity prices.

So, the challenge of rebalancing prices (and/or the price-setting mechanism) in a way capable of attracting the private sector was a formidable one. The discussion which follows uses process tracing to explore, in turn, how stakeholders engaged between 1999 and 2004 vis-à-vis efforts to transform the price-setting mechanism, and efforts to adjust price levels. As the discussion shows, in neither dimension was there any significant progress in moving towards a pricing regime capable of attracting private investment. Rather, paralleling the discussion of market structure, the result was 'churning': the pricing discourse was characterized by ongoing conflicts amongst stakeholders with divergent visions as to the way forward, and by the inability of any actor – including the regulator, NER, which had the formal authority – to craft a way forward that was capable of both winning the acquiescence of all stakeholders with veto power, and providing a pricing platform capable of underpinning private investment.

3.5.1   *Transforming the Price-Setting Mechanism*

With the establishment of the NER in 1995, South Africa's electricity prices began to be set via the classic mechanism whereby a regulated utility proposes an adjustment, and the regulator decides what adjustment to grant. The pricing challenges were formidable, given both the commitments to increase access to affordable electricity as a means of reducing poverty and the disconnect between the level of historical prices and the need for cost-reflective pricing if private investors were to be drawn into the system. Rather than confront these disconnects directly, between 1999 and 2003 the NER and Eskom directed much of their attention to the broader question of how the price-setting mechanisms themselves might be transformed.

The White Paper created expectations that there would be major changes. It suggested that 'the introduction of competition into the electricity supply sector along with restructuring, would help streamline the troubled market and could lead to greater efficiencies and further price reductions' (Chalmers 1998: 10). The price at which IPPs could sell power into the national transmission grid would be signalled through the publication of 'NER-approved tariffs for the purchase of co-generated and independently generated electricity on the basis of full avoided costs' (DME 1998: 54). Environmental costs were to be included in the pricing structure in order to prioritize environmentally friendly generation options (DME 1998: 54). The responsibility of appropriate tariff creation and further market research was left with the NER.

Consistent with this vision, in its 1999/2000 Annual Report, the NER stated that it would 'not license additional generation capacity that is based on inflexible long-term power-purchase agreement. This stance is based on the premise that customers should be protected against being deprived of the benefits of a future competitive electricity market' (PARI 2013: 13).

In September 2001, Eskom announced plans to phase out cross-subsidization between different tariff structures, and began to experiment internally with an in-house-designed Wholesale Electricity Pricing System (WEPS). The aim was to align tariffs with the actual cost of supply, with the new tariffs to be phased in over a five-to-ten-year period. But the plan did not address the tension between operational pricing and full-cost pricing, which was capable of supporting the huge capital costs associated with new investment. There was also concern that the plan would lead to higher prices for domestic users and smaller bulk buyers, but lower prices for larger bulk buyers, as the WEPS system also affected retail tariffs. Also unaddressed was the question of how electricity for indigent customers would be financed.

The NER expressed concern at the risks of abuse of a WEPS, stating that the challenge was 'to ensure that cost-reflectivity does not mean that utilities can be inefficient in running their business, yet be able to apply for a price rise' (Singh 2001: 50). COSATU also weighed in; in November 2001, it accused the government of reneging on an election pledge to cross-subsidize electricity tariffs to the poor. COSATU alleged that the Cabinet had previously announced that the subsidy system would only come under review in 2003, when social impact studies had been undertaken, a statement at odds with Eskom's announcement of a plan to remove subsidies (Kindra 2001: 9).

Again, the NER weighed in with its vision of the future. In December 2001, it offered assurances that it was looking at ways to prepare the South African ESI for a more competitive environment by transforming Eskom's internal power into a national power pool. The power pool would allow distributors to purchase power, either through a market or through a single wholesale operator. Other models under consideration included the Norwegian system of electricity trading with 'an independent transmission system and a power exchange open to all players' (Chalmers 2001e: 2). In 2002, the NER established a Multi-Market Model group to explore possibilities, and the group published a paper in the NER Quarterly Journal in 2003. However, no official policy regulations were released by the NER in this regard (du Toit 2003: 43, 44). The mechanism for price-setting remained what it had been since 1995.

3.5.2   *Adjusting Price Levels*

Alongside efforts to come up with a new market mechanism for electricity, everyday conflicts over price levels persisted in erupting. For the first four years of the NER's existence, all of Eskom's price increases had been below inflation – part of Eskom's pre-NER price compact to reduce the real price of electricity by 15 per cent from 1994 to 2000. Then, at the end of 1999, Eskom requested an above-inflation increase of 7 per cent (Chalmers 1999b: 1). A compromise was achieved of a 5.5 per cent increase, 1.5 per cent lower than Eskom's original request (Chalmers 1999b: 1).

In 2000, Eskom applied for a further 6.2 per cent increase in prices. The NER capped the increase at 5.2 per cent, with NER chief executive Xolani Makwanazi stating that 'this is a signal that we want to commit to affordable electricity. If we start showing price spikes we will scare off investors who depend on cheap electricity and that could have a huge impact on the economy.' Makwanazi revealed that the most important deciding factor for the price increases was the inflation rate (Bailey 2000: 1).

In March 2002, Minister of Public Enterprise Jeff Radebe announced in Parliament that 'the government and Eskom are considering ways to make electricity cheaper and more accessible'. One of the major problems faced in restructuring prices was that of unpaid bills; these amounted to over R2 bn, R277 m of which were owed by municipalities (Stuart 2002: 6).

In March 2003, Eskom announced plans to increase its tariffs at a rate above inflation. The increase in tariffs was to fund a capital expenditure project aimed at the mining sector over five years. This announcement was met with remonstrations from the National Consumer Union and other civil society and political groupings (Matyu 2003: 7). In April, the Deputy Minister of the DME announced the government's plans to provide R300 m worth of free basic electricity by July 2003 (wa Sekano 2003: 4).

Some actors within the private sector, such as Mike Schussler of Tradek, put forth the argument that South African regulators, including NER, 'were only listening to the parastatals and should have done more research before authorizing increases'. The Competition Commission had received several complaints about excessive price increases by Eskom and other parastatals (Wray 2003: 5).

At an April 2003 meeting of the Parliamentary Committee on Minerals and Energy, Dr Wolsey Barnard of the NER announced that South Africa could be facing a major energy crisis in the next four to eight years. In order to combat this, new generation capacity would have to be developed. At the time, Eskom was generating electricity at a rate of 10c a unit whereas the 'levelised cost' for a new coal-fired power station was about 25c a unit. At the same meeting, Professor Anton Eberhard noted: 'that just tells you that the price we have at the moment is economically unsustainable' (SAPA 2003: 6). In the presentation, representatives from the NER argued that the increase in prices was due to the need for new investment, not because of the possible restructuring of the organization (Loxton 2003: 9).

Eskom spokesperson Fani Zulu stated that there was 'upward pressure on the price of electricity' but, he said, 'over the years electricity prices had been kept artificially low'. Zulu projected that prices would have to increase in the future and that there was a choice to be made to either accept gradual increases or succumb to a 'big bang' in the future. A senior industry source who chose to remain anonymous said that 'current electricity pricing reflected an inherent contradiction in policy and was tantamount to letting politics trump economics. They want to restructure the industry and attract investment but they are not willing to allow market forces to set prices.' There was awareness from some industry insiders that Eskom was charging 'half the economic cost of electricity' (Wray 2003: 4).

In July 2003, Eskom applied for an 8.5 per cent increase in prices in order to better facilitate capacity development. The NER approved only a 2.5 per cent increase, stating, 'Eskom has the capacity to build new plants without increasing real prices now' and expressing the belief that 'there is no guarantee Eskom will be required to build new generation capacity' (Phasiwe 2003c: 3). Eskom stated that it had meant to invest the additional funds in the refurbishment of older power station as opposed to the development of new ones. The NER chief executive stated that whilst the development of new capacity was a serious issue to be dealt with at a national level, 'we do not agree with the principle that says increase electricity prices in order to accumulate massive monies for future investments' (Nxumalo 2003: 5).

In December of 2003, Eskom formally appealed against the price increase granted by the NER to the Minister of the DME, Phumzile Mlambo-Ncgucka (Phasiwe 2003d: 2). The NER responded by requesting that Eskom withdraw its appeal or risk losing the 2.5 per cent increase it had been granted (Phasiwe 2003e: 2).

In May, the national government upheld the NER's decision to allow only a 2.5 per cent tariff increase, even as it reiterated that new capacity was to be built by private companies. Industry analysts, however, said that such a low increase could deter private investment (Phasiwe 2004b: 2). At that time, South Africa had amongst the lowest electricity prices globally (Phasiwe 2004a: 2). Industry insiders suggested that the minimal increase was the by-product of 2004 being an election year. This stance was further supported by a statement from the DME that 'it did not want electricity prices to soar when government was trying to expand the economy' (Singh 2004: 40).

In October 2004 the NER granted a price increase of 6.4 per cent to Eskom; this increase had some analysts worrying about the inflationary pressures of rising electricity prices (Shezi 2004: 1). The increase came in the same week that the Minister of Public Enterprises, Alec Erwin, made his announcement that Eskom, not IPPs, would be the main champion of South African capacity development (Chalmers 2004: 13).

3.6   Conclusion

In 1998, South Africa signalled its intent to pursue a far-reaching agenda of electricity-sector reform. This chapter has explored the gap between reform intent and outcome – specifically, how ambitious agenda for change can be short-circuited by politics. The research has been focused on a subset of the broader agenda – namely the effort to address generation-supply constraints by attracting private investment – and, within that, on the political dynamics associated with efforts to clarify (a) what the market structure for electricity generation should be, and (b) how electricity purchased from electricity generation providers should be priced.

As process-tracing analysis has shown, whilst on the surface the reforms were supported by government, beneath that surface there were many unresolved conflicts amongst stakeholders. The result was six years of reform churning – six lost years at a time when, as per the 1998 White Paper, forward progress in terms of investment in new electricity generation capacity was required. In sum, the evidence laid out in this essay does not contradict its guiding hypothesis, namely that:

The inability to attract private investment into new electricity generation was a result of an inability to move beyond general principles and put in place a credible regulatory framework capable of attracting such investment. This failure was, in turn, a result of a failure to address contradictory perspectives on the reform principles of politically influential stakeholders, both within and outside government.

The South African reform process from 1998 to 2004 is a cautionary tale that highlights the need for the development of specific reform agendas that are responsive to country-specific contexts, including stakeholder interests and bargaining power. Failure to account for these domestic dynamics can lead to time wasted and, notwithstanding initial great expectations, a reform process that results in no significant changes to the structure of the ESI.

South Africa was hardly alone in its embrace of ambitious approaches to electricity-sector reform. Indeed, when it embarked on its reform efforts, the 'standard model' of electricity-sector reform that it pursued reflected the global conventional wisdom as to how electricity sectors should be modernized.[6] In recent years, though, there has been a substantial rethinking of this 'best practices' approach – both in the electricity sector, and more broadly.[7] South Africa's electricity-reform experience between 1998 and 2004 stands out, however, as an especially vivid example of where an over-enthusiastic embrace of reform without concomitant political commitment can lead.

But change processes are often circuitous – and the long-term consequences, for good and ill, can be different from what they initially might have seemed. We thus conclude by noting five post-scripts to the story told in this chapter. Each hints at possibilities for interpretation as to the underlying causal dynamics which build directly on the analysis and evidence presented here. Rather than speculate ourselves, we leave that exercise to the reader.

1)   As the White Paper predicted, in 2007 the lights did indeed go out across South Africa, resulting in heavy costs for the South African economy. The initial crisis eased after a few months as ongoing efforts at demand-side management (see below) took hold, but continued on and off until 2015, when new investments in electricity capacity began coming on stream (also see below).

2)   The evident crisis in electricity supply unlocked the log jam in electricity pricing. As Table 3.1 shows, between 2008 and 2012 prices more than doubled for most users. These higher prices led to substantial reductions in demand. They were also sufficient – indeed more than sufficient according to many, including advocates of cost-recovery pricing – to cover investment costs.

3)   In 2015 Eskom began bringing the Medupi power plant, with a capacity of 4,764 MW, on stream; this would be the first of two massive

---

[6] For a comprehensive presentation and discussion of the model, see Kessides (2004).

[7] For electricity, see Gratwick and Eberhard (2008), and an ongoing World Bank initiative on 'Rethinking Power Sector Reform'. For the broader rethink of 'best practices' approaches, see Andrews, Pritchett and Woolcock (2017), Levy (2014) and the rich variety of work by many other signatories to the Doing Development Differently manifesto (www.doingdevelopmentdifferently.com).

Table 3.1 *Average price of electricity in c/kWh*

	2005	2006	2007	2008	2009	2010	2011	2012
Redistributors	15.19	16.13	16.88	18.03	23.05	30.84	39.53	49.96
Residential	38.70	40.08	41.74	44.12	52.86	63.98	66.45	79.52
Commercial	21.88	22.69	23.50	24.61	31.29	40.97	52.63	51.21
Industrial	13.97	14.75	16.01	17.11	21.46	27.03	34.34	42.13
Mining	15.36	16.19	16.90	17.82	22.87	30.25	39.78	50.11
Rural	30.83	32.86	33.69	35.54	45.29	58.96	72.72	89.22

(Eskom 2012)

new coal-fired plants. The second, Kusile, with a capacity of 4,800 MW, began coming on stream in 2017. Interestingly, an examination of the historical record shows that Eskom had begun planning for these two power plants at least a year before the Cabinet's 2004 decision to reverse its earlier exclusion of Eskom from further investment in electricity generation.

4)   South Africa's ESI remains overwhelmingly vertically integrated, with the state-owned utility, Eskom, generating 95 per cent of the country's electricity (Fisher and Downes 2017: 3). By the mid-2010s, Eskom had become the centre of wave after wave of controversy. These included conflicts over the following issues: internal governance, with multiple, politically influenced suspensions and firings of senior executives and board members; massive proposed new investments in nuclear power plants, at estimated costs upwards of $100 billion – these were associated with allegations of non-standard procurement processes involving politically connected investors; restructuring coal supply contracts, which attracted allegations not only of non-transparent contracting, but of government pressure to transfer ownership of a major coal mine; and multiple other non-standard procurement processes.[8]

5)   Finally, alongside Eskom's massive investments in coal-fired generation capacity, other parts of government (units within the DME and South Africa's National Treasury) quietly initiated a programme to attract new IPP investments into renewable (wind and solar) electricity generation. As of 2014, close to $14 bn had been attracted into almost 4,000 MW of new wind and solar capacity. A multi-round competitive bidding process had brought the costs of wind power down from US14.1c per kWh in the first round to 7.5c in the third – and solar costs down from

---

[8] For two influential reports, see Bhorat et al. (2017) and Public Protector (2016).

34c per kWh to 10c.[9] However, Eskom, through which the renewable IPPs connect to the grid, has repeatedly put obstacles in the way of the expansion of this programme, which had become a significant, evident substitute for its own programme of nuclear and other investments.

At the time of writing, it remains very uncertain how the myriad controversies and scandals surrounding Eskom will be resolved.

Bibliography

Andrews, M. (2013). *The limits of institutional reform in development.* New York: Cambridge University Press.

Andrews, M., Pritchett, L. and Woolcock, M. (2017). *Building state capability: Evidence, analysis, action.* Oxford, UK: Oxford University Press.

Bailey, S. (2000, 7 November). NER reduces Eskom's tariff increase to 5.2%. *The Star*, p. 1.

Belinska, B. (2003). Overview of the current NER regulatory framework for independent power producers in the electricity supply industry. *National Energy Regulator Quarterly Journal*, 2: 2.

Bhorat, H., Buthelezi, M. Chipkin I., Swilling M. et al. (2017). *Betrayal of the promise: How South Africa is being stolen.* Johannesburg: State Capacity Research Project.

Carothers, T. and de Gramont, D. (2013). *Development aid confronts politics: The almost revolution.* Washington, DC: Carnegie Endowment for International Peace.

Chalmers, R. (1998, 28 December). Competition bid will give Eskom a boost. *Business Day*, p. 10.

Chalmers, R. (1999a, 9 June). NUM rejects gov'ts denials. *Business Day*, p. 3.

Chalmers, R. (1999b, 13 December). Compromise on electricity price hike. *Business Day*, p. 1.

Chalmers, R. (2000, 23 November). Power producer may be licensed next year. *Business Day*, p. 4.

Chalmers, R. (2001a, 3 April). Eskom's generation division gets new look. *Business Day*, p. 17.

Chalmers, R. (2001b, 11 April). Global utilities are set to pounce in SA. *Business Day*, p. 15.

Chalmers, R. (2001c, 4 July). State puts Eskom privatisation on the back burner. *Business Day*, p. 1.

Chalmers, R. (2001d, 1 October). Eskom unveils its new plan to restructure. *Business Day*, p. 3.

Chalmers, R. (2001e, 13 December). SA may get National Power Pool. *Business Day*, p. 2.

Chalmers, R. (2002a, 7 January). Three steps to be taken in reshaping power arena. *Business Day*, p. 1.

---

[9] See Eberhard, Kolker and Leigland (2014).

Chalmers, R. (2002b, 12 March). Eskom powering ahead despite challenges. *Business Day*, p. 21.

Chalmers, R. (2002c, 1 July). Eskom to be converted into a tax-paying public company today. *Business Day*, p. 12.

Chalmers, R. (2004, 24 October). Why the power is still with Eskom. *Business Day*, p. 13.

Chalmers, R. and Vermuelen, A. (1998, 18 December). Govt maps out energy deregulation. *Business Day*, p. 1.

COSATU. (2014). Tripartite alliance. COSATU. www.cosatu.org.za/show.php?ID=2051.

DOE (Department of Energy). (2014). About us. *Department of Energy.* ewww .energy.gov.za/files/au_frame.html.

DME (Department of Minerals and Energy). (1998). *White paper on Energy Policy for Republic of South Africa.* Pretoria: Department of Minerals and Energy.

DPE (Department of Public Enterprise). (2014). DPE overview. *DPE.* www .dpe.gov.za/about.

du Toit, E. E. (2003).The multi-market model for the introduction of independent power producers and private sector participation in the electricity supply industry in South Africa. *National Energy Regulator Quarterly Journal*, 2(1).

Eberhard, A. (2005). From state to market and back again – South Africa's power sector reforms. *Economic and Political Weekly*, 40(50): 5309–5317.

Eberhard, A. and K. Gratwick (2008). Demise of the standard model for power sector reform and the emergence of hybrid power markets. *Energy Policy*, 36: 3948–3960.

Eberhard, A., Kolker, J. and Leigland, J. (2014). *South Africa's renewable energy IPP program: Success factors and lessons.* World Bank: Public Private Investment Advisory Facility.

EGI-SA (Electricity Governance Initiative of South Africa Working Group) (2010). *The governance of power: Shedding light on the electricity sector in South Africa. Electricity Governance Initiative of South Africa.* http://electricitygovernance.wri.org/files/egi/EGI-SA%20report%20-%20The%20Governance%20of%20Power%20(Feb. 2010)– cover.pdf

Ensor, L. (2000, 28 September). Parliament to process Eskom bill next year. *Business Day*, p. 4.

Ensor, L. (2004, 26 August). Eskom wants clarity on new power producers. *Business Day*, p. 2.

Eskom. (1998). *Eskom annual report 1998.* Johannesburg: Eskom.

Eskom. (1999). *Eskom annual report 1999.* Johannesburg: Eskom.

Eskom. (2012). Copy of historical average prices. *Eskom.* www.eskom.co.za/search/Pages/Results.aspx?k=copy%20of%20historical%20average%20%20prices%204%20july%202012. (Accessed 19 June 2014).

Fisher, N. and Downes, G. (2017). South Africa. www.iea.org/ciab/South_Africa_Role_Coal_Energy_Security.pdf . (Accessed 31 October 2017).

Gratwick, K. N. and Eberhard, A. (2008). Demise of the standard model for power sector reform and the emergence of hybrid power markets. *Energy Policy*,

(36): 3948–3960. https://pesd.fsi.stanford.edu/sites/default/files/Demise_of_st andard_model_Sept08.pdf. (Accessed 29 October 2017).

Green, D. (2016). *How change happens*. Oxford: Oxford University Press.

Hirsch, A. and Levy,B. (2017). Elaborate scaffolding, weak foundations: Business-government relations and economic reform in democratic South Africa. Graduate School of Developing Policy and Practice, Occasional Working Paper Number 8. University of Cape Town.

IC Publications. (2000). Eskom's African expansion. http://www .thefreelibrary.com/ESKOM'S+AFRICAN+EXPANSION.-a0. (Accessed 20 January 2014).

International Energy Agency. (1998). World energy outlook. https://jancovici .com/wp-content/uploads/2016/04/World_energy_outlook_1998.pdf. (Accessed 29 October 2017).

Kessides, I. (2004). *Reforming infrastructure: Privatization, regulation and competition*. A World Bank Policy Research Report. Washington, DC: Oxford University Press and the World Bank.

Kindra, J. (2001, 15 November). Govt is breaking its promise, say unions. *Mail and Guardian*, p. 9.

Levy, B. (2014) *Working with the grain: Integrating governance and growth in development strategies*. New York: Oxford University Press.

Loxton, L. (2003, 10 April). Electricity tariff rises are inevitable this year, warns regulator. *Star*, p. 9.

Lunsche, S. (1999, 8 December). *Eskom, jewel in the R150bn crown. Business Day*, p. 4.

Marrs, D. (2001, 5 July). Plans for new Cape power plan on track. *Business Day*, p. 2.

Matyu, J. (2003, 12 March). Outrage over plan to hike Eskom tariff over inflation. *The Herald (EP Herald)*, p. 7.

Messerschmidt, J. (2014a). A quarter of a century of electrification – Part One. *EE Publishers*. www.ee.co.za/article/messerschmidt-a-quarter-of-a-century-of-electrification-part-one.html. (Accessed 1 November 2017).

Messerschmidt, J. (2014b). A quarter of a century of electrification – Part Two. *EE Publishers*. www.ee.co.za/wp-content/uploads/2014/04/energize-april-14-p-22–24.pdf. (Accessed 1 November 2017).

Morgan, K. (2002). The current role of the NER in regulating South Africa's electricity industry. *National Energy Regulator Quarterly Journal*, 1.

Nxumalo, F. (2003, 14 October). NER's dim view of Eskom plan. *Star*, p. 5.

Phasiwe, K. (2003a, 16 July). Eskom warns of power shortage. *Business Day*, p. 2.

Phasiwe, K. (2003b, 15 September). Eskom in upgrade to avert blackouts. *Business Day*, p. 2.

Phasiwe, K. (2003c, 13 November). Billions needed to light up SA's future. *Business Day*, p. 3.

Phasiwe, K. (2003d, 4 December). Eskom in appeal to minister over tariff. *Business Day*, p. 2.

Phasiwe, K. (2003e, 10 December). Regulator warns Eskom on tariff increase. *Business Day*, p. 2.

Phasiwe, K. (2004a, 20 May). Eskom still cheapest supplier of electricity in the world, but for how long? *Business Day*, p. 2.

Phasiwe, K. (2004b, 20 May). State peg's utility's tariff raise at 2.5%. *Business Day*, p. 2.

PARI (Public Affairs Research Institute). (2013). *Why the lights went out: Reform in the South African energy sector.* Written for the Graduate School of Development Policy and Practice. Johannesburg: PARI.

Public Protector. (2016). *State of capture.* Report No. 6 of 2016/17. Pretoria: Republic of South Africa.

SAPA. (2003, 10 April). Power to the people looks set to come at a higher price. *Star*, p. 6.

Singh, S. (2001, 30 November). Who will pay for the poor? *Financial Mail*, p. 50.

Singh, S. (2004, 23 January). Test still lies ahead. *Financial Mail*, p. 40.

Sonjica, B. (2008). Address by the Minister of Minerals and Energy, Ms Buyelwa Sonjica, MP: Joint Sitting of Parliament on electricity load shedding problem. http://oldgov.gcis.gov.za/speeches/2008/08013015151001.htm. (Accessed 31 October 2017).

South Africa, the Presidency. (2006). Electricity Regulation Act. Government Gazette 28992, Notice 660, 5 July 2006. Pretoria: Government Printer.

Steyn, G. (2006). *Investment and uncertainty: Historical experience with power sector investment in South Africa and its implication for current challenges.* Prepared for the Management Programme in Infrastructure Reform and Regulation (MIR) at the Graduate School of Business and the University of Cape Town. www.gsb.uct.ac.za/files/Eskom-InvestmentUncertainty.pdf. (Accessed 21 June 2013).

Stuart, B. (2002, 8 March). Cheap power planned. *Citizen*, p. 6.

Thompson, F. (2002, 30 April). Eskom revamp needs realism jolt. *Business Day*, p. 15.

Wa Sekano, P. (2003, 6 April). Free power switch-on boon for the poor. *City Press*, p. 4.

Wray, Q. (2003, 27 June). Watchdogs not reining in prices – Schussler. *Star*, p. 5.

Yanguas, P. (2018). *Why we lie about aid.* Chicago: University of Chicago Press.

4 Institutional Enablers of Energy System Transition: Lessons from Solar Photovoltaic Electricity in Eight African Countries

Valerie J. Karplus, Donald R. Lessard, Ninad Rajpurkar and Arun Singh

Abstract

In this chapter, we shall study the role of institutions in clean energy transitions in developing countries. Renewable energy (RE) for electricity generation has been proposed as a way to bridge the gap between affordable and clean-energy infrastructure. We shall examine the drivers of past and planned solar photovoltaic (PV) electricity-capacity expansion in eight African countries during a period of rapidly falling technology costs. The countries in our sample that experienced RE expansion do not have liberalized market-oriented electricity sectors, and many provide only limited policy support. Careful cross-case comparisons point to a set of financing, political/regulatory, value capture and technical capabilities that may help to explain RE outcomes. Although these findings are specific to the group of African countries we studied, they may hold lessons for other settings in the 'second wave' of RE development.

4.1 Introduction

An abundance of solar and wind resources in many African countries and the falling costs of renewable energy (RE) technologies inspire visions of isolated rural villages dotted with solar panels and megacities powered by grid-scale installations. Ideally, these technologies would increasingly displace more costly and polluting forms of energy. A wide range of recent studies have highlighted RE's potential to bridge the infrastructure gap in affordable and clean power in many African contexts (IRENA 2016c; SE4All 2019). This chapter studies the antecedents of past and planned development of renewable energy for power generation in eight African countries, focusing on the case of grid-connected solar photovoltaic electricity (PV). Specifically, we ask which institutional features are present (or absent) in countries with successful RE outcomes, and carefully examine possible channels by which the former influences the latter.

We start from the premise that institutions, which are the socially devised rules of engagement in politics, markets and society (North 1992), may influence the timing, pace and extent of RE development. Institutions vary across countries and affect the support, influence and protections granted to stakeholders – including government, utilities, financiers, non-RE and RE project developers, operators, rate payers and the broader civil society. The ways in which institutions emerge and shape the capabilities that actors develop, as well as how they resolve conflicts amongst stakeholder interests, have been largely outside the focus of existing literature on enablers of RE. Until recent years, RE development largely occurred in the relatively 'institutionally similar' economies of Western Europe and the United States – we term this the 'first wave'.[1] Whilst studies of these settings suggest that institutions mattered (Jenner, Groba and Indvik 2013; Jacobsson and Bergek 2004), current expansion of RE in the Middle East, Africa, Oceania and Latin America has occurred against the backdrop of wider institutional variation. We term this the 'second wave' of RE expansion.

The 'first wave' of RE deployment in the 1990s and early 2000s – which unfolded in Western Europe and the United States – was largely enabled by dedicated RE policy support, primarily R&D support, feed-in tariffs (FITs) and/or renewable portfolio standards (Reiche and Bechberger 2004; Butler and Neuhoff 2008; Jenner et al. 2013; Lema and Ruby 2007). Since then, costs of solar and wind technology have fallen – the combined effect of design innovation and of declining component costs and manufacturing scale in the lead development locations of China, Europe and the United States (Reichelstein and Yorston 2013). This has ushered in a 'second wave' of investment in RE that is becoming competitive against established, dispatchable forms of power generation, particularly in countries rich in RE resources.[2]

Technology cost and physical-resource potential are only part of the story. To be economically viable at a system level, RE technologies must be integrated into the electricity mix alongside other existing and

---

[1] Wind energy for electricity generation in China is a notable exception.

[2] In India, for example, tax exemptions and import duty waivers for solar components have been recently replaced by a new regime that taxes solar modules at 18 per cent, with lower increases for other components, amid consensus that solar technology no longer requires fiscal support to be competitive (Bridge to India 2017).

proposed generation types. The properties of RE create new challenges for the electricity system. RE resources are both uncertain and variable, and create a need for additional flexibility of operation. Strategies for increasing this flexibility can include expanding co-ordination across balancing nodes, and instituting more responsive grid dispatch, as well as physical measures such as load-following generation, storage, and/or responsive demand (Bird, Milligan and Lew 2013). As such, it is important to evaluate how performance of candidate RE technologies depend on the characteristics of the existing electricity system (Rose et al., 2016). For example, the value of RE may depend on the operational flexibility of other generation types, and projects can falter when expansion of trans-mission infrastructure and grid connections is delayed or fails to occur in the first place.

The countries in our sample exhibit significant variation in mea-sures of the ease of doing business, which serve as a proxy for the smooth functioning of the institutions that govern economic activity (World Bank 2016; WGIP 2016). We traced relationships between these differences and RE development in these countries. We found that the countries with the largest existing or planned RE pro-grammes also scored highly on a range of Doing Business metrics that correspond to broad-based institutional strength. By contrast, we found no systematic relationship between the extent of market-oriented reform in the power sector – unbundling, an independent regulator and spot markets – and RE development. Our results suggest that to enable RE expansion in its early stages, countries should take stock of, and augment as necessary, system-wide cap-abilities and incentives that enable RE development. Whilst these lessons may apply to grid-scale, off-grid and micro-grid systems, the focus of our study is on grid-scale RE expansion and our specific conclusions are limited to it.

We find evidence that if an enabler is weak or missing, project or programme design may be able to compensate – for instance, by involving patient capital or development agency funding to overcome high local lending costs and currency risk (as discussed in the example of Mozambique later in this chapter). However, addres-sing institutional deficiencies project-by-project, or even on a programmatic basis, may not provide a sustained and scalable solution. Instead, a constellation of capabilities must come together for sustainable RE growth at the national or regional level. Notably, whilst formal RE policy support may be less important in this 'second wave', the necessary institutional support may become more so, given the complex and rapidly changing political landscapes characteristic of some African countries.

Whilst not the primary focus of our inquiry, we find evidence that on-grid RE development may not advance efforts to expand energy access, because the institutional factors that favour RE development also support higher pre-existing levels of access. In the eight countries we examined, countries with the highest levels of electricity access also showed the strongest commitment to RE expansion, whilst countries with low levels of access emphasized RE less in their development plans. Challenges to utility operation, including electricity theft, low willingness-to-pay and perpetual insolvency, are typical of countries with limited electricity access, and are factors which affect a country's capability of supporting RE. We believe that this observation reflects the fact that there is substantial overlap in the capability sets required to enable electricity access and RE development, but we can by no means prove this, given our small sample. The fact that on-grid RE systems are most abundant where access levels are already high may suggest that managing a modern, inclusive electric grid and managing RE deployment draws on an overlapping set of capabilities.

Insights from this study can support African countries in their aims to expand clean and affordable energy, which form a central part of many national commitments to the 2015 Paris Climate Agreement (UNFCCC, 2015) and to Sustainable Energy for All (SE4All 2019). Clean energy transitions in the developing world, where much of the growth in greenhouse gas (GHG) emissions is expected to develop over the next ten to twenty years, will be essential to global efforts to mitigate climate change.

This chapter is organized as follows. Section 4.2 describes the global and African country-specific context for renewable energy development and outlines the motivation for studying the role of institutions. Section 4.3 describes the country case studies and develops cross-country comparisons. Section 4.4 offers our explanation for variation in RE development and attempts to distil general lessons that can be learned from the case studies. Section 4.5 concludes the chapter.

4.2   Context

4.2.1   *Global RE Trends and Technology Costs*

Renewable energy for electricity generation has expanded globally over the past fifteen years. Installed capacity for electricity generation that

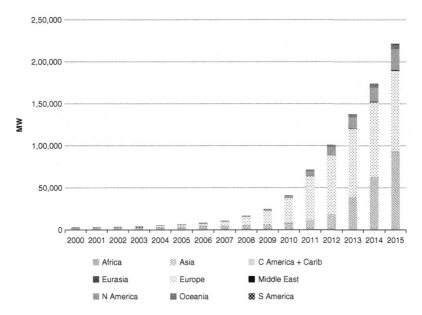

Figure 4.1 Installed solar PV capacity by region, 2000–2015
Source: IRENA (2016b)

relies on modern renewable energy sources,[3] in particular solar (PV or thermal) and wind, increased from 18.5 GW in the year 2000 to 659 GW in 2015, representing an compound annual growth rate of about 27 per cent (IRENA 2016b).

As noted above, the growth in RE capacity can be roughly divided into two waves. The 'first wave' gained momentum in the early 2000s, driven by policies designed to support renewable energy in its early stages. Expansion occurred mainly in Western Europe, the United States and later China. A 'second wave' has emerged since approximately 2011, driven by falling costs and physical-resource abundance in parts of Africa, the Caribbean and Latin America. Figure 4.1 shows capacity expansion in solar PV technology since 2000. Installations have expanded in Central America and the Caribbean, the Middle East, Oceania, South America and Africa over the 2011 to 2015 time frame. Whilst these capacity additions are small compared to total global solar PV capacity, they are large relative to the installed base in many countries.

---

[3] We consider the category of 'modern' renewable energy sources to consist of PV and concentrated solar power (CSP), wind and biomass. Amongst these sources, biomass is the most expensive and application is limited. Hydro- and geothermal energy sources are also considered to be renewable, and we categorize these sources separately.

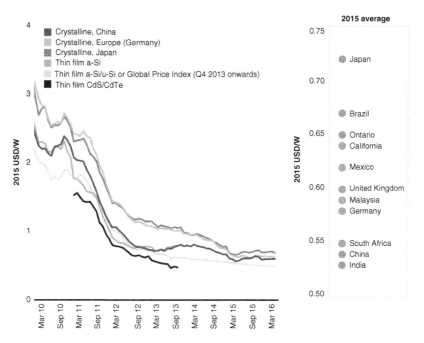

Figure 4.2 Global solar PV module price trends
Source: IRENA (2016a, 2016c)

In parallel with global capacity expansion, the costs of installed wind and solar electricity have fallen as manufacturing scale has increased and key components have become commoditized. The price of solar PV modules (an important component of installed cost) has fallen by about 21 percent for every doubling of cumulative production volume, corresponding to large price reductions over time as shown in Figure 4.2 (IRENA 2016c). According to the seventh edition of the International Roadmap for Photovoltaics (ITRPV 2016), solar PV producers are continuing to track the historic learning-curve rate of 21 per cent.

Yet other important components of cost, some of which depend on country-specific features, are a function of project location. Capital cost, which reflects country-specific risks as well as the identities, access and creditworthiness of the involved parties, affects the Levelized Cost of Electricity (LCOE) of renewable energy projects more strongly than for less capital-intensive alternatives, such as natural gas. The lowest bid[4]

---

[4] While LCOE is the average bottom-up cost estimate of solar power, the bid price is calculated using project-specific characteristics.

recorded for a solar PV project was in September 2016 in Abu Dhabi at $0.024/kWh, submitted by a consortium of Chinese module manufacturer JinkoSolar and Japanese developer Marubeni (Lacey, 2016).

4.2.2   RE Development in Africa

Africa is a large and diverse continent, with the level of economic and energy sector development varying widely across countries. The RE potential of Africa is projected to be substantially larger than the current and projected power consumption of the continent (Hermann, Miketa and Fichau 2014). According to the Africa Energy Outlook 2014 study, published by the International Energy Agency, the total on-grid power-generation capacity of Africa was 158 GW in 2012. The grid-based power-generation capacity in sub-Saharan Africa increased from about 68 GW in 2000 to 90 GW in 2012, with South Africa alone contributing to half of this capacity. Coal-fired generation capacity is about 45 per cent of the sub-Saharan total and is concentrated mainly in South Africa, followed by hydropower (22 per cent) and oil-fired power (17 per cent). Gas-fired power (14 per cent) is mainly located in Nigeria, with nuclear power (2 per cent) and other renewables (less than 1 per cent) contributing the balance.

Reliable and affordable energy is an important factor for the competitiveness of the industrial sector. Unreliable power supplies in Africa are considered one of the major obstacles to accelerating economic development. According to the Africa 2030 IRENA Report, more than thirty African countries experience regular outages and load shedding, with opportunity costs amounting to as much as 2 per cent of their GDP. Power shortages force industrial users to rely on diesel generators as a backup source of power.

Access to electricity is also a major challenge across the continent, with an estimated 600 million people lacking a source of electric power. Barring the northern region and South Africa, a large proportion of the population in the remaining regions lacks access to grid-connected electricity. The appropriateness of decentralized and centralized approaches to providing electric power is an open question. Renewable energy technologies can be deployed locally on a smaller scale to resolve the issue of electricity access to remote populations. These off-grid solutions can be deployed rapidly and customized to local needs in areas where grid extension does not make economic sense.

African countries differ widely in terms of economic profiles and development levels, resource endowments, energy access levels and institutional, technical and human-resource capacities. However, grid-connected energy remains more economic for regions with concentrated populations of users, even, or perhaps even more so, with RE as the source. This diversity influences the parameters for policy and projects in individual countries.

4.2.3   Institutions and RE: A Review of the Literature

A large literature has explored the drivers of modern RE development (Engelken et al. 2016; Garcia 2012; Ahlborg and Hammar 2014; Mohammed, Mustafa and Bashir 2013; Jacobsson and Johnson 2000). Whilst drivers are often classified into economic and non-economic categories – see for instance Garcia (2012), this distinction is not always helpful, as the costs of the system can reflect many non-economic factors (Jacobsson and Bergek 2004; Hekkert and Negro 2009). Here we focus on the dynamic interplay between technology (discussed above) and the institutions that underpin RE-enabling capabilities.

Beyond technology, institutions can affect the pace and direction of technology development. They can affect the conduct of business and governance, shaping conceptions of rights and authority, rule of law and contract enforcement. In our study, we adopt the Doing Business (DB) and World Governance Indicators (WGI) from the World Bank (World Bank 2016; WGIP 2016) as institutional indicators, and consider such indicators not just in isolation but in terms of how they combine to shape a nation's 'institutional context'.

Garcia (2012) notes that institutions enhance the investment climate for RE by ensuring general legal security – enforced property rights, observance of contracts and anti-corruption measures – as well as capable bureaucracy and predictable regulations for renewables, and by enabling competition. Similarly, Ahlborg and Hammar (2014) enumerate the barriers to RE expansion, and include weak institutions amongst other determinants such as: economy and finance; social dimensions; technical-system and local management; technology diffusion and adoption; donor dependency; and rural infrastructure and affordability. Mohammed et al. (2013) point to elements such as: cultural constraints; lack of education; unstable economies and low foreign investment; poor financial support and high credit costs; unsustainable RE policy; and poor capacity-building, as major barriers to RE development. These findings are echoed in Ika (2012), in which barriers are identified as institutional/ sustainability challenges, including: endemic corruption; capacity-building setbacks; recurring project costs; low political support and institutional capacity; lack of implementation capacity on the part of donors and recipients; incompatibility between countries and donors' management systems; and risk of collusion between the principal (agency bureaucrats or project supervisors) and the agents (project managers). A proposed solution is that project management for infrastructure development should avoid a universal one-size-fits-all approach, and instead treat projects as both technocratic exercises and political arenas for conflict, bargaining and trade-offs.

We map these identified factors in Figure 4.3, which draws motivation from Markard and Lüthi (2010). The puzzle pieces represent four interlocking sets of institutional factors, whilst the circles represent the presence or influence of these factors at different scales from local to global levels. We focus primarily on national-level capabilities that exist within each of the four institutional categories (examples of factors suggesting the presence or absence of these capabilities are given by the words overlapping the circles). However, we explicitly acknowledge that institutional environments can transcend national borders – for instance, if a local player is able to access financing on favourable terms through a partnership with a lender in a distant country with lower country risk. They can also vary widely within a country, and affect regional and even project-level conditions. For effective deployment of an RE project (which sits at the centre of our diagram), prior literature suggests that it is important for the different puzzle pieces to fit together and provide the required combination of institutional capabilities.

Building on this framework, we assess our case studies of eight African countries in terms of the set of capabilities alluded to in Figure 4.3. We consider interaction amongst technology and its cost drivers, energy system development priorities and the institutional set-up. As we will discuss below, the adoption of RE technologies in these countries appears to be driven primarily by expectations of growing energy demand, issues in access to grid-supplied electricity and the favourable economics of RE technologies, amongst other factors. The barriers include several factors outlined above, such as shortcomings in the legal and policy framework, corruption, lack of low-cost financing, technology-specific challenges and socio-cultural issues.

We hypothesize that institutional characteristics predating recent reductions in the cost of renewable energy may affect the location and scale of solar PV, and, more broadly, renewable energy development in Africa. A country's rule of law, enforceability of contracts, prevalence of corruption and stability of policy support influence the investment environment and the cost, and ease, of accessing capital. More direct financial considerations such as banking-sector stability, government guarantees and availability of foreign investment may also influence developers' appetite to operate in one country over another. The time and legwork involved in securing a project site and obtaining the necessary construction permits may also sway the decisions of location-agnostic overseas

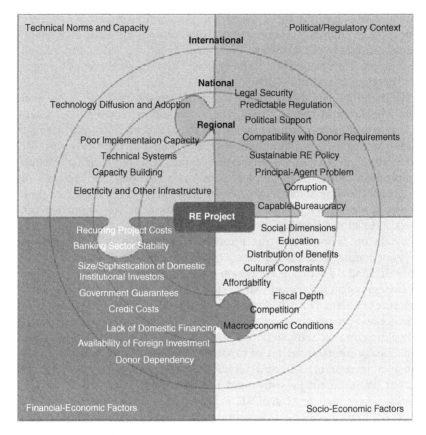

Figure 4.3 Map of factors affecting RE development, which arise from country-level RE capabilities. Extends ideas from Markard and Lüthi (2010).

investors. It is worth noting that institutional form shapes not only the decision of RE project investors and developers, but the environment for investment as a whole, including in the power sector. In addition to expecting slower RE development, we also expected to see more limited investment in power generation and grid infrastructure in the absence of strong institutions. Finally, institutions affect currency stability through the former's influence on economic performance and investment flows, directly impacting capital-intensive RE projects.

National institutions are only part of the story. Developers vary in their prospects for operating successfully within a country's institutional context. For instance, if a developer is able to tap into sources of low-cost

Figure 4.4 Map of Africa, depicting countries chosen for the study

capital or know-how, they may have a valuable competitive advantage in securing development rights and profiting from projects. Much of the expertise and technology required to install and operate grid-scale solar PV plants in Africa initially originated overseas, either in the form of purely private ventures or with the assistance of development aid. We can think of institutional enablers as interacting in complementary ways with government programmes to develop renewable energy, as well as with design choices within projects themselves.

4.3   Country Case Studies

We selected our country case studies as representing a diversity of geographic, socioeconomic, institutional conditions present across the African continent. Our country cases (Angola, Egypt, Ghana, Kenya, Morocco, Mozambique, South Africa and Tanzania) are shown on a map of Africa in Figure 4.4. Selected countries vary along many dimensions, including physical and economic size, composition of economic activities, creditworthiness of stakeholders (government, offtaker and developers amongst others), socioeconomic status and share of the population with electricity access.

4.3.1   Country Case Descriptions

Whilst our cases do not represent exhaustive combinations of these dimensions, they do contain substantial variation that can help us to bound influences. Basic statistics for the countries we study are included in Table 4.1. South Africa, Morocco and Ghana have a much higher share of population living in urban areas than Mozambique, Tanzania and Kenya. Customer density affects the ease of extending grid connections. Countries also vary widely in electricity access, from over 75 per cent with access in South Africa, Egypt, Ghana and Morocco to less than 36 per cent in Angola, Kenya, Mozambique and Tanzania. Per capita gross domestic product (GDP) varies widely, with South Africa and Angola highest and Tanzania and Mozambique lowest. South Africa and Mozambique, although they are neighbours, differ in per capita GDP by almost an order of magnitude. Angola's high average per capita GDP largely reflects the substantial contribution from the oil and gas industry to economic output. As it has the lowest life expectancy of the countries studied, Angola's per capita GDP numbers do not paint a representative picture of citizens' wellbeing.

The economies in our sample are also similar along several dimensions. Energy and natural resources, much of which are destined for export, account for a large share of economic activity in all countries. As Table 4.1 shows, with the exception of South Africa, countries are similar on measures of inequality (measured by the Gini coefficient), and literacy rates are similar except for South Africa (where they are higher) and Mozambique (where they are lower).

We chose our cases to span a variety of institutional contexts across the African continent. Our goal was neither to establish causality nor to be exhaustive, but instead to focus on probing associations amongst institutional context, RE-supporting capabilities and RE development outcomes. Our primary independent variables of interest provide measures of several widely recognized institutional enablers of economic activity in each country. We focus on several measures adopted from the World Bank's DB indicators as well as measures included in the WGIs. We focus on DB indicators related to starting a capital-intensive business, including time and procedures involved in establishing the business, registering property, obtaining construction permits and accessing domestic credit. The WGI measures capture regulatory quality, rule of law and control of

Table 4.1 *Comparison of macroeconomic and demographic indicators of sample countries*

	Angola	Egypt	Ghana	Kenya	Morocco	Mozambique	South Africa	Tanzania
Land area (sq. km)	1,246,700	997,939 (only 5% inhabited and cultivated)	238,537	569,259	710,850 (incl. Western Sahara disputed region)	799,380	1,219,090	883,749
Population (million)	24.3	87.2	26.4	45.6	33.9	25.8	54.0	50.8
2014 GDP – market price (US$ billion)	131.4	282.1	39.16	60.94	110.4	16.59	350.1	48.03
GDP growth rate	2012: 5.2% 2013: 6.8% 2014: 4.8%	2012: 2.2% 2013: 2.1% 2014: 2.2%	2012: 9.3% 2013: 7.3% 2014: 4.0%	2012: 4.6% 2013: 5.7% 2014: 5.3%	2012: 3.0% 2013: 4.7% 2014: 2.4%	2012: 7.2% 2013: 7.1% 2014: 7.2%	2012: 2.2% 2013: 2.2% 2014: 1.5%	2012: 5.1% 2013: 7.3% 2014: 6.8%
Sovereign credit rating	S&P: B (stable) Moody's: Ba2 (-ve) Fitch: B+ (stable)	S&P: B- (stable) Moody's: B3 (stable) Fitch: B (stable)	S&P: B- (stable) Moody's: B3 (-ve) Fitch: B (-ve)	S&P: B+ (-ve) Moody's: B1 (stable) Fitch: B+ (-ve)	S&P: BBB- (stable) Moody's: Ba1 (stable) Fitch: BBB- (stable)	S&P: B- (-ve) Moody's: B2 (on review) Fitch: B (stable)	S&P: BBB- (-ve) Moody's: Baa2 (-ve) Fitch: BBB- (stable)	Economist Intelligence Unit: B
GDP per capita (US$)	5,407	3,199	1,483	1,338	3,255	643	6,483	945
World Bank income-level classification	Upper-middle income	Lower-middle income	Lower-middle income	Lower-middle income	Lower-middle income	Low income	Upper-middle income	Low income
% of population below poverty line	30.1% (2008)	25.2% (2010)	25.2% (2005)	33.6% (2005)	8.9% (2007)	68.7% (2008)	53.8% (2010)	46.6% (2011)
Gini index	42.7 (2008)	30.8 (2008)	42.8 (2005)	48.5 (2005)	40.7 (2007)	45.6 (2008)	63.4 (2011)	37.8 (2011)
Literacy rate	71%	75%	71%	72%	67%	51%	93%	79%
Life expectancy (years)	52	71	61	61	71	55	56	64

Table 4.1 (*cont.*)

	Angola	Egypt	Ghana	Kenya	Morocco	Mozambique	South Africa	Tanzania
Urban population (% of total)	44%	43%	53%	25%	60%	32%	64%	31%
Major exports/ foreign currency earning sources	Crude oil (90% of exports, 50% of GDP), diamonds (5% of exports)	Crude oil, gas, refined petroleum, tourism, Suez Canal receipts	Gold, cocoa beans, crude oil	Tea, refined petroleum	Insulated wires, cars, fertilizers	Aluminium, refined petroleum, gas, coal	Gold, diamonds, platinum, coal, iron ore	Gold, raw tobacco, precious metal ore
Exports as % of GDP (2014)	59%	15%	39%	16%	35%	27%	31%	19%
Power consumption per capita (kWh)	375	1,700	346	160	866	444	4,328	105
Electricity access (% of population)	32%	99.8%	78.3%	36%	91.6%	21.2%	86%	15.5%
Average electricity price (US cents/kWh)	4.6	11.5	25.4	21.6	13.0	7.0	9.3	16.7

Note: Electricity access figures taken from the World Bank in 2014 (http://data.worldbank.org/indicator/EG.ELC.ACCS.ZS).

corruption. Measures for each country are provided in Table 4.2. The entries for countries that rank in the top four in each row are shaded light grey. Comparing across countries, Kenya, Morocco and South Africa rank highest in terms of DB 'Overall Rank'. Ghana, Morocco and South Africa are ranked in the top four most frequently amongst the indicators considered, with Egypt and Kenya ranking in the top four in a sparser subset of the categories. Angola, Mozambique and Tanzania did not rank in the top four by any of the metrics considered.

4.3.2   Measures of RE Deployment

We cannot isolate the impact of institutions on RE outcomes with such a small number of cases. Nevertheless, we can look for country characteristics that tend to coexist with robust RE development programmes, and qualitatively examine the relative influence of various characteristics on outcomes through detailed examination of our cases. We focused on several measures of renewable energy development in our sample countries. First, we discuss historical outcomes, specifically total RE capacity added (2000–2015) and RE as a share of total capacity additions (2000–2015). We also show growth in solar PV, which experienced steep cost declines (IRENA 2016a), over the same period. Second, we compute the shares of RE and solar PV, respectively, in capacity additions currently targeted by government plans. These outcomes are shown by country for absolute levels in Figure 4.5 and for shares in Figure 4.6.

South Africa dominated renewable capacity additions from 2000 to 2015, exceeding installations in the other seven countries by approximately two orders of magnitude. Most of the capacity installed was procured through the REIPPP (Renewable Energy Independent Power Producer Procurement) Programme, which hosted a series of competitive, RE-specific auctions for long-term power purchase agreements with a sovereign guarantee of payment by South Africa's National Treasury. The programme was originally launched during a period of power shortages in order to supplement efforts by the state utility (Eskom) to expand generation capacity. At the time, it was considered a desirable and measured supplement to ongoing construction of new coal-generation capacity, which was plagued by cost overruns (Worch et al., Ch. 2, this volume). Over successive bidding rounds, the levelized costs that prospective developers bid dropped substantially (Eberhard and Kåberger 2016) and the success of the programme prompted its expansion. Of the new 3.8 GW of generation capacity constructed in the country over this period, approximately 1.1 GW was new solar PV.

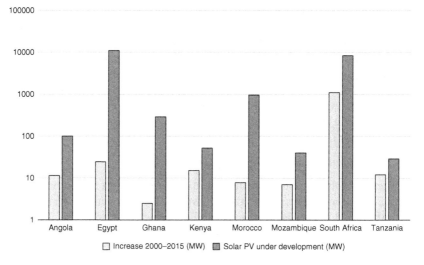

Figure 4.5 Solar PV capacity installations (MW) in the eight case-study countries. Note logarithmic scale on vertical axis. Source: IRENA Statistics, 2016a

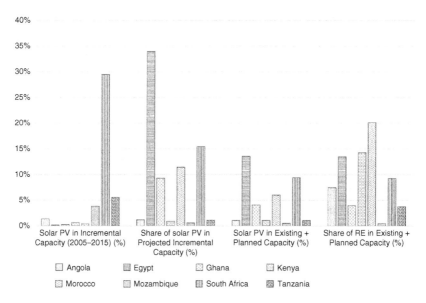

Figure 4.6 Measures of emphasis on solar PV or renewable energy in past and planned electricity-capacity expansion for the eight case-study countries. Source: IRENA, 2016a

Comparing countries on multiple measures of emphasis on solar PV in future development plans (see Figure 4.6), Egypt, Morocco and Ghana seem most likely to emerge as leaders next to South Africa in RE development. Solar PV factors most prominently in Egypt's system expansion plans (at 50 per cent of incremental capacity), whilst Ghana, Morocco and South Africa anticipate that it will contribute 10–15 per cent of new capacity. By contrast, Angola, Kenya, Mozambique and Tanzania place far less emphasis on solar. In terms of the share of solar PV in total expected generation, patterns are similar, with Egypt anticipating approximately 20 per cent solar PV in total electricity capacity; South Africa anticipates just under 10 per cent; whilst Morocco and Ghana are both around 5 per cent. Interestingly, the picture changes for a few countries when all types of RE are considered. Kenya, and to a lesser extent Angola and Tanzania, anticipate that other types of RE will contribute a substantial share of the total. After accounting for its large expected growth in wind capacity, with a target of 630 MW (which slightly exceeds the solar PV target of 500 MW), Kenya's share of non-dispatchable renewable energy in total capacity rises to approximately 1 per cent. Angola rises to 7 per cent and Tanzania to 4 per cent, from around 1 per cent for both countries in calculations for solar PV alone.

4.4   Explaining the Variation

The relationship between a country's solar resources (x-axis), planned total system capacity expansion (y-axis), and planned solar PV capacity expansion post-2016 (bubble size) is shown in Figure 4.7. The eight countries can be divided into essentially two groups: Angola, Kenya, Mozambique and Tanzania show little to no relationship between resource quantity and solar PV installations. By contrast, Egypt, Ghana, Morocco and South Africa have significantly greater emphasis on solar PV in energy development plans, with bubble size (which corresponds to planned solar PV capacity) roughly increasing with solar PV potential and planned electricity-system expansion.

In the following sub-sections, we examine potential antecedents of the development outcomes we observe. We are careful not to claim that our results are causal. However, we use the relationships we find as a starting point for elaborating potential channels for influence, which could become testable propositions for a future study.

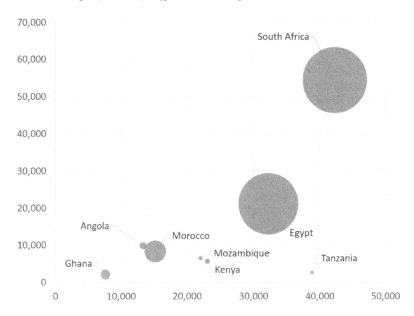

Figure 4.7 Planned solar PV capacity (bubble size) as it relates to solar PV potential (TWh/year, horizontal axis) and planned electricity-system expansion (MW, vertical axis).

4.4.1   The Roles of Resource Quality, Pre-Existing Infrastructure and Expansion Plans

Given that countries do not introduce RE in a vacuum, we examine the relationship between energy resources, pre-existing infrastructure and a country's past and future emphasis on solar PV (and RE) development. First, we find evidence that energy resources matter. Energy-resource quality, specifically solar PV potential, is expected to be a major driver of expansion because it affects capacity factor and therefore LCOE. We focus on absolute energy-resource quality (rather than area-normalized measures) because it directly influences the total amount of economically viable solar PV a country constructs. We find that, in general, capacity expansion is most intensive in solar-resource-rich areas. Tanzania is a notable exception. Mozambique, Kenya and Angola also plan more limited expansion than countries with a similar quality of solar resources, namely Morocco and Ghana. Whilst energy-resource quality appears to be important, it does not seem to explain the variation in capacity-expansion plans.

Second, choices on the quantity of solar PV to construct may be influenced by the availability and desirability of alternatives, both fossil-fired and renewable. Mozambique, South Africa, Angola and Tanzania are all planning to construct substantial additional hydropower capacity, utilizing domestic water resources. Rich wind resources in Morocco and Kenya have led to the inclusion of grid-scale wind-power installations in national plans, at 1,300 MW and 630 MW, respectively, whilst South Africa also plans an additional 1,000 MW of wind to augment the substantial existing capacity. Kenya has abundant, inexpensive geothermal resources, leading that country to include 1,646 MW in its electricity development plans. Mozambique has abundant coal deposits that it must clear in order to excavate more valuable sub-surface resources, prompting them to plan for 900 MW of coal-fired generation. Indeed, the combination of abundant solar resources and limited alternatives may be driving the large investments in grid-scale solar PV planned in Morocco and Egypt. Solar resources in these countries would not require substantial new grid infrastructure, as in both countries resources are co-located with population centres.

The rationale for increasing generation capacity could also partly explain prior and planned investments in solar PV. On this dimension, our sample counties vary: investment could be aimed at meeting growing demand from a grid-connected population (Egypt, Morocco) or at providing access to unserved populations (Kenya, Tanzania, Mozambique). Over a given time horizon, the scale of capacity expansion determines the size of the pie for various generation types. A larger pie could potentially mean larger solar PV in relative and absolute terms. Comparing across countries in our sample, those planning greater absolute electricity-capacity expansion also see solar PV playing a more prominent role. Relative system expansion, by contrast, shows no relationship with planned solar PV capacity, perhaps because rapid expansion rates are concentrated in countries where the starting level of electricity access is low and substantial expansion is planned to close the gap (Angola, Kenya and Mozambique). In Tanzania, even though it has limited electricity access, system expansion is planned on a much smaller scale, perhaps helping to explain why, despite abundant solar resources, planned solar PV expansion is expected to be limited in relative and absolute terms.

4.4.2   The Role of Institutions

The factors discussed above – resource quality, pre-existing infrastructure and expansion plans – cannot fully explain observed patterns of past or planned solar PV development. Prior literature has pointed to the role of institutions, alongside dedicated policy support, and the cost of technology as an important class of enablers of RE development (see Section 4.2.3). We add to our list of potential drivers a comparison of the institutional features in the eight countries, relying primarily on widely recognized indicators from the DB and WGI, summarized in Table 4.2.

A comparison of the eight countries reveals that RE development varies widely across institutional contexts. As a simple first cut, for each indicator we filter the countries that perform in the top half of countries in our sample (indicators are shaded in grey in Table 4.2). We then focus on the three countries that rank in the top half on the greatest number of measures of institutional performance: Ghana, Morocco and South Africa. These countries stand out for the most comprehensive coverage in terms of high rankings on institutional quality metrics; Egypt and Kenya have less coverage but compare favourably to Angola, Mozambique and Tanzania. Ghana, Morocco and South Africa are also three of the four largest developers of solar PV, and for Morocco and South Africa, this is true for all RE as well. Clearly, national institutions seem to be important, in particular for large-scale, grid-connected installations, which dominate solar PV expansion plans in these countries. Egypt, also relatively highly ranked but just outside the top three, is the fourth largest centre of solar PV development within the sample; and whilst Kenya's solar PV development is limited, it is one of the largest developers of all RE, with substantial shares of wind and geothermal alongside solar PV in capacity-expansion plans.

By contrast, Angola, Mozambique and Tanzania score weakest on these institutional measures. They also exhibit the lowest shares of RE development in past or planned construction. This evidence is suggestive of the role of institutions in enabling RE development, specifically through their influence on the emergence of a set of capabilities that combine to enable the steady growth of RE projects.

4.4.3   Energy Sector Institutions

In terms of the structure of the power sector in the sample countries, it might be expected that countries with an unbundled utility structure, higher existing private-sector participation, independent regulatory oversight, a cost-reflective tariff structure and a well-connected transmission network would attract more private-sector investment in the RE sector than countries which do not have these enabling factors. Evidence from our sample countries does not uniformly support this expectation, as summarized in Table 4.3.

Two of the countries with high levels of existing or planned RE development, South Africa and Morocco, have vertically integrated utilities that are government owned. The generation sector of South Africa is

Table 4.2 *Comparison of institutional quality measures across country cases: Highlighted cells indicate top four highest-ranked countries on each metric*

	Angola	Egypt	Ghana	Kenya	Morocco	Mozambique	South Africa	Tanzania
Business environment enabling factors								
Ease of doing business 2016								
Overall rank	181	131	114	108	75	133	73	139
Overall DTF	39.64	54.43	57.69	58.24	64.51	53.98	64.89	51.62
Select DB indicators								
Starting a business rank	141	73	102	151	43	124	120	129
DTF	76.79	88.24	83.73	74.47	92.06	80.23	81.18	79.58
No. of days	36	8	14	26	10	19	46	26
No. of procedures	8	7	8	11	4	10	6	9
Dealing with construction permits rank	108	113	132	149	29	31	90	126
DTF	66.65	65.97	62.32	59.37	77.65	77.58	69	62.85
No. of days	203	179	216	146	91	111	141	205
No. of procedures	10	20	15	15	13	10	19	18
Registering property rank	169	111	77	115	76	105	101	133
DTF	40.87	57.84	66.12	56.63	66.32	58.99	60.79	51.37
No. of days	190	63	46	61	30	40	23	67
No. of procedures	7	8	5	9	5	6	7	8

Table 4.2 (cont.)

	Angola	Egypt	Ghana	Kenya	Morocco	Mozambique	South Africa	Tanzania
Getting credit rank	*181*	*79*	*42*	*28*	*109*	*152*	*59*	*152*
DTF	5	50	65	70	40	25	60	25
Enforcing contracts rank	*185*	*155*	*116*	*102*	*59*	*184*	*119*	*64*
DTF	26.26	44.60	54.00	56.25	62.34	27.32	53.18	61.66
No. of days	1,296	1,010	710	465	510	950	600	515
WGI 2014 measures								
Regulatory quality percentile rank	*16.83*	*25.00*	*50.96*	*42.31*	*52.40*	*37.98*	*63.94*	*41.35*
Governance score (−2.5 to +2.5)	−0.96	−0.75	−0.04	−0.34	−0.01	−0.39	0.32	−0.34
Rule of law percentile rank	*11.06*	*31.25*	*59.13*	*37.50*	*56.25*	*21.63*	*63.94*	*39.42*
Governance score (−2.5 to +2.5)	−1.10	−0.60	0.02	−0.45	−0.06	−0.84	0.16	−0.41
Control of corruption percentile rank	*3.37*	*32.21*	*50.96*	*16.35*	*50.48*	*27.88*	*54.33*	*22.60*
Governance score (−2.5 to +2.5)	−1.45	−0.59	−0.21	−0.94	−0.26	−0.70	−0.11	−0.80

Notes: DTF: Distance to Frontier score (0–100, 100 – best, 0 – worst). Shading indicates that a country scores in the top four on a particular indicator.

Table 4.3 *Power-sector institutions in the eight case-study countries*

	Angola	Egypt	Ghana	Kenya	Morocco	Mozambique	South Africa	Tanzania
Utility structure	Recently unbundled into separate generation, distribution and transmission companies	Unbundled – seven generation, nine distribution companies and one transmission company	Unbundled into separate generation, transmission and distribution companies	Unbundled into separate generation, transmission and distribution companies	Vertically integrated utility controlling 29% generation, 100% transmission and 58% distribution	Vertically integrated, government owned	Vertically integrated, government owned	Vertically integrated, government owned
Private-sector participation	Only in generation	Generation and distribution	Only in generation	Only in generation	Generation and distribution	Only in generation	Only in generation	Only in generation
Private-sector share in total capacity	-	Generation – 10% of 27% capacity Distribution – 1% of capacity	Generation – 10% of 27%	26%	38%	-	3.4%	41%
Independent regulator	Yes, since 2002	Yes, since 1997	Yes, since 1997	Yes, since 2007	No (draft law approved in Sept. 2015)	No	Yes, since 2004	Yes, since 2006
Tariff regime	Heavily subsidized	Subsidized, tariffs being increased gradually to eliminate subsidies	Subsidized tariffs being increased to a cost-reflective structure	Cost-reflective tariffs set by regulator based on type of consumer. Feed-in-Tariff (FIT) regime for small-scale renewable projects (IPPs). For other large-scale projects, tariffs agreed by IPPs and offtaker, with approval from regulator	Fixed by decree from prime minister. Subsidized tariffs lower than generation cost	Heavily subsidized	Eskom applies to regulator for approval of revenue (based on return on regulatory asset base and pass-through costs). Tariffs based on approved revenue and forecasted sales approved by the regulator	Low-usage customers subsidized, higher tariffs for general usage. Tariffs being increased to recover utility losses

dominated by the state-owned company Eskom, with private-sector share at only 3.4 per cent. Morocco does not have an independent regulatory authority for the power sector. Tariffs in South Africa are determined based on an application to the regulator for approval of revenue and forecasted sales. In Morocco, tariffs are fixed by a decree from the prime minister, and are subsidized. Both countries have a relatively well-developed transmission network connecting the power-generation sources with the respective load centres.

Egypt, on the other hand, has an unbundled utility structure, although private-sector participation is limited to the generation sector (10 per cent of capacity). An independent regulator exists for the power sector; however, currently subsidized tariffs are gradually being increased to reflect generation costs. The transmission network is concentrated along the River Nile and its delta, where most of the population of the country is located. Ghana and Kenya also have an unbundled utility structure. The private sector accounts for more than a quarter of the generation capacity in both countries, and both also have an independent power-sector regulator. Kenya has a cost-reflective tariff structure set by the regulator, whilst Ghana is gradually increasing tariffs to recover generation costs. The transmission system of the latter is not very well developed, with Ghana's grid connecting the major regions but yet to reach remote inaccessible rural areas. The Kenyan grid primarily connects the Nairobi region with the surrounding counties; eight large counties with dispersed populations have yet to be connected to the grid.

Tanzania has a vertically integrated utility, TANESCO (Tanzania Electricity Supply Company, Limited); however, it has the largest share of private-sector participation in the power-generation sector amongst the sample countries in percentage terms (41 per cent). It has an independent regulator, with tariffs gradually being adjusted to recover utility losses. The transmission grid only covers large urban centres in the country. Angola and Mozambique have no private-sector participation in the power sector, although their governments have allowed investment in the generation sector. Mozambique has a vertically integrated utility, whereas Angola has recently unbundled its utility into separate companies for generation, transmission and distribution. The tariff regime is heavily subsidized in both countries and the grid is divided into independent systems, with no single national grid. The fact that RE development and the degree of power sector reform show no strong association suggests that electric power sector structure did not play a decisive role in development of RE sources in the sample countries. Despite having vertically integrated utility structures, both South Africa and Morocco have been able to attract significant private-sector participation in the RE sector.

In terms of regulatory oversight, we do not find an independent regulator in all countries with ambitious past or planned RE development. Morocco's power sector, which ranks amongst the top three in terms of planned RE capacity expansion, currently lacks this function. All other countries, including those with low levels of RE development, have an independent regulator. Countries such as Angola and Egypt have had appointed power-sector regulators for a long time, but tariffs are still heavily subsidized in these countries, partly for political reasons.

4.4.4   The Role of Public Support for RE

Public policy or fiscal support for renewable energy development by itself does not seem to be a stable predictor of RE expansion within our sample. Table 4.4 shows the status of major types of RE incentive programmes in the case-study countries. Egypt, Ghana and Kenya have both feed-in tariffs (FITs) and fiscal support, yet planned solar PV capacity in Kenya remains modest. Kenya has had a FIT in place since 2010; however, the system has been criticized for uncertainty in project pricing and a lack of transparency and there have been claims that it stifles competition (Newsbase 2016). In late 2016, policy makers announced that the FIT would be scrapped in favour of competitive auctions, modelled on South Africa's approach. Ghana's FIT has also not been sufficient to enable RE development. When first introduced, the FIT attracted a pipeline of twenty-nine projects totalling over 2 GW. However, in 2015 the government limited the project size to 20 MW and total installations to 150 MW, amid concern that the country's electric grid was not going to be able to absorb the new capacity (News .Ghana.com 2015), which highlighted the importance of complementary system-wide RE integration capabilities. Recent efforts to extend the time horizon for FITs from ten to twenty years are not likely to increase installations in the face of the new transmission capacity constraints. Both the Ghanaian and the Kenyan cases illustrate how the terms, and even the existence, of public support for RE can be subject to change, reflecting policy and regulatory unpredictability, and undermining stable expansion of RE sources. This is an example of how institutional factors can work at cross-purposes with dedicated RE support. It contrasts sharply with the experience of early RE markets in Western Europe and China, where dedicated support played a critical enabling role (Reiche and Bechberger 2004; Butler and Neuhoff 2008; Jenner et al. 2013; Lema and Ruby 2007). Similarly, Tanzania, which offers fiscal support for RE projects but has relatively incomplete institutions, has seen comparatively limited development.

Table 4.4 *Public support for RE in the eight case-study countries*

	Angola	Egypt	Ghana	Kenya	Morocco	Mozambique	South Africa	Tanzania
Feed-in tariffs for RE	No	Yes	Yes	Yes	No (EnergiPro scheme: projects up to 50 MW receive incentive tariffs and grid access)	No	No (FIT was explored, but rejected in favour of competitive tenders)	No (Small Power Producers Programme has FIT for projects < 10 MW)
Fiscal incentives for RE	No	Yes	Yes	Yes	No	No	Yes	Yes
Competitive auctions	No	No	No	Yes – under-development	No	No	Yes	No

Our cases underscore that the credibility, stability and comprehensiveness of the set of system-wide capabilities required to enable RE, which depends on the institutional context, is more important than subsidies or other forms of RE-specific policy support. In countries where one or more of the institutional capabilities are lacking, forms of RE support that create new and dedicated channels for RE development may be more effective than targeted policy support, to the extent that they prioritize RE and enhance system-wide co-ordination. South Africa, which established dedicated procurement auctions, and Morocco, which offers incentive tariffs and grid access, have had significantly greater success in developing RE in the absence of FITs. In South Africa's case, a dedicated office for renewable energy procurement was established, with the tacit support of the state-owned utility Eskom, during a period of electricity shortages. At the time, Eskom planners saw RE as complementary rather than threatening. Abundant solar resources in South Africa, combined with global module-cost reduction and competitive bidding, ensured that the prices Eskom paid to procure solar electricity continued to fall, and the company extended grid connections to utilize these resources. Besides, the National Energy Regulator of South Africa guaranteed that the full cost of power purchase agreements (PPAs) would be directly passed on to ratepayers, ensuring that Eskom was financially unaffected. The South African government, under pressure to act on climate change by reducing its economy's reliance on coal and other fossil fuels, highlighted the RE procurement auctions as a major pillar of domestic climate-change mitigation efforts. Morocco's RE development has similarly benefited from the direct support of King Mohammed VI, who has declared targets for the share of electricity generated from RE that increase to 52 per cent by 2030 as part of the nation's plans to tackle climate change.

Beyond evidence that RE support and institutional setting interact to determine RE outcomes, we also found that policies and programmes can incentivize development when they build in institutional elements that are weak or absent in a particular national context. We found evidence consistent with this mechanism in every country we studied. Our findings are perhaps most relevant for the large-scale, grid-connected solar PV projects that could displace urban and industrial usage of diesel generators and coal, which rank amongst the least climate-friendly energy options. All of our case-study countries rank lower on institutional quality indicators compared to the industrialized nations where the first wave of RE development occurred. We see evidence in some countries that FITs, fiscal incentives, dedicated procurement and even single projects may have worked in countries precisely because the respective initiative compensated for the most consequential institutional gaps. This may help to explain why South Africa and Morocco have both seen the most substantial investments in RE. In Mozambique, where RE development is minuscule, the only project to date relies on grant funds from the Swedish International Development Cooperation Agency to circumvent foreign-exchange risk and bring down the otherwise prohibitively high project LCOE to permit a sufficiently low tariff level. No doubt such an approach to RE expansion would not be viable at scale.

4.5   Conclusion

This chapter examined the relationship between country-specific institutional characteristics and observed outcomes for RE development in eight diverse country contexts across Africa. The institutions we considered ranged from broad and fundamental enablers of commerce in a country (indicators of contract enforceability, for instance) to electricity-sector-specific institutions (extent of unbundling, existence of an independent regulator), to RE-specific supporting policies (FITs, renewable portfolio standards). Our finding that the first category – broad economic enablers, spanning multiple categories – is the most important antecedent for RE development is supported by evidence from countries with relatively large existing and planned levels of RE. The fact that the second and third categories are not uniformly present suggests that a set of institutions that are at least minimally viable in supporting the capabilities needed to attract RE may be an important antecedent of its development. The second and third categories may also be influential, especially once the first category of enabling institutions is in place; we offer this inter-dependency as a proposition for other scholars to test.

Our exploration provides evidence that these combined capabilities are comprised of four categories: financing capabilities, political/regulatory capabilities, value capture capabilities and technical capabilities. Dedicated support for renewable energy falls within the group of political/regulatory capabilities, but we find evidence that these policies can only work if the other elements of this combined capability set are in place. Further, these capabilities can exist and have an enabling effect in systems that vary widely in their structure and governance. The operative question is 'where do (or could) these capabilities reside?' and not 'what single, one-size-fits-all prescription, if adopted, would give rise to these capabilities?' Institutions can be considered as the catalysts, or the scaffolding, that allows capabilities to come into being, to mature and to evolve over time. In general, we find evidence that function matters more than form – for instance, whether the electricity sector is vertically integrated or unbundled seems to be unrelated to the RE outcomes we examine. Indeed, our results encourage stakeholders to take stock of a country's broader institutional setting and existing capabilities, before advancing consensus prescriptions to restructure the electricity sector, with the aim of facilitating RE integration.

In the coming decades, much of the growth in electricity demand is expected to occur in developing countries. Assuming the global components of RE cost continue to fall, we can expect RE to figure prominently in the energy system development plans of countries that have rich physical RE resources and system topologies amenable to grid connection and integration, making the all-in cost of project development attractive relative to prevailing tariffs. To realize this potential, policy makers will benefit from taking stock of institutional enablers *in countries* and supplementing them as needed with enablers *in projects or policies*, and from asking whether or not they provide the value capture, system-wide coordination and dynamic risk-mitigation capabilities to incentivize developers to initiate new projects.

Our observations regarding the role of institutions have at least two major implications for national RE development efforts. First, in the long term, countries can improve RE development prospects by augmenting the set of capabilities, supported by national and energy sector institutions, that allow the improving economics of RE to translate into its widespread, cost-effective adoption. Underlying fragilities caused by incompleteness of underlying national institutions are a major, but perhaps too often overlooked, source of project risk, even in countries where early development has been successful. An example of this is South Africa, which after multiple successful bidding rounds found state-run utility Eskom refusing to sign off on contract payments for RE developers. A feature of the original RE procurement programme – its independence from Eskom – turned into a bug when the scale and future prospects of RE were perceived as a potential threat to Eskom's business, in particular its nuclear energy development plans (Interviews with Authors 2016). As a result, the future of RE development in South Africa went on pause, adversely impacting investors and developers.

The South African case illustrates an important step required for RE to reach scale – side-stepping or neutralizing the resistance to RE that would follow from the reallocation of rents its expansion would imply (Smink, Hekkert and Negro 2015; Lauber and Jacobsson 2016). Leadership and co-ordination from the top helps here, and in this regard, Morocco may prove to be more successful, although long-term RE development will depend on the sustained commitment of the King. Egypt's FIT programme and additional direct procurement of (mostly Middle Eastern) large-scale solar PV reflects institutional enablers embedded in these programmes, but anticipated investments could be scaled back dramatically if national institutions do not offer the necessary long-term support. Indeed, our study suggests that any form of government RE support that does not either build in or benefit from stable institutional conditions could sharply limit RE development over the long term. Efforts to 'patch in' institutions within dedicated RE-support programmes should be accompanied by efforts to strengthen national institutions in ways that stabilize incentives for RE investment.

Second, the goal of greening the energy supply may be usefully decoupled from the goal of expanding electricity access. Our case-study comparisons suggest that RE is most likely to make a significant contribution to climate-change mitigation in countries that have relatively well-developed institutions, encompassing the spectrum of required capabilities, high willingness-to-pay and high expected electricity demand growth. Institutionally, it may be easier – and more cost-effective from an environmental standpoint – to intro-duce RE as part of efforts to expand electricity generation on a large scale in places with high levels of electricity access and relatively well-off populations. It may take a centralized, strategic effort to pave the way for the system-wide changes needed to support RE expansion at scale – including securing grid connections and operational rights for new generation assets alongside incumbent energy types. To the extent that such projects displace coal or other fossil generation, they will have a larger environmental impact. By contrast, extending basic electricity to distributed rural households may involve a smaller quantity of electrons, a less-developed grid and locally unique insti-tutional gaps. Whilst solar PV or other renewable energy types may indeed rank amongst the most cost-effective options for extending access, this decision should be informed by local costs, conditions and alternatives.

Our analysis suggests several directions for future research. Whilst our sample of countries included major African markets with existing or planned RE development, expanding the scope to all countries in Africa would probe the durability of our findings. For now, we emphasize that our conclusions should not be generalized beyond the eight countries we studied. Moving beyond installed capacity would also allow insight into how institutions influence operation of RE and impacts on long-term development. Successful expansion and integration of RE requires the support of multiple complementary functions – national planning, avail-ability of finance, project procurement, grid connection and dispatch/operation. Given that development of RE is still at a relatively early stage in the eight countries we considered, we focused on installed capacity, but future work should consider generation. Metrics of interest could include grid-connected capacity as a share of the total, as well as curtailment – the amount of wind spilled as a result of institutional and technical constraints.

With costs expected to fall further, RE will come within the reach of ever more markets around the world. Many developing countries are rich in RE resources. In developing countries where dispatchable resources are prone to fuel shortages and price fluctuations, RE may prove more reliable and cost competitive, especially if combined with low-cost storage. The latest estimates indicate that the technology's potential in Africa is enormous (IRENA 2016c). Our case studies suggest that realizing this potential will require careful attention to be paid to whether or not dedicated policy or programmatic support, and existing system-wide RE financing, political/regulatory, value capture and technical capabilities, enabled by national institutional contexts, combine in ways that incentivize sustained RE expansion. In this sense, the 'second wave' may look very different from the 'first wave' of RE development. Even the markets where RE development began may benefit from taking stock of the fit between dedicated RE support mechanisms and national institutions for clues on how to accelerate clean-energy transitions.

Acknowledgements

This research was sponsored by Eni, through the MIT Energy Initiative. We thank the four anonymous reviewers for their constructive comments.

References

Ahlborg, H. and Hammar, L. (2014). Drivers and barriers to rural electrification in Tanzania and Mozambique – Grid-extension, off-grid, and renewable energy technologies. *Renewable Energy*, 61 (2014): 117–124. http://dx.doi.org/10.1016/j.renene.2012.09.057

Bird, L., Milligan, M., and Lew, D. (2013). *Integrating Variable Renewable Energy: Challenges and Solutions.* NREL/TP-6A20-60451 (September), 14. Washington, DC: National Renewable Energy Laboratory. http://doi.org/NREL/TP-6A20-60451

Bridge to India. (2017, 22 May). GST to cause significant disruption to the solar sector. *India Solar Weekly.* https://bridgetoindia.com/gst-cause-significant-disruption-solar-sector/

Butler, L., and Neuhoff, K. (2008). Comparison of feed-in tariff, quota and auction mechanisms to support wind power development. *Renewable Energy*, 33(8): 1854–1867. https://www.sciencedirect.com/science/article/pii/S0960148107003242 http://documents.worldbank.org/curated/en/2016/04/26218214/independent-power-projects-sub-saharan-africa-lessons-five-key-countries

Eberhard, A. and Kåberger, T. (2016) Renewable energy auctions in South Africa outshine feed-in tariffs. *Energy Science and Engineering*. https://onlinelibrary .wiley.com/doi/full/10.1002/ese3.118

Engelken, M., Romer, B. Drescher, M., Welpe, I. M., and Picot, A. (2016). Comparing drivers, barriers, and opportunities of business models for renewable energies. *A review. Renewable and Sustainable Energy Reviews*, 60 (2016): 795–809. http://dx.doi.org/10.1016/j.rser.2015.12.163

Garcia, C. (2012). Policies and institutions for grid-connected renewable energy: 'Best practice' and the case of China. *Governance: An International Journal of Policy, Administration, and Institutions*,26(1) (January 2013): 119–146.

Hermann, S., Miketa A. and Fichaux, N. (2014). *Estimating the renewable energy potential in Africa*. IRENA-KTH Working Paper. International Renewable Energy Agency, Abu Dhabi.

IEA. (2014). *Africa energy outlook: A focus on energy prospects in sub-Saharan Africa*. World Energy Outlook Special Report. Paris: International Energy Agency. https://www.iea.org/publications/freepublications/publication/WE O2014_AfricaEnergyOutlook.pdf

Ika, L. (2012). Project management for development in Africa: Why projects are failing and what can be done about it. *Project Management Journal*, 43(4): 27–41. 10.1002/pmj.21281

Interviews with Authors. (2016). Conducted by members of the research team with stakeholders in Morocco, Mozambique and South Africa. Transcripts available upon request.

IRENA. (2016a). *The power to change: Solar and wind cost reduction potential*. Abu Dhabi: International Renewable Energy Agency. www.irena.org/DocumentD ownloads/Publications/IRENA_Power_to_Change_2016.pdf

IRENA. (2016b) Trends in renewable energy. Renewable Energy Data and Statistics. *IRENA*. http://resourceirena.irena.org/gateway/dashboard/

IRENA. (2016c). *Solar PV in Africa: Costs and markets*. Abu Dhabi: International Renewable Energy Agency. www.irena.org/DocumentDownloads/Publication s/IRENA_Solar_PV_Costs_Africa2016.pdf

ITRPV. (2016). *International technology roadmap for photovoltaic (ITRPV): 2015 results including maturity reports*. Frankfurt am Main: ITRPV/VDMA. www .itrpv.net/.cm4all/iproc.php/ITRPV%20Seventh%20Edition%20including% 20maturity%20report%2020161026.pdf

Jacobsson, S., and Bergek, A. (2004). Transforming the energy sector: The evolution of technological systems in renewable energy technology. *Industrial and Corporate Change*, 13(5): 815–849. https://doi.org/10.1093/icc/dth032

Jacobsson, S., and Johnson, A. (2000). The diffusion of renewable energy technology: an analytical framework and key issues for research. *Energy Policy*, 28(9): 625–640.

Jenner, S., Groba, F. and Indvik, J. (2013). Assessing the strength and effectiveness of renewable electricity feed-in tariffs in European Union countries. *Energy Policy*, 52: 385–401. http://doi.org/10.1016/j .enpol.2012.09.046

Lacey, S. (2016, 20 September). Jinko and Marubeni Bid 2.4 Cents to Supply Solar in Abu Dhabi. How Low Can Solar Prices Go? Green Tech Media https://

www.greentechmedia.com/articles/read/jinko-solar-and-marubeni-bid-2-4-ce
nts-for-solar-power-plant-in-abu-dhabi/

Lauber, V. and Jacobsson, S. (2016). The politics and economics of constructing,
contesting and restricting socio-political space for renewables – The German
Renewable Energy Act. *Environmental Innovation and Societal Transitions*, 18:
147–163. https://doi.org/10.1016/j.eist.2015.06.005

Lema, A., and Ruby, K. (2007). Between fragmented authoritarianism and policy
coordination: Creating a Chinese market for wind energy. *Energy Policy*, 35(7):
3879–3890. http://doi.org/10.1016/j.enpol.2007.01.025

Markard, J. and Lüthi, C. (2010). Institutional and organizational contexts for
sustainable innovation in sanitation. Cities of the Future Conference. Boston:
Water Environment Federation, 889–903.

Mohammed, Y. S., Mustafa, M. W. and Bashir, N. (2013). Status of renewable
energy consumption and developmental challenges in Sub-Sahara Africa.
Renewable and Sustainable Energy Reviews, 27, 453–463. (http://dx.doi.org/10
.1016/j.rser.2013.06.044)

Newsbase. (2016, Oct. 20). Kenya moves to swap FiTs for competitive auctions.
REM – Renewable Energy, 42 (531). http://newsbase.com/topstories/kenya-
moves-swap-fits-competitive-auctions

North, D. (1992). *Transaction costs, institutions, and economic performance*. San
Francisco, CA: ICS Press.

Reiche, D., and Bechberger, M. (2004). Policy differences in the promotion of
renewable energies in the EU member states. *Energy Policy*, 32. www
.sciencedirect.com/science/article/pii/S0301421502003439

Reichelstein, S., and Yorston, M. (2013). The prospects for cost competitive
solar PV power. *Energy Policy*, 55: 117–127.

Rose, A., Stoner, R., and Pérez-Arriaga, I. Prospects for grid-connected solar PV
in Kenya: A systems approach. Applied Energy, 161, 583–590. (http://doi.org/
10.1016/j.enpol.2012.11.003)

SE4All (Sustainable Energy for All). (2019). Action agenda. https://www.se4all-
africa.org/seforall-in-africa/country-actions/action-agenda/

Smink, M. M., Hekkert, M. P., and Negro, S. O. (2015). Keeping sustainable
innovation on a leash? Exploring incumbents' institutional strategies. *Business
Strategy and the Environment*, 24(2): 86–101. https://doi.org/10.1002/bse.1808

Tsakhara, P. (2015, March 16). Presentation on the Tanzanian solar PV-hybrid
workshop held in Berlin, Germany. TANESCO. www.giz.de/fachexpertise/do
wnloads/2015-tanesco-presentation-tansania.pdf

WGIP. (2016). *Worldwide Governance Indicators Project*. http://info.worldbank.org
/governance/wgi/index.aspx#home

World Bank. (2016). *Doing business 2016: Measuring regulatory quality and
efficiency*. Washington, DC:World Bank. DOI:http://10.1596/978-1-4648-
0667-4. Licence: Creative Commons Attribution CC BY 3.0 IGO.

5 Harnessing Africa's Energy Resources through Regional Infrastructure Projects

Amy Rose, Ignacio Pérez-Arriaga, Robert Stoner and Richard de Neufville

Abstract

Regional electricity systems, or power pools, can reduce the cost of providing electricity and improve system reliability through co-ordinated use of energy resources. Realizing these benefits requires a strong political will to co-operate combined with careful market design supported by technical, economic and institutional analysis. In this chapter, we present some of the unique motivations for power pools in Africa, describe the current status of pooling arrangements on the continent, study in detail the regulation of transmission in the Southern African Power Pool (SAPP) and identify some improvements to the present rules. Our approach combines mathematical modelling of the SAPP system using linear programming with analysis of regional institutions and their role in promoting efficient investments as well as efficient market behaviour. We have investigated several market-design questions, such as how to identify, implement and allocate costs for necessary regional transmission investments. Our regulatory proposals developed for the SAPP could be feasible options for other regional systems in Africa that face similar institutional and technical challenges in developing regional infrastructure.

> We strongly believe that the optimal solution for the energy crisis in Africa is to go regional.
>
> *Professor Mosad Elmissiry, Head of Energy Programmes, NEPAD (World Energy Council, 2015)*

5.1 Challenges in the Development of Energy Resources in Africa

Despite an abundance of energy resources, electric power systems in Africa have been slow to develop. Forty-five per cent of the population in sub-Saharan Africa remains without access to electricity (IEA 2016a). Those with access often experience poor reliability, hampering economic growth. Companies in sub-Saharan Africa experience an estimated 8.4 electrical outages per month, resulting in an approximate loss of 8.3 per cent of annual sales (Enterprise Surveys 2017). Reliability concerns have prompted over 50 per cent of firms to own or share a private generator. Affordability is a second concern for electricity consumers. A survey of electricity tariffs in twenty-seven African countries found that average tariffs consistent with full recovery of economic costs are only affordable for 70 per cent of current consumers (Briceño-Garmendia and Shkaratan 2011). The study found that if countries expanded electricity access to the 634 million people who remain unconnected to the centralized grid, these tariffs would only be affordable for 25 per cent of newly connected households.

A key challenge in terms of providing reliable and affordable electricity access throughout Africa is that energy resources, though plentiful, are not uniformly distributed (Figure 5.1), and demand in individual countries is often too low to capture economies of scale for new projects. The Congo River alone has the estimated potential to produce 1,400 TWh per year, equivalent to over three times the annual consumption in all of sub-Saharan Africa in 2010 (IEA 2013; World Bank 2015). Abundant coal resources are concentrated in the south of the continent, whilst most of the natural gas and oil reserves are found in West and North Africa. Due to significant economies of scale in generation and transmission infrastructure, resources are often not economic to develop unless at scale. However, the efficient scale for new projects is oversized for many individual countries in sub-Saharan Africa. The Program for Infrastructure Development in Africa estimates that at least twenty countries have demand that falls below the efficient level for a single power plant (AfDB 2010).

Financing is another barrier to harnessing Africa's energy resources. Average public expenditure on energy infrastructure in sub-Saharan Africa is US $5 billion per year, far less than the estimated $27 billion needed annually to meet growing demand over the next thirty years (Castellano et al. 2015; Eberhard et al. 2011). Funding from the private sector, official development assistance and, most recently, Chinese investments add an additional $11 billion per year (World Bank 2016; Gutman, Sy and Chattopadhyay 2015). However, these funds tend to be concentrated in a small number of countries, namely, South Africa, Kenya, Ethiopia, Nigeria, Tanzania and Ghana. Outside of these areas, utilities faced with limited financial resources

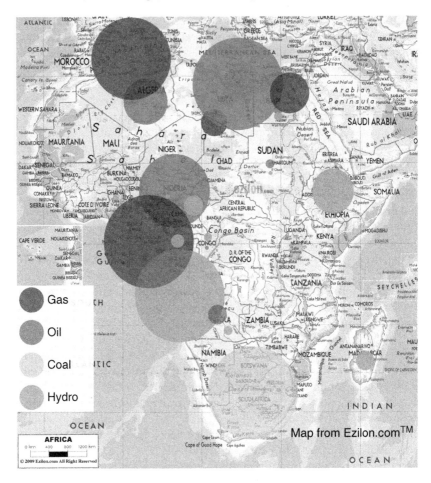

Figure 5.1 Relative concentration of energy resources in Africa. The size of the circle indicates relative size of proven reserves as of end of 2011. Units are million tonnes (Oil and Coal); trillion cubic feet (Gas); TWh/yr (Hydro). Authors' representation based on WEC (2004; 2013)

and low levels of consumer demand have tended to deploy technologies such as diesel generators that can be built in smaller increments but may have more expensive per-unit energy costs. The level of MW of generation capacity and of kilometres of transmission lines per million inhabitants in sub-Saharan Africa is much lower than in any other region of the world (World Bank 2017a).

5.2 Regional Integration as an Alternative Development Strategy

There is growing interest in regional integration as a potential strategy with which to overcome the barriers of scale and financing that individual countries face in developing reliable and affordable electricity supplies across the African continent. Africa now hosts one regional power pool, with two more in advanced stages of development.

5.2.1 Benefits of Regional Integration

Regional pooling of demand can enable African utilities to capture economies of scale for larger projects with lower per-unit costs (Olmos 2013). Large projects need sufficient consumer demand to guarantee investors can recover their costs through revenues. By creating a larger consumer market across multiple countries, projects that are oversized or risky for a single country may be economically feasible for a regional market.

Regional integration can also enable resource sharing and better utilization of the most efficient generators by allowing resource-rich countries to export power to countries with limited resources (World Bank 2008). The former are able to earn extra revenues through power sales and the latter can benefit from access to lower-cost energy supplies and potentially avoid some need for new investments. Resource sharing can also reduce the cost of providing reserves. By sharing reserves, countries with asynchronous demand profiles can reduce their total reserve requirements compared to a case in which each country must provide its own reserves.

Finally, regional integration can improve security of supply for participants. In the case of some contingencies, such as the failure of a power plant or transmission line, regional systems can rely on a larger network of support to restore power supplies. In the longer term, regional integration helps shield individual systems from the effects of fuel-price spikes or droughts by diversifying the energy resources used for electricity production.

Studies of regional power trade in Africa estimate that regional integration could reduce annualized costs by 3–10 per cent or $2.7 billion (Rosnes, Vennemo and Pöyry 2009). McKinsey & Co. estimate that regional integration could save African consumers nearly $10 billion per year in lower capital and operating costs (Castellano et al. 2015). The ability to share reserves and diversify fuel supplies could also enable greater deployment of renewable energy. The International Renewable Energy Agency estimates renewable penetration in southern and western

Table 5.1 *Installed capacity by generation source and per thousand inhabitants for each power pool in 2015 (The category 'Other' refers to wind, solar and biomass technologies)*

		SAPP	EAPP	WAPP
Installed capacity	(MW)	61,556	62,622	15,558
Hydro share	(%)	19	26	31
Thermal share	(%)	77	71	68
Other share	(%)	4	2	0
Capacity per person	kW/1,000 inhabitants	207	128	45
Electric power consumption	kWh/capita	1,073	506	172

Source: Platts (2010); Global Energy Observatory (n.d.); World Bank (2017b); World Bank (2017c).

Africa could reach 46 per cent and 52 per cent respectively by 2030 if countries co-ordinated investments and operations (Miketa and Merven 2013a; Miketa and Merven 2013b).

5.2.2   *Present Status of Regional Integration in Africa*

As of 2017 there are three regional power pools in Africa: the Southern African Power Pool (SAPP), West African Power Pool (WAPP), and Eastern Africa Power Pool (EAPP). There are proposals for a Central African Power Pool and a Comité Maghrebin de l'Electricité (COMELEC) in northern Africa, but these organizations are still in their infancy. Figure 5.2 shows how the five regional power pools might span the continent. Table 5.1 compares the installed capacities and levels of consumption for each power pool.

At the regional level, thermal generation sources account for the majority of installed capacity in each pool. However, this picture is skewed by dominant thermal-based countries with a large fraction of installed capacity in each region: South Africa in SAPP (77 per cent); Egypt in EAPP (59 per cent); and Nigeria in WAPP (53 per cent). Excluding these countries, the portion of installed capacity from hydropower increases to 69 per cent in SAPP, 53 per cent in EAPP and 37 per cent in WAPP.

The SAPP area has the highest rates of electricity consumption and installed capacity per inhabitant, followed by EAPP and WAPP. Similar to the regional generation mix, dominant countries in each region drive these values and any inter-regional differences. If South Africa, Egypt and

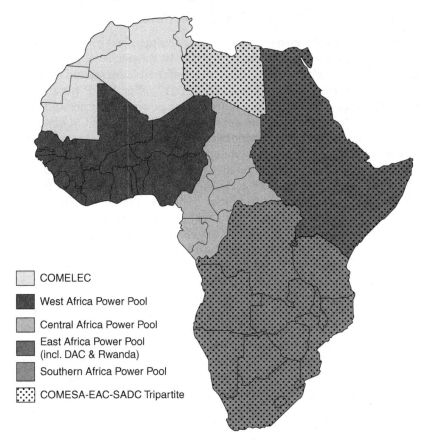

COMELEC

West Africa Power Pool

Central Africa Power Pool

East Africa Power Pool
(incl. DAC & Rwanda)

Southern Africa Power Pool

COMESA-EAC-SADC Tripartite

Figure 5.2 Grouping of African countries into five regional power pools. To date, only the southern, eastern and western pools are in advanced stages of formation

Nigeria are excluded, the values for installed capacity per 1,000 inhabitants and per capita consumption are significantly smaller and fairly similar across the three regions.

We chose to study the SAPP in detail because it is the oldest and most advanced regional electricity market in Africa. It has been operating for over twenty years, allowing time for experiential learning and new challenges to emerge. The EAPP and WAPP are still in the process of establishing regional trading platforms, market rules and regional institutions. These two organizations look to other regional markets, including the SAPP, for guidance on how to design and implement their own systems.

5.2.2.1   *Southern African Power Pool (SAPP)*

The SAPP was established in 1995 by the twelve members of the Southern African Development Community (SADC). Its mission is to 'provide the least cost [*sic*], environmentally friendly and affordable energy and increase accessibility to rural communities' (SAPP 2017). The SAPP has sixteen member utilities, including two independent power producers and two independent transmission companies. Angola, Tanzania and Malawi are termed 'non-operating' members because these countries are not connected to the regional transmission network.

In 2015, regional trade accounted for less than 10 per cent of electricity consumed (IEA 2016b). Market development is fairly advanced in the SAPP. Members can choose from four trading arrangements: long-term bilateral contracts, short-term or over-the-counter bilateral contracts, day-ahead and intra-day market trades. Despite the SAPP's progress in developing competitive short-term markets, long-term bilateral contracts are the basis for cross-border trading, accounting for over 94 per cent of power traded in the 2014–15 trading year.

Insufficient generation and transmission capacity is a critical challenge for the SAPP. In 2015, the capacity shortfall reached 8,247 MW (17 per cent of peak demand). The region is now strongly promoting energy efficiency and demand-side management programmes to relieve supply constraints and reduce load shedding (SAPP 2015). Large hydropower projects including the Cahora Bassa North Bank Extension (Hussain 2015) in Mozambique (1,245 MW), Batoka Gorge (NEPAD 2017) in Zambia and Zimbabwe (1,600 MW), and Inga 3 (PR Newswire 2016) in DRC (4,800 MW) could alleviate regional supply constraints. Investments in transmission are critically needed to relieve congestion and connect planned generation projects to the regional market (SAPP 2005).

The SAPP's officials are also focused on strengthening regional institutions and regulatory and policy frameworks. There is no regional grid code and, as a result, members do not have the basic assurances, such as full open access to the transmission network, that are necessary to promote competition and facilitate trade (Magombo et al. 2008). A key step in advancing regulatory and policy harmonization would be to grant more rule-making authority and resources to the Regional Electricity Regulators Association (RERA).

5.3   Regional Transmission as a Critical Area for Study

The regional transmission network is an essential part of any electricity system because it facilitates power exchanges between network users.

Absent adequate interconnections, the benefits of regional integration cannot be realized. In fact, the EAPP master plan found that over 75 per cent of the estimated $1,200 million per year cost savings from co-ordinated generation and transmission expansion could be captured through investments in regional transmission interconnections alone (SNC-Lavalin International Inc. and Parsons Brinckerhoff 2011). Whilst transmission is critical to realize the benefits of integration, international experience suggests that necessary investments will not take place unless regional rules are in place for network planning, cost sharing and management.

Regional planning can identify beneficial projects that may not be economically feasible or justified in national infrastructure plans. Particularly for transmission, national planning mandates generally do not include objectives such as facilitating cross-border trade, or evaluate the impacts that planned network reinforcements may have on other areas. Therefore, some degree of centralized or co-ordinated planning is needed in order to identify investments that satisfy regional needs rather than only the needs of each country.

For projects of regional scope, the costs of designing and implementing a project tend to be high and the benefits are often distributed amongst multiple agents including consumers, generators and other transmission companies spread across a number of countries. Because network benefits can be widely dispersed, there is generally no single agent willing to undertake the investment, since they will only capture a fraction of the benefits. Therefore, some sound method of allocating costs for regional transmission projects is needed to avoid opposition to new investments by those who might be left worse off, with flawed cost-allocation rules even for efficient network investments (i.e. those that provide a net benefit to the region). No opposition to an efficient transmission project is a good start in terms of getting the project implemented and its cost recovered. Project sponsors could negotiate payments amongst potential beneficiaries but this is not ideal. This process may limit the types of projects being developed to only those with a small number of easily identified beneficiaries and with very large margins of benefits over costs. Projects that meet this criterion may not correspond to those that are most beneficial or needed in the region. Further, failure to negotiate an agreement could stall projects that are otherwise justified.

Finally, the physical laws governing power flows may result in a situation whereby injections or withdrawals from a network user located in one country impact power flows across lines in several other countries. Therefore, the regional network should be managed in a co-ordinated fashion to avoid technical failures and promote the efficient use of generation and transmission infrastructure.

5.3.1   Research Approach

Previous authors have conducted technical studies of the transmission network using mathematical optimization or simulation techniques.[1] These studies identified new investments that were needed to promote trade or ensure system reliability. Other studies looked at the role of regional institutions to promote co-ordinated planning and operations (Magombo et al. 2008; UN ECA 2013; Zhou 2012).

Our study adopts an integrated approach, combining technical and institutions analysis to the difficult problem of identifying and promoting investments in necessary transmission infrastructure. This integrated approach to market design can better identify opportunities to improve transmission regulation and indicate which regulatory strategies are most suitable for a particular region. We demonstrate how such an approach can be applied through a detailed study of the design and operation of the SAPP. We draw from principles of sound regulatory practice, power-systems engineering, microeconomic theory and international experience to develop proposals for transmission planning, regulatory approval and cost allocation that are feasible to implement in southern Africa's multi-national system.

A key component of this analysis is a linear programming model of the SAPP power system. This economic dispatch model optimizes the hourly output of generation plants and flows across each transmission line to meet demand over a sample period (one week) at lowest cost, subject to technical, policy or regulatory constraints formulated as linear equations. The generation and demand characteristics in each country are represented as a single node. Power flows across the regional network are represented using a simplified transportation model.[2] Additional information on the model design and complete formulation can be found in Rose (2017).

Whilst this analysis is focused on the SAPP, the same integrated approach could be generalized to other regional markets in Africa. Where possible, we also examined existing transmission regulation and

---

[1] See, for example, previously cited studies by SNC Lavalin International Inc. and Parsons Brinckerhoff (2011); Rosnes et al. (2009); Miketa and Merven (2013a); and Castellano et al. (2015).

[2] This type of representation only includes Kirchhoff's first law: the sum of the power flowing into a node is equal to the sum of power flowing out of it.

regional institutions in the EAPP and WAPP systems but did not include mathematical modelling of these entities.

5.3.2 Regional Context: Transmission Regulation in the SAPP

The SAPP presents a compelling case study of the need for a regional approach to developing the regional transmission network. When the market was developed in 1995, the region had a generation-capacity surplus of 22 per cent over peak demand, due primarily to excess supplies in South Africa and DRC. At the same time, countries in the north had just experienced a prolonged drought that threatened electricity supplies. Regional integration provided an opportunity for some member countries to capitalize on excess capacity through trade and for others to improve reliability by diversifying the energy resources they relied on for electricity. Both of these goals required new investments in transmission interconnections in order to link all countries to the regional network and strengthen existing connections.

After twenty years of operation, the necessary transmission investments have not taken place and insufficient transmission is now cited as an urgent issue by regulators, system operators and utilities alike.[3] Three countries are still isolated from the regional grid and in 2015 less than 60 per cent of energy matched in the day-ahead market was actually traded, due to transmission constraints (SAPP 2015). The region's 'central corridor' (comprised of Botswana, Zimbabwe and Zambia) experiences high levels of congestion that limit trade between South Africa and its northern neighbours, and some of the highest-priority generation projects including the Cahora Bassa North Bank Extension in Mozambique, Batoka Gorge in Zambia and Zimbabwe, and Inga 3 in DRC may be at risk if necessary transmission connections are not developed to transmit the power from these sites. Regional officials attribute the slow progress in developing network reinforcements to a lack of co-ordination in the planning process and the use of flawed methods in allocating network costs (Zhou 2012; Musaba 2010; Chikova 2009).

A key challenge in terms of developing the regional grid in southern Africa is that no regional body has the authority to identify and promote necessary projects. According to the SAPP's Transmission Planning Criteria – a set of non-binding technical standards and procedural

[3] The system operator is responsible for managing day-to-day grid operations and ensuring the real-time technical viability of the system. The SAPP Coordination Centre serves as the regional system operator and is responsible for running the regional market, managing the regional transmission network and co-ordinating with national system operators to ensure system safety.

rules – member countries are responsible for conducting their own network planning studies. In cases where a new line may impact other systems, network owners are instructed to conduct joint studies. The guidelines do not specify how systems owners should determine if a project impacts another system or the process for conducting joint studies (i.e. what information must be shared? How will disputes be resolved?). The SAPP's Planning Sub-Committee is nominally responsible for identifying and evaluating regional network investments as part of its indicative regional planning study, which is updated every two years; but this unit is reported to be in need of additional training before it can undertake regional planning activities. The only official regional Pool Plan was produced in 2007 by the consultants Nexant (Nexant 2007). The Planning Sub-Committee also needs criteria with which to evaluate and prioritize candidate projects. For generation projects, the SAPP has seven selection criteria and a scorecard to evaluate and rank candidate submissions (SAPP 2005). There are no equivalent assessment criteria for transmission projects. The Planning Criteria state that priority transmission projects should be selected based on 'least life cycle cost option' and 'other parameters as specified by SAPP', which implies the application of some type of cost–benefit analysis. For lines designed to improve reliability, the criteria state that these should only be selected if the expected reduction in costs for non-served energy exceeds the project's costs. However, there are no guidelines on how to evaluate other types of benefits or compare and rank lines that offer different types of benefits.

In lieu of centralized network planning from the Planning Sub-Committee, the SAPP Coordination Centre is trying to co-ordinate network development by promoting a short list of priority projects. These projects are identified and selected based on consultations with national utilities and system operators rather than the results of centralized planning and the application of a multi-criteria assessment or cost–benefit analysis. Table 5.2 lists the primary objectives and current status of the SAPP's Priority Projects.

Of the twelve projects identified by the SAPP, one is complete, two are under construction and the majority of those remaining have not progressed past initial proposals or feasibility studies. This lack of progress is due, in part, to the fact that the SAPP does not have a 'champion' responsible for promoting a project after it is deemed beneficial (Magombo et al. 2008).

Another reason why the region has not succeeded in developing necessary and beneficial projects is that current regulations do not guarantee that the full cost of the investments will be recovered. The SAPP uses a method called MW-mile (or MW-km, to be described in Section

Table 5.2 *Status of priority transmission projects in southern Africa*

Primary objective	Project name	Capacity (MW)	Expected date	Status
Interconnect non-operating members	WESTCOR (Angola, DRC, Namibia, Botswana, South Africa)	3,000	2012	Abandoned
	Zambia-Tanzania-Kenya	400	2007	Work on ZAM-TAN link; feasibility study on TAN-KEN link
	Mozambique-Malawi	300	2008	Implementation planning
	Namibia-Angola	400	2012	Feasibility study
	DRC-Angola	600	2016	Feasibility study
Relieve congestion	ZIZABONA (Zimbabwe, Zambia, Botswana, Namibia)	600	2008	Implementation planning; Special Purpose Vehicle established in Namibia
	Central Transmission Corridor (Zimbabwe)	300	2008	Feasibility study review
	Kafue-Livingstone Upgrade (Zambia)	600	2014	Commissioned 2016
Integrate new generation	Mozambique Backbone (CESUL)	3,100	2017	Implementation planning
	2nd Mozambique-Zimbabwe	500	2017	Feasibility study
	2nd Zimbabwe-South Africa	650	2008	Feasibility study
	2nd DRC-Zambia	600	2009	Construction

Source: SAPP (2012); Ndhlukula et al. (2015)

5.4.2.1) to allocate costs for using the regional network. This method has two fundamental flaws. First, as it is implemented in the SAPP, it only applies to the fraction of each transmission line used for wheeling.[4] The costs for the fraction of lines that are unused or not used for wheeling are not allocated and must be recovered through national network charges or privately negotiated cost-sharing agreements between generators and

---

[4] Wheeling means that the electricity that transits a line in a given service area is neither injected nor withdrawn in that service area. For example, transactions between Mozambique and Botswana must be wheeled through an intermediate country because they are not adjacent.

major load centres. For example, the sponsors for the new ZIZABONA transmission project propose to recover its investment costs through charges included in long-term power purchase agreements between the national utility of Zambia, as the seller, and the national utilities of South Africa, Namibia and Botswana, as buyers.[5] These agreements generally require extensive negotiations and may not guarantee cost recovery for the entire adopted economic life of the investment (the physical life for a transmission line before it requires substitution of critical components could exceed forty years). Cost-allocation negotiations can take a long time or become stalled, because countries have their own schedules, priorities and differences in capabilities and expertise. Second, the MW-km method uses commercial transactions between network agents to determine how much each agent uses the regional network. This transaction-based approach is fundamentally flawed because, in a well-designed market, commercial transactions do not impact system operations and network use.[6]

As a result of uncoordinated planning, and flawed transmission-pricing and cost-allocation methods at the regional level, some more recently built lines have been generally developed by private profit-seeking entities or coalitions of network users under their own initiative. For example, the Mozambique Transmission Company (MOTRACO) is jointly owned by the national utilities of Mozambique, Swaziland and South Africa. It was created to supply power from South Africa to the Mozal aluminium smelter in Mozambique. The project sponsors often restrict the use of these lines by external utilities. Table 5.3 lists the existing cross-border interconnections in the SAPP and highlights any restrictions associated with specific lines. Blank entries indicate no known restrictions on the use of the line. As the table shows, many of the lines grant priority access to specific utilities or do not allow lines to be used by external agents for wheeling.

The SAPP is now seeking support from external agencies to prepare and package priority projects and to develop a new method for computing regional network charges. The World Bank recently established a Project Advisory Unit at the SAPP Coordination Centre to accelerate project implementation. This unit will co-ordinate with national governments, conduct analytic work and help screen, select, prepare and monitor the implementation of priority projects. Other organizations, including the United States Agency for International Development (USAID) and

---

[5] The name ZIZABONA was derived by taking the first two letters of the following country names: Zimbabwe, Zambia, Botswana and Namibia.

[6] For further discussion on the flaws of transaction-based network pricing methods, please see Rivier et al. (2013).

Table 5.3 *SAPP transfer limits and restrictions on use of privately owned and operated transmission lines*

From	To	Transfer capacity (MW)	Restrictions
Zambia	DRC	500	CEC has priority
Zambia	Zimbabwe	1,400	
Zambia	Namibia	300	
Zimbabwe	Mozambique	450	
Zimbabwe	Mozambique	70	
Zimbabwe	Botswana	350/600	Higher northward transfer; ZESA, BPC and Eskom have priority
Zimbabwe	Botswana	250	
Botswana	South Africa	650	ZESA, BPC, Eskom have priority
Botswana	South Africa	150	
Botswana	Namibia	70	
Mozambique	South Africa	2,000	No wheeling; Eskom supply only
South Africa	Mozambique	1,450	No wheeling; Eskom supply to Mozal; EDM and SEC have priority on remaining capacity
South Africa	Mozambique	250	
South Africa	Mozambique	150	
South Africa	Swaziland	230	No wheeling; Eskom supply to Mozal; EDM and SEC have priority on remaining capacity
South Africa	Swaziland	1,450	
South Africa	Lesotho	230	
South Africa	Namibia	250	
South Africa	Namibia	500	
Swaziland	Mozambique	1,450	No wheeling; Eskom supply to Mozal; EDM and SEC have priority on remaining capacity

Source: Africa Greenco (2017)

the New Partnership for African Development Agency (NEPAD), are also involved in efforts to prepare and package regional projects (SAPP 2014). The Coordination Centre is also seeking support from the energy consultant Mercados Energeticos to develop a new model for transmission pricing. These activities are valuable but do not address the underlying problems that network planning is not co-ordinated at the regional level and that no regional entity has the resources and authority to oversee the development of the regional network and allocate network costs. Without a legislated mandate from the SADC, regional entities can only serve in an advisory role to member utilities and governments.

5.4   Proposed Transmission Regulation to Promote Regional Investments

As the SAPP case study demonstrates, the necessary investments in regional transmission infrastructure will not take place without leadership from regional institutions and common rules and procedures for network planning and cost sharing. We propose a regional approach to network development that should include the following:

1. A regional planning authority responsible for identifying efficient investments.
2. A regional regulator responsible for approving new lines and allocating network costs amongst network users.
3. A system of network charges that allocates costs in proportion to how much each user benefits from the regional network and guarantees full cost recovery for efficient network investments.
4. Regional rules and procedures that strike a balance between maximizing regional benefits and interfering as little as possible in local decision making.

The following sections discuss how this approach could be implemented in African power pools.

5.4.1   Regional Planning

The regional transmission network can be developed based on proposals from local systems or through a process of centralized planning. Under the first model, no single entity is responsible for overall regional network planning. National transmission owners or coalitions of transmission owners can propose new reinforcements. Relying on local systems for network proposals could be effective in regions that resist ceding power to a regional planning authority. However, the proposals will likely be projects in which the beneficiaries are easily identified and concentrated amongst a few systems willing to form a coalition. These projects may not reflect the most beneficial series of investments, because local systems are unlikely to organize around projects for which the benefits are widely distributed amongst many systems or difficult to quantify because the marginal benefit to each system would be very small. Therefore, there is a consensus that a fair amount of centralized authority is needed for regional transmission planning (IEA 2002; Hogan 2011; MIT 2011).

Under centralized planning, the regional system operator, or some other specialized institution with sufficient experience and technical expertise, is responsible for proposing new lines. Centralized planning does not preclude local authorities from the planning process. In fact, including national authorities is important to assure the regional plan accurately reflects anticipated changes in the power system and fosters support amongst national decision makers. One way to include national interests in the planning process is to require the regional entity to consider all proposals from national transmission owners, system operators and regulators and provide a justification if a proposal is rejected.

Amongst African power pools, proposals for new lines come from regional expansion plans, regional system operators and coalitions of network users. To date, regional expansion plans have had very little influence on investment decisions. These plans are not updated regularly, carry no obligations for compliance amongst member countries, and have so far been developed by external consultants rather than regional planning authorities. The EAPP, SAPP and WAPP have each established a regional planning authority to facilitate the development of the regional network, but these entities have yet to commence planning activities. Table 5.4 compares the status of regional planning institutions in each power pool.

In southern Africa the Planning Sub-Committee is tasked to update a regional expansion plan every two years. However, the most recent plan was created in 2009 by the consultant Nexant. Similarly, the WAPP's Master Plan and upcoming Revised Master Plan are developed by external consultants rather than the region's own Engineering and Operating Committee. In east Africa, the Planning Sub-Committee's authority is limited to co-ordinating national plans rather than developing a regional plan. Its effectiveness in this role may be limited, however, because it does not have the authority to compel countries to adjust their national plans. The only regional plan for EAPP was developed by the consultants SNC-Lavalin.

Regional planning efforts can be improved by strengthening the authority and capabilities of planning bodies in each power pool to identify and evaluate necessary investments. These entities need training to enable them to conduct their own planning studies that can be regularly updated and to evaluate proposals from network users and system operators. This is a key area in which international and multilateral financial support could be leveraged to finance training for local planning authorities rather than paying for intermittent studies by external consultants.[7] In the case of east Africa, the EAPP Planning Sub-Committee needs an expanded mandate to conduct regional planning studies.

---

[7] The leading financial institutions for the SAPP, WAPP and EAPP master plans were the World Bank, European Investment Bank, and African Development Bank, respectively.

Table 5.4 *Comparison of regional institutions created to support the development of the regional network in African power pools*

	EAPP	SAPP	WAPP
Regional planning institution	Planning Sub-committee	Planning Sub-Committee	Engineering and Operating Committee
Institution's mandate	Co-ordinate master plans and development programmes of member countries	Develop a Pool Plan every two years highlighting potential cost savings from regional co-ordination	Review member plans and develop regional network plan to promote greater efficiency and reliability of electricity supply
Implementation	No authority to force changes in national plans; most recent Master Plan (2011) developed by SNC-Lavalin	More training needed for regional planning studies; most recent Pool Plan (2009) developed by Nexant	No planning studies yet; most recent Master Plan developed by Tractebel (2011); ECOWAS (Economic Community of West African States) has a legislated mandate to promote priority projects

Source: SNC-Lavalin International Inc. and Parsons Brinckerhoff (2011); Musaba (2010); EAPP (2016); SADC (2006); WAPP (2005); Tractebel Engineering (2011)

5.4.2   *Regulatory Oversight*

As the experience in African power pools suggests, detailed technical planning studies or strong coalitions of users in support of a project do not necessarily lead to investments in regional transmission. Further, they do not prevent network users or coalitions of users from making investment decisions that may be sub-optimal from a regional perspective. For these reasons, a regional regulatory body should oversee the development of the regional network. This entity should play three key functions: (1) approve proposals for new lines, (2) guarantee satisfactory remuneration for new lines and (3) establish a method to allocate costs amongst network users.

Before discussing how the regulator could fulfil each of these responsibilities, it is important to distinguish between two types of transmission investments: regulated lines and merchant lines. Regulated lines are approved, according to some prescribed criteria, and guaranteed some level of remuneration by regulators. Any regional or national entity could propose a new line for approval as a regulated line. In practice almost all built lines are regulated. Merchant lines, by contrast, are developed by private, profit-seeking companies under their own initiative. These projects are not part of the centralized planning process and are not guaranteed any remuneration from the regulator. As seen in southern Africa, merchant lines are generally subject to restrictions on their use by giving the project sponsors either priority or exclusive access to use the line. Since it is not normally possible to control the path of power flows in a meshed network, the only way to compensate merchant investors by flows created in their lines by third parties is to charge them whatever fee may correspond.

Regardless of the type of investment, all lines should be subject to some kind of regulatory approval according to well-defined criteria established in regional rules. For regulated lines, the regulatory test should determine if a particular reinforcement is justified, measured by its net benefit to the region (i.e. the surplus of societal benefit provided by the line over its cost), where societal benefit must be understood in a broad sense, including economic, security-of-supply, environmental and competition enhancement factors.[8] This typically involves demonstrating the investment is justified based on a cost–benefit analysis and conducting any additional studies requested by the regulator to test different uncertainty scenarios and demonstrate the project is superior to alternatives. In addition to passing a cost–benefit analysis, the regulator should ensure the proposed line does not have any outstanding issues that may prevent it from being completed such as siting and permitting issues, social opposition, overly complex technical design or excessive time to build. In cases where proposed projects overlap, the regulator should approve the project with the highest social benefit (a well-developed transmission expansion plan should consist of the ensemble of projects that jointly result in maximum social benefit). For merchant lines, the test can be less stringent. The proponents of the line need only demonstrate that it is not detrimental to the network and does not interfere with other anticipated investments already under way.

Once approved, construction for regulated lines can be undertaken by the project's sponsor or through a competitive bidding auction. In general, competitive bidding is preferable, because the winning company would be paid according to their bid, avoiding the need for the regulator to compute benchmarks for the cost of constructing different kinds of

---

[8] For more information on assessing the benefits of regional transmission investments, see von der Fehr et al. (2013).

lines. If not enough competition is expected, the regulator can set the remuneration rate based on the project's estimated cost (which must include an adequate rate of return for the investor). The regulator should be responsible for establishing a method to allocate costs amongst network users for regulated lines. This will be discussed in more detail in Section 5.4.3.

Amongst African power pools, the level of regulatory oversight for transmission investments varies considerably. The WAPP requires any entity proposing a new regional line to consult with the ECOWAS Regional Electricity Regulatory Authority (ERERA) for authorization. This body is tasked with evaluating each proposal, considering it in 'respect of the regional network development plan' and proposing solutions if deviations are likely to negatively influence the regional market. It is also responsible for approving formulae for calculating network tariffs. Eastern Africa's Independent Regulatory Board (IRB) is also responsible for setting network tariffs, but investors do not have to consult with or seek approval from IRB to build new regional lines. Southern Africa has the weakest regulatory oversight for transmission investments. The SAPP Coordination Centre, rather than RERA, is responsible for the region's set of non-binding technical criteria for new investments as well as designing and implementing the network tariffs for regional trade. No entity is responsible for approving new investments or co-ordinating proposed investments amongst member countries.

Importantly, none of the African power pools require new projects to be approved by a regional regulator or some other regional body that can in turn guarantee that the full costs of the investment will be recovered. This is an essential step that would be required in order to reduce investment risk for necessary transmission projects. Each power pool could expand the authority of their respective regional regulators to include approving new lines. Alternatively, the region could give this responsibility to another regional institution or use ad hoc committees representing concerned countries. To avoid conflicts that may delay needed projects, the regional rules should stipulate that once a project is approved as a regulated line, national entities should not be able to oppose it.

5.4.3   *Network Cost Allocation*

Transmission cost allocation involves assigning the costs of a new or existing transmission facility amongst the network users. The design of the cost-allocation method is critically important because poorly designed schemes could prevent necessary investments from taking place. For example, if costs are concentrated amongst users that derive little benefit from a new line, these users may refuse to pay for its construction. Cost-allocation schemes could also distort or deter efficient trade if, for example, users are charged differently depending on the national boundary in which they are located or the party with whom they are trading. Basic principles derived from a combination of microeconomic theory, power-system engineering, sound regulatory practice and years of trial and error in actual systems (Pérez-Arriaga and Smeers 2003) suggest that any well-designed method should contain the following characteristics: (1) it recovers the full cost of the network, (2) it allocates costs in proportion to benefits, (3) the format of the implementation of the charge (e.g. charge per unit of energy produced or consumed, charge per capacity contracted or used, annual charge based on some other criterion) avoids interfering with cross-border trade, (4) it separates cost allocation from commercial transactions, (5) it uses a technically sound method to approximate network benefits and (6) it is feasible to implement in a real system. This method should result in a single network charge that would grant the user access to the entire regional network. More recently, another important criterion has been added which recommends charges should be announced ex ante and remain in place for a reasonable period of time (e.g. 10 years) (MIT 2011).

Translating these principles into practice is an active area of interest amongst African power pools, all of which are in the process of designing, implementing or replacing their regional transmission-pricing schemes. The EAPP has not published a regional cost-allocation scheme yet and may still be in the process of designing one. The WAPP recently announced it intends to adopt the MW-km method, but this has not been implemented. As previously mentioned, the SAPP uses the MW-km method but is currently looking to replace it.

5.4.3.1   Evaluation of Possible Cost-Allocation Methods

We tested several transmission-pricing methods for the existing SAPP network and three new network investments, to identify which method or combination of methods is the best option for the regional system. In all cases the purpose of the method is to determine how much each country should be allocated of: (i) the total cost of the SAPP transmission network; (ii) the cost of some important new network investments.

Table 5.5 *Simplified description of transmission cost-allocation methods evaluated in this study*

Method	Description
Beneficiary Pays (BP)	Costs allocated based on expected increases in revenues or decreases in costs that each user obtains as a result of the line. Costs and revenues are measured by injections or withdrawals times the nodal price with and without a new line.
Average Participations (AP)	Costs allocated in proportion to network usage, approximated using a heuristic rule that assumes any injections or withdrawals can be traced through the network by assuming power splits at each node in proportion to actual historic network flows.
Postage Stamp	Costs allocated in proportion to each user's injections and withdrawals from the network.
Transits	Each country is responsible for paying the cost of its own network plus some compensations countries must pay each other for using external networks. Compensations are calculated using aggregate national data including load, generation, imports and exports.
MW-km	Costs allocated based on contribution of each transaction to power flows, calculated by simulating network flows with and without the transaction. The change in flows across each line is multiplied by the cost of the line and its length.

The methods tested represent the best-known approaches in practice today in regional markets. Table 5.5 describes the approach used in each method evaluated. More information on the theory behind each method and mathematical equations used to calculate network costs can be found in Rose (2017).

An important limitation of the Beneficiary Pays (BP) method is that it cannot be applied to transmission assets that were installed many years ago (e.g. five or more), since removing a line that has been in use for many years creates a meaningless counterfactual under present generation and load conditions. If the line did not exist, another line may have been built instead, or generators and loads might have evolved in time differently. Therefore, we have applied this method only to the case of new investments, which is actually the most relevant problem in practice.

For the allocation of the total costs of the existing SAPP transmission network we have employed the four methods that use network usage as a proxy for benefits. The challenge with using network usage as a proxy for

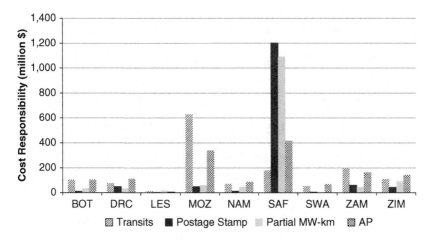

Figure 5.3 Comparison of network cost-allocation results obtained from different transmission-pricing methods for the existing SAPP regional network (AP – Average Participations). For comparison, the costs have been aggregated to reflect the total cost to each country

benefits is that it cannot be measured directly. The only parameters that can be measured are injections and withdrawals at each node, and flows across each line. Therefore, each usage-based method adopts a different approach to translating these data into approximate network usage. Amongst the usage-based pricing methods, Average Participations (AP) adheres most closely to principle (4) of transmission cost allocation (it is based on the actual flows in each line and how these flows really split at each node, not on computer simulations based on the hypothesized behaviour of flows, based on commercial transactions or questionable assumptions) and we have used it as a basis for comparison with other methods.

The results of the cost-allocation problem can vary significantly depending on the method selected. Figure 5.3 compares the allocation of costs to SAPP countries obtained by each method for the existing SAPP network.

By assuming each country pays for their own network plus some compensations or payments based on net imports and exports, the Transits method obtains the closest results to those obtained from AP. Leaving aside the fact that there is no unique definition of 'transit' that makes sense consistently,[9] in this particular case the difference between

---

[9] For detailed information on some of these methods, and the Transits and AP methods in particular, see Florence School of Regulation (2005). For each proposed definition of

the two methods stems from the fact that Transits only approximates cost causality in proportion to total network use rather than the use of individual lines. This simplification can impact an agent's cost responsibility because it does not account for the fact that some lines are more expensive than others. The cost-allocation results for Mozambique and South Africa demonstrate the impact of this simplification amongst SAPP users. In the simulated period, Mozambique is responsible for 30 per cent of total energy imbalances (domestic generation does not equal domestic load) in the region and is therefore responsible for 30 per cent of total wheeling charges in addition to its own network costs. These charges are applied to cover wheeling payments to South Africa and Namibia. Namibia has several expensive interconnections, including one with South Africa that is the second most expensive in the region. However, the AP results indicate that Mozambique only contributes to flows across a small number of mostly inexpensive adjacent lines and only marginally impacts flows across lines connected to Namibia. As a result, the charges calculated using AP are lower than those obtained with the Transits method. Similarly, the Transits method underestimates South Africa's cost responsibility because it does not account for the fact that South Africa contributes to flows across many of the most expensive lines in the regional network.

The MW-km and Postage Stamp (PS) methods diverge the most compared to AP. Under these methods, the majority of charges are levied on South Africa because it is the biggest consumer and producer and, therefore, has the biggest share of injections and withdrawals. In addition, under the MW-km method South African network users are responsible for most of the charges associated with bilateral transactions because they are co-signers on most of the region's bilateral contracts.

Clearly the method selected to allocate network costs can have a significant impact on how much users in each country must pay. This is especially important for new lines, for which a new project may not be developed if stakeholders do not agree on how the project's costs will be shared. To examine how each method performs for a new investment, the cost-allocation problem is applied to several new projects being proposed in southern Africa. Figure 5.4 compares the allocation of costs to SAPP countries obtained for the ZIZABONA project under different pricing methods. The ZIZABONA project is a joint venture between the national utilities of Zimbabwe, Zambia, Botswana and Namibia, which, it is estimated, will cost $223 million in total (Horvei 2012). Its primary

'transit' in the technical literature, it is easy to find an example that shows that the definition makes no sense.

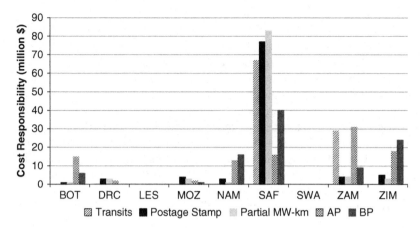

Figure 5.4 Comparison of network cost-allocation results obtained from different transmission-pricing methods for the ZIZABONA project (BP – Beneficiary Pays). For comparison, the costs have been aggregated to reflect the total cost to each country

objective is to allow these four member countries to increase trade with each other and the wider SAPP area, and South Africa in particular. The project is expected to ease congestion through the central corridor connecting Zimbabwe and South Africa and, as a result, also within South Africa. The ZIZABONA project is really a cluster of projects consisting of three transmission lines and five substations spread over the four member countries.

Comparing the results obtained from BP to those obtained from other methods, several problems are immediately apparent. First, the results obtained for the Transits, PS and MW-km methods are largely independent of how each agent benefits from the new lines. Both PS and MW-km overcharge South African consumers and producers compared to how much these agents are expected to benefit from the ZIZABONA lines.

The Transits method only captures changes in net compensations between countries and not how each country benefits from the project. The biggest change is in South Africa, because the ZIZABONA project reduces the total power wheeled through that country, reducing the total compensation it will receive. This results in higher overall network payments for South Africa. Zambia's network costs increase to cover its portion of the ZIZABONA project, but these increases are not matched by increased compensation from other countries because wheeling through Zambia is not expected to increase. Most other countries are expected to pay or receive the same compensation with and without the project.

Average Participations also diverges from BP in some instances, revealing the shortcomings of using network usage as a proxy for economic benefits. For example, under AP, the South African load pays nothing for the ZIZABONA project because, according to the heuristic rule of 'tracing flows' into South Africa, domestic users are not expected to use the lines. However, the BP analysis reveals that these consumers are benefiting through lower nodal prices during peak hours. The new lines allow increased trade amongst other countries, reducing South Africa's exports and allowing lower-cost generators to meet domestic load. In other cases (i.e. Botswana, Zambia), AP allocates costs to users that are not benefiting economically from the project because their costs or revenues remain the same with and without the line. However, the divergence between AP and BP was, on average, much smaller than differences using other methods.

5.4.3.2   *Recommended Network Cost-Allocation Method*

Based on the evaluation of how each method performed for different types of investments, we recommend that costs for existing lines and new lines approved as regulated lines should be fully recovered through a system of regional charges. For new lines, these charges should be calculated using BP. Rather than attempting to quantify and monetize all possible transmission benefits, the evaluation should account for the most significant benefits that are relevant for the region. Von der Fehr et al. (2013) present a catalogue of such benefits and demonstrate how they could be measured in a regional system.

The charges determined through BP should be in place for a reasonable amount of time, for instance ten years, to reduce uncertainty for investors and network users. After a line has been commissioned for many years, the magnitude, distribution and nature of its benefits may change. Rerunning the BP analysis cannot provide meaningful results because there is no viable scenario without the line. Therefore, the usage-based method of AP should be adopted to allocate costs for existing lines. The AP calculation should be based on actual power flows from the most recent year of operation. To avoid discontinuities, the charges for new and existing lines should transition gradually over a small number of years.

Merchant lines or lines built and financed by coalitions of network users for their own use can recover their costs through privately negotiated contracts with network users. Because insufficient transmission capacity is an ongoing constraint for market trading and potential investments in new generation plants, these lines should be subject to open-access rules for regulatory approval. This means the owners must allow any member to use the line. Actually, in a meshed alternating current network it is impossible to prevent the power from flowing all over the place following Kirchhoff's laws. In this case, the owners can be allowed to earn revenues based on the same system of regulated payments used for other regional lines (e.g. AP). However, for merchant lines, these payments are not guaranteed to recover the entire cost of the line, and it has been shown that in most cases they will not.[10]

5.4.4   Balancing Regional and National Interests

Regional planning must strike a balance between maximizing regional benefits and interfering as little as possible in local decision making. An effective way to strike this balance is to distinguish between domestic and regional transmission facilities. Under this distinction, any regulator or system operator anticipated to be affected by a regional line could participate in the decision-making process for its construction and the costs for regulated regional lines would be allocated using a regional cost-allocation scheme. The decision-making process and associated costs for domestic lines could be left to local authorities.

African power pools do not have a clearly defined process to determine which lines should be considered regional and, therefore, included in regional planning studies. Master plans developed for the EAPP, SAPP and WAPP represent the full national transmission networks in some countries and only part of the network in others. These studies include all cross-border lines and some intra-national lines close to 'areas of interest' (i.e. large power plants or interconnection nodes) (SNC-Lavalin International Inc. and Parsons Brinckerhoff 2011). This approach may fail to identify lines that are significantly used in cross-border trade and, conversely, may include lines that are not used much for regional trading. Note, however, that some level of arbitrariness always exists in these definitions, as nobody can unambiguously determine the origin or the end of power flows.

To improve regional planning and cost-allocation efforts, a transparent procedure should be in place to define the regional network. Regional facilities could include all cross-border lines and any intra-national lines that are used to facilitate regional trade. An independent regional entity, such as the regional system operator, should be responsible for conducting the analysis. For example, the regional authority can simulate power flows under different anticipated supply-and-demand scenarios to

---

[10] For a detailed discussion of the reasons why a transmission network based on merchant lines will be necessarily underdeveloped, please see Rivier et al. (2013).

estimate the utilization of intra-national lines by 'external' agents located outside of the area where the line is built. If this usage exceeds some pre-defined threshold, the line would be considered part of the regional network. The definition of the regional network should be updated regularly, every three to five years, to account for changes in system operations. The regional authority must evaluate any recommendations from national transmission owners or system operators for lines to be included as part of the regional network and provide a justification if the line is rejected. Regional transmission charges would only apply to those lines identified as part of the regional network.

A second challenge for regional transmission regulation is that each country has its own rules in place for calculating and allocating network costs. On the one hand, applying one network charge for domestic lines and a second, regional charge for using regional lines could distort invest-ment and trade behaviour amongst network users. On the other, harmo-nizing network charges amongst all member countries may be politically unacceptable. One way to address this issue is to implement payments for the regional network through a system of national charges. Under this system, each user's transmission charge is calculated without considering national borders, and based on some regional pricing method (we recom-mend the methods of BP and AP). These charges are then aggregated ex post to a single national charge. In other words, after the regional pricing method is applied, all of the charges to users in Country A would be aggregated to a single national charge that Country A must pay. National authorities are then free to allocate this charge amongst their respective network users. If the cost-allocation method is applied to individual users before charges are aggregated, the resulting national charges will avoid the estimation errors seen with other methods, such as Transits, that only look at gross national activity and miss interactions amongst individual network users. Similar to regional charges, the design of national charges should, as much as possible, allocate costs to beneficiaries, avoid basing charges on commercial transactions and be in place for a reasonably long time. In addition, the same method should be used to allocate costs associated with national and regional networks to avoid distorting regional trade.

5.5   Conclusions

Regional integration presents an opportunity for African countries to reduce the cost of providing electricity and improve system reliability through co-ordinated use of energy resources. These objectives have led to the development of regional power pools amongst neighbouring coun-tries in southern, eastern and western Africa. In each case, significant investments in regional infrastructure are needed to realize the benefits of integration. Investments in regional transmission pose a particularly difficult challenge because they must be planned, managed and paid for through a co-ordinated regional process.

Amongst African power pools, the necessary investments in regional transmission are slow to take place. We apply an integrated approach, combining technical, economic and institutional analysis to identify existing barriers to the development of regional transmission infrastructure, and propose regulatory and institutional changes to address these barriers. Examinations of regional regulations and institutions in the EAPP, SAPP and WAPP reveal that insufficient co-ordination in regional planning and flawed transmission-pricing rules are critical challenges to the development of transmission infrastructure. We propose that the regional network should be developed based on a system of centralized planning that accounts for any direct proposals from members of the power pool, under the supervision of a regional regulator. Some interaction between the members and the regional institutions may be needed, as in the end the members have the last word regarding the construction of a line in their territories. Business models for network development should be expanded to include regulated lines that are guaranteed satisfactory remuneration from the regulator through a fixed rate of return or bid-based auction. An examination of different network cost-allocation methods reveals that the MW-km method currently in use in the SAPP and proposed in the WAPP is not allocating network costs efficiently. The methods of BP and AP present technically and economically sound alternatives that could be implemented in a regional system.

To accommodate differences in national transmission planning and tariff practices, first, a distinction should be made between regional and domestic transmission facilities. Regional network planning and pricing rules should only apply to those facilities identified as part of the regional network. Second, charges should be implemented through a system of national charges, allowing each country flexibility to allocate costs amongst network users according to a method of its choosing.

References

AfDB (African Development Bank). (2010). *Programme for infrastructure development in Africa – Interconnecting, integrating, and transforming a continent.* Tunis: AfDB.

Africa Greenco. (2017). *Feasibility study.* London: Africa Greenco.

Briceño-Garmendia, C. and Shkaratan, M. (2011). *Power tariffs: Caught between cost recovery and affordability*. Policy Research Working Paper: no. WPS 5904. World Bank. https://openknowledge.worldbank.org/handle/10986/3671

Castellano, A. et al. (2015). *Brighter Africa: The growth potential of the sub-Saharan electricity sector*. New York City, NY: McKinsey & Co.

Chikova, A. (2009). Energy trading in the Southern African Power Pool. Presentation March 2009. Durban: Southern African Power Pool.

EAPP (Eastern African Power Pool). (2016). The Eastern Africa Power Pool Independent Regulatory Board (EAPP-IRB) establishment. Eastern African Power Pool. http://eappool.org/independent-regulatory-board/

Eberhard, A., Rosnes, O., Shkaratan, M. and Vennemo, H. (2011). *Africa's power infrastructure: Investment, integration, efficiency*. Technical Report, Washington, DC: The World Bank.

Enterprise Surveys. (2017). Infrastructure. Enterprise Surveys. Washington, DC: The World Bank. www.enterprisesurveys.org/data/exploretopics/infrastructure

Florence School of Regulation. (2005). *A study on the Inter-TSO compensation mechanism*. Florence: European University Institute. Energy Regulators. www.energyregulators.eu/portal/pls/portal/docs/1/19428531.PDF

Global Energy Observatory. (n.d.) http://GlobalEnergyObservatory.org/

Gutman, J., Sy, A. and Chattopadhyay, S. (2015). *Financing African infrastructure: Can the world deliver?* Washington, DC: Brookings Institution.

Hogan, W. (2011). *Transmission benefits and cost allocation*. Cambridge, MA: Harvard University. https://sites.hks.harvard.edu/fs/whogan/Hogan_Trans_Cost_053111.pdf.

Horvei, T. (2012). ZIZABONA transmission project. Presentation to Investors Roundtable Meeting, Swakopmund, 12 July.

Hussain, M. Z. (2015). *Mozambique – Energy sector policy note*. Washington, DC: The World Bank. http://documents.worldbank.org/curated/en/13571146818 0536987/Mozambique-Energy-sector-policy-note.

IEA (International Energy Agency). (2002). *Security of supply in electricity markets: Evidence and policy issues*. Technical Report. Paris: OECD/IEA, Paris.

IEA (International Energy Agency). (2013). *Key world energy statistics*. Paris: OECD/IEA.

IEA (International Energy Agency). (2016a). *World energy outlook 2016*. Paris: OECD/IEA.

IEA (International Energy Agency). (2016b). *World energy statistics and balances*. Paris: OECD/IEA.

Magombo, G., Kügel, L., and Julião, F. (2008). Survey on the status of policy, institutional and regulatory frameworks of the electricity supply industry (ESI) in the Southern African Development Community (SADC) region. Technical Report. Submitted by AECOM International Development to USAID/ Southern Africa. Gaborone, Botswana: USAID.

MIT (Massachusetts Institute of Technology). (2011). *Transmission expansion. In MIT Study on the Future of the Electric Grid*. Cambridge, MA: Massachusetts Institute of Technology, pp. 77–108. http://mitei.mit.edu/system/files/Electric_Grid_Full_Report.pdf.

Miketa, A. and Merven, B. (2013a). *West African Power Pool: Planning and prospects for renewable energy.* Abu Dhabi: International Renewable Energy Agency.

Miketa, A. and Merven, B. (2013b). *Southern African Power Pool: Planning and prospects for renewable energy.* Abu Dhabi: International Renewable Energy Agency.

Musaba, L. (2010). *The Southern African Power Pool.* Harare: Southern African Power Pool.

Ndhlukula, K., Radojičić, T., and Mangwengwende, S. (2015). *Analysis of infrastructure for renewable power in Eastern and Southern Africa.* Technical Report. Abu Dhabi: International Renewable Energy Agency.

NEPAD (New Partnership for Africa's Development). (2017). Batoka Gorge Hydro Electric Scheme: Zambezi River in Zambia and Zimbabwe. Project Information Memorandum. New Partnership for Africa's Development. www .nepad.org/publication/batoka-gorge-hydro-electric-scheme-zambezi-river-zambia-and-zimbabwe.

Nexant. (2007). SAPP Regional Generation and Transmission Expansion Plan Study. Draft final report, Main Report, Volume 2, submitted to SAPP Coordination Center. Harare: Southern African Power Pool.

Olmos, L. (2013). Regional markets. In Ignacio Pérez-Arriaga (Ed.), *Regulation of the power sector.* 1st ed. London: Springer.

Pérez-Arriaga, I. and Smeers, Y. (2003). Guidelines on tariff setting. In F. Lévêque (ed.), *Transport pricing of electricity networks.* Boston: Kluwer Academic Publishers.

Platts. (2010). *UDI world electric power plants data base.* Washington, DC: Platts.

PR Newswire. (2016, 21 January). Further delays with Inga III hydroelectric project in DRC. *PR Newswire.* www.prnewswire.com/news-releases/further-delays-withinga-iii-hydroelectric-project-in-drc-300207721.html

Rivier, M., Pérez-Arriaga, I., and Olmos, L. (2013). Electricity transmission. In Ignacio J. Pérez-Arriaga (Ed.), *Regulation of the power sector.* 1st edition. London: Springer.

Rose, A. (2017). Improving the performance of regional electricity markets in developing countries: The case of the Southern African Power Pool. Doctoral dissertation, Massachusetts Institute of Technology. Cambridge, MA: MIT.

Rosnes, O., Vennemo, H., and Pöyry, E. (2009). *Powering up: Costing power infrastructure spending needs in sub-Saharan Africa.* Technical report, AICD Background Paper 5, Africa Region, Washington, DC: The World Bank.

SNC Lavalin International Inc. and Parsons Brinckerhoff. (2011). Regional power system master plan and grid code study. East African Power Pool (EAPP) and East African Community (EAC).

SADC. (2006). *Revised inter-governmental memorandum of understanding.* Gaborone: Southern African Development Community (SADC).

SAPP. (2005). SAPP priority projects for investor consideration and funding. Presentation to the SAPP Executive Committee, 21 November. Harare: Southern African Power Pool (SAPP).

SAPP. (2012). *SAPP 2012 annual report.* Harare: Southern African Power Pool (SAPP).

SAPP. (2014). *Draft terms of reference for cooperation between Southern African Power Pool (SAPP) and United States Aid Agency (USAID) and the World Bank regarding assistance to SAPP in establishing project management capability.* Harare: Southern African Power Pool (SAPP).

SAPP. (2015). *SAPP 2015 annual report.* Harare: Southern African Power Pool (SAPP). www.sapp.co.zw/annual-reports.

SAPP. (2017). Vision and objectives. *SAPP.* Harare: Southern African Power Pool (SAPP). www.sapp.co.zw/

Tractebel Engineering. (2011). Final report volume 4: Executive summary. In *Update of the ECOWAS revised master plan for the generation and transmission of electrical energy.* Accra: Economic Community of West African States.

UN ECA. (2013). *Assessing regional integration in Africa (ARIA VI): Harmonizing policies to transform the trading environment.* Addis Ababa: United Nations Economic Commission for Africa (UN ECA). http://libguides.uneca.org/con tent.php?pid=675909.

von der Fehr, Nils-Henrik M., Meeus, L., Azevedo, I., He, X., Olmos, L., and Glachant, J.-M. (2013). *Cost benefit analysis in the context of the energy infrastructure package.* Florence School of Regulation. Florence: European University Institute.

WAPP (West African Power Pool). (2005). *Articles of agreement of the West African Power Pool organization and functions.* Accra: West African Power Pool.

World Bank. (2008). *Building regional power pools: A toolkit.* Technical Report. Washington, DC: The World Bank.

World Bank. (2015). *World development indicators: Electricity production, sources, and access.* Washington, DC: The World Bank.

World Bank. (2016). Investment in energy with private participation (current US$). *Private participation in infrastructure database.* Washington, DC: The World Bank.

World Bank. (2017a). *Linking up: Public-private partnerships in power transmission in Africa.* Washington, DC: The World Bank.

World Bank. (2017b). Population, total. Washington, DC: The World Bank. https://data.worldbank.org/indicator/sp.pop.totl

World Bank. (2017c). Electric power consumption (kWh per capita). Washington, DC: The World Bank. https://data.worldbank.org/indicator/EG .USE.ELEC.KH.PC

WEC. (2004). *World energy resources: 2004 survey.* London: World Energy Council (WEC).

WEC. (2013). *World energy resources: 2013 survey.* London: World Energy Council (WEC).

WEC. (2015). The world is getting ever more connected. *World Energy Focus* 15 (September). London: World Energy Council (WEC).

Zhou, P. (2012). *Regional infrastructure development master plan: Energy sector master plan.* Technical Report August.Gaborone: Southern African Development Community Secretariat.

6 Centralized vs. Decentralized Generation in Zambia: Meeting Electricity Demand in the Context of Climate Change

Malik Ismail, Murray Metcalfe and Madeleine McPherson

Abstract

This chapter investigates the feasibility of large-scale central-ized renewable generation and residential solar photovoltaic electricity (PV) in addressing Zambia's electricity deficit, caused by droughts which are in turn attributable to climate disturbances and the nation's rapidly increasing electricity demand. Specifically, it was found that centralized solar gen-eration when optimally located could produce generation/cost ratios as low as \$0.042/kWh, comparable with existing hydro generation cost ratios of \$0.02-\$0.03/kWh. For the decentral-ized generation scenarios, which analyzed the potential of on-grid and off-grid solar PV generation in Lusaka, Zambia's capital, it was observed that a fully decentralized approach is not economically feasible, as electricity would be 6 to 12 times as costly as the existing rate. A series of hybrid scenarios, with varying combinations of centralized and decentralized genera-tion, were also analyzed, with the 70 percent centralized, 30 percent decentralized scenario being found to best address Zambia's electricity shortage. This approach would both pro-vide affordable power and enable quicker implementation, greater consumer autonomy, easier planning, and diversified sources of funding. It would also enhance Zambia's ability to become a continental leader in renewable energy.

Introduction

There is little doubt that Africa will be a center of the multiple trends of substantial population growth accompanied by urbanization, climate change, and (hopefully) economic growth. A study by McKinsey and Company found that electricity demand in sub-Saharan Africa will grow by 4.5 percent annually, with commercial and industrial, and residential demand growing by 4.1 percent and 5.6 percent per annum respectively (Castellano et al. 2015). Even if one questions the specifics of growth projections by governments and commercial entities, preparing for growth seems an imperative for African countries, and specifically for those planning the evolution of energy systems in countries and individual cities.

As part of a broader project we have been examining the impacts of these trends and factors on the energy infrastructure of and options for Zambia, and its capital, Lusaka. With Africa's temperature predicted to increase more rapidly than the global average, climate change will clearly be an increasingly important challenge to surmount (Onishi 2016). Zambia, in particular, is expected to see an increase of 1–2 degrees Celsius, resulting in more droughts and a prolonged reduction in hydroelectric generation potential (Future Climate for Africa 2016; Yamba et al. 2011; Fant et al. 2015). And Lusaka, in particular, will be extremely susceptible to the impact of drought, as "70 percent of Lusaka's workforce are engaged in agricultural activity and urban agriculture is a major source of livelihoods," and this is heavily reliant on stable precipitation (Future Climate for Africa 2016). This anticipated rise in temperature could be economically catastrophic for Zambia's capital.

Where does energy regimen fit into this equation? Given a lack of focus on both the geospatial analysis of renewable energy in Zambia and rooftop-solar analysis in Lusaka, this chapter aims to apply methodologies from multiple bodies of work to determine the optimal mitigation strategy, given cost and socioeconomic factors, for Zambia's electricity shortage between 2015 and 2030, and through that to offer a perspective potentially relevant to other African nations. We will apply multi-criteria decision-making frameworks to assess the technical and socioeconomic impact of various centralized and decentralized renewable energy solutions to address Zambia's drought-induced electricity shortage. While broad, our analytic framework is not (and, we argue, cannot be) comprehensive – further layering of institutional, regulatory, and political structures are also important components of the discourse but are not explicitly addressed here.

The chapter will draw from three research themes – centralized vs. decentralized generation, the estimation of urban rooftop potential, and economic and political feasibility – as well as build on previous work (McPherson et al. 2018) which analyzed the generation potential of both rooftop solar in Lusaka and centralized solar and wind sites. We will attempt to address the best solutions for a dense urban setting like

Lusaka, and those of more general applicability to Zambia at the country scale.

This chapter investigates the ability of three renewable energy alternatives: large-scale solar and wind centralized generation; decentralized rooftop-solar photovoltaic panel systems; and a hybrid combination of the two to augment the existing energy infrastructure in Zambia, and address both the rapidly growing electricity demand and the electricity deficit caused by droughts due to climate disturbances. The authors approached this problem through a systems engineering lens, examining the technical and financial feasibility of a set of potential solutions, as well as their socioeconomic benefits, in order to determine the most effective way of mitigating Zambia's electricity shortage.

The chapter consists of three parts. The first section summarizes the existing electricity situation in Zambia and planned government initiatives to tackle the energy crisis. The second summarizes the methodologies used in this chapter to examine the efficacy of various generation solutions. Section 6.3 presents an analysis of whether a centralized, decentralized, or hybrid solar photovoltaic and wind generation solution is the most effective way of addressing Zambia's electricity shortage. The chapter concludes that a 70 percent centralized solar and 30 percent decentralized solar approach is optimal for addressing Zambia's electricity deficit until 2030.

6.1   Electricity in Zambia

6.1.1   Current and Future

A southern African nation of 14 million people, Zambia has been growing rapidly in recent years. Its economic growth of 6 percent GDP annually has yielded increased foreign investment in new infrastructure, spurring job creation (International Renewable Energy Agency 2013; Africa-EU Renewable Energy Programme 2015b). Coupled with the nation's rapid population growth of 3.06 percent, Zambia's capital, Lusaka, is regarded as one of Africa's fastest-growing cities. Lusaka's electricity demand has grown by 6 percent annually over the past decade, surpassing the available supply (International Renewable Energy Agency 2013; African Review of Business and Technology 2015). Lusaka's population is expected to increase twenty-fold by 2100, reaching a population of approximately of 37 million (Hoornweg 2015). Growth of this type could potentially result in an additional 34,000 gigawatt-hours of electrical load.

6.1.2   *Zambia's Electricity Suppliers, Demand, and Growth*

Three companies are responsible for distribution, transmission, and generation in Zambia: the public utility ZESCO, the Copperbelt Energy Corporation (CEC), and the Lunsemfwa Electricity Company (Zambia Development Agency 2014). Collectively, these companies supply a load that peaks at 1,960 MW with 54.5 percent purchased by the CEC, 30.4 percent by residential users, and other economic sectors consuming the remaining 15.1 percent (Hill 2015; Energy Regulation Board 2015).

However, this demand has been far from stagnant. Driven by greater economic and commercial activity in several industry sectors including agriculture, manufacturing, and mining (Zambia Development Agency 2014), Zambia's electricity demand increased 3 percent annually between 2004 and 2014. Between 2014 and 2015, electricity consumption increased by 6.8 percent, from 10,720.5 GWh in 2014 to 11,449.9 GWh in 2015 (Energy Regulation Board 2015). This trend is expected to continue, with the Zambian government projecting annual increases in electricity demand between 150 and 200 MW (Zambia Development Agency 2014).

Other studies also suggest rapid growth in electricity demand for the nation over the coming decades. The UN Renewable Readiness Assessment (RRA), conducted in 2013, anticipates "the electricity demand in Zambia is expected to reach 3544 MW by 2030 in low case scenarios and 5406 MW in high case scenarios" (International Renewable Energy Agency 2013). This would result in commercial and industrial demand in the region increasing by approximately 270 percent, and residential demand increasing by approximately 410 percent between 2010 and 2040 (Castellano et al. 2015). The study also found that every 1 percent in GDP growth corresponds to an average electricity demand increase of 1.67 percent excluding residential demand (Castellano et al. 2015). Projections of peak demand in Zambia between 2010 and 2030, using growth rates from various independent studies, can be seen in Figure 6.1 below. The projected growth rate for Zambia is comparable to the 6 percent annual increase in electricity demand observed between 2001 and 2009 (Zambia Development Agency, 2014).

6.1.3   *Zambia's Existing Generation*

Zambia possesses about 40 percent of the water resources found in the fifteen countries comprising the Southern African Development Community. Reflecting this, Zambia's electricity companies have extensively developed and utilized hydropower plants for electricity generation.

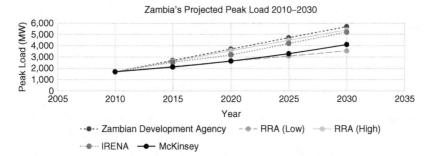

Figure 6.1 Peak-load forecast for Zambia from various studies (International Renewable Energy Agency 2013; Zambia Development Agency 2014; Miketa and Merven 2013; Castellano et al. 2015)

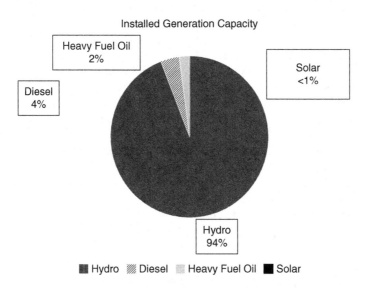

Figure 6.2 Installed electricity generation mix by type, 2015 (Energy Regulation Board 2015)

In 2015, 94 percent of the nation's 2,410.66 MW installed generation capacity was hydro, as seen in Figure 6.2 (Zambia Development Agency 2014; Energy Regulation Board 2015). However, although Zambia has 6 GW of additional "unexploited hydro power potential," the country's "strong reliance … on hydro exposes the power system to seasonal climate variation known to include droughts and floods, which can greatly hamper hydropower generation" (International Renewable Energy Agency 2013; Zambia Development Agency 2014).

6.1.4   *Effect of Climate Change*

Increased droughts and temperature increases induced by climate change over the past two years have reduced the water levels feeding several of Zambia's hydro plants, greatly restricting generation (Hill 2015; Onishi 2016). For example, in April 2016, the Kariba Dam, which typically supplies upwards of 40 percent of Zambia's national load, operated at quarter-capacity due to its water level, which was at 13 percent of capacity relative to 51 percent of capacity at the same time the previous year (Africa-EU Renewable Energy Programme 2015a; *Mail and Guardian Africa* 2016). The country's dependence on hydropower has resulted in electricity deficits (defined simply as the incremental electricity required beyond existing generation to meet demand) near 1,000 MW, more than half of the 1,960 MW peak demand (Hill 2015; Chutel 2016).

These shortages, resulting in ongoing scheduled and unscheduled blackouts, have had significant economic repercussions for Zambia, exacerbating an already fragile situation. Francis Ndilla, the head of the energy committee at the Zambia Chamber of Commerce and Industry, said that "climate change had had a direct effect already of slowing down our economic development" (Onishi 2016). In fact, according to the International Renewable Energy Agency (IRENA), the economic cost of these power outages is significant, reducing GDP by as much as 5 to 7 percent (Miketa and Merven 2013).

The impact of the shortages has been felt across industries in Zambia. Already faced with declining revenue, copper companies have seen their profitability greatly impacted by rising production costs induced by blackouts (Onishi 2016; Bariyo 2015). To reduce costs and mitigate impact to the bottom line, thousands of copper miners were laid off, further exacerbating the country's average income issue (Onishi 2016). Economic hardship caused by climate-change-induced electricity shortages has also been experienced by Good Time Steel, Zambia's largest steel maker, which was, for the first time in its history, unprofitable in 2015. Power cuts resulted in frequent breakdowns in machinery, causing Good Time Steel to lose one-third of its production capacity and preventing it from meeting production deadlines (Onishi 2016). Similarly, the fishing and honey industries have seen revenue decline significantly because of the droughts (*Mail and Guardian Africa* 2016; BBC 2016).

6.1.5   Zambian Government Initiatives

Given this predicament, the Zambian government began implementing various initiatives to mitigate its drought-induced electricity shortage in 2014 and 2015. In the short term, Zambia became a net importer of electricity; between 2014 and 2015, Zambia's electricity imports increased sixty-one-fold, from 12.82 GWh to 785.15 GWh, "buying 148 MW from Aggreko Plc on a continuous basis, while at night importing 150 MW from the Southern African Power Pool and 100 MW from EDM of Mozambique" (Energy Regulation Board 2015; Hill 2015). In the long term, the government approved the $843 m Maamba Collieries, a 300 MW coal-fired power plant, and participated in the World Bank's Scaling Solar Initiative to reduce nations' reliance on hydroelectric power by diversifying the sources of generation (World Finance 2016; Chutel 2016). The latter is a program which "aims to make privately funded grid-connected solar projects operational within two years and at competitive tariffs, by bringing together developers, financiers and governments to plan and execute utility-scale solar projects in Africa" (The World Bank 2017).

Despite the additional generating capacity yielded by these initiatives, planned generation projects, and the hydro generation potentially returning to pre-drought levels, IRENA predicts that in a high-demand growth scenario, Zambia will still see a potential power deficit of 1,000 MW by 2030, 18 percent of projected demand, assuming Zambia strives to be self-sufficient and does not import electricity (International Renewable Energy Agency 2013). Should climate-change-induced drought persist, and hydro generation continue to be affected, Zambia could potentially experience a generation deficit of 2,000 MW by 2030, which would greatly harm the nation's economy and stagnate growth. However, we will argue there are a range of energy solutions, some derived from innovative, decentralized, and renewable approaches, that could help address these impacts. We turn now to discuss those.

6.1.6   Generation Alternatives

For the purposes of this chapter, centralized generation is defined as large-scale, grid-connected projects (>10 MW) such as a solar or wind farm. On-grid decentralized generation is defined as consumer-owned, small-scale rooftop-solar generation (<20kW), which is connected to the grid and does not have a battery-storage component. Off-grid decentralized generation is taken to be consumer-owned, small-scale rooftop-solar generation (<20kW) that is not connected to the grid. These off-grid

Global Solar Irradiation in Zambia

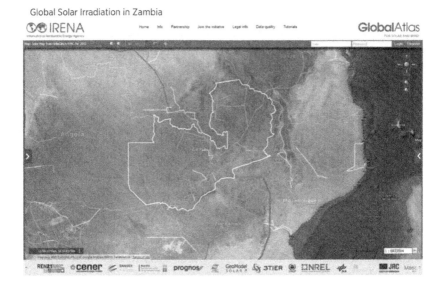

Figure 6.3 Map of solar irradiation and transmission infrastructure in Zambia (International Renewable Energy Agency 2013)

systems are assumed to use batteries to store and supply electricity during time of low solar irradiance.

In many African nations, the emphasis over substantial periods of time has been on traditional, large-scale centralized approaches to electricity generation (Wheeler 2008). In the case of Zambia, although the government has invested heavily in developing the country's substantial hydro resources, the nation also has significant non-hydro renewable energy resources that have remained undeveloped despite their ability to greatly diversify its energy mix. In fact, Zambia possesses excellent solar power potential, with an average of 2,000–3,000 hours of sunshine per year (Africa-EU Renewable Energy Programme 2015c). With daily irradiation levels as high as 8 kWh/m^2 relative to a national average of 5.5 kWh/m^2, the Lusaka region has some of the greatest solar development potential, as seen in the GIS map of Zambia's solar resources in Figure 6.3 (Africa-EU Renewable Energy Programme 2015c).

The RRA found that "given Zambia's ample solar, wind and geothermal resources and its central position in the SAPP [Southern African Power Pool], the country could play a leading role in expanding non-hydro renewable energy in both the SAPP and Eastern African Power Pool (EAPP)" (International Renewable Energy Agency 2013).

In addition to copious renewable resources, Zambia also has significant coal supplies, with an estimated 30 million tons of untapped reserves. With copper companies only requiring 2,000 tons annually, coal could act as a reliable alternative for the foreseeable future (International Renewable Energy Agency 2013). Conversely, Zambia has no oil resources, and therefore spends $0.5b, or 2.3 percent of its GDP, annually importing crude oil from Tanzania. Although coal is easily accessible and has comparable generation and investment costs to hydropower, it has significantly greater lifecycle greenhouse gas emissions, which contribute to global warming and potentially further exacerbate the rising temperatures and droughts occurring both globally and in the region (Miketa and Merven 2013; National Renewable Energy Laboratory 2013).

Therefore, the coupling of abundant solar and wind resources, their limited contribution to climate change, and the rapidly declining costs of renewable technology have the potential to greatly increase the resilience of Zambia's electricity system to drought and climate change.

Existing literature has explored certain aspects of the renewable energy alternatives in Zambia. Some papers have assessed the total renewable generation needed to meet Zambia's existing demand (International Renewable Energy Agency 2013; Miketa and Merven 2013), while others have discussed the economic feasibility of decentralized and centralized generation in the context of existing demand on country-specific (Thiam 2010; Sanoh et al. 2012; Ohiare 2015; Parshall et al. 2009; Kemausuor et al. 2014), regional (Castellano et al. 2015), and global scales (Levin and Thomas 2011; Levin and Thomas 2016; D'Agostino, Lund, and Johannes 2016; Sanoh et al. 2012; Ohiare 2015; Sanoh et al. 2014; Levin and Thomas 2013). Another body of work has explored the potential of urban rooftop solar in meeting electricity demand in global cities (Singh and Banerjee 2015; Khan and Arsalan 2016; Kabir, Endlicher, and Jägermeyr 2010; Yuan et al. 2016; Byrne et al. 2015). From a political and economic perspective, Jacobson and Delucchi have analyzed the required policies and cost needed to implement renewable energy generation (Jacobson and Delucchi 2009). A detailed literature review can be found in the paper by McPherson et al. (McPherson et al. 2018).

However, given the lack of focus on either the geospatial analysis of renewable energy in Zambia and rooftop-solar analysis in Lusaka, or addressing the impact of climate change, it is clear that there exists a research gap between the current literature and work exploring the mitigation of Zambia's energy situation. Therefore, this chapter brings together four previously distinct fields for application in Zambia in the context of climate change and drought:

1. Centralized vs. decentralized generation
2. Geospatial analysis of potential renewable generation locations
3. The estimation of urban rooftop potential
4. Economic and political feasibility

6.2   Methodology

6.2.1   Section Overview and Summary

This section presents detailed methodology for assessing future energy scenarios and options for Zambia. The efficacy of Zambia's various renewable alternatives is determined using a three-step process developed previously (McPherson et al. 2018). First, load profiles, projections, and existing generation from IRENA were used to establish a base-case scenario for Zambia between 2015 and 2030. Second, the potential of rooftop-solar generation in Lusaka and centralized generation in rural Zambia were estimated using geospatial and temporal data and compared against Zambia's load profile to determine the ability of these solutions to meet the generation shortage over the next fifteen years. This analysis assumed that Zambia's large hydro plants are equipped with enough storage capacity to balance the grid and dynamically alter hourly generation to meet demand throughout the day, thus mitigating the operational effects of intermittent renewable energy sources (McPherson et al. 2018). Third, a socioeconomic analysis of various generation solutions and development paradigms, considering both transmission and technology costs, was conducted, the method for which is described in Section 6.2.2.

6.2.2   Establishing the Base-Case Scenario

Load profiles and projections from 2015, 2020, and 2030, given by IRENA in their SAPP report, were used to establish the baseline demand (McPherson et al. 2018). These projections segmented demand profiles into industry, rural, and urban segments, and considered their hourly fluctuation by season. The annual load projections can be seen in Table 6.1.

The analysis in this chapter compared demand profiles with generation on a monthly basis. To calculate the baseline deficit in 2015, 2020, and 2030, the load forecasts were coupled with the estimated electricity supplied by existing and in-plan generation projects. It was assumed

Table 6.1 *Zambia total demand by season (top) and customer segment (bottom) in 2015, 2020, and 2030 (Miketa and Merven 2013)*

Year	Pre-winter (MW)	Winter (MW)	Post-winter (MW)
2015	1,964	2,538	2,008
2020	2,482	3,192	2,537
2030	4,043	5,200	4,133

Year	Industry (GWh)	Urban (GWh)	Rural (GWh)	Total (GWh)
2015	10,467	6,349	343	17,158
2020	13,358	8,103	438	21,899
2030	21,759	13,198	713	35,671

that all projects were completed on schedule and that generation of a new project began on January 1st of its first year of operation. By 2030, Zambia will have 6,393 MW of large hydro capacity, 91 MW of small hydro capacity, and 640 MW of coal capacity.

For hydro plants in Zambia, electricity output was estimated using a dry-year capacity factor of 39.7 percent for large hydro plants (> 32 MW), and 41.4 percent for small hydro plants (≤ 32 MW), to model a scenario of persistent drought in Zambia over the next fifteen years (Miketa and Merven 2013). These capacity factors were determined by taking a weighted average of the dry-year capacity factors given by IRENA. Monthly fluctuation for hydro generation was used, following historical fluctuations observed in 2014. For coal generation, a capacity factor of 88 percent was assumed for existing and planned projects, as per IRENA's report (Miketa and Merven 2013). The load projections and existing and in-plan forecasts were then combined to provide a base-case scenario and identify the annual deficits in 2015, 2020, and 2030. Tables of all planned and existing generations and their respective capacity factors can be found in the Appendix (Tables 6.7, 6.8, and 6.9).

6.2.3   Identification of Optimal Solar and Wind Generation Sites

To identify the optimal solar and wind generation sites in Zambia, GRETA was used. This is a novel modeling algorithm which provides hourly solar and wind resource data using NASA's Modern-Era Retrospective Analysis for Research and Applications (MERRA) (McPherson et al. 2018). GRETA provides this data by 1/2° latitude by 2/3° longitude grid cells, and assumes that the solar panel used is a First

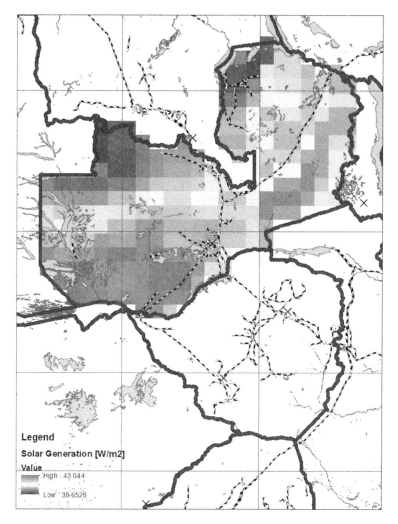

Figure 6.4 GRETA solar irradiance data (left) and average wind-power-capacity factor (right) (McPherson et al. 2018)

Solar FS-395 panel with a 12 percent efficiency, while the wind turbine is a Vestas V112, with 3,075 kW capacity (McPherson et al. 2017; McPherson et al. 2018). The average solar irradiance and wind output from GRETA for Zambia can be seen in Figure 6.4.

GRETA was used to identify the five best solar and wind generation latitude–longitude grid cells in Zambia. The cells chosen, the grid cell

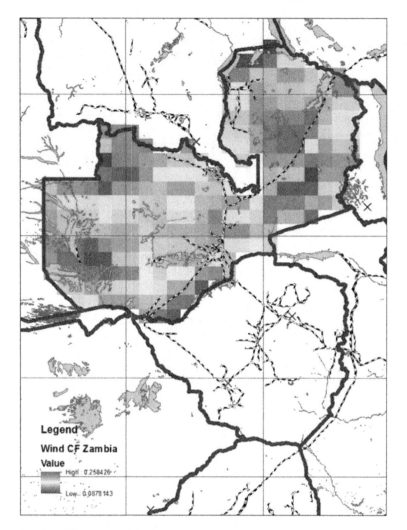

Figure 6.4 (cont.)

corresponding to Lusaka, and the capacity factor of the resources in these locations can be seen in Table 6.2.

To determine the total generation potential in each of the selected latitude–longitude cells, land-use data was considered. For centralized generation in rural areas, the total available area for solar and wind generation was determined by multiplying the available area of appropriate land types (from GIS spatial data [Anon 2016]) by land-use

Table 6.2 *Grid cells with the five largest irradiance and average wind-power values*

	Solar				Wind		
Grid cell	Latitude–longitude	Average irradiance (W/m^2) for FS-395 panel	Capacity factor	Grid cell	Latitude–longitude	Average power for Vestas V112 turbine with 3075 W capacity	Capacity factor
146–310	−17.0, 26.67	43.0	32.6%	151–317	−14.5, 31.33	795	25.8%
146–309	−17.0, 26.0	42.8	32.5%	150–316	−15.0, 30.67	749	24.4%
147–310	−16.5, 26.67	42.7	32.4%	156–316	−12.0, 30.67	731	23.8%
148–307	−16.0, 24.67	42.6	32.3%	157–316	−11.5, 30.67	730	23.7%
145–309	−17.5, 26.0	42.6	32.3%	158–317	−11.0, 31.33	724	23.5%
149–313 (Lusaka)	−15.5, 28.67	41.5	31.4%				

factors, which account for shading, the shape of the area, and geographic constraints (Ong et al. 2013; McPherson et al. 2018).

For Lusaka, urban land-use data was utilized to determine the total available rooftop area for solar generation, considering shading coefficients, solar irradiance, panel efficiency, and urban growth between 2015 and 2030 (McPherson et al. 2018).

6.2.4   Project Cost

Project cost, comprised of technology costs and transmission costs, was utilized to determine the cost of power ($/kWh) of various solutions, enabling the filtering and prioritizing of specific centralized and decentralized projects.

6.2.5   Centralized Generation Projects

Given that renewable centralized generation projects would be in rural locations, the total cost of a centralized project was estimated by aggregating the equipment cost of solar panels or wind turbines, the cost of new transmission lines to connect a given project to the grid, and the cost of adding conductors to existing transmission towers. The methodology used for determining the cost of transmission infrastructure can be found in the paper by McPherson et al. (McPherson et al. 2018).

6.2.6   Large Centralized Solar

The cost of utility-scale centralized solar generation projects was determined using a National Renewable Energy Lab (NREL) pricing benchmark study which assessed utility and residential solar photovoltaic (PV) prices in the United States. Despite studies conducted by IRENA regarding utility-scale solar PV costs in Africa, no equations for trend lines or explicit values for data points were provided for the change in cost per watt as project size increases (Taylor and So 2016). Therefore, NREL data was used as a proxy in the absence of detailed African-specific data. The full methodology for determining the price of centralized solar generation can be found in the Appendix.

6.2.7   Large Centralized Wind

The technology cost of a wind project was calculated by multiplying the total project size in MW by $2.075/MW, the median price per megawatt of a wind farm, according to IRENA (Secretariat 2012). Data from IRENA were used as specific cost data were not available for Zambia.

6.2.8   Decentralized Rooftop Solar

An IRENA report on the technology costs of rooftop solar PV panels and their associated components was used to estimate the cost of grid-connected and off-grid decentralized generation projects in Lusaka (Taylor and So 2016). Central to these estimates was the assumption that on-grid solar PV would not require battery storage as consumers could access grid-based electricity when their solar panels are not generating, whereas off-grid solar PV would require battery storage as consumers would not be connected to the electricity grid. According to the IRENA report, a 100 W off-grid rooftop PV system would cost approximately $10/W inclusive of battery storage (Taylor and So 2016). A similar on-grid system would cost approximately $6/W without the battery and charge controller (Taylor and So 2016). The total cost of various on- and off-grid solutions in Lusaka was determined by multiplying the above costs by the total generation potential in Lusaka. It is important to note that the exact development and institutional costs of designing, overseeing, and implementing electricity distribution level infrastructure for on-grid generation scenarios were not calculated, as the complex modeling of individual rooftop connections was beyond the scope of this chapter. However, given that these connections can cost upward of $750 per connection, the overall feasibility of the expensive nature of grid-connected rooftop generation is discussed later in Section 6.4 (Castellano et al. 2015).

6.2.9   Cost of Power

The annual cost of power for the various centralized and decentralized scenarios was determined on a per kWh basis, considering operating and maintenance costs, as well financing costs, using the following formula (Wallace 2016):

$$g\left(\frac{\$}{kWh}\right) = \frac{C \cdot R}{E} + \frac{k \cdot C}{E} + \frac{S_A}{E} + \frac{T_A}{E} \tag{6.1}$$

Where:
- g is the cost per unit electric power
- E is the total electric power produced annually in kWh
- C is the total capital cost of the project (sum of project cost and transmission infrastructure costs)

- **R** is the capital cost recovery factor
- **k** is the maintenance factor

The capital cost recovery factor was determined using the following formula (Wallace 2016):

$$R = \frac{r}{1 - (1 + r)^{-n}} \tag{6.2}$$

Where:
- **R** is the capital cost recovery factor
- **r** is the real rate of return
- **n** is the project lifetime

Values for the maintenance factor and interest rate were taken from accepted literature. The maintenance factor, which considers operating and maintenance costs, was assumed to be 10 percent of the annual capital cost payment for decentralized solar, as per IRENA (Castellano et al. 2015; Taylor and So 2016). An interest rate of 6 percent was utilized, again in accordance with the IRENA study (Taylor and So 2016).

6.2.10 Transmission Costs

It was assumed that transmission lines were 330 kV double circuit, with each line having 400 MW capacity (McPherson et al. 2018). A double circuit factor of 1.6 and a cost per kilometer of $200,000 were also assumed in accordance with literature values (McPherson et al. 2018).

6.2.11 Limitations

There are a few limitations of the methodology outlined in this chapter. As mentioned previously, the cost estimate for the decentralized on-grid scenarios excluded the costs associated with developing necessary distribution infrastructure in Lusaka, which could cost upwards of $750 per connection (Castellano et al. 2015). As discussed later in the chapter, this exclusion was made due to the highly complex nature of the modeling required to determine Lusaka's distribution system costs. However, despite this exclusion, the additional connection costs support the argument we shall make in Section 6.4 that from a pure cost perspective, centralized generation is more feasible than decentralized generation.

Secondly, the cost estimates for the centralized generation scenarios exclude the curtailment costs, as well as the capital required for additional distribution and transmission assets, such as substations and circuit protection assets. The use and cost of utility storage as well as their effect on hydro generation are also not explored in this chapter; these costs could be upward of $150–$180 m for a 100 MW utility-scale battery-storage facility (Adams 2017). Additionally, Zambia-specific utility solar PV costs were not available for use in cost estimates, which could vary from the NREL proxy used by an increase of up to 30 percent, the justification for which is discussed in the Appendix. Furthermore, the methodology in this chapter does not include a simulation of grid operation or configurations; nor does it consider the efficacy of micro-grids, an exclusion also seen in other institutional reports (Castellano et al. 2015). A full dispatch model analysis for Zambia using some of the methodologies highlighted in this chapter, coupled with electric vehicle analysis, can be found in the paper by McPherson et al. (McPherson et al. 2018).

6.3   Results and Discussion

Coupling the methodology outlined above, and in the paper by McPherson et al., three sets of broad renewable energy strategies for Zambia were examined: fully centralized solutions in rural Zambia, fully decentralized solutions in Lusaka, and hybrid solutions comprised of centralized and decentralized components (McPherson et al. 2018). These solutions were compared in terms of their efficacy in addressing Zambia's deficit of 7,839, 4,769, and 7,503 gigawatt-hours in 2015, 2020, and 2030 respectively (McPherson et al. 2018).

6.3.1   Centralized Generation Scenarios

The results discussed for a fully centralized generation approach to mitigating Zambia's deficit are a summary of an analysis conducted by McPherson et al. (McPherson et al. 2018).

In their paper, they conducted a scenario analysis using solar and wind centralized generation sites from the ten best MERRA grid cells discussed in Section 6.2.3, examining 102 potential centralized solar generation sites in the top solar cells and 213 potential wind sites in the top wind cells (McPherson et al. 2018). Nine scenarios, each with a different approach for selecting the generation sites to develop, were then applied to the identified solar and wind sites to determine the best centralized generation approach to have used in 2015 to eliminate Zambia's deficit, and for use in 2020 and 2030.

As mentioned previously, Zambia's projected deficit in 2020 will be lower than in 2015 by 39 percent. Given that the deficit will approach 2015 levels again by 2030, analysis was only conducted for the deficit in

Table 6.3 *Centralized generation-site selection scenarios*

Scenario	Description
A) Proximity to transmission infrastructure	
A1	Only solar generation sites in the solar grid cell closest to existing transmission infrastructure were considered for development
A2	Only wind generation sites in the wind grid cell closest to existing transmission infrastructure were considered for development
A3	50 percent of the generation was from wind sites, and 50 percent from solar sites in the wind and solar grid cells respectively closest to existing transmission infrastructure
B) Resource quality	
B1	Generation sites with the highest capacity factor were developed until the deficit was eliminated
C) Dispersion	
C1	One generation site, with a maximum capacity of 400 MW, was selected from each GRETA cell (10 total sites). If the aggregate generation of the selected sites was higher than the deficit (i.e. yielding a surplus), all the selected projects were scaled down proportionally to eliminate the surplus
D) Project cost	
D1**	The most expensive individual projects were selected for development until the deficit was eliminated
D2	Generation sites with the lowest individual cost were selected until demand was met
E) Generation/cost ratio	
E1	Generation sites with the highest generation/cost ratio were selected until the deficit was eliminated
E2**	Generation sites with the lowest generation/cost ratio were selected until the deficit was eliminated

** Highest-cost scenarios were included in models to assess the sensitivity of the total cost of deficit elimination to site location, size, and quality.

2015, as this represented the worst-case scenario for Zambia and the situation they might face in fifteen years, according to projections.

From the nine scenarios in Table 6.3 and Figure 6.5, the three most cost-effective scenarios (A1, B1, and E1) were further analyzed, considering four criteria: overall cost, resource quality (measured by capacity factor), average monthly shortage (the average shortage in months where there are generation deficits), and generation dispersion (the number of grid cells which have generation sites for a given scenario). These three scenarios solely prioritized centralized solar generation. Applying a decision matrix, it was determined that Scenario E1 is the optimal centralized

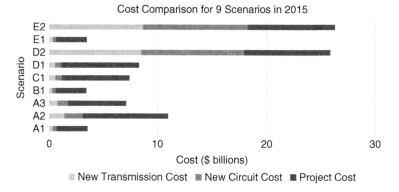

Figure 6.5 Cost comparison of large centralized generation scenarios, 2015 (McPherson et al., 2018)

development paradigm among those considered for Zambia in order to address its generation shortage and minimize the subsequent economic impact.

Under Scenario E1, which was comprised solely of centralized solar generation in four grid cells located in the west of the country, the cost of power considering only project costs was calculated to be $0.035/kWh, which is moderately more expensive than the cost of existing centralized hydro generation of $0.02-$0.03/kWh (International Renewable Energy Agency 2013). Even if transmission infrastructure costs are included, the cost of power in Scenario E1 rises to $0.042/kWh, which would still be highly profitable to a developer, assuming they receive a similar purchasing power agreement of $0.06/kWh from the Zambian government as Neoen.[1]

From a planning perspective, given the deficit relief provided by planned generation in 2020, capital project timing can still be optimized by government overseers, working with appropriate developers and financing sources, as seen with Zambia's participation in the Scaling Solar program and the resulting Neoen and First Solar[2] projects (First Solar 2018; Scaling Solar 2017).

6.3.2 Rooftop Solar

Solar home systems in Lusaka have the potential to contribute to reducing the generation deficit that Zambia faces. According to McPherson et al., there is enough rooftop capacity in Lusaka to have up to 12,755 GWh

---

[1] Neoen is a "French developer and independent power producer" (Lusaka Times, 2017a).
[2] First Solar is an American developer and independent power producer.

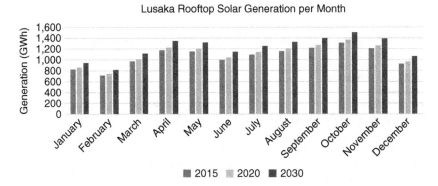

Figure 6.6 Maximum Lusaka roof top solar generation per month in 2015, 2020, and 2030, assuming all applicable rooftops have solar PV

and 14608 GWh of solar PV generation potential in 2015 and 2030, providing a potential alternative to addressing Zambia's deficit (McPherson et al. 2018). The upper bound of generation potential identified in the paper by McPherson et al. is used in the following analysis (see Figure 6.6).

As mentioned earlier in the chapter, two decentralized rooftop-solar configurations in Lusaka were considered for analysis – grid-connected and off-grid. The grid-connected scenario assumes that homes and businesses with solar PV panels are electrified, and therefore would be able to supply electricity back into the grid to help address Zambia's national deficit. Inherent in this assumption is the development of distribution infrastructure in Lusaka, which can cost up to three times more than transmission infrastructure, but is not calculated in this chapter as electricity distribution planning is highly complex and beyond the scope of this research (Castellano et al. 2015). However, the general impact of these costs is discussed more broadly later in this section. The off-grid scenario assumes that a rooftop-solar solution would only supply Lusaka's electricity demand (McPherson et al. 2018). Central to this approach is the assumption that all off-grid solar panels would only supply existing electricity customers in Lusaka, and that the city's electrification rates would stay constant at 70.6 percent between 2015 and 2030 (Republic of Zambia Central Statistical Office 2015). If the electrification rate did rise, the total cost of addressing the deficit would increase; however, the cost per kilowatt-hour would remain the same. Additionally, as only 32 percent of rooftop area would need to be covered to address Lusaka's current

Table 6.4 *Total cost and cost of power for decentralized generation scenarios in Lusaka*

	2015	2020	2030
100% grid-connected			
Penetration rate	61%	36%	51%
Cost ($M USD)	$17,100	$10,400	$16,360
Cost of power ($/kWh)	$0.188	$0.188	$0.188
70% grid-connected, 30% off-grid			
Penetration rate	71%	39%	51%
Cost ($M USD)	$23,650	$13,650	$19,640
Cost of power ($/kWh)	$0.260	$0.246	$0.225
50% grid-connected, 50% off-grid			
Penetration rate	92%	50%	63%
Cost ($M USD)	$34,160	$19,420	$26,570
Cost of power ($/kWh)	$0.375	$0.350	$0.305
100 percent off-grid			
Penetration rate	17%	21%	32%
Cost ($M USD)	$7,750	$10,350	$17,060
Cost of power ($/kWh)	$0.313	$0.313	$0.313

load under a fully off-grid decentralized scenario, even if electrification rates did increase, there would still be ample rooftop area to supply the additional load.

Table 6.4 lists the total cost, and the cost of power of various fully decentralized rooftop-solar scenarios in Lusaka for addressing Zambia's deficit. A penetration rate, calculated by dividing the necessary rooftop generation by the total potential rooftop generation, was determined for each scenario, such that the total deficit in 2015 would be 0 GWh. We note two key elements at work. Firstly, the price of solar home systems was assumed to be stagnant between 2015 and 2030 to give a conservative estimate of the technology cost; however, the price will realistically decrease as mentioned earlier. Secondly, as discussed previously, the 100 percent off-grid scenario was assumed to only address Lusaka's electricity demand, and therefore the penetration rate was chosen such that the entirety of Lusaka's electricity demand would be met between 2015 and 2030.

Although the aggregate cost for the 100 percent off-grid scenario is significantly lower than the other decentralized scenarios, the result is misleading. As per McPherson et al., Lusaka's load only comprised 12 percent of Zambia's total electricity demand in 2015, and therefore the 100 percent off-grid scenario would require fewer solar panels to supply this load. Conversely, scenarios with an on-grid component would aim to mitigate the entirety of the national deficit, and therefore require more solar panels and so have a higher aggregate cost. On a per-kilowatt-hour basis, the 100 percent off-grid scenario is one of the most expensive, which can be attributed to the unit price of a storage unit adding 67 percent, or $4, in costs, as mentioned earlier in the chapter.

Regardless, a fully decentralized approach would be highly expensive and unaffordable to existing consumers, costing between six and twelve and a half times more than conventional hydro and coal generation in Zambia, without even considering connection or distribution infrastructure costs. Although other business models exist, such as a private firm installing and leasing units back to consumers, the high technology costs would necessitate high contract fees, purchasing power agreements, or charges to the consumer to cover costs. Furthermore, urban electrification is a resource-intensive, arduous, and slow process, and therefore there would likely be delays in its implementation, postponing the ability of urban rooftop solar to address Zambia's deficit and exacerbating the economic implications of electricity shortages. Additionally, consumers would need to be aware of the benefits of buying solar panels to realize uptake and address the deficit, requiring proper public education policies to be implemented. This is discussed further in Section 6.4.

Given the high cost of power, and the potential uptake and development hurdles of a fully decentralized solution, Zambia needs to either focus solely on centralization of solar generation, or to adopt those systems, augmented with a combination of grid and off-grid connected PV solar on rooftops in Lusaka. We address this latter hybrid scenario below.

6.3.3   Hybrid Generation Scenario

A series of hybrid generation approaches were analyzed based on cost and generation reliability and were compared to the fully centralized approach discussed previously. This section also includes an important discussion about non-cost implications, such as institutional, political, and socio-economic factors, which need to be considered when deciding the optimal approach to address Zambia's electricity deficit.

Three hybrid combinations of centralized and decentralized generation were analyzed – 70 percent centralized and 30 percent decentralized (70/30), 50 percent centralized and 50 percent decentralized (50/50), and 30 percent centralized and 70 percent decentralized (30/70). The centralized generation component assumes the E1 approach, a fully solar scenario with generation sites in western Zambia, which was previously determined to be the optimal centralized scenario. The decentralized component assumes that Lusaka's load is entirely supplied by off-grid generation, with the remainder of national demand supplied by on-grid rooftop-solar generation in Lusaka. As such, for each scenario total generation is unchanged, but the role of decentralized solutions varies.

The decentralized generation assumption regarding on- and off-grid was made because it would be the fastest decentralized solution for Zambia to implement relative to other decentralized approaches, while still addressing the national deficit. There were two reasons for this.

Firstly, off-grid rooftop solar can be rapidly deployed, taking on average between 1 – 3 days to install, thus enabling Lusaka's electricity needs to be addressed in a few years with non-grid solutions (Maehlum 2014). The uptake of these solar panels by consumers and businesses can be incentivized through government subsidies, microfinance, and public awareness programs, as seen in Bangladesh (Khandker et al. 2014). This is further discussed in Section 6.4.

Secondly, the on-grid component would be implemented expediently, relative to other decentralized approaches, as there is less on-grid generation, thus fewer grid-connections and less urban distribution planning and capital investment needed (Castellano et al. 2015). This deployment can be realized through various methods, including the consumer purchasing the panels directly, companies acting as intermediaries and leasing panels to consumers, or through government subsidies, the latter of which has been recently observed in Uganda. This is discussed in further detail in Section 6.4.

Although, independently, this amalgamated on- and off-grid decentralized generation approach would be one of the most expensive options in terms of upfront capital investments, as illustrated in Table 6.5, a hybrid approach leads to reduced power costs. This is attributed to the fact that it requires fewer resources to plan and build distribution infrastructure, which, as mentioned previously, can cost up to three times more than transmission infrastructure. It is important to note that these costs only account for system costs, and do not include the institutional costs associated with planning, as these data are not publicly available. This exclusion is widely accepted, having also been made by other institutional planning reports such as those by IRENA and McKinsey (Miketa and Merven 2013; Castellano et al. 2015). If the cost for technical assistance and project supervision for distribution and transmission projects in Lusaka is used as a proxy, then planning costs account for approximately 5 percent of the overall system costs and have a marginal impact on the results discussed in this chapter (The World Bank 2013).

Table 6.5 *Comparison of parameters for hybrid and centralized generation approaches in 2015*

Parameters	Centralized (E1)	70/30	50/50	30/70
Total cost[3]	$3.5 B	$10.6 B	$13.4 B	$16.2 B
Dispersion*	4	5	5	4
Mean monthly deficit (GWh/mo.)	−59.99	−46.59	−47.09	−48.09
Number of months with deficit	7	7	7	7
Cost/kWh	$0.042	$0.119	$0.149	$0.178

* The number of GRETA grid cells which have generation sites

As with the centralized and decentralized analysis, only the 2015 scenarios were compared for the hybrid generation scenarios due to their potential to address Zambia's deficit until 2030.

Although a fully centralized approach has the cheapest cost in terms of power, it is the least resistant to extended generation shortages in the four scenarios. This is because, as mentioned previously, all the generation sites are concentrated in the west of the country and therefore susceptible to the same natural events, such as extensive cloud cover. This lack of geographic dispersion of generation sites, as seen by the lower dispersion value relative to other scenarios, resulted in the centralized scenario having the largest average deficit during months when there was not enough sunlight. Conversely, the hybrid scenarios which have generation sites in western Zambia and in Lusaka have lower monthly deficits due to the geographic dispersion of generation sites. The more dispersed the generation sites are (i.e. the more GRETA cells covered), the lower the number of generation sites affected by the same natural events occurring in a part of the country, and, therefore, the less susceptible the system is to extensive generation shortages.

To account for the various parameters in Table 6.5, a Pugh decision matrix[4] was used to identify the optimal approach to Zambia's deficit, with each parameter having equal weight due to their individual importance (Table 6.6).

Consistent with existing literature on centralized and decentralized generation alternatives, a 100 percent centralized generation approach

---

[3] Figures are 2015 cash prices and do not account for inflation.

[4] A quantitative method for selecting a solution from several options by comparing across criteria. Each criterion is given a weighting and the solution with the highest total score is chosen as the optimal solution.

Table 6.6 *Decision matrix for hybrid and centralized generation approaches in 2015*

Parameters	Centralized (E1)	70/30	50/50	30/70
Total cost	1.00	0.33	0.26	0.21
Dispersion	0.80	1.00	1.00	0.80
Mean monthly deficit	0.78	1.00	0.99	0.97
Number of months with deficit	1.0	1.00	1.00	1.00
Total score	3.58	3.33	3.25	2.98

would be the most effective solution from a purely cost-of-power basis (Taylor and So 2016). However, there are other aspects of renewable resource development that need to be analyzed as well, namely the time required to implement the generation projects, consumer autonomy, ease of planning, and sources of funding, which will be discussed in Section 6.4.

6.4   Beyond the Costs: A Case for the 70/30 Scenario

Considering the implications of the various generation scenarios for the additional factors of resource development (implementation time, consumer autonomy, ease of planning, and sources of funding) we selected the 70/30 scenario (70 percent centralized, 30 percent decentralized) as the representative optimal solution for Zambia. This is because this approach enables utilities to provide cheap centralized power for the general population in the short term, while simultaneously helping the government to lay the groundwork for greater urban electrification in the long term. Furthermore, this scenario enables the Zambian government to leverage existing relationships with international developers, such as Neoen, in order to deploy large-scale centralized generation quickly, while simultaneously providing consumers in Lusaka with greater autonomy through off-grid options, and yielding a less strenuous planning process for the government. It is notable that off-grid approaches would constitute about 90 percent of decentralized generation (see Figures 6.7 and 6.8).

6.4.1   *Implementation Time*

Given the detrimental economic impact of Zambia's impending generation deficit and the inability of planned hydro and coal projects to fully

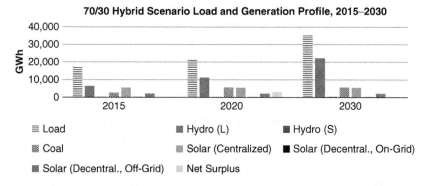

Figure 6.7 70/30 hybrid scenario load and generation profile, 2015–2030

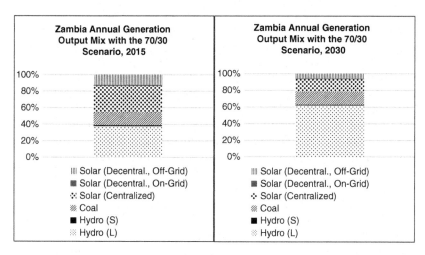

Figure 6.8 Zambia annual generation output mix with the 70/30 hybrid scenario. 2015 (left), 2030 (right)

mitigate the country's electricity shortage over the next fifteen years, it is imperative that additional generation be developed quickly. The 70/30 approach's inclusion of off-grid decentralized generation enables a quick (less than one year) partial mitigation of the shortage. Given the time required for financing, site surveying, and construction of necessary project and transmission infrastructure, the development of centralized generation would take, at minimum, two years, likely longer, even via world-renowned initiatives such as the World Bank's Scaling Solar

Program, as seen with the Neoen and First Solar projects in Zambia (Scaling Solar 2017). In comparison, off-grid decentralized rooftop solar, being consumer owned, takes approximately three days to install, assuming public support and affordability – a fraction of the time – and it has the potential to be scaled up quickly, similar to Off-Grid Electric in Tanzania, and M-Kopa in Kenya, the latter of which has installed over 500,000 rooftop-solar panels in Kenya since 2011 (Maehlum 2014; McKibben 2017; Muhatia 2018). The ability for consumers to rapidly deploy these systems in the nation's capital yields the potential for Lusaka's load to be fully addressed by 2020, which would cut the projected national deficit in half, and reduce the economic impact of drought and government spend on importing electricity. Thus, given its expedient nature, the 70/30 approach is clearly advantageous over a lengthier, fully centralized approach.

The quick implementation time for rooftop-solar systems hinges on the ability of the Zambian government to raise awareness about the benefits of these systems and provide financial incentives/support for deploying them. The latter are discussed later in this section. Various approaches have been tried to effectively raise public awareness regarding the benefits of solar panels in the developing world. One of the most effective solutions has been in Bangladesh, where the Infrastructure Development Company Limited (IDCOL), a company established by the Government of Bangladesh, worked with the government and private sector to raise public awareness through the distribution of publicity materials and case studies of successful rooftop-solar implementations and their benefits (Khandker et al. 2014). This approach, coupled with declining prices of solar rooftop systems, has been directly correlated with rising solar PV demand in the nation, resulting in over 3 million rural homes adopting rooftop PV over ten years, with 50,000 new homes adopting systems every month (Khandker et al. 2014). The approaches adopted in, and lessons learned from Bangladesh could prove to be invaluable for the Zambian government and its partners as they strive to increase uptake of rooftop-solar PV systems in Lusaka.

6.4.2   Consumer Autonomy

The dependence of consumers and businesses in Lusaka on Zambia's historically unreliable electricity system, frequently subject to shortages and high-power losses, has inhibited consumer and economic autonomy, often resulting in a reduced national GDP (International Renewable Energy Agency 2013). Although consumers and large businesses have access to backup diesel generators, these are often expensive to operate, subject to fluctuating fuel prices and contribute to global warming (International Renewable Energy Agency 2013). The 70/30 approach, via its off-grid decentralized rooftop-solar component, would provide homeowners and businesses in Lusaka with previously inaccessible urban electricity resilience and autonomy, reducing the impact of shortages on the economic capital of Zambia. Furthermore, depending on the terms of the financing (which are discussed in Section 6.4.5), it could enable consumers to be more financially independent, as they would be paying off their newly acquired solar home system (an asset they would own) instead of a utility electricity bill. The implementation of off-grid solar panels in Lusaka would also benefit the national economy, as electricity previously supplied to the capital could be diverted to other industrial sectors, such as manufacturing.

6.4.3   Ease of Planning

The planning of a national transmission and urban electricity distribution network can be a highly complex and resource-intensive process. By leveraging centralized, off-grid decentralized, and on-grid decentralized generation, the 70/30 approach minimizes this complexity relative to other mitigation strategies for three reasons.

Firstly, the Zambian government would be able to utilize its experience with, and partnerships developed through, its previous participation in the World Bank's Scaling Solar program to expediently plan the centralized component of the 70/30 solution and partner with established developers. Leveraging this experience would further propel Zambia into developing a leadership role within sub-Saharan Africa in centralized renewable power.

Secondly, as mentioned previously, the incorporation of off-grid decentralized solar in the 70/30 approach enables Lusaka's electricity demand to be addressed in a quicker and less resource-intensive manner with reduced planning. Coupled with proper educational policy to engender public awareness of the benefits of rooftop solar, this off-grid solar component of the deficit mitigation strategy would enable Zambia to eliminate approximately half of the electricity deficit by 2020. Additionally, this approach could build off of the existing momentum to electrify 22,000 rural homes and 1,000 rural businesses by 2022 through Zambia's rural electrification program (Lusaka Times 2017b). Doing so would enable major stakeholders to test and learn various policies and educational strategies to maximize uptake of rooftop-solar panels.

Thirdly, the ability of centralized solar, off-grid decentralized solar, and planned and existing generation to address Zambia's electricity shortage by 2020 eliminates the need to expedite the development of on-grid decentralized generation in Lusaka. Instead, the 70/30 approach encourages the government of Zambia to take the necessary time to properly conduct urban distribution planning studies in Lusaka, acquire funding, and develop the requisite policy. It also allows the government to identify other institutional intermediaries, such as IRENA, to help build the necessary capabilities to successfully conduct on-grid decentralized planning on a city-wide scale.

Effective and efficacious planning for the 70/30 scenario will require the collaboration of local, municipal, and federal governments to develop holistic and long-term renewable energy legislation to address Zambia's electricity needs over the coming decades, as identified by a European Union assessment of renewable energy accessibility in Zambia (European Union 2016). This collaboration, which is often challenging due to the politics, human capital, and timelines involved, will necessitate the creation of an appropriate budget that incorporates the capital needed to conduct technical studies, and build the subsequent infrastructure to provide state-of-the-art protection for grid assets. As per the EU recommendation, the legislation should also include plans for renewable energy education, raising public awareness of the benefits of rooftop-solar technology, and mandating the development and proliferation of technical renewable energy talent at local universities (European Union 2016). This strategy would build on existing efforts, such as the establishment of solar labs by the University of Zambia, and provide the nation with leading renewable energy knowledge capital in southern Africa (African Review 2014).

6.4.4   Cost of Power

Through the 70/30 scenario consumers would have two disparate ways of purchasing power: coupled large centralized generation and on-grid rooftop solar, and off-grid decentralized rooftop solar panels. The availability of two approaches would allow implementation of a range of consumer income levels and financial situations.

Although the off-grid solar generation would cost approximately $0.30 per kilowatt-hour, roughly a tenfold increase relative to existing utility electricity costs in Zambia, consumers would be benefiting from the autonomy, speed of electricity access, and reliability, which has a major impact on quality of life for homes and businesses in Lusaka, as discussed below (International Renewable Energy Agency 2013). Additionally, this cost could be greatly decreased or subsidized, which is further discussed in Section 6.4.5. Furthermore, as stated previously, the cost of rooftop-solar PV will likely decrease by over 50 percent over the coming decade, and when coupled with private and public funding sources (discussed below), will be more competitive for consumers to purchase.

Electricity from grid-connected generation (large centralized and on-grid decentralized) would cost $0.047/kWh in the 70/30 scenario, comparable to existing utility electricity costs, and would therefore be affordable for most Zambians who currently purchase electricity. In fact, until 2020 the cost of grid-connected electricity would be closer to $0.042/kWh as the more expensive on-grid decentralized solar generation would not be implemented until after 2020. Furthermore, rooftop solar panels will likely reduce in price over the coming years, as their mass production in emerging markets such as China becomes more ubiquitous, further reducing the cost of grid-connected electricity (Taylor, Ralon, and Ilas 2016).

6.4.5   Sources of Funding

Multiple sources of funding will be needed to acquire the capital investment necessary to fully mitigate Zambia's generation shortage. The 70/30 scenario has advantages over a fully centralized scenario in terms of enabling Zambia to build on its existing investor base, and diversify funding sources while being cost-effective. This can be attributed to the development of both centralized and decentralized generation, which can be funded by different sets of stakeholders.

For utility-scale centralized solar projects there are two areas of financing needed: the generation projects themselves and the associated transmission infrastructure. Historically, several sub-Saharan African countries have struggled to acquire funding because projects were not financially viable or had poor cost transparency (Castellano et al. 2015). To mitigate this, Zambia should leverage existing international initiatives, such as the World Bank's Scaling Solar program, to access funding sources and reach agreements with developers for centralized solar projects, like the recently announced First Solar project (International Finance Corporation 2016). The Zambian government would pay solar developers, such as First Solar, a very attractive twenty-five-year purchasing power agreement (PPA) at a fixed rate (most recently $0.06/kWh) for the entirety of the contract (International Finance Corporation 2016). The developers would maintain responsibility for asset financing and construction (International Finance Corporation 2016). Given the numerous investors and developers who have shown an interest in developing large, centralized solar projects in Zambia, the funding and agreement process could, in an ideal case, be expeditious (Scaling Solar 2017).

This interest from developers was demonstrated in early 2017, when twenty-one companies submitted a "Request for Qualification" as part of the Scaling Solar Program to develop a 300-MW solar plant in Zambia (Kenning 2017). However, detailed case studies have shown large-scale infrastructure projects, across a range of types of participants and developed country players and interest, have been laboriously slow and disappointing, and in some cases worse (Gil and Pinto 2017).

There are a few possibilities for the funding sources of the additional transmission infrastructure, in addition to the government developing a new federal budget and using tax dollars, which could be an arduous and time-consuming process. These include the Zambian government diverting resources currently spent on importing electricity, taking a loan from the World Bank or a similar international financing organization, or privatizing part of the new transmission infrastructure to expedite construction (Castellano et al. 2015). Again, historical results suggest caution in terms of expectations overall and certainly in terms of speed.

To speculate on reasons for optimism, grid-connected rooftop solar could be financed by a renewable feed-in tariff (REFIT) program, similar to that of Uganda, but for rooftop solar PV, whereby home and commercial owners would purchase and finance their solar panels and the government would pay the owners a fixed amount for the electricity they produce on a per kWh basis established through a nationally standardized REFIT contract (Couture et al. 2010; Electricity Regulatory Authority 2016). Tax dollars would fund the government payments, so appropriate legislation and oversight would need to be established to ensure the seamless operation of a REFIT program. The urban distribution infrastructure in Lusaka necessary to connect the rooftop solar panels to the grid, along with their studies and planning, would also need to be funded by the government.

As mentioned previously, off-grid rooftop solar would be financed by home and business owners themselves. The government could help promote such programs and offer subsidies as deemed appropriate, as seen in India, where the World Bank gave a $625 m loan to the State Bank of India to provide "discounted finance for rooftop solar installations on factories and institutions," and in Uganda, where subsidies of $5.5/W were provided on solar equipment purchased by households (The World Bank Group 2017; Elmer Hansen, Brix Pedersen, and Nygaard n.d.). Furthermore, private-sector institutions, such as Off-Grid in Tanzania and Ivory Coast, can lease out rooftop solar panels, enabling consumers to have a rooftop-solar system for $8 per month, eliminating the barrier of high upfront costs that often inhibits lower-income customers from accessing solar panels (McKibben 2017).

6.4.6 Industry Building and Fostering Entrepreneurship in Zambia

The 70/30 scenario, or another hybrid approach, would also help create a solar PV marketplace and could enable Zambia to become a continental leader in renewable energy, partially driven by the development of latent entrepreneurial skills among young Zambians. The fact that other countries harbor similar ambitions and latent skill sets only amplifies the power of this approach broadly across Africa.

The mass introduction of off-grid rooftop solar panels in Lusaka could ideally enable the creation of a solar PV marketplace, which would enable Zambians to accrue several benefits. Firstly, the marketplace would reduce the price of solar panels, making them more affordable to the general consumer (Barbose and Darghouth 2016; Taylor et al. 2016). Secondly, the establishment of a marketplace would invite additional suppliers to enter the market, increasing competition and so further reducing the average price per unit (Barbose and Darghouth 2016; Melitz and Ottaviano 2008; Taylor et al. 2016). Thirdly, an established marketplace with credible vendors and advertising would seamlessly augment initiatives taken by the government to increase awareness of the benefits of solar panels. If done correctly, these marketing tactics could further drive demand for solar home systems, which would subsequently improve electrification rates more rapidly and thus improve the average quality of life (Barbose and Darghouth 2016).

Again, caution is required, even as successful case studies unfold in Zambia and elsewhere on the African continent. Nonetheless, a 70/30 approach could, we assert, position Zambia as a continental leader in renewable generation, both on a centralized and an urban scale, and potentially create new working relationships with other countries in the region, such as South Africa, that are also pursuing the development of renewable energy generation (Roelf 2017). The deployment of rooftop solar in Lusaka could enable it to be the first city on the continent entirely powered by this means, while the additional centralized solar generation could result in Zambia having a notable level of installed renewable sources relative to other African nations. These two feats would reinforce Zambia's expertise in this sector, making it an attractive market for foreign investment, and helping to increase an already rapidly growing GDP.

Additionally, the successful implementation of the 70/30 approach would strengthen Zambia's technical knowledge capital in renewable energy, and create the opportunities for entrepreneurial activities and the building of innovative energy enterprises. We have been struck by the desire of students and other young people to find ways to participate in, and eventually lead, these organizations. This reflects trends and opportunities across other infrastructure sectors, such as transportation and housing, where Africa could leapfrog approaches to infrastructure used in the developed world (Metcalfe 2018). There is an immediate mandate for engineering schools in Zambia and sub-Saharan Africa to include these entrepreneurship and leadership skills in their engineering curriculum plans, as they adapt them to the substantial challenges – and opportunities – facing Africa in the twenty-first century (Ibrahim, Luo, and Metcalfe 2017).

6.5   Conclusion

Zambia's dependence on hydro generation for electricity has left it exposed to climate fluctuations and drought, resulting in significant electricity deficits and economic implications in recent years. As discussed in this chapter, Zambia has the resources needed to address its generation shortage, but they need to be cultivated in the most effective manner. This chapter recommended that the optimal solution is a hybrid approach for incremental generation of 70 percent centralized solar generation and 30 percent decentralized solar generation (90 percent off-grid and 10 percent on-grid) between now and 2030. This approach diversifies the sources of energy and recognizes renewables can play a part in bridging the gaps that are sure to materialize, while realistically appreciating the capacity and power of centralized approaches. This approach would not only mitigate the nation's impending electricity crisis, but additionally, it might effectively be applied to African countries facing similar challenges. In the right circumstances it could position Zambia as a continental leader in renewable energy and create a base for renewable energy proliferation in Africa over the coming decades. However, while the opportunity may be there, making it happen will be a significant undertaking, given it requires bridges to be built between various large-scale players and fledgling start-up enterprises.

Although this chapter assumed the unlikely occurrence of Zambia experiencing fifteen consecutive dry years between 2015 and 2030, research has indicated that sub-Saharan Africa will experience more drastic and intense precipitation patterns over the coming years. So, while there may not be a fifteen-year shortage of electricity, there will be shortages over prolonged periods of months and years that will need to be addressed. Although this chapter will likely not directly influence policy, we hope that it initiates discourse and additional research around the most sustainable ways for African countries heavily impacted by climate change, such as Zambia, to address electricity shortages and build a resilient energy sector.

Acknowledgments

This work was conducted at the University of Toronto, Faculty of Applied Science and Engineering. It was supported through the Division of Engineering Science and the Department of Civil Engineering, and through the Engineering Education for Sustainable Cities in Africa (EESC-A) project, which is funded by the University of Toronto through the Dean's Strategic Fund, the Connaught Global Award, and the Learning and Education Advancement Fund. The authors and our collaborators greatly appreciate this institutional support.

Appendix 1
6A.1 Existing and Planned Generation

Table 6.7 *Existing and planned large hydro projects in Zambia with dry-year capacity factors (Energy Regulation Board 2015; Miketa and Merven 2013)*

Large hydro project name	First year	Capacity (MW)	Dry season C.F. (IRENA)
Kafue Gorge	Existing	990	36%
Kariba North	Existing	720	Not available
Kariba North Extension	Existing	360	29%
Victoria Falls	Existing	108	Not available
Kalungwishi	2018	220	30.1%
Kafue Gorge Lower	2019	750	35.5%
Lunsemfwa	2018	255	39.6%
Devil's Gorge	2019	500	44.9%
Batoka Hydro Power Project	2020	1,200	44.9%
Itzehi-Tezhi Power Plant	Existing	120	42.4%
Mumbotula Fall	2021	301	44.9%
Mpata Gorge	2023	543	44.9%
Mambililma Falls	2025	326	44.9%
Total		**6,393**	**39.7%**

Table 6.8 *Existing and planned small hydro projects in Zambia with dry-year capacity factors (Energy Regulation Board 2015; Miketa and Merven 2013)*

Small hydro project name	First year	Capacity (MW)	Dry season C.F. (IRENA)
Lusiwasi	Existing	12	44.9%
Chishimba Falls	Existing	6	Not available
Lunzua River	Existing	14.8	Not available
Shiwang'andu	Existing	1	Not available
Ikelengi	Existing	0.75	Not available
Mulunguish	Existing	32	Not available
Lunsemfwa	Existing	24	39.6%
Total		**90.55**	**41.4%**

Table 6.9 *Existing and planned coal projects in Zambia*

Coal	First year	Capacity (MW)	Dry season C.F.
Maamba Collieries	Existing	300	88%
EMCO Thermal	2018	340	Not available
Total		640	

Appendix 2
6A.2 Determining the Cost of Centralized Generation

As the NREL study mentioned in the chapter only contained pricing data for projects up to 100 MW, the cost of a solar project greater than 100 MW in Zambia was determined by segmenting the project into multiple 100 MW projects (Fu et al. 2016). For example, if a project was 400 MW, for pricing purposes it was broken into four 100 - MW projects to determine the project price. A linear regression model based on the NREL data, seen in Figure 6.9, was used to estimate the price for projects between 1 MW and 100 MW in size.

Although the NREL cost estimate is approximately 30 percent lower than that provided by IRENA for Africa, it is like values provided by IRENA for the global average cost of utility solar per watt (Taylor et al. 2016). Furthermore, although the cost of utility solar is currently higher in Africa relative to the global average, IRENA projects that costs will decrease as the solar PV market in Africa matures and competition

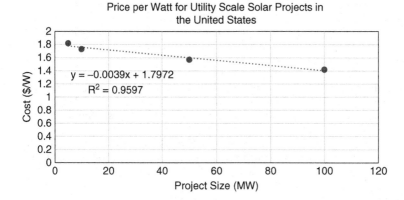

Figure 6.9 Linear regression cost model for utility-scale solar PV

increases (Taylor et al. 2016). It is therefore likely that the cost of utility-scale solar PV in Africa converges with the average global cost over the coming years, which, according to a report by IRENA, will be $0.63/W by 2025, more than a 50 percent reduction of the current cost provided by NREL (Taylor et al. 2016). So, although the NREL cost value used in this analysis is lower than the cost seen currently in Africa, it is likely a conservative estimate for the cost of solar power in Zambia over the next fifteen years.

References

Adams, R. (2017). There's less to Tesla's big Australian battery deal than meets the eye. *Forbes* [Online]. www.forbes.com/sites/rodadams/2017/07/07/mega hype-over-tesla-battery-capable-of-providing-nameplate-power-for-less-than-80-minutes/#4e97ddb54919

Africa-EU Renewable Energy Programme. (2015a). Zambia – renewable energy potential. *RECP.* [Online]. www.africa-eu-renewables.org/market-informa tion/zambia/renewable-energy-potential/

Africa-EU Renewable Energy Programme. (2015b). Zambia overview. *RECP.* [Online] www.africa-eu-renewables.org/market-information/zambia/

Africa-EU Renewable Energy Programme. (2015c). Zambia: Renewable energy potential. *RECP* [Online]. www.africa-eu-renewables.org/market-information/ zambia/renewable-energy-potential/

African Review. (2014). University of Zambia to establish solar laboratories. *African Review* [Online]. www.africanreview.com/energy-a-power/renewables/ university-of-zambia-to-establish-solar-laboratories

African Review of Business and Technology. (2015). Aurecon secures Lusaka grid overhaul contract. *African Review* [Online]. www.africanreview.com/ener gy-a-power/transmission/aurecon-secures-lusaka-grid-overhaul-contract

Anon. (2016). *World land cover ESA 2010* [Online]. Available at: www.arcgis.co m/home/item.html?id=7173340debc240a9b7ee5aec230e099c

Barbose, G. and Darghouth, N. (2016). *Tracking the sun IX: The installed price of residential and non-residential photovoltaic systems in the United States*. Berkeley, CA: Lawrence Berkeley National Laboratory.

Bariyo, N. (2015, August 3). Zambia copper producer halts production over power shortages. *Wall Street Journal* [Online]. www.wsj.com/articles/zambia-copper-producer-halts-production-over-power-shortages-1438613847

BBC. (2016). Zambia's drought hits honey farmers. *BBC News* [Online]. http://www.bbc.com/news/business-37128951

Byrne, J., Taminiau, J., Kurdgelashvili, L. and Kim, K. N. (2015). A review of the solar city concept and methods to assess rooftop solar electric potential, with an illustrative application to the city of Seoul. *Renewable and Sustainable Energy Reviews* 41 (January): 830–844.

Castellano, A., Kendall, A., Nikomarov, M., and Swemmer, T. (2015). *Brighter Africa: The growth potential of the sub-Saharan electricity sector*. McKinsey and Company.

Chutel, L., (2016). *Zambia plans to have sub-Saharan Africa's cheapest solar power*. *Quartz Africa* [Online]. http://qz.com/700187/with-hydropower-running-dry-zambia-turns-to-the-sun/

Couture, T. D., Cory, K., Kreycik, C., and Williams, E. (2010). *A policymaker's guide*. Golden, CO: National Renewable Energy Laboratory.

D'Agostino, A. L., Lund, P. D. and Johannes, U. (2016, February 23). The business of distributed solar power: A comparative case study of centralized charging stations and solar microgrids. *Wiley Interdisciplinary Reviews: Energy and Environment* 5(6): 640–648.

Electricity Regulatory Authority (2016). *Uganda renewable energy feed-in tariff (REFIT)*. Kampala: Electricity Regulatory Authority.

Elmer Hansen, U., Brix Pedersen, M., and Nygaard, I. (n.d.) *Review of solar PV market Ddevelopment in East Africa*. Roskilde, Denmark: UNEP Riso Centre, Technical University of Denmark.

Energy Regulation Board. (2015). *Statistical bulletin 2015*. Lusaka: Energy Regulation Board.

European Union. (2016). *Support to the Zambia energy sector: increased access to electricity and renewable energy production*. European Union [Online]. https://ec .europa.eu/europeaid/sites/devco/files/aap-financing-zambia-c-2016-5043-an nex1_en.pdf

Fant, C., Gebretsadik, Y., McCluskey, A., and Strzepek, K. (2015, April 18). An uncertainty approach to assessment of climate change impacts on the Zambezi River Basin. *Climatic Change* 130(1): 35–48.

First Solar. (2018). *First solar overview*. [Online] www.firstsolar.com/en/About-Us/Overview

Fu, R., Chung, D., Lowder, T., et al. (2016). *U.S. solar photovoltaic system cost benchmark: Q1 2016*. Golden, CO: National Renewable Energy Laboratory (NREL).

Future Climate for Africa. (2016). *Baseline assessment for Lusaka – Prepared for FRACTAL*. Cape Town: FRACTAL.

Gil, N. and Pinto, J. (2017). *Between accountability and ambition: Organizational duality in public goods provision in emerging markets*. Manchester: University of Manchester.

Hill, M. (2015, September 22). Zambia's electricity shortfall widens to half of peak demand. *Bloomberg* [Online]. www.bloomberg.com/news/articles/2015–09-22/zambia-s-electricity-shortfall-widens-to-half-of-peak-demand

Hoornweg, D. (2015). *A cities approach to sustainability*. Phd thesis. Toronto: University of Toronto.

Ibrahim, N., Luo, C., and Metcalfe, M. (2017). *Developing Africa's future city engineers*. Proceedings of the Development and Investment in Infrastructure (DII) Conference Series, Johannesburg.

International Finance Corporation (2016). Scaling solar delivers low-cost clean energy for Zambia. *IFC*. www.ifc.org/wps/wcm/connect/news_ext_content/if c_external_corporate_site/news+and+events/news/scaling+solar+delivers+lo w+cost+clean+energy+for+zambia

International Renewable Energy Agency (2013). *Zambia renewable readiness assessment 2013*. Abu Dhabi: International Renewable Energy Agency.

Jacobson, M. Z., and Delucchi, M. A. (2009, November 1). A path to sustainable energy by 2030. *Scientific American*: 58–65.

Kabir, M. H., Endlicher, W., and Jägermeyr, J. (2010). Calculation of bright rooftops for solar PV applications in Dhaka Megacity, Bangladesh. *Renewable Energy, August*, 35(8) (August): 1760–1764.

Kemausuor, F., Atkins, E., Adu-Poku, I., and Brew-Hammond, A. (2014). Electrification planning using Network Planner tool: The case of Ghana. *Energy for Sustainable Development* 19 (April): 92–101.

Kenning, T. (2017). Zambia's IDC prequalifies 12 bidders for 300 MW solar auction. *PV Tech*. www.pv-tech.org/news/zambias-idc-prequalifies-12-bid ders-for-300 mw-solar-auction

Khandker, S. R., Samad, H. A., Sadeque,Z. K. M. et al. (2014). *Surge in solar-powered homes: Experience in off-grid rural Bangladesh*. Washington DC: The World Bank.

Khan, J., and Arsalan, H. M. (2016). Estimation of rooftop solar photovoltaic potential using geo-spatial techniques: A perspective from planned neighborhood of Karachi, Pakistan. *Renewable Energy* 90 (May): 188–203.

Levin, T., and Thomas, V. M. (2011, December 5). Least-cost network evaluation of centralized and decentralized contributions to global electrification. *Energy Policy* 41:286–302.

Levin, T., and Thomas, V. M. (2013). A mixed-integer optimization model for electricity infrastructure development. *Energy Systems, March* 4(1):79–98.

Levin, T., and Thomas, V. M. (2016, February 4). Can developing countries leapfrog the centralized electrification paradigm? *Energy for Sustainable Development* 31: 97–107.

Lusaka Times. (2017a). French company secures 25-year power purchase agreement for a 54 MW solar project in Zambia. *Lusaka Times* [Online].

www.lusakatimes.com/2017/03/14/french-company-secures-25-year-power-purchase-agreement-54-mw-solar-project-zambia/

Lusaka Times. (2017b). Rural Electrification Authority gets $26.5 million credit facility from World Bank. *Lusaka Times* [Online]. www.lusakatimes.com/2017/11/21/rural-electrification-authority-gets-26–5-million-credit-facility-world-bank/

Maehlum, M. A. (2014). Solar panels and installation time. *Energy Informative* [Online]. Available at: http://energyinformative.org/solar-panels-installation-time

Mail and Guardian Africa. (2016, April 9). Hunger, power cuts deal Zimbabwe, Zambia severe blow as Lake Kariba hits record low. *Mail and Guardian Africa* [Online]. http://mgafrica.com/article/2016–04-09-hunger-power-cuts-deal-zimbabwe-zambia-severe-blow-as-lake-kariba-hits-record-low

McKibben, B. (2017, June 26). The race to solar-power Africa. *The New Yorker* [Online]. www.newyorker.com/magazine/2017/06/26/the-race-to-solar-power-africa

McPherson, M., Ismail, M., Hoornweg, D., and Metcalfe, M. (2018). Planning for variable renewable energy and electric vehicle integration under varying degrees of decentralization: A case study in Lusaka, Zambia. *Energy*, 151: 332–346.

McPherson, M., Sotiropoulos-Michalakakos, T., Harvey, D. L. D., and Karney, B. (2017). An open-access web-based tool to access global, hourly wind and solar PV generation time-series derived from the MERRA reanalysis dataset. *Energies*, 10(7) (March).

Melitz, M. J., and Ottaviano, G. I. P. (2008). Market size, trade, and productivity. *The Review of Economic Studies*, 75(1): 295–316.

Metcalfe, M. (2018). Entrepreneurship and African urban infrastructure: Seeking the intersection. Presentation at the 1st International Conference on New Horizons in Green Civil Engineering, Victoria.

Miketa, A., and Merven, B. (2013). *Southern African Power Pool: Planning and prospects for renewable energy.* Abu Dhabi: International Renewable Energy Agency.

Muhatia, A. (2018, January 17). Outdated policies, high taxes discourage uptake of solar. *The Star* [Online]. www.the-star.co.ke/news/2018/01/17/outdated-policies-high-taxes-discourage-uptake-of-solar_c1699093

National Renewable Energy Laboratory. (2013). *Life cycle greenhouse gas emissions.* Golden, CA: National Renewable Energy Laboratory (NREL).

Ohiare, S. (2015). Expanding electricity access to all in Nigeria: A spatial planning and cost analysis. *Energy, Sustainability and Society* 5(8) (December).

Ong, S., Campbell, C., Denholm, P., Margolis, R., and Heath, G. (2013). *Land-use requirements for solar power plants in the United States.* Lakewood, CO: National Energy Research Lab.

Onishi, N. (2016). Climate change hits hard in Zambia, an African success story. *New York Times* [Online]. www.nytimes.com/2016/04/13/world/africa/zambia-drought-climate-change-economy.html

Parshall, L., Pillai, D., Mohan, S., Sanoh, A., and Modi, V. (2009). National electricity planning in settings with low pre-existing grid coverage: Development of a spatial model and case study of Kenya. *Energy Policy*, June 37(6) (June): 2395–2410.

Republic of Zambia Central Statistical Office. (2015). *2015 Living conditions monitoring survey report*. Lusaka: Central Statistical Office.

Roelf, W. (2017). Sun, wind and water: Africa's renewable energy set to soar by 2022. *Reuters* [Online]. www.reuters.com/article/us-africa-wind power/sun-wind-and-water-africas-renewable-energy-set-to-soar-by-2022-idUSKBN1DF1T8

Sanoh, A., Parshall, L., Sarr, O. F., Kum, S., and Modi, V. (2012). Local and national electricity planning in Senegal: Scenarios and policies. *Energy for Sustainable Development* 16(1) (March):13–25.

Sanoh, A., Selin Kocaman,A., Kocal, S., Sherpa, S., and Modi, V. (2014). The economics of clean energy resource development and grid interconnection in Africa. *Renewable Energy* 62 (February): 598–609.

Scaling Solar. (2017). Zambia – testimonials. Scaling solar [Online]. www.sca lingsolar.org/active-engagements/zambia/

Secretariat. (2012). *Renewable energy technologies: Cost analysis series, wind*. Abu Dhabi: International Renewable Energy Agency (IRENA).

Singh, R., and Banerjee, R. (2015). Estimation of rooftop solar photovoltaic potential of a city. *Solar Energy* 115 (May): 589–602.

Taylor, M., Ralon, P., and Ilas, A. (2016). *The power to change: Solar and wind cost reduction potential to 2025*. Abu Dhabi: International Renewable Energy Agency.

Taylor, M., and So, E. Y. (2016). *Solar PV in Africa: Costs and markets*. Abu Dhabi: International Renewable Energy Agency.

Thiam, D.-R.(2010). Renewable decentralized in developing countries: Appraisal from microgrids project in Senegal. *Renewable Energy* 35(18) (August): 1615–1623.

Wallace, J. S. (2016). *Cost of electric power produced*. Toronto: University of Toronto.

Wheeler, D. (2008). *Crossroads at Mmamabula: Will the World Bank choose the clean energy path?* Center for Global Development.

The World Bank. (2013). *Project appraisal document on a proposed credit in the amount of SDR 70.1 million (US $105 million equivalent) to the Republic of Zambia for the Lusaka Transmission and Distribution Rehabilitation Project*. Washington, DC: The World Bank.

The World Bank. (2017). *Scaling solar. The World Bank* [Online]. www.scalingso lar.org/

The World Bank Group. (2017, December 7). *India transforms market for rooftop solar. World Bank* [Online]. www.worldbank.org/en/news/feature/2017/12/07/india-transforms-market-for-rooftop-solar

World Finance. (2016). Maamba collieries aims to bridge the power shortfall in Zambia. *World Finance* [Online]. www.worldfinance.com/infrastructure-invest ment/project-finance/maamba-collieries-aims-to-bridge-the-power-shortfall-i n-zambia

Yamba, F. D., Davison, F., Walimwipi, H. et al. (2011, June 23). Climate change/ variability implications on hydroelectricity generation in the Zambezi River Basin. *Mitigation and Adaptation Strategies for Global Change* 16(6): 617–628.

Yuan, J., Farnham, C., Emura, K., and Lu, S. (2016). A method to estimate the potential of rooftop photovoltaic power generation for a region. *Urban Climate* 17 (September):1–19.

Zambia Development Agency. (2014). *Energy sector profile*. Lusaka: Zambia Development Agency.

7   Delivering Healthcare Infrastructure and Services through Public–Private Partnerships: The Lesotho Case

Mark Hellowell

Abstract

Many governments in Africa are establishing public–private partnerships (PPPs) to provide healthcare infrastructure and services. We know very little about how healthcare PPPs are planned and implemented in Africa, and even less about the associated outcomes. This paper begins to address this gap through a detailed case study of an innovative, ambitious and complex partnership contract in Maseru, Lesotho. The scheme has been labelled 'the future of healthcare delivery on the African continent' and encompasses the design, build, partial financing and full operation of a new hospital facility alongside a wide range of core clinical services. This chapter draws on documentary data to evaluate the main features of the contract, the procurement process and monitoring arrangements and the outcomes in terms of benefits and costs. A key finding is that payments to the private operator are far higher than was expected pre-contractually, and have become a major source of budgetary uncertainty, as well as a demanding call on government's healthcare resources. We conclude that successful social infrastructure PPPs in Africa will require considerable investments in contract management skills, strong budgeting institutions and mechanisms, and enhanced (and more independent) scrutiny of plans and forecasts of financial impacts.

7.1   Introduction

Many governments in Africa are seeking to establish public–private partnerships (PPPs) to provide social infrastructure and services. There is a substantial body of research on PPPs in high-income countries, but we know very little about how these initiatives are planned and implemented in these low- and middle-income countries (LMICs), and still less about the associated outcomes. These are important lacunae given the distinctive set of challenges that long-term, complex and capital-intensive transactions may give rise to in African countries. This paper begins to address these gaps through a detailed case study of a project in Lesotho, in southern Africa. This is an 'integrated' PPP scheme (see Table 7.1) that incorporates the financing and construction of a 425-bed national referral facility (the Queen 'Mamohato Memorial Hospital), a gateway clinic and three urban 'filter' clinics alongside a comprehensive range of clinical services to be delivered over a sixteen-year period. The contract is unusual in that it combines the private delivery of new healthcare infrastructure with a wide range of clinical activities. As such, it was described as 'an innovative and sustainable model for governments across sub-Saharan Africa' by Jean Philippe Prosper, Director for Eastern and Southern Africa at the International Finance Corporation (the private finance arm of the World Bank Group), and as 'the future of healthcare delivery on the African continent' by Richard Friedland, chief executive officer of Netcare, the majority shareholder of the eventual private operator (International Finance Corporation 2010; Netcare Limited 2012). This chapter draws on documentary data to evaluate:

1. The financial, contractual and technical features of the contract
2. The structure of the market through which it was established and the adequacy of the monitoring and evaluation arrangements
3. The outcomes in terms of benefits and costs for the wider healthcare system. [1]

The article concludes with an outline of policy implications for decision-makers and practitioners in Africa.

7.2   Challenges and Opportunities of the PPP Model in Africa

The financial case for the PPP model resides in its ability to allocate the risks of delivering infrastructure and services more effectively than alternative methods. This requires that three conditions are met, all of which are dependent on the state's contractual and commercial abilities (Iossa and Martimort 2012).

---

[1] The author was part of a team of researchers that conducted an evaluation of the World Bank's role in the project as part of the Bank's *Implementation and Completion Report* (*ICR*) (World Bank 2013). Much of the data collected as part of that assignment is owned by the Bank and is not in the public domain. The case study reported in this chapter is therefore based on an analysis of publicly available data (including the *ICR* itself).

Table 7.1 *A typology of public–private partnerships in the healthcare sector*

PPP category	Common term (examples)	Definition
Service	Operating contract (Spain, Cambodia, Vietnam, UK, Nigeria; many instances of primary care contracting in various African countries).	A private operator is contracted to operate and deliver (wholly or partly) publicly funded healthcare in a publicly owned facility.
Facility/ finance	PFI, PPP, P3 (Australia, Brazil, Canada, Chile, Mexico, France, Italy, Portugal, South Africa, UK).	A public agency contracts a private operator to design, build, finance and operate a hospital facility. Most clinical services within this are provided by government.
Integrated	PPP (elective and diagnostic treatment centres in England, the 'Alzira' hospital model in Spain,[2] hospital and primary care services in Maseru, Lesotho).	A private operator builds or leases a facility and provides free (or heavily subsidised) healthcare services to a defined population.
Co-location	Co-location (England, Lesotho, Nigeria, Mexico, Spain).	A public agency allocates a portion of a hospital's land or premises for use by a private operator in exchange for payment and specified benefits to the agency.

Source: Adapted from Montagu and Harding (2012)

First, the payment to the operator must be determined by whether, and the extent to which, the infrastructure and services specified in the contract are available for use, and are at the agreed standard (Farquharson, de Mastle and Yescombe 2011). If the payment is linked to key performance indicators that are well specified and measurable, adequate arrangements are in place for monitoring and verifying performance and contractual relations are equitable between the parties (Lonsdale and Watson 2007), then failures to achieve specified outcomes should result in financial losses for the private operator. It has a strong incentive to avoid losses and, so, to deliver on its obligations.

Second, as the payment mechanism places a ceiling on the operator's total revenues, there is an incentive for the operator to minimise production costs (thereby maximising profits). A distinctive feature of PPPs is that they 'bundle' together a range of activities – the design, construction, operations and maintenance of assets, alongside a range of services – in

---

[2] A comprehensive evaluation of the globally influential 'Alzira' model can be found in Accerete, Stafford and Stapleton (2012).

a single contract, such that the operator has the *capability*, as well as the incentive, to exploit economies of scope (Iossa and Martimort 2012), e.g. by investing in innovations which lower production costs (Barlow and Köberle-Gaiser 2009).

Finally, if, in addition, the structure of the market permits an adequate level of competition between bidders, if bidders are able to foresee the opportunities to minimise production costs through the exploitation of economies of scope, and if state purchasers are sufficiently well resourced to negotiate effectively, then this incentive framework should generate downward pressure on the prices quoted by bidders, and therefore the final contract price borne by taxpayers.

The emphasis placed on risk and incentives in the financial case for PPPs reflects the fact that large-scale government investment projects are frequently characterised by higher than expected costs and/or lower than expected benefits. Flyvbjerg, Holm and Buhl (2002) attribute this to strategic behaviour by government actors in a context in which information is poor, and there are inadequate processes of independent scrutiny and challenge. For example, state planners may deliberately underestimate future costs and overestimate benefits in order to increase the likelihood that favoured initiatives are able to proceed (*strategic misrepresentation*). Other factors originate in strategic behaviour by market actors, which is facilitated by asymmetric information. For example, in a conventional procurement in which the risk of cost overruns is borne by the state, the bidder has an incentive to offer a lower price than it actually intends to charge, such that the 'wrong' bids are selected (a case of *adverse selection*). Similarly, in the post-contractual phase, the operator may take actions that reduce, in ways that the state may find it difficult to observe or counteract, the quantity or quality of output (a case of *moral hazard*).

Transferring financial risk to the operator can address some of these problems. When the operator bears a risk, it has an incentive to reduce the magnitude and severity of it. If actual production costs are higher than those the operator expected at the time of contract close and/or revenues are lower, e.g. because the quality of its services are verifiably lower than those contractually specified, it will fail to achieve its expected rate of return. This generates an accountability environment that may, more often than for alternative delivery mechanisms, lead to infrastructure being delivered on time and on budget, and human-resource practices and management that reduce the erosion of social surpluses attributable to moral hazard (Hellowell, Vecchi and Caselli 2015).

The operator of a PPP is financed with a mixture of equity and debt, but mostly debt. In cases where the costs of project delivery vary considerably from those expected at the time a deal is agreed, the operator may default on its debt, with serious implications for its shareholders and, in extreme cases, its lenders. As a result, lenders have an incentive to assess the robustness of business plans before contracts are signed, ensuring that forecasts of costs and revenues are robust, and risks are appropriately allocated. Lenders are unlikely to accept at face value the forecasts of managers and will seek independent advice when undertaking forecasting, due diligence and risk assessment. The involvement of lenders – as a source of independent scrutiny and challenge – plays a key role in addressing adverse selection, which is of benefit to shareholders and may lead to relatively good outcomes for the public sector (Hellowell et al. 2015).

However, evidence shows that PPPs provide only a partial solution to problems of strategic behaviour – on both the provider and the purchaser side. The structure of the market before and after contracts are signed has been highlighted as an important variable in determining the distribution of *market power* between the parties (Colla et al. 2015). In particular, the degree of contestability during and after the procurement process can influence the types of contract relationships that develop, the nature of operation and how the economic gains from the partnership are divided. Where it is difficult to achieve competition in procurement, or it is difficult to cancel contracts in operation, due to the absence of other providers, private operators may have significant market power, with the effect that the ability of government purchasers to safeguard their interests (and/or those of service users) is reduced within the partnership.

7.2.1   *Potential Sources of Higher Costs*

In addition to these limitations, there are several features of the PPP model which may generate additional financial costs. The most important of these are transaction costs and costs of using private capital. The majority of economic theorists examining these issues have taken a social welfare perspective when considering costs, e.g. Grout (2003); Reiss (2005); and Iossa and Martimort (2012). Hence, analysis has generally focused on whether PPPs are likely to reduce consumption of society's real resources in comparison with alternative procurement options – and has not focused on whether the prices by the government purchaser are likely to be lower (Hellowell, Vecchi and Caselli 2015). There has been very little theoretical research on the latter question, despite its relevance for decision-makers. A notable exception is Ross and Yan (2015), in which it is recognised that the government's objective may be to get a project delivered for the lowest financial cost *to the* government, rather than the maximisation of total social surplus.

7.2.1.1   Transaction Costs

The Transaction Cost Economics (TCE) framework, pioneered by Oliver Williamson (1985; 1990), has been used to provide an account of why complex contracts are likely to be associated with higher transaction costs than other forms of delivery (Lonsdale 2005). In this framework, economic actors – buyers and sellers – are seen to be constrained by bounded rationality, while the self-interest orientation of all actors is characterised by opportunism, or 'self-interest seeking with guile' (Williamson 1985, pp. 47–48). When opportunism on the part of buyers and sellers is combined with bounded rationality, either of the parties is liable to take advantage of gaps in the other's knowledge to further their interests, at the expense of efficiency (Guasch et al. 2014; Lohmann and Rötzel 2014; Qu and Loosemore 2013).

The impact of these behavioural factors on outcomes is dependent on two dimensions of the transaction: *asset specificity*, i.e. the extent to which investments by the parties are specific to the transaction, and *uncertainty*, i.e. the extent to which current objectives are subject to change. In a private finance contract, both asset specificity and uncertainty are relatively high. In the former case, both parties face considerable switching costs if they wish to withdraw from the deal (see Section 7.3 for an example). In the latter case, the duration and scope of contracts ensure that, in a rapidly changing industry such as healthcare, there is a strong likelihood of contractual incompleteness, and a need for renegotiation during the contract (Lonsdale 2005). In this context, the TCE framework predicts that the processes of contract negotiation, and of monitoring and evaluation, will be extensive and involve substantial financial costs for both buyers and sellers.

There is some empirical evidence that supports this prediction. Dudkin and Välilä (2005), for example, showed that a sample of PPPs undertaken in the UK generated higher transaction costs in the pre-contractual phase – about 10 per cent of the capital expenditure value of the project, on average, for both contracting authorities and preferred bidders, and up to 5 per cent of that value for losing bidders – than other forms of procurement. They attributed this to their longer-term character, greater financial complexity and emphasis on risk-sharing, all of which tend to increase tendering and negotiating costs, and will often lead to limited competition both *in* and *for* the market, i.e. during procurement processes.

7.2.1.2   The Private Cost of Capital

The rates of return on private capital (debt and equity) may generate financial costs that are higher than those of other delivery mechanisms

(Hellowell and Vecchi 2012). The interest cost on private finance has been an important focus of academic research and official audit (e.g. McKee, Edwards and Atun 2006; National Audit Office 2015). This is normally a multiple of the interest rate that the government pays on its own borrowing. However, it is unclear that this is a relevant comparator, since borrowing is only one source of a government's income, alongside taxes, fees, asset sales, interest on cash holdings and so on, and hence the sources of funds for the marginal project are a weighted combination of these. Determining the right approach to estimating the cost of capital for government varies according to who is doing the analysis. From the perspective of a Ministry of Finance, the cost of capital is, in economic terms, equal to the opportunity cost – the value of the *next best* alternative government project. In contrast, from the point of view of a Ministry of Health (MoH), or an individual healthcare organisation, the cost of loans from national/sub-national governments, or from debt instruments issued directly by the organisation, may be more relevant comparators.

In both cases, evidence shows that the private operator's weighted average cost of capital will often be in excess of this (Colla et al. 2015). In Africa, where domestic banks hold only short-term deposits and other liabilities, an additional problem is the high price of long-term domestic loans. Most social infrastructure projects require a repayment period of at least fifteen years to be affordable (Hellowell and Vecchi 2012). Hence, while long-term financing is essential, it is often not available in sub-Saharan Africa where, for instance, loan tenors are commonly five years or less; even where longer-term financing is available, commercial lending interest rates are typically high in comparison with prices for comparable instruments in high-income countries (Irving and Manroth 2009).

7.2.2   Government Costs and Risks

Private finance contracts generate costs for the public sector over many years, but these are not well captured by the budgeting system. In most developing countries, even a medium-term expenditure framework involves a planning horizon of just three years (Fölscher 2007). For larger infrastructure projects, the associated costs for the public sector may be low (or zero) in this period, however high they may be thereafter. The fact that the cost of projects is deferred to future budgeting periods may adversely influence the *selection, specification and scale* of investments, making it more difficult for allocative efficiency and long-run financial sustainability to be achieved. The scale of costs for government and service users that PPPs can give rise to, and their impact on sustainability, is a common theme in studies of PPPs globally (Monteiro 2013; Acerete et al. 2012; Koppenjan and Enserink 2009; Shaoul, Stafford and Stapleto 2011).

However, it is evident that, in Africa, the consequences of adverse selection may often be more severe than in the comparatively well-resourced welfare states of OECD countries.

7.2.3   Summary

The section above allows three theoretical propositions to be advanced in relation to the opportunities and challenges associated with the PPP model in Africa. The first is that, because of the financial incentives they generate, PPPs may generate positive outcomes in terms of the efficiency and quality of services delivered. The second is that positive outcomes are likely to be moderated (and adverse outcomes exacerbated) by weaknesses in the commercial capacities of the state. The third is that contract prices will be high, as finance prices are subject to upward pressure from capital market constraints, while budgeting inadequacies that fail to capture these mean that PPPs will often impact adversely on the sustainability of the state's financial position.

The following case study provides evidence in relation to these theoretical propositions.

7.3   Case Study: A Large 'Integrated' PPP for a New Referral Hospital in Maseru, Lesotho

In January 2007, the Government of Lesotho initiated the tender for a contractor to replace the ageing national referral hospital, the Queen Elizabeth II, and upgrade a network of primary care facilities. On 27 October 2008 it signed a contract with Tsepong, a consortium led by Netcare Hospital Group, a South African healthcare provider, to design, build, finance and operate a 425-bed national referral facility, the Queen 'Mamohato Memorial Hospital (QMMH), and a gateway clinic adjacent to the hospital. The project would also cover the refurbishment and re-equipment of three urban 'filter' clinics: Qoaling, Mabote and Likotsi (Vian et al. 2013) (see Table 7.2).

As at financial close, the total capital expenditure requirement of the project was estimated by Tsepong at US\$134.98 million (in 2017 dollars). In return for delivering the specified assets and providing a comprehensive range of clinical services in the hospital, Tsepong receives a *unitary fee* from the government, covering interest payments and profits for the private operator and the cost of infrastructure-related and clinical services. This is identified in the contract as

Table 7.2 *Details of funding sources, funding uses, revenues and returns*

SOURCES

	Maloti '000	%
Government grant (excl. VAT)	400,000	34.3
Commercial debt – drawdowns	589,830	50.6
Commercial debt – capitalised Interest	70,622	6.1
Mezzanine debt		
DBSA (Development Bank of South Africa)	56,207	4.8
Netcare	37,472	3.2
Shareholders' Contribution		
Local Empowerment Enterprises Equity	6,245	0.5
Netcare equity	4,164	0.4
TOTAL	**1,164,541**	**100**

USES

	M'000	%
Building costs	737,121	63.3
Equipment	208,183	17.9
Commissioning costs	98,854	8.5
Capitalised interest	70,622	6.1
Other	49,761	4.3
TOTAL	**1,164,541**	**100**

REVENUES AND RETURNS

		%
The contractually specified unitary fee	255,550	
Equity Internal Rate of Return (after Advance Company Tax)		25.2
Interest rate on mezzanine debt		13.1
Interest rate on commercial debt		11.62

Source: Government of Lesotho (2009)

US$29.61 million (in 2017 dollars). In principle, this is payable *as, when, and to the extent that* the outputs specified in the contract are delivered at the agreed standard. Independent monitors were appointed to evaluate the quality of construction and operations, and structures were established in the contract for joint oversight by Tsepong and the government. Use of the facility is free to patients at the point of delivery, except for a small co-payment (which is waived for those on low incomes) in respect of some services. These fees ultimately go to the government, though Tsepong retains 10 per cent of the fees to cover its administration costs (Vian et al. 2013).

The terms of the contract required both the government and the operator to contribute to the capital expenditure requirement (Downs et al. 2013). Direct government capital of M400 million was provided to co-finance construction, and a further M86 million was paid for improvements to the construction site itself. Private capital of M765 million financed the majority of capital expenditure. Of this, a loan provided by the Development Bank of Southern Africa (DBSA) accounted for 86 per cent of the capital expenditure, at an interest rate of 11.62 per cent. The DBSA and Netcare also provided subordinated debt, of M56.2 million and M37.5 million respectively, which accounted for 12.2 per cent of total capital expenditure. This portion of the debt, which is 'junior' to the senior tranche – so that, if Tsepong experiences a cash-flow shortfall, payments to senior debt are prioritised over those to the mezzanine debt – was provided at an annual interest rate of 13.1 per cent (Government of Lesotho 2009).

Finally, Netcare and a group of regional investors, based in both Lesotho and neighbouring South Africa, provided equity capital of M10.41 million. Of this, Netcare provided M4.16 million and local investors M6.25 million. Hence, Netcare is the largest shareholder, with 40 per cent of equity. When the contract was signed, the forecast internal rate of return (IRR) on all shareholder capital was 25.2 per cent. It should be noted, however, that actual returns may have been higher or lower than this rate, and this information is not in the public domain.

These returns are higher than is normal for comparable PPPs in the advanced economies. In the UK, for example, IRR on equity capital has been in the range of 12–18 per cent (Hellowell 2013) – and research has shown that this range has been sufficient to provide shareholders with excess returns – illustrated, for example, in high windfall profits when shares are sold in the secondary market. This supports the proposition that economic variables common to developing countries, such as capital market constraints, macroeconomic risk and political uncertainty, increase the cost of capital on PPPs in such contexts – and thus the final cost of contracts to the relevant government.

Of great importance for the evaluation of the project is its capital structure: a debt-to-equity ratio of 86/14. This is normal for a health-sector PPP in a high-income country, but high for a contract that incorporates full clinical services provision, and located in a country where experience with PPP is limited. A high debt-to-equity ratio (gearing) has various short-term advantages for the main contractual counterparties. For the public purchaser, a higher gearing lowers the operator's cost of capital and reduces the minimum fee that the operator is able to accept – since, for a given fee, the operator will achieve a higher return to equity with higher gearing. However, the fact that the operator is so thinly capitalised reduces its ability to bear risk, making it less likely that scheduled debt payments can be made if cash flows fall below the expected level. This increases the probability that the sponsor will default on its debt – an eventuality that did in fact occur, as will be described in sections below.

7.3.1   Service Provision and Operator Remuneration

The three filter clinics began operating in May 2010, and the hospital opened in October 2011. The care delivered within these facilities includes the full range of services normally expected in a referral hospital of this scale in Africa, though it omits some services that a large hospital would normally provide in a high-income context, including treatments such as transplants, joint replacements, dialysis, cardiac surgery (with the exception of emergency procedures), chemotherapy and radiotherapy, obstetrics and gynaecology, plastic surgery and dentistry (Vian et al. 2013).

The contract specifies that the operator will be paid an annual unitary fee (see Table 7.3). The fee can be adjusted if services are verifiably failing to meet basic standards, as outlined in a range of key performance indicators applying to each listed service (Vian et al. 2013). To this extent, the structure of the deal resembles that of an 'availability-based' contract as commonly used in more developed economies, such as Australia, Canada and the United Kingdom. However, a distinctive feature of this contract is that the fee can vary according to the level of activity. It can do so within defined parameters according to the extent that outputs specified in the contract are delivered by the operator.

There is a minimum number of patients (the lower-demand parameter) and a maximum number (the upper-demand parameter) to be treated per year. These parameters are broken down into inpatients and out-patients (Vian et al. 2013).[3] The contract defines the penalties to be levied if there is 'under-performance' in service provision, i.e. the number of treatments is lower than the demand parameter, and also defines the additional fees to be paid if there is 'over-performance', i.e. the number of treatments is greater than the upper-demand parameter.

---

[3] In effect, the fee is set to provide Tsepong with sufficient income to finance the functions of the business, including expected returns to equity and debt, for the actual level of activity. In health financing terms, the fee resembles a retrospective global budget rather than a prospective treatment-based payment. However, in accordance with the principle of risk transfer, this also includes an element of performance-based payment.

Table 7.3 *Demand parameters for inpatients and outpatients*

	Lower parameter	Upper parameter
Inpatients	16,500	20,000
Outpatients	258,000	310,000
Total	274,500	330,000

Source: Vian et al. (2013)

In each of the years of operation, the number of patients treated by Tsepong has been higher than the upper parameter in respect of both inpatients and outpatients. In 2011 and 2012, Tsepong chose to defer fees for these treatments. However, it has chosen to invoice the government for additional treatments performed since the beginning of 2013. Patient numbers exceeded the upper parameter by 25 per cent in that year (see Table 7.6 for the financial impact of this).

In addition, the contract defines the mechanism by which the fee is adjusted for inflation. This mechanism has two notable features. First, the index is applied to the entire fee, so that the indexed proportion of the fee is greater than the proportion of Tsepong's costs that vary with inflation (Government of Lesotho 2009). This 'over-indexation' reduces the fee in the early years of the contract, but increases the total payment to be made over the contract period, and creates a risk for the government that inflation will be higher on average than forecast at the point of financial close (while Tsepong's nominal returns are exposed if the opposite occurs). Second, the index is weighted towards the Lesotho Consumer Prices Index (CPI) and a Composite Medical Index (consisting of Lesotho CPI plus the difference between South African Medical CPIX and South African CPIX (the X standing for the inclusion of mortgage costs) (Marriot 2014), and thus fails to define a fee that is in step with Tsepong's costs.

This is a concern for the MoH because its own budget is unlikely to move in step with the fee – the key parameters of which are general and medical inflation in South Africa. Conversely, it creates a risk for Tsepong that its production costs are not reflected in the unitary fee. For example, if there are changes in the price of local labour and supplies, these may not be adequately captured in the index, with the result that the fee would be too low to finance the functions of the business. This occurred in 2013, when the government implemented a substantial increase in civil service wages, along with a re-grading process that also increased labour costs.

The implementation of these policies led to pressure on Tsepong to increase wages in an attempt to avoid the aggravation of existing recruitment and retention problems, and to maintain adequate levels of qualified staff (see Section 7.3.5 for more detail).

7.3.2   The Nature of the Market through Which the Contract Was Established

Only two consortia, both anchored by South African hospital operators, Netcare and Life Healthcare, submitted responses to the government's Request for Proposals (RfP) document (Downs et al. 2013). At the conclusion of the RfP evaluation process, it was determined that both bids had significant weaknesses and that neither was compliant with RfP objectives (Government of Lesotho 2007). As a result, on 30 October 2007, the government asked for stronger and more detailed bids for the project in a request for Best and Final Offers (RfBAFO). It is apparent from this document that the government was, at this point in the procurement process, proposing a *materially different project* from the one implemented – in terms of its nature, scale and costs, of the proportion of private financing involved, and of the annual payment that the government perceived that it was able and willing to make.

The most notable points that emerge from this comparison are:
1. In the RfBAFO, the expected total capital expenditure requirement (capex) is identified as approximately M500 million, including VAT. This is less than half the capital expenditure requirement recorded in the financial model, of M1.165 billion. Although clear evidence is lacking, it appears that the government decided to add a further filter clinic, a gateway clinic and a number of additional services, such as a neonatal intensive care unit, laparoscopy, neurosurgery, and MRI facilities, to the output specification at some point during the period of non-competitive exclusive negotiations with Tsepong, implying that the technical solutions related to these outputs, and associated prices, were determined in the absence of competition.
2. At the time of the RfBAFO, it was expected that public capital of M400 million, including VAT, would account for 80 per cent of capex. It was anticipated that only 20 per cent of the capital (or M100 million) would be raised by the operator. In the financial model of 20 March 2009, Tsepong records the proportions as 34.3 per cent public finance against 65.7 per cent private finance, or M765 million in private-sector equity and loans.

Table 7.4 *Comparison of financial values between RfBAFO and financial close*

Financial variables	Financial values expected at RfBAFO (30 October 2007)	Financial values recorded at financial close (20 March 2009)★
Capital expenditure	M500 million	M1,165 million
Public versus private financing	M400/M100 million (80% public versus 20% private)	M400/M764.5 million (34.3% public versus 65.7% private)
Expected unitary fee	180.4	M255.6

★ Note all figures are in 7 April 2007 monetary values
Sources: The Kingdom of Lesotho, New Referral Hospital Public Private Partnership, Request for Best and Final Offers, 30 October 2007; and Tsepong (Pty) Ltd, Kingdom of Lesotho, New Referral Hospital Financial Model, Financial Close Version 6.01.

3. In the RfBAFO, the government recorded its assessment of the affordable fee at M180.4 million per year, excluding VAT. In contrast, the financial model specifies the initial unitary fee (stated in 7 April 2007 terms) as M255.6 million, excluding VAT.[4]

The key points of this comparison are summarised in Table 7.4.

Clearly, these points are related: the growth in the capital expenditure requirement during the final months of negotiation increased the proportion of private financing required, and, together with certain additional services, and changes in the cost of capital, led to an increase in the initial unitary fee.

On 14 December 2007, the Netcare-led consortium was appointed the preferred bidder. This was followed by a ten-month period of bilateral negotiations, and the contract was signed on 27 October 2008, with financial close on 20 March 2009. It was during this non-competitive period that the above-mentioned changes to the scale and structure of the contract were agreed. Thus, there is a question about the extent to which the output specification and contract price can be regarded as having been competitively determined. It is notable that, in other government procurement markets, making changes of this scale during the preferred bidder process would be unlawful. For instance, under European Union procurement regulations, bidders may only 'fine tune, specify and clarify' their bids at this stage, reflecting a concern that such negotiations can undermine the degree of competition.

---

[4] Because of the 100 per cent application of an inflation index, discussed below, the actual amounts paid from the first year of operation in 2011/12 were considerably higher than this amount.

In addition, during this period of final negotiations, the DBSA changed its financing terms, from 7 to 11.62 per cent (Government of Lesotho 2009). Again, it is notable that this change – ostensibly, a result of changing base rates during the early onset of the global financial crisis – was made in the absence of any competitive pressure, either on the borrower (Tsepong) or on the lender (the DBSA).

7.3.3   The Institutional and Organisational Capacity Surrounding the Contract

The contract includes provisions for an extensive monitoring framework to assess Tsepong's performance against a large number of key performance indicators. There are five key strands to this framework:

1. An independent monitor has been employed to conduct quarterly assessments of performance, and make recommendations about the appropriate penalty (if any) to be applied to the unitary fee.
2. Internal monitoring is conducted by Tsepong, which drafts a monthly report on aspects of performance such as the volume of services provided, patient and family satisfaction, local economic empowerment indicators and staff training.
3. The Ministry of Health is allowed to monitor performance; though in practice, it has very limited capacity to do so (UNICEF and World Bank 2017).[5]
4. A Joint Services Committee, with representation from Tsepong and the government, is tasked with reviewing performance towards specified targets, and considering the case for any needed modification of the PPP agreement.
5. The private operator must obtain and maintain accreditation by COHSASA, the Council for Health Service Accreditation of Southern Africa. If Tsepong fails to maintain accreditation, the Ministry of Health has a right to terminate the contract.

(List adapted from Vian et al. 2013)

This is perhaps the strongest element of the contractual management system. In order to achieve accreditation, healthcare providers need to achieve a compliance rate of 80 per cent against International Health Standards, with all areas designated as 'critical' being compliant. The

---

[5] Currently only two full-time MoH employees manage all of its outsourced services, including the QMMH, which collectively account for over 52 per cent of the total amount it spends (UNICEF and World Bank 2017).

new hospital obtained the COHSASA accreditation for compliance in November 2013 with an overall score of 94 per cent. The three filter clinics were accredited by COHSASA earlier in 2013 with a score of 89 per cent (Vian et al. 2015). This accreditation had not been previously attained by any health facility in Lesotho, and by only one other public hospital in the region outside South Africa. The accreditation process should give the MoH comfort that the hospital is delivering a high standard of medical care. The standards required by COHSASA are considered demanding by regional standards. However, COHSASA cannot hold Tsepong to account over its delivery of the contract. This part of the monitoring arrangements can exert pressure on Tsepong to deliver high-quality care, but it cannot ensure that the incentive framework intended to be generated by the contract's payment mechanism is effective.

7.3.4   *The Outcomes from the Project: Infrastructure, Service Delivery and Budgetary Impact*

The filter clinics opened in May 2010, and the hospital in October 2011. In both cases, construction was completed ahead of schedule, indicating that the contract was successful in transferring asset-related risks to Tsepong. There is also evidence that Tsepong is delivering services of higher quality than were provided in the old Queen Elizabeth II hospital (Table 7.5).

There is strong evidence that the introduction of robust management systems and protocols have played an important role in the achievement of higher quality and quantity of care in the new facilities. For example, Vian et al. (2015) show that, at both the hospital and the filter clinic sites, new policies and guidelines have enhanced the quality of services delivery by outlining and setting standards and holding individual staff accountable for compliance.

However, there is a question about whether these positive outcomes have been driven by the payment mechanism itself or, conversely, Tsepong's willingness to perform effectively (combined, perhaps, with the need to achieve COHSASA accreditation). It is evident that the MoH has limited ability to deploy the contract as a regulatory mechanism (World Bank 2013), creating the potential for moral hazard, and undermining the incentives at the heart of the financial case for the PPP (as described above). At the same time, the project is clearly of very high strategic value for Netcare *as a multinational corporation*. At a presentation to investors in March 2012, Richard Friedland, CEO of Netcare, said of the PPP:

Table 7.5 *Comparison of clinical outcomes and productivity at the PPP in 2012 compared with equivalent measures in the former public facilities*

	PPP facilities	Former public facilities	% difference
Hospital beds	390	409	-5
Filter clinic beds	24	8	200
Total beds	414	417	-1
Inpatient admissions (hospital)	23,341	15,465	51
Inpatient days (hospital)	116,648	91,808	27
Outpatient visits (incl. filter clinics)	374,669	165,584	126
Deliveries (incl. filter clinics)	7,431	5,116	45
Average length of stay (days)	5	5.94	-16
Bed occupancy rate %	82	61	33
Death rate (incl. filter clinics) %	7.1	12	-41
Maternity death rate (incl. filter clinics) %	0.21	0.24	-10
Paediatric pneumonia death rate (hospital) %	11.9	34.4	-65
Stillbirth rate (hospital) %	3.1	4	-22
Survival of very low birth weight infants (=1,500 g) %	69.8	n/a	n/a
C-section rate (incl. filter clinics)%	26.8	7.2	272
Patient satisfaction rate (incl. filter clinics) %	86	70.7	22

Source: Adapted from World Bank (2013)

We see this [the Lesotho PPP] as the future of healthcare delivery, not just on the rest of the African continent but in our own country [South Africa] as well. (Netcare 2012)

It is surely beneficial to have in place a private operator that has a strong corporate commitment to good project performance. And it is of significance that an operator may be motivated to achieve a successful project in the absence of financial incentives to do so. One might, however, have concerns that such motivation may not be sustained over the contract period, in which, for example, corporate strategies may change as macroeconomic developments occur, and new personnel, with less personal association with the project, become influential.

7.3.5 Budgetary Impact

It is notable that the government and its advisers chose to proceed with the PPP contract, despite the increase in the annual unitary fee from the 'affordability threshold' of M180.4 million to M255.6 million during the final stages of bidding – a 42 per cent increase. Overall, the amounts paid to Tsepong by the MoH during the operation of the contract have been considerably higher than was forecast at the point of financial close. This is for four main reasons:

1. The payment is inflation-indexed. The related adjustment is applied to the entire unitary fee – and other parts of the payment – rather than only that proportion of the payment relating to Tsepong's variable costs, i.e. the costs that are affected by changes in the price level (Yescombe 2017). The result of this 'over-indexation' is to make the unitary charge lower in the early years and higher in the later years than would otherwise be the case. This factor alone led to a 68 per cent increase in the fee, from M255.6 million in 2008/09, to M439.4 million in 2015/16, net of VAT (UNICEF and World Bank 2017).

2. The unitary fee recorded in the financial model is net of VAT; but, in fact, the MoH must pay a rate of 14 per cent on the contract price (Vian et al. 2013). Hence, MoH expenditure on the contract, gross of VAT, was M517 million in 2015–16.

3. The contract sets the annual 'upper-demand parameters' at 20,000 for inpatients and 310,000 for outpatients. Treatment of patients in excess of these parameters leads to higher payments, of M9,491.64 (including VAT) per inpatient and M57 (including VAT) per outpatient. In practice, the volume of treatment has exceeded these upper-demand parameters (by several thousand inpatients, and several tens of thousands of outpatients) in every year of the contract's operation up to the latest year for which we have data (2015/16). The Ministry of Finance has not budgeted for the additional services to be paid, and it has only partially paid them or paid them with a substantial delay (UNICEF and World Bank 2017).

4. There are a number of other elements of the cost. As noted in (3), the government has not always been able to execute the payment on time, and Tsepong has the right to charge interest on any outstanding fees. In addition, there have been several instances of Tsepong defaulting on the DBSA loan, due to missed or delayed payments. As a consequence of this, the DBSA has charged Tsepong late-payment fees, and these have been passed on to the government in the form of higher costs. In addition, there remain several issues affecting the PPP that are currently under arbitration – including, among others, interest charged on late payments, some components of the payments for additional treatments, the inflation rate for patient co-payments, and the rise in health workers' salaries in 2013. In 2013, the government increased salaries for doctors (by 40 per cent), assistant nurses (by 70 per cent), and full nurses (by 50 per cent). Netcare claimed that this

Table 7.6 *Actual MoH expenditure on Tsepong*

Financial year	Invoiced amount (M)	Actual expenditure (net of VAT) (M)	Actual expenditure (gross of VAT) (M)	% Annual increase in invoiced amount	Amounts invoiced minus actual expenditure (gross of VAT) (M)	% Annual increase in actual expenditure
2012/13	435.55	409.86	463.35	–	−27.8	–
2013/14	575.3	463.58	533.41	32	41.89	13.1
2014/15	598.12	482.44	555.12	4	43	4.1
2015/16	641.99	439.42	517.01	7.3	124.98	−8.9-

Source: Invoices submitted via Tsepong to the MoH, via UNICEF and World Bank (2017)

was 'unforeseen conduct' by the government, and made a claim for compensation (UNICEF and World Bank 2017). As Tsepong is entirely dependent on the PPP contract for its income, and the level of this income is indexed by a formula that is only weakly linked to changing wages in the local market for clinical labour, it did not increase its own staff salaries equally. That has created staff recruitment and retention problems for Netcare, as well as periodic industrial action by staff. In addition, it is clear that, once settled, these issues could eventually have significant financial implications for the MoH. As Table 7.6 shows, the combination of these four factors has led to great volatility in the amounts invoiced by Tsepong. The table also highlights that there has been an increasing tendency for the MoH to pay less than the amounts invoiced by Tsepong (particularly in relation to 2015/16, in which none of the payments due for treatments above the upper-demand parameter have been paid; UNICEF and World Bank 2017). This raises the question of whether the shortfall in payments will at some stage have to be corrected, with potentially significant financial implications for the MoH.

There is a clear view among some development stakeholders that rising expenditures on Tsepong have rendered the PPP contract financially unsustainable, especially when set against the priority of addressing the burden of HIV/AIDS in the country – the prevalence of which is, at 26.4 per cent, more than four times the average for sub-Saharan Africa (UNICEF and World Bank 2017). The QMMH is not accredited to provide treatment and follow up for HIV-positive patients, though its filter clinics can do so.[6] It is also evident that from the perspective of broader efforts to strengthen the healthcare system in Lesotho, the

---

[6] HIV/AIDS is, by a considerable margin, the major cause of mortality in Lesotho, with 41.4 per cent of deaths (adults and children included) in Lesotho attributed to HIV/AIDS in 2014 (UNICEF and World Bank 2017).

decision to prioritise high-end services in the capital over rural clinics and preventive medicine is a dubious one. Overall, QMMH doctors constitute close to half of all the doctors in Lesotho (UNICEF and World Bank 2017). When accounting for district population, per capita expenditure on health in Maseru (at M995 per capita) is double the amount of the second-place district, Qacha's Nek (M460) (ibid). While there is pressure on the government to re-allocate doctors to under-served districts to ensure patients have sufficient access to needed healthcare, it is evident that the non-discretionary nature of the payment to Tsepong makes such a move towards allocative efficiency harder to achieve.

7.4   Concluding Discussion

Theory and evidence both predict that the PPP model will deliver good outcomes in terms of the cost and quality of infrastructure and services (proposition 1). However, they may create additional costs and risks for government (proposition 2) – and such adverse outcomes are likely to be aggravated when government capacity is limited and there is a lack of providers capable of delivering the contract (proposition 3). The case study outlined in this chapter largely validates these propositions. In Lesotho, new healthcare facilities were delivered on time, to budget and in accordance with the output specification. In addition, early analyses of the hospital's performance indicate higher levels of utilisation, clinical quality and patient satisfaction than pertained in the previous national referral hospital, Queen Elizabeth II. Although it is not possible to know whether the prices paid for these outcomes are higher than would have been achieved via alternative delivery mechanisms, proposition 1 is substantially borne out.

However, the case study also highlights the scale of the additional financial risks that PPPs can give rise to, and their potential to impact on the state's capacity to achieve allocative efficiency, in line with proposition 2. Further, the case supports proposition 3, which predicts that, in a context of limited government and market capacity, and ineffective scrutiny of plans for, and behaviour in relation to, the contract, such PPPs can pose a threat to the ability of policy-makers to meet their wider social objectives. In this case, the government and its advisers chose to proceed with the PPP despite strong evidence that the future costs were rising well beyond the level regarded as affordable ex ante. It is also apparent that the structure of the contract has served to generate highly volatile expenditures and a great deal of budgetary uncertainty, and is likely to continue to do so over the contract period.

Debates about whether a particular asset or service is 'affordable' are complicated by the fact that 'affordability' has no precise economic meaning. In standard welfare economics, an individual's willingness to pay for goods or service is the focus of study, and economists are generally not interested in whether someone has the ability to pay. However, in the public-policy literature, analysis of affordability normally focuses on what has to be forgone in order to obtain the goods under consideration, and whether this is reasonable or excessive. In the health sector, what is forgone may be regarded as excessive if it compromises in some way the ability of government to address priority health needs. Precise information on those forgone benefits, especially in relation to allocations to address the country's HIV/AIDS burden, is necessary to assess more comprehensively whether the costs borne by the government of Lesotho are 'affordable'.

For advocates of private-sector-oriented development policy, this is an important learning point. Private finance – and engagement with the private sector more generally – can play an important role in helping governments address their social infrastructure gap, potentially improving both investment decisions and service delivery. But this may also create avenues for self-interested state and private-sector employees to take actions that undermine the public interest. Development agencies that advocate for the expansion of PPPs in such settings should ensure that governments have adequate budgetary capacity to support the substantial expenditures that large-scale capital-intensive PPPs can generate. Governments in the African region should ensure that highly ambitious projects, such as the one studied in this chapter, proceed only on the basis of rigorous and independent scrutiny of project plans and forecasts, and that they have adequate budgetary institutions and mechanisms in place to support the expenditures generated. Major investments in these areas may be required, alongside those relating to asset delivery and the management of the project over the long term.

References

Acerete, B., Stafford, A. and Stapleton, P. (2012). New global health care PPP developments – A critique of the success story. *Public Money & Management*, 32 (4), 311–314.

Barlow, J. and Köberle-Gaiser, M. (2009). Delivering innovation in hospital construction: Contracts and collaboration in the UK's Private Finance Initiative hospitals program. *California Management Review*, 51: 126–143.

Colla, P., Hellowell, M., Vecchi, V. and Gatti, S. (2015). Determinants of the cost of capital for privately financed hospital projects in the UK. *Health Policy*, 119(11): 1442–1449.

Downs, S., Montagu, D., da Rita, P., Brashers, E. and Feachem, R. (2013). *Health system innovation in Lesotho*. San Francisco, CA: UCSF and PricewaterhouseCoopers.

Dudkin, G. and Välilä, T. (2005). Transaction costs in public-private partnerships: A first look at the evidence. EIB Economic and Financial Report 2005/03. Luxembourg: European Investment Bank.

Farquharson, F., de Mastle, C. T. and Yescombe, E. (2011). *How to engage with the private sector in public-private partnerships in emerging markets*. Washington, DC: World Bank Group.

Flyvbjerg B., Holm, M. and Buhl, S. (2002). Underestimating costs in public works projects: Error or lie? *Journal of the American Planning Association*, 68(3), 279–95.

Fölscher, A. (2007). Budget methods and practices. In A. Shah (Ed.), *Budgeting and budgetary institutions*. Washington, DC: The World Bank.

Guasch, J. L., Benitez, D., Portabales, I. and Flor, L. (2014). The renegotiation of PPP contracts: An overview of its recent evolution in Latin America. International Transport Forum Discussion Papers, no. 2014–18, George Mason University, Washington, DC.

Government of Lesotho (2007). New referral hospital public private partnership, request for best and final offers, 30 October 2007. Maseru, Lesotho: Government of Lesotho.

Government of Lesotho (2009). New referral hospital public private partnership – Financial model (v6.01). Maseru, Lesotho: Government of Lesotho.

Grout, P. (2003). Public and private sector discount rates in public-private partnerships. *Economic Journal*, 113, C63–C68.

Hellowell, M. (2013). PFI redux? Assessing a new model for financing hospitals. *Health Policy*, 113 (1–2), 77–85.

Hellowell, M. and Vecchi, V. (2012). An evaluation of the projected returns to investors on 10 PFI projects commissioned by the National Health Service. *Financial Accountability and Management*, 28(1), 77–100.

Hellowell, M., Vecchi, V. and Caselli, S. (2015). Return of the state? An appraisal of policies to enhance access to credit for infrastructure-based PPPs. *Public Money & Management*, 35(1), 71–78.

International Finance Corporation (2010). *Lesotho: New public-private partnership set to boost access to health care for the poor*. Washington, DC: World Bank Group.

Iossa, E. and Martimort, D. (2012). Risk allocation and the costs and benefits of public-private partnerships. *The RAND Journal of Economics*, 43(3): 442–474.

Irving, J. and Manroth, A. (2009). *Local sources of financing for infrastructure in Africa*. Washington, DC: World Bank.

Koppenjan, J. F. M. and Enserink, B. (2009). Public–private partnerships in urban infrastructures: Reconciling private sector participation and sustainability. *Public Administration Review*, 69: 284–296. http://dx.doi.org/10.1111/j.1540-6210.2008.01974.x

Lohmann, C. and Rötzel, P. G. (2014) Opportunistic behavior in renegotiations between public-private partnerships and government institutions: data on public-private partnerships of the German armed forces. *International Public Management Journal*, 17(3), 387–410.

Lonsdale, C. (2005). Contractual uncertainty, power and public contracting. *Journal of Public Policy*, 25(2), 219–240.

Lonsdale, C. and Watson, G. (2007). Managing contracts under the private finance initiative. *Policy and Politics*, 35(4), 683–700.

Marriot, A. (2014). *A dangerous diversion: Will the IFC's flagship health PPP bankrupt Lesotho's Ministry of Health?* London: Oxfam GB.

McKee, M., Edwards, N. and Atun, R. (2006). Public–private partnerships for hospitals, *Bulletin of the World Health Organization*, 84, 890–896.

Montagu, D. and Harding, A. (2012). A zebra or a painted horse? Are hospital PPPs infrastructure partnerships with stripes or a separate species? *World Hospitals and Health Services*, 48(2): 15–19.

Monteiro, R. (2013). *Implementing a framework for managing fiscal commitments from Public Private Partnerships*. Washington DC: The Financial and Private Sector Development Network.

National Audit Office (2015). The choice of finance for capital investment. Available at: www.nao.org.uk/report/the-choice-of-finance-for-capital-investment/ (Accessed 19 March 2015).

Netcare Limited (2012). Transcript from the results presentation for the six months ended 31 March 2012. Available at: www.netcare.co.za/Portals/0/Investor%20Relations/Financial%20Results/2012%20-%20Interim%20results/Transcript%20of%20presentation%20results.pdf?ver=2017-05-15-140106-787 (Accessed 24 November 2014).

Qu, Y. and Loosemore, M. (2013). A meta-analysis of opportunistic behaviour in public-private partnerships: manifestations and antecedents. In S. D. Smith and Ahiaga-Dagbui, D. D. (Eds.), *Procs 29th Annual ARCOM Conference*, 2–4 September Association of Researchers in Construction Management, Reading, UK, pp. 415–424.

Reiss, A. (2005). Is the PPP model applicable across sectors? *EIB Papers*, 10 (2): 10–30.

Ross, T. and Yan, J. (2015). Efficiency vs. flexibility in public-private partnerships. *Journal of Comparative Policy Analysis*, 17(5): 448–466.

Shaoul, J., Stafford, A. and Stapleton, P. (2011). NHS capital investment and PFI: from central responsibility to local affordability. *Financial Accountability & Management*, 27: 1–17.

UNICEF and World Bank. (2017). *Lesotho: Public health sector expenditure review 2017*. Washington DC: The World Bank.

Vian T., McIntosh N., Grabowski A. and Brooks B. (2013). *Endline study for Queen 'Mamohato Hospital Public Private Partnership (PPP): Draft final report*. Boston, MA: Boston University.

Vian, T., McIntosh, N., Grabowski, A., Limakatso Nkabane-Nkholongo, E. and Jack, B. W. (2015). Hospital public–private partnerships in low resource settings: Perceptions of how the Lesotho PPP transformed management systems and performance. *Health Systems & Reform*, 1(2), 155–166.

Williamson, O. (1985). *The economic institutions of capitalism*. New York, NY: The Free Press.

Williamson, O. (1990). Transaction cost economics and organisation theory. In O. Williamson (Ed.), *Organisation theory: From Chester Barnard to the present and beyond*. New York, NY: Oxford University Press.

World Bank. (2013). *Implementation completion and results report on a grant in the amount of $6.25 million to the Kingdom of Lesotho for a new hospital PPP project (p104403)*. Washington DC: World Bank Group.

Yescombe, E. R. (2017). *Public private partnerships in sub-Saharan Africa: Case studies for policymakers*. Dar es Salaam, Tanzania: Uongozi Institute. Available at: www.africaportal.org/publications/public-private-partnerships-in-sub-saharan-africa-case-studies-for-policymakers-2017/ (Accessed 1 July 2017).

8 Achieving Long-Term Financial Sustainability in African Infrastructure Projects

Anne Stafford, Pamela Stapleton and Cletus Agyemin-Boateng

Abstract

In this chapter we set out to consider what is needed to ensure that Africa's infrastructure remains financially sustainable throughout its life cycle. Managing the operational phase is at least, if not more, crucial than ensuring a project is constructed in the first place, but evaluation, particularly in relation to affordability, is weak even at the global level. We identify that in Africa there are frequently weak systems of governance, fragile and risky political institutions and lack of financial management capacity. We empirically examine five Ghanaian projects in electricity generation, water desalination, and the use of private finance to deliver and operate university buildings, to demonstrate financial and accountability shortcomings. We identify four methods that could improve financial sustainability for African infrastructure projects: namely, the establishment of independent infrastructure agencies; training and salary support of competent government technical staff; a move to more transparent decision-making; and the introduction of project monitoring and contingency planning.

Keywords: Financial sustainability, affordability, project evaluation, project choice, contract specification, performance monitoring, governance, accountability, utilities, university facilities

8.1 Introduction

Africa faces a huge infrastructure gap of around $93bn per year, with a number of difficult challenges including missing regional links, problematic economic geography and many fragile states (Foster and Briceño-Garmendia 2010). Attempts over past decades to address these challenges through the introduction of competitive restructuring and privatisation have shown that care is needed to ensure that appropriate regulatory oversight is both in place and given time to achieve effectiveness, and that many African states have not yet completed this process (Kessides 2005). In addition, institutional regulation still remains weak in many jurisdictions (Estache and Wren-Lewis 2009; Tan 2011). Further reform is still needed in many countries to ensure appropriate pricing policies are in place that properly enable the poor to access services and to balance regulatory commitment with flexibility in privatisation agreements so that there can be public confidence in infrastructure delivery (Kessides 2005). As a consequence, infrastructure investment remains risky and raising finance for infrastructure purposes is difficult. Moreover, Foster and Briceño-Garmendia (2010) note that around a third of infrastructure needs relate to ongoing maintenance costs. Inefficiencies in operation and maintenance mean that infrastructure services cost twice as much in Africa as they do in Asia and South America, with the provision of stable and affordable power supply the greatest challenge.

The development of sustainable infrastructure in Africa, therefore, depends, not only on the successful project management of complex mega-structures to construction completion, but also on the financial sustainability of the project throughout its full lifecycle. Whilst consideration of the *ex ante* case for projects and the construction phase is important, managing the operation and maintenance phase is also crucial, given that these infrastructure projects have long lives, typically cannot operate without government subsidy and, following structural reform, usually involve private finance that needs to be serviced. This chapter focuses on overall project evaluation from a financial perspective, rather than assessing projects as a series of separate milestones, in order to assess how and why problems have arisen. It then considers how better financial sustainability could be achieved.

Ensuring that projects have sustainable finances over the long term has proved to be difficult for many countries in the developed world and is, therefore, much more difficult for African governments. The fragility of political institutions in many African countries, and fragmentation across countries, means that in many cases governments are dependent on the international community for financial investment, construction capability and project and financial management know-how. The international community includes institutions such as the World Bank, global consultancy firms and Western governments with development budgets. Regional banks, notably the African Development Bank, are also important. In recent times, countries such as China and Brazil have not only expanded their financial investment into Africa, but have also brought in their own national construction workers and project managers, so retaining control of project implementation. This dependence on the international community creates a number of governance and sustainability issues for African projects.

Weak systems of governance mean that the projects put forward by the international community are not measured against appropriate benchmarks. The African context, where limited ability of users to pay is coupled with institutional inefficiencies, requires a different regulatory framework (Laffont 2005; Estache and Wren-Lewis 2009; Tan 2011). Projects can be divided into those which are necessary for economic growth, such as transport and energy, and those which bring about social improvement, such as water, healthcare and housing projects. However, rather than developing a portfolio of suitable projects to meet this economic and social need, often large 'showpiece' projects may be chosen instead, such as extensive highways and bridges, vast dam projects, or new, well-equipped hospitals. These look good for politicians, who are able to deliver on promises of shiny new roads and buildings, but do nothing to foster the development of mundane projects, such as the widespread provision of electricity, water and housing, which would raise economic and social standards for a wider group of the population.

Unlike developed economies, in which the government is perceived as low risk by contractors, many African governments tend to be seen as high-risk entities. Consequently the political uncertainty makes investment in mega-projects very difficult, as constructors will prefer less risky private-sector investment. But infrastructure investment typically needs government subsidy as a minimum, and, therefore, many African governments are reliant on international financial institutions, such as the World Bank, for investment. The amount and quality of the supporting material provided by such institutions has increased over recent years; however, the focus remains on the provision of technical documentation to follow and apply in relation to contract management, rather than on the 'softer' skills of decision-making, negotiating, challenging and evaluating, which are also important in terms of ensuring that African countries enter into infrastructure projects that are financially achievable and sustainable in the long term.

Lack of financial management capacity in many African governments means that there may be poor understanding of the true cost of borrowing finance to invest in infrastructure projects. Politicians focus on the short-term delivery of the infrastructure, but the operational period is typically in the region of twenty to forty years, in order to allow payback to the providers of finance, who increasingly come from the private sector. The cost of interest payments for projects is high, typically at least three times the original capital cost of the investment. In addition, volume and cost forecasts may not be accurate, not least due to lack of professional expertise (Tan 2011). Costs tend to be understated in business cases in order to secure project approval, leading to affordability issues once projects are operational, no matter whether it is the government or direct users who are making the payments. The consequences can be severe. Projects may be constructed but only operated for a short time, as the operator pulls out of the project, as has happened, for example, in a number of West African water projects. Only part of a large-scale project may be completed, for example, in relation to Nigerian electricity provision, where the cost of initial projects has been so high (for both the government and direct users) that further expansion to other neighbourhoods has failed to take place. The budget for other services may be cut to keep the major project running, for example in relation to hospitals, where running costs have been much higher than forecast during the procurement process, leading to cuts in primary healthcare budgets (see Hellowell, Chapter 7 in this volume).

A full understanding as to what might comprise best practice for long-term financial sustainability of infrastructure projects must, therefore, include aspects of both the practical day-to-day financial management of projects through the maintenance of suitable information systems, and also consideration of the governance and accountability systems (Shaoul, Stafford and Stapleton 2012). But the evidence to date shows us that across the globe, governments do not tend to follow good practice in relation to the financial sustainability of privately financed infrastructure projects. They avoid putting the debt on the public balance sheet (Benito, Montesinos and Bastida 2008); they do not consider the full cost of infrastructure projects (English 2006); they fail to challenge the private sector in relation to risk transfer and the high returns that that sector makes at the expense of public affordability (Edwards and Shaoul 2003); and they override their governance and accountability systems (Stafford and Stapleton 2017). These issues occur across the world, but are exacerbated in African emerging economies due to both the existence of less capacity to implement and maintain strong systems of accountability and governance, and political interference (Laffont 2005; Estache and Wren-Lewis 2009; Levy 2014).

This chapter focuses on the long-term financial sustainability of privately financed projects, considering particularly how projects are chosen; ability to pay (here we define affordability in terms of the public procurer's ability to pay, although we note that user affordability is also important in the African context); contract specification; and governance and accountability. We examine five Ghanaian projects in three different sectors to demonstrate the financial and accountability problems in the African setting. In line with the spirit of this book, we seek to 'work with the grain' (Levy 2014) towards finding 'good fit' approaches suitable for achieving better practice for financial sustainability in infrastructure projects.

8.2   Examining Financial Sustainability in Privately Financed Infrastructure Projects

To understand what makes an infrastructure project financially sustainable, we need to go beyond understanding 'success' for an infrastructure project as consisting of construction completion and operational launch. Most previous reviews have used a disciplinary perspective and either a global or a Western viewpoint, with findings relating to the context of private companies working to a lesser or greater extent with the public sector, that is, in the context of public–private partnerships (PPPs), which we define in the broadest possible way to include any arrangement where the private and public sector come together. The private sector brings extensive construction and project-management skills and know-how, plus financial investment to the project. All infrastructure projects, whether designated as PPPs or not, involve the public sector to some extent, as there is usually a regulatory role and subsidies are often an integral element of both construction and operation, meaning that a framework to provide governance and accountability for public money is required.

Initial project-management literature reviews have focused on what are seen to be the critical success factors, which have included the need for a stable investment environment, projected financial and economic viability and appropriate risk allocation (Zhang 2005; Li et al. 2005). A small number of African reviews fit into this category. Eberhard et al. (2011) identify the factors listed above as important in their analysis of success factors in the power industry, as do Montgomery, Bartram and Elimelech (2009) in their review of the rural water industry. Osei-Kyei and Chan (2015, 2016) examine the success and failure factors for a number of African transport and infrastructure projects, noting in addition to the previous factors the importance of a high level of participation by local investors. More critical commentary comes from Flyvbjerg (2014), who notes that mega-projects are increasing in size and frequency, but not in terms of performance, which he describes as 'dismal', with higher costs and fewer benefits than anticipated. In effect, Value for Money (VFM), that is, purchasing at the minimum price to achieve the maximum efficiency and effectiveness, tends not to be achieved in practice.

There have been various international calls for a wider evaluation of long-term infrastructure contracts which go beyond the monitoring of whether narrow utilitarian outcomes are achieved (Broadbent and Laughlin 2003; Hodge and Greve 2007; Jeffares, Sullivan and Boivard 2013) and which assign more importance to political and governance dimensions (Skelcher 2010; Hodge and Greve 2017). However, Hodge and Greve (2017) confirm that most analysis of financial performance has been based on *ex ante* business cases rather than actual operational performance, with few empirical studies available. They agree with Hare's (2013) assessment that available evidence assessing financial performance is mixed, in that some groups, notably practitioners, claim policy success, whilst academics are more sceptical. Financial evaluation of privately financed infrastructure projects in African countries, or in emerging economies more generally, is extremely sparse.

Given this chapter's focus on the financial sustainability of infrastructure projects, our review concentrates on evaluation of the financial aspects, including project choice, contract specification, operating costs and governance and accountability of infrastructure projects, together with wider consideration of political and governance dimensions.

8.2.1   *Project Choice and Cost Projection*

We would expect to see evidence of planning for infrastructure spending at government level, although the detail and transparency of plans are dependent on the prevailing political economy. African countries dependent on World Bank or other international financial institution financing need to develop plans identifying the need for, and benefits to be delivered by the project, as well as an assessment of affordability. Usually a financial model is used to assess project viability, therefore giving the impression of efficiency and rational decision-making. However, the methodology for calculating *ex ante* project costs has some widely recognised flaws, not least because it is known to be malleable and subject to political influence. The figures used for input to financial models are by necessity forecasts, which can be inaccurate in terms of both projected usage and costs. Forecasting is known to often be over-optimistic or to contain errors (Flyvbjerg, Skamris Holm and Buhl 2005; Bain 2009). The UK National Audit Office (NAO 2013) noted over-reliance on quantitative model outputs rather than a tendency to also consider a wider range of qualitative features and exercise judgement.

Significantly it reported that the UK, a world leader in the use of private finance, still has insufficient data on project performance to underpin the main assumptions in the financial model.

Risk assessment is another important part of infrastructure cost, both for the government and for any private partner. Macro-level risks, which include regulatory, network and political risks (Quiggin 2004; Li et al. 2005), can be problematic due to the level of uncertainty characterised by typical infrastructure projects (Lonsdale 2005a). Project-specific risks, such as the construction risk, can be transferred to the private-sector partner, who is expected to manage them better than the public sector, so that costs should be lower. For PPPs, volume-based risks, such as demand risk, may be transferred to the private partner but may not transfer as anticipated, particularly if actual volumes are significantly different to forecasts. Risk assessment is also a consideration for the providers of finance, whether they are private lenders or an international financial institution, such as the International Finance Corporation (IFC). Financiers seek a favourable balance between risk and returns and this influences the nature of PPP agreements over the needs of public stakeholders (Asenova and Beck 2010; Demirag et al. 2010). A particular concern is that too much emphasis may be placed on risk allocation rather than on ensuring that projects are affordable over the long term.

In terms of good practice, the UK's NAO (2009) notes that whilst private finance can deliver benefits, it is not suitable at any price or in every circumstance. It suggests that the public sector should do more to act as 'intelligent customers', using the four key enablers of accurate data; skills, capacity and experience; effective accountability; and project assurance, as well as the ability to strike strong deals (NAO 2011). A good example is Farooqi and Siemiatycki's (2012) report on key findings from a case study of 28 VFM evaluations in Ontario, Canada, which finds that the planning process in Ontario weights political risk very highly. Some projects that could demonstrate technical delivery of VFM through transfer of revenue and operation risk have not been permitted to go ahead for political reasons. Instead, VFM appraisal is used to confirm that the PPP model is the correct decision, for example, the transfer of construction risks from government to private-sector partners drives VFM results.

8.2.2   Contract Specification

Good contract specification is crucial to ensure that both parties are clear on the facilities and services to be delivered, how these will be monitored and measured, what the payment mechanisms are and what penalties will be instigated for non-compliance. Given that contracts are both legally binding and necessarily incomplete due to the long time frame, good contract negotiation and monitoring are needed from the government side. However, as such contracts are often 'one-offs' from the government perspective, there may be a lack of skills and public resources, both in negotiating appropriately and then monitoring and using performance data. This means that contracts may not set out all the necessary information, for example, how operating risks are to be allocated between parties or how penalties are to be applied (Edwards et al. 2004).

8.2.3   *Cost of Operational Projects*

Public–private partnerships have long lives and costs must be affordable over the long term. There may be a need to pay back the capital cost, depending on how the project is financed, plus cover maintenance costs. This means there is the potential for affordability problems, especially where availability fees, which include the high cost of finance, must be paid. Projects also need to be managed efficiently over their operational lifetime. Creating good working conditions between public and private partners is challenging. Studies on UK and Irish projects found that co-operative working was limited and managers had to deal with supplier opportunism (Lonsdale 2005b; Reeves 2008; Stafford and Stapleton 2017), although English and Baxter (2010) found that in an Australian prisons case trust between partners developed over time. Issues included poor transparency and restricted access to contract detail, a lack of skills and public resources devoted to monitoring and using performance data, payment mechanisms which do not deliver budget certainty nor mitigate against costs to the public sector and numerous conflicts of interest. Many individual studies report the difficulties of *ex post* risk management (Edwards and Shaoul 2003; Shaoul 2003; English 2005; English and Walker 2004; Hodge 2004).

Studies of healthcare PPPs, especially Spanish exemplars, indicate that competent learning from cross-national experience is complex, as close attention to the nature of institutional factors and operational costs is necessary (Acerete, Stafford and Stapleton, 2011, 2012; Acerete et al. 2015). These studies differ from wider assessments, such as the European health observatory (Rechel et al. 2009), in that they pay closer attention to the underlying finances. Here, findings show that the expected costs of UK Private Finance Initiative (PFI) hospitals and roads, and Spanish roads, are higher than anticipated (Shaoul, Stafford and Stapleton 2008; Acerete, Shaoul and Stafford 2009; Acerete et al. 2010) and that returns to the private sector are excessive (Hellowell and Vecchi 2012; Vecchi,

Hellowell and Gatti 2013). This is despite risk transfer being lower than expected, and minimal in some cases, with government guarantees provided.

It is difficult to empirically determine in financial terms that a project has delivered VFM. This would require a calculation over the whole life of a PPP, with a comparison to an identical project acquired through conventional public procurement. Due to the long length of PPP contracts, we have not yet reached this point in time, even assuming we can find suitable public-sector comparators. Some evidence from a study of two terminated UK crossings (Shaoul, Stafford and Stapleton 2011) shows that accurate forecasting of volumes and the provision of extra infrastructure at low or no cost to the project is key: the Dartford Crossings project, an early form of PPP-style contract, was successful due to high, and higher than expected, traffic flows; low and stable tolls; and the opportunity for the private sector to collect tolls from previously toll-free infrastructure, where the assets were transferred across as part of the project deal. In contrast, the low-volume Skye Bridge project was a failure, costing the Scottish government £7 m in subsidies and £27 m to terminate early. The estimated additional cost of private finance was £18 m. These projects add further weight to the argument that, once all elements are considered, infrastructure contracts are expensive in terms of what they deliver.

8.2.4 Governance and Accountability of Infrastructure Projects

Proper systems to evaluate governance and accountability of public infrastructure are important for ensuring that governments are held to account for public spending. In a democratic country, the people should be able to see that expenditure has been made as intended by government. Infrastructure projects mean that very large sums of public money are being spent, a large proportion of which may be outside the control of the public sector. Moreover, as English et al. (2010) note, effective evaluation should not just take the form of a passive watchdog noting compliance, but should take on the role of a sheepdog, containing a coaching and mentoring role to drive improvement.

But the evaluation systems in place fall short. The UK's NAO and the Australian state audit offices, in particular, do carry out evaluation, but on an ad hoc basis. The UK NAO has commented on the lack of a 'truly robust and systematic evaluation of actual performance' of PFI projects at either project or programme level (NAO 2009), whilst in Australia gaps in governance and contract management limit assurance and visibility of operational effectiveness of infrastructure projects (VAGO 2013). From an academic perspective, English (2007), in relation to Australian projects, and Edwards et al. (2004) and Shaoul, Stafford and Stapleton (2007; 2008), in relation to UK shadow toll roads and hospitals, report an over-focus on technical, systems-based compliance, rather than evaluation of *ex post* risk transfer and VFM, and a lack of a routine programme for evaluation. In recent years, some frameworks for examining governance and accountability have been developed (Demirag and Khadaroo 2011; Shaoul, Stafford and Stapleton 2012), but as yet, have been little used. Findings are patchy and context-specific. Some findings argue that new forms of hybrid infrastructure projects can lead to more, and strengthened, accountability mechanisms in comparison to existing public arrangements (Grimsey and Lewis 2002; Willems 2014). Other studies find little overall accountability (Acerete et al. 2011) or a focus on the detail, rather than the project overview (Andrew 2007).

Overall, the public sector remains vulnerable to dependence on private-sector monitoring and performance data (Shaoul, Stafford and Stapleton 2010, 2012). The complex organisational structures make data collection very difficult, as it is hard to find, and then follow, a trail through the groups of companies and their multiple subsidiaries and related companies. There is also leeway in judgement and choice of determining level of aggregation, presentation and public disclosure of performance data. The public sector also tends to lack adequate monitoring capacity.

8.2.5 Summary

Privately financed infrastructure projects, even when successful, are costly due to high finance costs, raising questions around affordability. When they fail, the risks and costs are widely dispersed. The evidence so far shows us that there is limited data or evaluation of financial sustainability of infrastructure projects internationally, with a paucity of operational evaluation of African projects. Forecasts have proved to be unrealistic in the past, leading to higher costs and, for PPPs, less risk transfer than anticipated. Moreover the financial models used to appraise and report infrastructure projects are not neutral constructs as they have certain biases built in. Care is needed when assessing, reporting and comparing projects as robust figures are difficult to come by. Overall we need greater transparency of both process and outcomes.

8.3   Examining the Financial Sustainability of Infrastructure Projects in Africa

We now turn to examine the procuring, financing, contracting and monitoring practices used for five infrastructure projects in Ghana. The research method is documentary analysis of publicly available information, including project brochures, material available on government and project websites, and news items. Some further information was acquired through private communications. We discuss the issues raised by each mini-case and consider how an understanding and implementation of good practice could lead to more financially sustainable outcomes.

8.3.1   Procurement of an Electricity Generation Project in the Energy Sector

Africa's major infrastructure efficiency gap is in energy, where capacity runs at around 10 per cent of that elsewhere in the developing world (Eberhard, Foster and Briceño-Garmendia 2008). There is a desperate need to generate secure electricity supplies through increased capacity, rather than reliance on short-term leases for emergency power supplies (Foster and Briceño-Garmendia 2010). However, involving the private sector in the delivery of power is problematic, as institutional, regulatory and administrative processes remain weak and under-developed. Foster and Briceño-Garmendia (2010) note that whilst there are few cancellations of projects, renegotiations are common and projects are very costly.

Following public pressure due to frequent power failures, Ghana sought to alleviate its electricity supply problem by entering into a \$510 m Build Own Operate Transfer (BOOT) contract with the UAE-based Africa Middle East Resources Investment (AMERI) Group LLC in March 2015. The project was procured through sole-sourcing, which is permitted under the Ghanaian Public Procurement Act,[1] because, although it has an emphasis on competitive tendering as it helps to achieve competitive pricing and ensures VFM, the checks and balances mean that the normal process is necessarily lengthy. The project aimed to supply ten gas turbines, described as supplying amounts varying between 230 and 330 MW of electricity, which AMERI Group would own and operate for five years before transferring the plant to the government of Ghana. As an emergency project designed to be fulfilled within ninety days, the project was signed off very quickly with limited public transparency.

---

[1] Available at the Ghanaian Public Procurement Authority website: www.ppaghana.org/

The contract also involved a government guarantee in the form of a letter of credit for $51 m. The gas turbines then took eight months to be delivered, following which they needed to be connected into the power grid, which took another four months.

The energy policy think-tank African Centre for Energy Policy (ACEP) disapproved from the start, and an investigation by a Norwegian newspaper,[2] following up potential fraud committed by a Norwegian citizen involved as a director of the AMERI Group, led to assertions that the true cost of the project should have been $360 m, as AMERI simply subcontracted the deal at a price of $360 m for purchasing the turbines and operating them through the power network. In January 2017, a change in government led to the setting up of a commission to investigate the VFM aspects of the deal. The resulting Ministry of Energy report reviewed the agreement, found that the delay in implementing the project meant that it failed to meet the classification of an emergency project and recommended that the contract should be renegotiated, restructured and amended to take account of the fact that the cost to the Ghanaian government appeared to be grossly inflated.[3] It indicated that the difference of $150 m between the $510 m charged to the government over the five-year contract and the $360 m cost for the subcontract amounted to an excessive commission for AMERI. AMERI, though, has continued to claim that the price is fair.[4]

This project raises the issues of procurement, contract specification, VFM and affordability. The use of sole-sourcing for this project, whilst permitted under the Ghanaian Public Procurement Act for emergency projects, meant that normal public procurement practices were not followed, as they were too time-consuming. A transparent and efficient procurement process brings benefits in terms of low transaction costs, competitive pricing and VFM (Chan et al. 2009; Tadelis and Bajari 2006). The selection of bidders, criteria applied for expenses and tendering procedure can be subject to public examination and review (Beh 2010). Transparency, especially, enables the public to challenge

---

[2] See Amund Bakke Foss, Rolf J. Widerøe and Harald Henden, 'Ghana's Minister of Power signed deal with a man from Oslo wanted for fraud and organizzed crime. The deal was worth 510 million dollars', *VG*, 29 August 2018. www.vg.no/nyheter/innenriks/ghana/g hana-s-minister-of-power-signed-deal-with-a-man-from-oslo-wanted-for-fraud-and-organized-crime-the-deal-is-worth-510-million-dollars/a/23577965/

[3] Available here: 'Report on AMERI power purchasing agreement', *GhanaWeb*, 27 March 2017, www.ghanaweb.com/GhanaHomePage/NewsArchive/FULL-TEXT-Report-on-AMERI-Power-Purchasing-Agreement-522780

[4] 'AMERI insists $510 m power deal fair', JoyOnline, 20 October 2017, www.myjoyonline.com/business/2017/October-20th/ameri-insists-510m-power-deal-fair.php

unfair public officials and make them more accountable, as mistakes, errors in judgement and bad practices can be reviewed (Sarfo and Baah-Mintah 2013). However, sole-sourcing creates opportunities for abuse, and has been cited as creating avenues for corruption, including inflation of prices to facilitate kickbacks and bribery (Osei-Afoakwa 2013).

In this case, the lack of transparency about the contract specification makes it difficult to establish what might have been a good price for the contract, as prices quoted range from the $220 m quoted in the Norwegian press for the simple purchase of ten gas turbines through to $350 m as the amount paid to the subcontractor, to $440 m as the price quoted by the government at the time of the contract signing for the cost of supplying the turbines, and $510 m for the full BOOT contract. So it seems that a significant sum was included to cover the cost of AMERI financing the deal over the five-year period of the contract. However, the quick signing of the agreement indicates that little due diligence was carried out, and instead, that the government had entered into the agreement precisely because outright purchase of gas turbines as an emergency measure was not affordable. The sole-sourcing procurement route followed means that the process of project choice was circumvented, and the potential excessive cost of the project indicates a lack of oversight by Parliament in agreeing the project. Given the story was first broken by foreign media, freedom of information legislation would help national media to effectively perform its watchdog role of holding government to account.

8.3.2   Procurement of a Water Desalination Plant

Addressing Africa's water needs is another area where the continent lags behind other developing regions, such as South Asia. Banerjee et al. (2008) note that access to piped water has remained largely the same since 1990. Whilst there have been attempts to use private participation to improve water infrastructure, mainly using management or lease contracts, these have been problematic and controversial, with 40 per cent being cancelled before completion (Foster and Briceño-Garmendia 2010). Ghana was the location for an early failed contract, where urban water delivery was under a private-sector management contract (see Agyemin-Boateng 2004). More recently Accra, with a population of around 3 m, has been struggling with a water demand of around 800,000 m^3 per day, and the Ghana Water Company Ltd (GWC) has been forced to operate a system of water rationing.

In 2011, the government entered into a new $126 m twenty-five-year BOOT contract for a desalination plant with Abengoa, a Spanish company, and the Japanese Sojitz Corporation.[5] Revenue over the period was estimated to be $1.3bn. The World Bank gave the project an investment guarantee of $179 m. The aim of the project was to ensure a stable water supply for 500,000 residents of Accra at an affordable price. It was sole-sourced due to the need for quick delivery and because new technology was being used – this would be the first desalination plant in West Africa. The project has the capacity to desalinate 60,000m^3 per day. The water agreement between the GWC and the private partners requires GWC to pay for the electricity required for the plant, and to pay 6.5 Ghanaian cedi (GHc) (around $1.44) per cubic metre produced. However, sale of water to domestic customers in Ghana is regulated by the Public Utilities Regulatory Commission (PURC). Due to poverty reduction targets, tariffs are set low at 1.5 GHc (around $0.33), meaning that the GWC makes a loss of around 5 GHc (around $1.11) for each cubic metre of water produced by the desalination plant. Monthly electricity costs are estimated to be around 1.5 m GHc (around $331,000).

This case again raises the issues of procurement, especially project choice, VFM and affordability. Water desalination plants are a costly way of providing water for citizens. A controversial PPP water desalination plant, in Melbourne, Australia, completed in 2012, has added AUS$200 (around $150) a year to the water bill for each Melbourne resident, even though for the first few years no water was produced.[6] However, water desalination plants are increasingly coming to be seen as a way of drought-proofing water supply at a time when climate change is introducing increasing uncertainty over levels of rainfall, which was the rationale for the Melbourne project.[7] It is unclear what feasibility studies were carried out for the Ghana project. A further consideration in Ghana is that there is considerable unmet water demand. Although an existing water treatment plant was being expanded at the time of the project, the government was apparently able to present a strong case for the additional water desalination project given that the increased output from the existing plant would still be insufficient to meet demand. However, in contrast to the business case presented for the Melbourne

[5] 'Ghana Water losing GHc6m monthly to Teshie desalination plant', Citi FM Online, 2 October 2017, http://citifmonline.com/2017/10/02/ghana-water-losing-ghc-6m-monthly-to-teshie-desalination-plant/.

[6] J. Ferguson, 'Billions in desalination costs for not a drop of water', *The Australian*, 18 October 2014: www.theaustralian.com.au/national-affairs/billions-in-desalination-costs-for-not-a-drop-of-water/news-story/1dc59f33b788c609e67c001786048fca.

[7] For the Victorian Desalination Project, see: www.dtf.vic.gov.au/sites/default/files/2018-01/Project-Summary-for-Victorian-Desalination-Project.pdf.

plant, the lack of transparency around PPP projects in Ghana means that details must be gleaned from the media.

Affordability for both the citizen and the government are concerns for this project. The citizen is protected by PURC, which sets the tariffs charged by the GWC. However, given that GWC is a national company, it stands to reason that citizens in other parts of the country, where water supply is profitable for GWC, must be subsidising this project. Of more concern is the financial pressure that this unsustainable contract is putting on the GWC. Assuming the plant is working to capacity, each month it is subsidising the contract by GHc 300 m ($67 m). Moreover, the desalination technique is power-hungry. The media report that the GWC is unable to pay its monthly electricity bill of around GHc 1.5 m ($330 k), meaning that the electricity company is also in financial straits. In addition, under the terms of a BOOT contract, the public sector is required to pay an availability fee to the private-sector partner and the media report that, as GWC has been unable to pay this fee, a large debt is building. It is therefore likely that this project will need to go into renegotiation in order for it either to be restructured to put it in a sustainable financial position going forward, or cancelled, so that the investment and associated charges can be repaid. Such an event will require input from the World Bank, who provided an investment guarantee. The poor financial sustainability evident from the start of operations raises questions about the quality of the oversight and governance of the choice of investment, and the decision-making process, in particular as to who should bear responsibility for ensuring that forecasts are realistic, and that projects are economically affordable. Given that other examples of failed private provision of water and electricity supply in Africa exist, for example, Estache and Wren-Lewis's (2009) description of failure in the privatisation of water and electricity in Mali, and the previous failure of a water contract in Ghana (Agyemin-Boateng 2004), it is clear that there is very limited learning taking place.

8.3.3 University Procurement Using Private Finance

Here we examine three infrastructure projects relating to the University of Ghana. Information sources include publicly available information from news websites, supplemented by some privately obtained information, including cost projections and conversations with relevant parties. The issues addressed include project procurement, contract specification, operational costs, monitoring and accountability.

8.3.3.1   Using Private Finance to Build Student Accommodation and Related Service Delivery

In the mid-2000s, the University of Ghana cited an acute shortage of student residential accommodation and inadequate public funding as the reasons for using private funding to build additional student accommodation. The university set up a new shell company, which entered into a partnership with a private shell company set up to deliver new student accommodation through a thirty-five-year Build Operate Transfer (BOT) contract. The private company engaged a consortium of six banks to fund an equivalent of $26 million for the development of hostel facilities for the university. The university provided an equivalent of approximately $4 million through its shell company.

The new accommodation was built and made available to students to rent. However, the project soon ran into financial difficulties. In order to recover the cost of the investment, the private company had to charge a rental of around three times as much as the rent for the old university-financed accommodation, although students found little difference in terms of quality of facilities and services between the two sets of accommodation. But the university management did not allow the private company to charge the full economic rent and, consequently, it will be unable to recoup all the investment made within the thirty-five-year time frame stipulated in the contract. Moreover, the company claimed that it was unable to rent all the rooms.

This led to a renegotiation of the contract very shortly after inception, as the initial contract signed between the two contracting parties failed to anticipate future problems and, therefore, had no available remedies to solve such problems as they occurred. As the contract failed to deal with situations whereby the private partner was unable to earn enough to finance the debt and repay it at the end of the contract, the private company had no option but to renegotiate with the university for a new agreement. The outcome saw the conversion of the BOT contract to a lease contract between the private company as the lessor and the university as the lessee.

Whilst renegotiation of PPP contracts is not new, and may come in different forms (see Whitfield 2010), the change from the initial BOT agreement to a lease agreement appears as problematic and bad business for the public-sector partner, namely, the university. The BOT contract would have led to the university becoming the owner of the accommodation when the contract ended after a period of thirty-five years. The BOT contract also saw demand and operations risks transferring from the university to the shell company. With the university becoming a lessee, it now bears the risks and associated costs of under-occupation and maintenance.

There was poor monitoring of the contract implementation. Evidence from publicly available documents suggests that a claim made by the CEO of 'reduced patronage of students for the accommodation' is arguable. This is because, every year, the private company puts notices in front of its main office on the university campus and on the notice boards of its accommodation blocks to inform students that there are no available rooms to rent out. This evidence indicates that if the university had critically analysed the main reason given by the private company for the change in agreement, it would probably have refused to renegotiate on the terms proposed by the private sector, and thus it could have maintained the initial BOT agreement. However, the university failed to perform its responsibility, showing a clear lapse in the management of the said contract.

Ineffective contract management is a public accountability challenge (Forrer et al. 2010; Andon 2012; Fombad 2013). Thus, the manner in which the PPP is overseen and managed during implementation is important for its success. Anything short of that may undermine the objectives of the contract, including any desire to achieve VFM (Demirag and Khadaroo 2008; Andon 2012). In other words, for the aims of the PPP to be realised, the contracting authority must play its crucial contract management role from the inception of the project, and on throughout its remaining life.

8.3.3.2   *Using Private Finance to Deliver a University Centre*

In 2015, the University of Ghana entered a $64 m twenty-five-year BOT contract with Africa Integras, the African investment arm of a US corporate, the Christie Company, to build a new centre.[8] This was designed to be an iconic symbol of progress and success for the university, creating a number of faculty buildings, plus student dorms. Whilst specific information on guarantees for this project is not available, Africa Integras usually relies on occupancy guarantees or land grants for project backing.

There are a number of fundamental financial shortcomings with regard to this project. First, it is denominated in US dollars, creating additional risk for the project due to uncertainty over movements in the currency exchange rate over its lifetime, which could impact on the guarantees given for it, as well as create long-term contingent liabilities. Second,

---

[8] See for information on the Christie Company: www.christiecompany.com/africa-integras/ and 'University of Ghana signs landmark $64MM USD PPP investment contract with Africa Integras', *University of Ghana*, 26 June 2015, www.ug.edu.gh/news/university-ghana-signs-landmark-64mm-usd-ppp-investment-contract-africa-integras.

although the loan is denominated in US$, the local inflation rate is running at around 16 per cent; considerably higher than the anticipated US inflation rate. This means that foreign currency exchange differences are likely to increase significantly over time, considerably adding to the overall cost of the project to be borne by the university. Third, costs are being incurred before the building is complete, as ground rent of $8 m is being paid throughout the construction period. As the university has no means of generating income until the buildings are complete, the rent adds to the total project cost for the university. Fourth, and most significantly, project viability is in doubt. Construction on this project stopped prior to completion and there are news reports of a dispute between the current and previous vice-chancellors of the university as to whether proper due diligence was carried out.[9] At the very least, the project shows a lack of financial capacity in the university. No business case was prepared, which would have demonstrated at least some of the financial shortcomings. There is a lack of any oversight from a relevant government body, which, again, would have identified any such shortcomings. Overall, there is little concern for stewardship of public resources.

8.3.3.3   *Using Private Finance to Deliver a University*
                Medical Centre

For this project, the university has worked with government to deliver a university medical centre using private finance. Under the government's 'innovative public debt management' programme, the government borrowed the money, which is backed with sovereign debt guarantees, and then lent the money to the company set up by the private partner to be responsible for the project. This 'innovative' transaction has the effect of cancelling out the debt on the government balance sheet, but creates asymmetrical activity as the government does not state the debt on the balance sheet, but still takes the 'credit' for getting the project built. As it has turned out, this particular project has been very expensive. No serious thought was given to the process of getting the centre up and running at capacity. Serious financial projections were only made when the construction had almost been completed and it had become clear that, on

---

[9] See 'US $64 million UG infrastructure project stalls', *GhanaWeb*, 5 December 2017, www.ghanaweb.com/GhanaHomePage/business/US-64-million-UG-infrastructure-project-stalls-606844 and 'University of Ghana's assets to be auctioned over $64 million – Napo reveals', *GhanaWeb*, 26 February 2018, www.ghanaweb.com/GhanaHomePage/NewsArchive/University-of-Ghana-s-assets-to-be-auctioned-over-64m-loan-Napo-reveals-629611.

completion, only 10 per cent of its capacity could be used during the first year of operation, although 100 per cent of the costs were being paid for. Government and the university both see successful delivery of an iconic project as a symbol of success, but both pay little attention to cost and affordability. Although in theory systems are in place for governance and accountability, they are overridden by the president and vice-president of the university.

The university BOT projects all display similar themes, whereby the provision of an iconic facility is prioritised over effective decision-making and VFM considerations. There are weak procurement practices that do not match up to the usual minimum that is required in developed economies of a robust business case. There is a lack of transparency and related oversight and scrutiny, meaning that poor decisions are being made. In financial terms, there is a failure to match costs with revenues, resulting in problems around financial sustainability and affordability. These projects highlight the need for better governance and financial management capacity in both the university and the government.

8.4 What Changes Are Needed to Make Investment Sustainable?

These Ghanaian cases highlight the complex issues that need to be addressed if Africa is to tackle its huge infrastructure gap. Structural reform means that international finance institutions increasingly require private finance to be used in infrastructure projects, in order to make up the infrastructure deficit referred to at the start of this chapter. Projects such as ensuring a secure electricity supply are essential for economic growth, whilst a stable water supply is needed for social development. But too often, too much is spent on vanity projects and/or on projects where the finances do not stack up from the start. Whilst a public procurer can enter into a number of these projects because, in the short term, there are limited upfront costs, over time, the high finance costs, coupled with the larger than anticipated running costs of projects and potential caps on user payments, mean that within a few years the project becomes unviable for the public procurer. This makes it even more difficult to afford future projects and creates a downwards financial spiral.

What has the potential to make the African situation even worse is that Western consultants and institutions continue to recommend a private finance policy that, as we have noted above, actually performs poorly in Western circumstances. Even though there are successful projects, these are delivered at a high cost, whilst the many failed projects disperse risks and related costs to many parties and users. And these findings occur in countries where there are meant to be strong institutional systems in place, meaning that governments apparently follow the required practices in terms of carrying out the necessary processes for decision-making based on a robust business case, proper implementation and *ex post* scrutiny to assure accountability. It is, therefore, hardly a surprise that African infrastructure projects reflect the same problematic outcomes, but that these are magnified due to greater challenges around politics, governance and financial sustainability in the relevant countries.

In particular, the capacity to understand and, therefore, cope with the structural and financial issues is lessened, thus increasing the chance of signing unaffordable projects. Whilst development funding has been made available for capacity-building in financial management, too often proponent investors focus on creating awareness of PPPs – in that the benefits of project delivery are sold – but the costs and VFM aspects are not well explained or understood. Indeed, often the issues of forecasting and affordability appear to be very much downplayed. Conflicts of interest abound, as consultants and investors have a vested interest in encouraging governments to take up their recommended projects and, therefore, deliver a revenue and profit stream over the long term. Efforts to develop financial management capacity are underway, supported by the World Bank, the Africa Capacity Building Foundation and the International Federation of Accountants. However, low public-sector pay means that qualified staff migrate to the private sector, where pay levels are set at the market rate. In addition, finding skilled financial jobs in finance ministries is difficult as, frequently, these posts are political appointments and are occupied by unqualified staff.[10]

How then, do we find a way forward for Africa to build financially sustainable infrastructure? As noted earlier, strong systems of governance and accountability are important, as is the political context. Estache and Wren-Lewis (2009) suggest that developing models to better understand mitigation between different institutional weaknesses may lead to improved regulatory policy; for example, multiple principals may increase accountability. In relation to governance, Levy's 'with the grain' approach suggests that 'successful reforms need to be aligned with a country's political and institutional realities' (Levy 2014: 142). Rather than grand schemes aiming for complete public-sector reform, he recommends that, for African countries with highly personalised political systems, where it is the elite who are rewarded, narrower strategies targeting

---

[10] Georgina Guedes and Keith Nuthall, 'Building crucial financial management and reporting capacity isn't just about importing good practice, but ensuring it's needed and then customising it for each country', ACCA, www.accaglobal.com/uk/en/member/member/ accounting-business/2017/04/in-focus/capacity-building.html

specific issues can achieve better traction. In relation to accountability, we draw on Ostrom's notion of collective action (Ostrom 2010), whereby she moves beyond a hierarchical and confrontational principal–agent attitude to a consideration of how humans bring together their motivations and capabilities to create solutions to institutional problems. Such a concept seeks to develop a multi-stakeholder approach, where all those involved in the project have a stake in ensuring efficiency and effectiveness.

8.5   Actions to Improve Financial Sustainability

Placing the need to achieve affordable projects and financial sustainability within the context of Africa's political and governance realities, we make four interrelated recommendations for improving financial sustainability in infrastructure projects.

First, establishing an independent infrastructure agency to oversee project selection and choice. Such a move would help to develop good and efficient governance processes (UNECE 2008). Professional expertise on different aspects of infrastructure decision-making, such as finance, legal and engineering know-how, can all be located centrally and then be made available to advise on specific sectors and regional projects as required (Rachwalski and Ross 2010). Such a scheme, given that it does not require wide-scale public-sector reform, stands a greater chance of success, and a number of African countries already have infrastructure agencies set up. However, achieving independence from political personalities remains a challenge.

This is linked to the second recommendation: the need for competent government professionals, especially finance professionals, who have a good understanding from a public-sector perspective of forecasting, costing and affordability in infrastructure projects, and so can challenge potentially unrealistic projections created by private-sector contractors. At present, low pay tends to mean qualified personnel quickly leave for the private sector and the related market rates of pay. Improvements in financial management capacity can be made by careful targeting of mid-tier technical roles. To circumvent the problem of limited public funds with which to pay market rates to public officials, a small cadre of technical experts can be created who earn the market rate based on their qualifications and experience. This approach follows Levy's (2014) description of successful reform in Sierra Leone, which targeted a small number of technical professionals, whilst not aiming to reform either the top jobs (due to their political nature) or the very many at the bottom (seen as low-paid patronage jobs where market rates are not appropriate). To create such a group of well-qualified individuals, there are funds available from the World Bank and other international financial institutions, earmarked for financial management training, plus professional assistance given from global accounting institutions. Over time and with political support, public agencies can benefit from using such 'expert groups' in infrastructure implementation.

The third recommendation, again related to the previous two, is that there should be a move towards transparent decision-making based on the preparation of a business case by the infrastructure unit. One problem noted with our case examples was the use of sole-sourcing based on minimal underlying information, which led to poor decisions being made. One part of the rationale for this approach was that infrastructure projects were needed urgently and, therefore, sole-sourcing was a way to achieve quick results. The evidence that the use of sole-sourcing, based on poor underlying information, did not necessarily result in quick implementation and certainly resulted in its being expensive, means that there is the opportunity to deliver something better. Introducing decision-making for infrastructure projects based on standard preparation of a business case by a suitably qualified infrastructure agency, at the very least, would mean that projects were prepared from a public-sector perspective, and that some acknowledgement of whole-life costs would be included, although forecasts would still be tricky. Such an approach is in line with the 'public management lite' piecemeal reform suggested by Levy (2014), which aims to deliver incremental improvement.

Finally, there is a need for better project monitoring in order to address issues of accountability. This could also be coupled with contingency planning. Monitoring gives opportunities for involvement on the part of all stakeholders, including the private partners, contractors, public sector and users, all of whom can contribute to feedback on a project's processes, operations, costs and affordability. Ideally there should then be public-sector oversight by a unit independent of the procuring agency, which links in to standard governmental accountability regimes; however, such regimes tend to be weak in the African context. Returning to the themes of 'public management lite' and incremental improvement, it may be that the infrastructure agency should be charged with including a section for the management of operational evaluation. Given that there may be a need to challenge the operational practices employed by infrastructure contractors (such as overcharging on volume, changing the conditions of the contract, etc.) the professional staff employed in the infrastructure agency would be best placed to do this.

Whilst solving the challenge of achieving financial sustainability for infrastructure projects is not easy, the above recommendations suggest ways in which incremental, rather than wholesale, reform can be realised. The aim is not to replicate the sustainability measures and governance structures of the developed world, which are themselves less than perfect. Rather, it is to bring about small improvements that lead to stable and robust practices being established in order to deliver and evaluate infrastructure projects. Together such measures can deliver sustainable economic development for African nations.

References

Acerete, B., Shaoul, J. and Stafford, A. (2009). Taking its toll: the cost of private roads in Spain. *Public Money and Management*, 29(1):19–26.

Acerete, B., Shaoul, J., Stafford, A. and Stapleton, P. (2010). The cost of using private finance for roads in Spain and the UK. *Australian Journal of Public Administration*, 69(S1): S48–S60.

Acerete, B., Stafford, A. and Stapleton, P. (2011). Spanish healthcare Public Private Partnerships: the 'Alzira model'. *Critical Perspectives on Accounting*. 22, 533–549.

Acerete, B., Stafford, A. and Stapleton, P. (2012). New global healthcare PPP developments: A critique of the success story. *Public Money and Management*, 32(4): 311–314.

Acerete, B., Gasca, M., Stafford, A. and Stapleton, P. (2015). A comparative policy analysis of healthcare PPPs: Examining evidence from two Spanish regions from an international perspective. *Journal of Comparative Policy Analysis*, 17(5): 512–518.

Agyemin-Boateng, C. (2004). Implications of the private sector involvement in the Ghana urban water delivery for the various stakeholders: The accounting perspective. Unpublished MSc. Dissertation, University of Manchester, Manchester.

Andon, P. (2012). Accounting-related research in PPPs/PFIs: present contributions and future opportunities. *Accounting, Auditing & Accountability Journal*, 25(5): 876–924.

Andrew, J. (2007). Prisons, the profit motive and other challenges to accountability. *Accounting, Auditing & Accountability Journal*, 18(8): 877–904.

Asenova, D., and Beck, M. (2010). Crucial silences: When accountability met PFI and finance capital. *Critical Perspectives on Accounting*, 21(1): 1–13.

Bain, R. (2009). *Toll road traffic and revenue forecasts*. Robert Bain.

Banerjee, S., Wodon, Q., Diallo, A., Pushak, T., Uddin, H.,Tsimpo, C. and Foster, V. (2008). *Access, affordability and alternatives: Modern infrastructure services in Africa*. Washington, DC: World Bank. https://openknowledge .worldbank.org/handle/10986/12558 License: CC BY 3.0 IGO.

Beh, L. S. (2010). Development and distortion of Malaysian Public-Private Partnerships–Patronage, privatised profits and pitfalls. *Australian Journal of Public Administration*, 69(s1).

Benito, B., Montesinos, V. and Bastida, F. (2008). An example of creative accounting in public sector: The private financing of infrastructures in Spain. *Critical Perspectives on Accounting*, 19, 963–86. 10.1016/j.cpa.2007.08.002.

Broadbent, J. and Laughlin, R. (2003). Public private partnerships: an introduction. *Accounting, Auditing & Accountability Journal, 16*(3): 332–341.

Chan, A. P., Lam, P. T., Chan, D. W., Cheung, E. and Ke, Y. (2009). Potential obstacles to successful implementation of public-private partnerships in Beijing and the Hong Kong special administrative region. *Journal of Management in Engineering, 26*(1): 30–40.

Demirag, I., and Khadaroo, I. (2008). Accountability and value for money in private finance initiative contracts. *Financial Accountability & Management, 24*(4): 455–478.

Demirag, I., and Khadaroo, I. (2011). Accountability and value for money: a theoretical framework for the relationship in public–private partnerships. *Journal of Management & Governance, 15*(2): 271–296.

Demirag, I., Khadaroo, I., Stapleton, P. and Stevenson, C. (2010). *Public private partnership financiers' perceptions of risks.* Edinburgh: Institute of Chartered Accountants of Scotland.

Eberhard, A. A., Foster, V. and Briceño-Garmendia, C. (2008). *Africa – Underpowered: The state of the power sector in Sub-Saharan Africa.* Africa infrastructure country diagnostic (AICD) background paper; no. 6. Washington, DC: World Bank. http://documents.worldbank.org/curated/en/1 42991468006934762/Africa-Underpowered-the-state-of-the-power-sector-in -Sub-Saharan-Africa

Eberhard, A., Rosnes, O., Shkaratan, M. and Vennemo, H. (2011). Africa's power infrastructure: Investment, integration, efficiency. Directions in Development; Infrastructure. Washington, DC: World Bank. http://docu ments.worldbank.org/curated/en/545641468004456928/Africas-power-infrastructure-investment-integration-efficiency

Edwards, P., and Shaoul, J. (2003). Partnerships: for better, for worse? *Accounting, Auditing & Accountability Journal, 16*(3): 397–421.

Edwards, P., Shaoul, J., Stafford, A. and Arblaster, L. (2004). *An evaluation of the operation of the private finance initiative in roads and hospitals.* Report to the Association of Chartered and Certified Accountants, ACCA Research Report No. 84, 2004.

English, L. M. (2005). Using public–private partnerships to achieve value for money in the delivery of healthcare in Australia. *International Journal of Public Policy, 1*(1): 91–121.

English, L. M. (2006). Public private partnerships in Australia: An overview of their nature, purpose, incidence and oversight. *UNSWLJ, 29*(3): 250–262.

English, L. M. (2007). Performance audit of Australian public private partnerships: legitimising government policies or providing independent oversight? *Financial Accountability & Management, 23*(3): 313–336.

English, L., and Baxter, J. (2010). The changing nature of contracting and trust in public-private partnerships: The case of Victorian PPP prisons. *Abacus, 46*(3): 289–319.

English, L. M., Guthrie, J., Broadbent, J. and Laughlin, R. (2010). Performance audit of the operational stage of long-term partnerships for the private sector provision of public services. *Australian Accounting Review, 20*(1): 64–75.

English, L. and Walker, R. G. (2004). Risk weighting and accounting choices in public-private partnerships: Case study of a failed prison contract. *Australian Accounting Review*, 14(33): 62–77.

Estache, A. and Wren-Lewis, L. (2009). Toward a theory of regulation for developing countries: Following Jean-Jacques Laffont's lead. *Journal of Economic Literature*, 47(3): 729–70.

Flyvbjerg, B., (2014). What you should know about megaprojects and why: An overview. *Project Management Journal*, 45(2): 6–19.

Flyvbjerg, B., Skamris Holm, M. K. and Buhl, S. L. (2005). How (in)accurate are demand forecasts in public works projects? The case of transportation. *Journal of the American Planning Association*, 71(2): 131–146.

Fombad, M. (2013). Accountability challenges in public-private partnerships from a South African perspective. *African Journal of Business Ethics*, 7(1): 11.

Forrer, J., Kee, J. E., Newcomer, K. E. and Boyer, E. (2010). Public–private partnerships and the public accountability question. *Public Administration Review*, 70(3): 475–484.

Foster, V. and Briceño-Garmendia, C. (2010). *Africa's infrastructure: A time for transformation*. World Bank.

Grimsey, D. and Lewis, M. K. (2002). Evaluating the risks of public private partnerships for infrastructure projects. *International Journal of Project Management*, 20(2): 107–118.

Hare, P. (2013). PPP and PFI: The political economy of building public infrastructure and delivering services. *Oxford Review of Economic Policy*, 29(1), 95–112.

Hellowell, M., and Vecchi, V. (2012). An evaluation of the projected returns to investors on 10 PFI projects commissioned by the National Health Service. *Financial Accountability & Management*, 28(1): 77–100.

Hodge, G. (2004). The risky business of public-private partnerships. *Australian Journal of Public Administration*, 63(4): 37–49.

Hodge, G. A. and Greve, C. (2007). Public–private partnerships: An international performance review. *Public administration review*, 67(3): 545–558.

Hodge, G. A. and Greve, C. (2017). On public–private partnership performance: A contemporary review. *Public Works Management & Policy*, 22(1): 55–78.

Jeffares, S., Sullivan, H. and Bovaird, T. (2013). Beyond the contract: The challenge of evaluating the performance(s) of public-private partnerships. In C. Greve and G. Hodge (Eds.), *Rethinking public–private partnerships: Strategies for turbulent times*. London: Routledge, p. 166–187.

Kessides, I. N. (2005). Infrastructure privatization and regulation: Promises and perils. *The World Bank Research Observer*, 20(1), 81–108.

Laffont, J. J. (2005). *Regulation and development*. Cambridge, UK: Cambridge University Press.

Levy, B. (2014). *Working with the grain: Integrating governance and growth in development strategies*. Oxford: Oxford University Press.

Li, B., Akintoye, A., Edwards, P. J. and Hardcastle, C. (2005). The allocation of risk in PPP/PFI construction projects in the UK. *International Journal of project management*, 23(1): 25–35.

Lonsdale, C. (2005a). Post-contractual lock-in and the UK Private Finance Initiative (PFI): The cases of National Savings and Investments and the Lord Chancellor's Department. *Public Administration*, 83(1): 67–88.

Lonsdale, C. (2005b). Risk transfer and the UK Private Finance Initiative: A theoretical analysis. *Policy & Politics*, 33(2): 231–249.

Montgomery, M. A., Bartram, J., and Elimelech, M. (2009). Increasing functional sustainability of water and sanitation supplies in rural sub-Saharan Africa. *Environmental Engineering Science*, 26(5): 1017–1023.

NAO (2009). *Private finance projects.* A paper for the Lords Economic Affairs Committee, available at: www.nao.org.uk/wp-content/uploads/2009/11/HL_Private_Finance_Projects.pdf

NAO (2011). *Lessons from PFI and other projects.* Report by the Comptroller and Auditor General, HC 920 Session 2010–2012. London: The Stationery Office.

NAO. (2013). *Review of the VFM assessment process for PFI.* Briefing for the House of Commons Treasury Select Committee, available at: www.nao.org.uk/wp-content/uploads/2014/01/Review-of-VFM-assessment-process-for-PFI1.pdf .

Osei-Afoakwa, K. (2013, 7 January). The antecedents and the prospects of public procurement regulation in Ghana. *Developing Country Studies (IISTE)* 3(1). Available at SSRN: https://ssrn.com/abstract=2197273

Osei-Kyei, R. and Chan, A. P. (2015). Review of studies on the critical success factors for Public–Private Partnership (PPP) projects from 1990 to 2013. *International Journal of Project Management*, 33(6): 1335–1346.

Osei-Kyei, R. and Chan, A. P. (2016). Developing transport infrastructure in Sub-Saharan Africa through public–private partnerships: Policy practice and implications. *Transport Reviews*, 36(2): 170–186.

Ostrom, E. (2010). Beyond markets and states: Polycentric governance of complex economic systems. *Transnational Corporations Review*, 2(2): 1–12.

Quiggin, J. (2004). Risk, PPPs and the public sector comparator. *Australian Accounting Review*, 14(33): 51–61.

Rachwalski, M. D. and Ross, T. W. (2010). Running a government's P3 program: Special purpose agency or line departments? *Journal of Comparative Policy Analysis*, 12(3): 275–298.

Rechel, B., Erskine, J., Dowdeswell, B., Wright, S. and McKee, M. (2009). *Capital investment for health: Case studies from Europe.* Copenhagen, Denmark: World Health Organization.

Reeves, E. (2008). The practice of contracting in public private partnerships: Transaction costs and relational contracting in the Irish schools sector. *Public Administration*, 86(4): 969–986.

Sarfo, P. A. and Baah-Mintah, R. (2013). Assessing the effect of the Procurement Act (663) on the public financial management in Ashanti region. *American Journal of Rural Development*, 1(4): 91–98.

Shaoul, J. (2003). A financial analysis of the National Air Traffic Services PPP. *Public Money and Management*, 23(3): 185–194.

Shaoul, J., Stafford, A., and Stapleton, P. (2007). Evidence-based policies and the meaning of success: The case of a road built under Design Build Finance and Operate (DBFO). *Evidence & Policy: A Journal of Research, Debate and Practice*, 3(2): 159–179.

Shaoul, J., Stafford, A., and Stapleton, P. (2008). The cost of using private finance to build, finance and operate hospitals. *Public Money and Management*, 28(2): 101–108.

Shaoul, J., Stafford, A., and Stapleton, P. (2010). Financial black holes: The disclosure and transparency of privately financed roads in the UK. *Accounting, Auditing & Accountability Journal*, 23(2): 229–255.

Shaoul, J., Stafford, A., and Stapleton, P. (2011). Private finance: Bridging the gap for the UK's Dartford and Skye bridges? *Public Money and Management*, 31(1): 51–58.

Shaoul, J., Stafford, A. and Stapleton, P. (2012). Accountability and corporate governance of public private partnerships, *Critical Perspectives on Accounting*, 23(3): 213–229.

Skelcher, C. (2010). Governing partnerships. In G. Hodge, C. Greve and A. Boardman (Eds.), *International handbook on public-private partnerships*. Cheltenham: Edward Elgar, pp.292–304.

Stafford, A. and Stapleton, P. (2017). Examining the use of corporate governance mechanisms in operational Public-Private Partnerships: Why do they not deliver public accountability? *Australian Journal of Public Administration* Special Issue on PPPs, 76(3): 378–91.

Tadelis, S., and Bajari, P. (2006). Incentives and award procedures: Competitive tendering vs. negotiations in procurement. In N. Dimitri, G. Piga and G. Spagnolo (Eds.), *Handbook of procurement*. Cambridge, UK: Cambridge University Press, pp. 121–139.

Tan, J. (2011). Infrastructure privatisation: Oversold, misunderstood and inappropriate. *Development Policy Review*, 29(1): 47–74.

UNECE (United Nations Economic Commission for Europe). (2008). *Guidebook on promoting good governance in public-private partnerships*. New York and Geneva: United Nations.

VAGO (Victoria Auditor General's Office). (2013). *Operating water infrastructure using public private partnerships*. PP 248 Session 2010–2013, Melbourne, Australia. www.audit.vic.gov.au/report/operating-water-infrastructure-using-public-private-partnerships?section=30950–operating-water-infrastructure-using-public-private-partnerships-message.

Vecchi, V., Hellowell, M. and Gatti, S. (2013). Does the private sector receive an excessive return from investments in health care infrastructure projects? Evidence from the UK. *Health Policy*, 110(2): 243–270.

Whitfield, D. (2010). *Global auction of public assets*. Nottingham, UK: Spokesman Books.

Willems, T. (2014). Democratic accountability in public–private partnerships: The curious case of Flemish school infrastructure. *Public Administration*, 92(2): 340–358.

Zhang, X. (2005). Critical success factors for public–private partnerships in infrastructure development. *Journal of Construction Engineering and Management*, 131(1):3–14.

9　A Proactive Social Infrastructure Model for Future Mixed-Use Housing in Egypt

Wafaa Nadim

Abstract

Egypt's population of 96 million is expected to double within the next twenty to thirty years. Given that Egypt has failed to meet a continuous increase in housing demand since the 1950s, there has been an expansion of informal housing, informal adaptation of formal housing and informal mixing of residential and non-residential uses. Whilst informal interventions may allow better access to affordable housing, they do not abide by building codes or regulations; thus, they burden existing infrastructure, and negatively affect the physical and psychological well-being of society.

This chapter investigates the potential for a dynamic response to a society's changing housing needs. A case study in an informal area of the Greater Cairo Region (GCR) sought to define means of informal interventions in order to capitalize on lessons learned, and to inform future mainstream housing developments in Egypt.

It concludes that a proactive flexible and adaptable mixed-use housing model may help respond to the socio-economic and demographic dynamics of households. However, the compatibility of non-residential activities requires investigation, and any necessary measures taken before mixing with residential. This model also anticipates a reduction in commuting, which would alleviate traffic congestion and strengthen community ties.

9.1　Introduction

Urbanization rates are increasing worldwide; it is anticipated that 66 per cent of the world's population will be urban by 2050. Africa, the poorest and least developed continent in the world, is arguably also the continent that is witnessing the fastest population growth; its population

254

is projected to rise from 1.2 billion to 2.4 billion by 2050 (UN 2015). This challenge is further exacerbated by rising urbanization rates of African countries, which range between 2 per cent and 6 per cent (CIA 2017). So, there is additional pressure on African nations to provide efficient housing as a major social infrastructure asset.

Egypt's challenge, as stated above, is not a recent phenomenon. The increase in rural-urban migration since the 1950s has caused housing demand to rise, and Egypt's inability to respond to that challenge has led to ever more informal interventions and the informal adaptation of government-provided housing, particularly in the Greater Cairo Region (GCR) (Kardash 1983; Salama 1995; Sims 2010; Nadim 2016a).

The GCR is the largest metropolitan area in Africa and is one of the most crowded in the world (ECORYS 2010). It is argued that the population of informal housing areas in the GCR increased from 6.3 million in 1993 to 8.3 million in 2000, suggesting that 60 per cent of GCR inhabitants live in informal settlements (Kipper and Fischer 2009; Sabry 2010). According to CAPMAS (2016), informal areas in Cairo account for 21 per cent of the total urban area, whereas in the GCR they make up 47.3 per cent of that area.

Informal interventions in Egypt have long attracted scholarly attention. Research into this area has investigated a wide spectrum of needs: spatial/ physical, social and/or financial (Habraken 1998; Kardash 1993; Tipple 1996; Sims 2010; GIZ 2013). Whilst the extant literature provides a rich seam of data documenting housing challenges, there is, however, no evidence that any attempt has been made to provide proactive, dynamic and holistic solutions, which would not only allow housing provisions to respond and adapt to the changing socio-economic and demographic needs of households (Nadim, Bock and Linner 2014), but would also achieve increased efficiency and social sustainability (Casey 2005).

This chapter explores housing supply as a crucial social infrastructure provision (Casey 2005). A case study in one of GCR's informal areas is used to define and quantify its inhabitants' basic needs, with the aim of informing a proactive housing model for future mainstream housing developments in Egypt. It posits that future housing models should be adaptable, forming a nucleus for mobility, as well as acting as an economic centre for cohesive neighbourhoods. This holistic and proactive model is suggested as an alternative to informal interventions. It is anticipated that such a model would improve quality of life and increase not only household income but also, of course, access to housing. What is more, the concomitant reduction in commuting would not only increase and strengthen community ties; it would also be of significant help in raising the standard of living.

9.2   Socio-Economic Dynamics of Housing in Egypt

With a 2 per cent annual growth rate, Egypt's population of 96 million inhabitants (CAPMAS 2017) makes housing provision a particularly challenging proposition. Added to the increasing anticipated annual demand of around 500,000 units (Colliers 2015), is an estimated existing shortfall of more than 2.4 million housing units. It is this unmet demand that has led to an unprecedented and blunt expansion of informal interventions (Sims 2010; Nadim, Bock and Linner 2014).

This informal phenomenon in Egypt first emerged in the 1950s, largely due to the previously stated increase in rural-to-urban migration (Fahmy 2004; Salama 1995), but there was also considerable expansion in the period between the Arab–Israeli wars of 1967 and 1975 (Sims 2010). Since the 1950s, successive governments have taken on the responsibility of providing housing for the poor and the middle classes, to ensure social justice (AlSayyad 2011). This action was also influenced by the need to combat slums, which was done by exploiting and benefiting from the expansion and popularity of prefabricated components imported from the then Soviet Union. So in this context, it was reported that the first housing typologies in Egypt were modelled on Russian modernist solutions (AlSayyad 2011). The very first public housing project in Egypt was conceived in 1948, and by 1965 almost 15,000 housing units, ranging between 45 m^2 and 65 m^2 in area, had been constructed. These were mainly reserved for low-income families and low-ranking government employees, who were charged marginal rental fees (Sims 2010).

In the second half of the twentieth century, the Egyptian government, in collaboration with international aid organizations, embarked on several initiatives to meet the demand for affordable housing. These ranged from fully finished and semi-finished apartment blocks to the core houses built as part of the sites and services scheme of the late 1960s and early 1970s. The site and services plots and core houses are often referred to as 'self-help' housing schemes. They were later deemed to have been unsuccessful and were subsequently discontinued (Sims 2010; Nazmy 2011). Further attempts to alleviate surging housing problems followed, such as the National New Towns Policy in 1977. However, due to weak service provision and a lack of attractions, the new towns that were constructed under this scheme failed to reach their planned capacity, achieving only 17.6 per cent of their target population size (Sims 2010; GOPP 2017). This is attributed to the fact that the majority of households preferred to stay in the existing overcrowded cities, rather than move to new towns with poor basic services (GOPP 2017). This created a large market for informal interventions in the existing cities; by the 1990s, such interventions had become very difficult, if not impossible, to combat. These informal interventions either took the form of complete informal areas or informal adaptations of the government-provided 'formal' housing which included horizontal and/or vertical extensions to housing units and/or informal alterations of units from residential to non-residential activity. All of which expanded the informal sector.

The term 'informal sector' dates from the 1970s, but has been replaced by the 'informal economy', which better acknowledges the importance and magnitude of this sector in relation to the formal economy (ILO 2005). The informal sector arguably offers sustainable employment growth at a relatively low cost per job created (El-Mahdi 2002). Informal workers may be categorized as 'visible', e.g. street vendors; 'working indoors', e.g. in shops, workshops, etc.; or the 'least visible', i.e. those working from home, a category that is reported to mainly consist of women (Chen 2012). Informal work is very common in informal areas in Egypt; it is either integrated into it (Bredenoord and Lindert 2010; Majale 2008) from the beginning of the informal intervention, or arrives at a later stage as 'residential' spaces are converted to become 'non-residential'.

Whilst informal interventions have the advantage of accommodating the various financial capabilities of households and creating job opportunities, they also have disadvantages; for example, they often lead to the creation of overcrowded and unhealthy living spaces, which burden the existing infrastructure and are even unsafe in some areas (Fahmy 2004; Sims 2010; GIZ 2013; Nadim et al. 2014; Nadim 2016a; GOPP 2017).

9.3 Urban Poverty and Housing Affordability

Poverty can be defined in either absolute or relative terms. Absolute poverty exists when people lack the basics of nutrition, health, sanitation and housing (UNESCO 2017), whereas relative poverty is typically defined in relation to the economic status of other members of society. Both definitions are criticized for focusing on the economic aspect of poverty, whilst paying no attention to its social and cultural aspects (UNESCO 2017). Additionally, the results of the different poverty studies were criticized for contradicting each other and were therefore considered misleading. This is attributed to the fact that different methodologies are used to define the poverty line, as well as the tendency of many methods to ignore the important segment of the population that lives in slums and in informal areas. Various household surveys found this segment of the population prioritized access to healthcare, jobs and a simple shelter over nutritious food, education and quality of life (Sabry 2010; GIZ 2013).

Affordable housing has been defined as accommodation that meets the needs of a range of low- and moderate-income households, and that is priced low enough to allow other essential basic living costs to be met (Abelson 2009). It is also defined as the stock at the lower end of the market that targets a wide range of delivery models (Whitehead 2007; Guran and Whitehead 2011). The debates in extant literature over different models for calculating housing affordability have tended to focus particularly on those that are one-dimensional, i.e. largely dependent on price-to-income ratio (JICA 2008). To illustrate this problem, according to the United States Department of Housing and Urban Development (HUD), total housing costs at or below 30 per cent of gross annual income are considered affordable (HUD User 2019)), whilst Demographia, on the other hand, considers the median multiple of 3.0 or under as a measure of affordability (Demographia 2019. These measurement methods lack theoretical underpinning, and overlook the dynamics of the changing needs of households (Li 2012).

The fact that housing-market competition denies poorer households access to housing has prompted governments worldwide to intervene and provide affordable homes. This policy has been pursued under the expectation that a society's welfare will improve if minimum standards are achieved for all households (Whitehead 2007). But conversely, whilst the provision of homes and neighbourhoods aims to sustain and support members of a society, there is the risk that it may also burden and oppress them if the dynamics of living are not considered in the design of those living spaces (Turner 1980; Evans 2003). So, housing provision should not merely denote the provision of a stock of houses; instead it should encapsulate a holistic approach that considers the dynamics of the whole community in order for it to be effective and productive (Turner 1980; Evans 2003). In this context, several initiatives around the world have been devised that aimed to ensure the availability of affordable housing by encouraging self-help housing provision.

9.4   Self-Help Housing

9.4.1   Self-Help International Initiatives

Self-help housing arguably dates back to the period 1918–29, when it emerged first in Europe, and then in the Soviet Union before its promotion in the developing world in the 1970s (Harris 1999; Rakodi 1989). The emergence of self-help was largely in response to the severe housing shortages and political unrest in the aftermath of the First World War in Europe. Aided or assisted self-help was described as a 'pragmatic' and 'untheorized scheme' (Harris 1999), whereby households received external support with which to build their homes. In general, self-help support took the form of sites and services provision, or core houses on plots within the sites and services scheme, whilst technical assistance and housing micro-financing schemes were also offered (Bredenoord and Lindert 2010); in addition, building regulations were enforced (Harris 1999).

In support of self-help, the United Nations (UN) urged governments to provide intensive and extensive assistance in order to build effective communities (UN 1964). The supporters of the self-help approach perceived its main aim as going beyond the mere building of houses, and instead creating a process of community education; thus, fostering a healthy atmosphere of cooperation and human conviviality. This, in turn, would allow people to work together towards a solution for their common problems in a constructive way (Fathy 1962; Rizvi 1966). There were, however, opponents of self-help housing amongst many local planners and governments internationally, who criticized such schemes as an 'aesthetic blight on rural and suburban landscapes' (Harris 1999).

In Germany, owner-built homes were pejoratively known as '*Wildsiedlungen*' or 'wild settlements'. Similarly, there was political reluctance towards self-help in Britain, where it was perceived as 'antagonising the building industry and trades'; the housing was also seen as unattractive and the product of anarchist schemes (Harris 1999; Kowaltowski 1998). The most substantial and successful self-help projects were in the Soviet Union, where free plots were offered to households to build their own homes, and a 2 per cent incentive was given to those who could provide a down payment of 30 per cent in cash or labour; such householders were also awarded a 10-year tax exemption. East Prussia, furthermore, financed and supervised construction, and arranged for the delivery of building material at a discounted price to those who invested their own labour (Harris 1999). In 1949–50, Canada developed the 'build-your-own-home' policy, which offered technical assistance, including construction courses together with on-site inspections and guidance. And in Stockholm, a municipal scheme of standardized prefabricated houses known as 'Magic Houses' was offered on the condition that home-builders accepted close supervision and constructed their homes within a defined time schedule (Harris 1999).

In order to ensure greater success for self-help, there were calls for such schemes to consider the environment, the culture and socio-economic needs of a community, in addition to the technical skills needed for successful development; this was anticipated to provide means to produce appropriate housing, whilst also developing a sense of community identity and enabling self-governance (Bredenoord and Lindert 2010; Nientied and Linden 1988; Rakodi 1989). It was also argued that a simple design, one that facilitates progressive and incremental expansion and improvement over time, is a key factor to affordable housing (Mukhija 2014).

9.4.2   Self-Help Housing in Egypt

Egypt launched several aided self-help core housing projects in the 1970s and '80s, but many were considered to have been failures and were cancelled (El-Batran and Arandel 1998; Sims 2010). This lack of success was largely attributed to the inherent perception that 'self-help', whether it took the form of sites and services or core housing within the sites and services scheme, produced 'sub-standard' housing (Kardash 1993).

A more recent and ongoing example of a self-help project is 'Ibny Baitak', or the 'build-your-own-home' initiative – a sites and services provision. It started in 2005 as part of the national housing project's strategy to reduce the expansion of informal housing. The project provides sites, with services, of 150 m^2 each, but households can only build on 50 per cent of their site, and are allocated a maximum of a ground floor and two upper floors. The project incentive was 150,000 LE (around $8,500) to be paid to the household in three instalments, subject to a pre-defined time frame. The project has faced and continues to face challenges, however. These have included scarcity of water during construction, lack of lighting for construction during night shifts, lack of proper transportation for labourers and theft of materials (Nazmy 2011). Post-construction problems have included the unavailability of infrastructure and a lack of basic services. Furthermore, the unit price is now unsuitable, which makes it unaffordable for the targeted households. In addition, households were not satisfied with the resultant net area of 63 m^2 (Ahmed, Moussa and Gaeiss 2014; Nazmy 2011). It was also noted that ground floors had been informally converted into commercial activities to compensate for the lack of basic services in the area, which, consequently, turned the housing schemes into mixed-use areas.

9.5   Mixed-Use Urban Development

9.5.1   Mixed-Use International Initiatives

Mixed urban living and working is an old model for traditional city life, which allows diversity in population density, land use, and social and cultural diversity (Kaur 2010; Trading Economics 2015). In this context, Rowley (1996) criticizes zoning and segregation of land uses as 'the determined neatness of planners', rather than the 'proper growth of a community'.

Work–life integration was common until the beginning of the twentieth century; at that time, families worked together and means of transportation were limited. It was arguably the onset of the industrial age and the proliferation of factories that caused the separation between work and life to emerge (Khallash and Kruse 2012).

Mixed use may occur centrally on the district, or at neighbourhood level in public spaces, or even within buildings (Kaur 2010). Major benefits of this model include a reduced need to travel, its contribution to urban diversity and vitality and its promotion of security and crime prevention (Trading Economics 2015). Nevertheless, some activities are considered 'not suitable for mixing', such as heavy industries (Trading Economics 2015.) However, Dolan (2012) is of the view that 'hazardous' activities may still be permitted if completely separated from living spaces and if building codes are complied with.

There have been calls in the developed countries for the re-integration of work and life, particularly as new technologies allow people to work from home and are changing work patterns. Furthermore, if workers are not bound to a specific work schedule, this may reduce barriers between managers and employees, leading to a 'boss-less' organizational setup (Khallash and Kruse 2012). On a social level, it is anticipated that this will improve family ties, which were previously negatively affected by the pattern of separation between work and home (Bailyn et al. 2001).

Building on the above, mixed-use housing may be a means of improving quality of life, as it provides better access to jobs within workers' own block of housing, or nearby; this encourages income generation, which allows access to housing for low-income households (JICA 2008).

9.5.2 Mixed-Use Initiatives in Egypt

A popular mixed-use housing initiative in Egypt is the Herafeen, an artisan region for servicing cars. The project encompasses apartment blocks which ground floors are reserved for car workshops, whilst the first to the fourth floors are residential. The residential unit areas range between 60 and 70 m^2, and consist of a small reception room, kitchen, two bedrooms and a bathroom. This initiative has been described in extant literature as 'unsuccessful' (Sims 2010); however, the reasons for this are not evident. When investigated by the research team, inhabitants attributed the 'failure' of the project to a number of reasons which can be categorized under spatial design and urban planning. From a social and cultural perspective, and since the mixed-use project was industrial in nature, i.e. focusing on servicing cars, households did not perceive the resultant constellation as a suitable environment for the females in their families, as they could be subjected to unwanted attention from the workers in the workshops. From the design/urban perspective, challenges included lack of basic services, lack of occupational health and safety measures, small unit areas, poor quality of finishing material, and streets that were too narrow to accommodate the serviced cars, which caused further obstruction of traffic, particularly on work days. As a result, inhabitants either moved out, selling their apartments as storage space for the workshops, or informal alterations were made to the original design to increase the living space available. So, it may be argued that the project did not achieve its goal, particularly as those currently working there are not necessarily living there as well, as had originally been intended.

The above reviews may lead one to conclude that the Egyptian government's initiatives for self-help and/or mixed-use initiatives have been unsuccessful. But against that, the informal/unplanned interventions that have relied on incremental building and mixed uses arguably seem to have been more successful than the formal interventions.

The following section uses a case study based in an informal area of GCR to record and document the ways in which people have informally adapted their built environment in response to their various changing needs. The intention is to focus on the positives whilst noting ways to avoid the negatives, as lessons learned for future mainstream housing models.

9.6   The Case Study: Informal and Incremental Mixed-Use Interventions

Saqiet Mikky is located in Giza, one of the GCR's urban governorates on the west bank of the Nile. Formerly agricultural land, it gradually became an informal urban area encompassing informal multi-storey apartment blocks of up to twelve floors or more. Located in the northern part of the case study area are apartment blocks built by the government in the 1970s. These comprise a ground floor and a maximum of five upper floors each. The majority of inhabitants in the case study are low-income families with a relatively poor quality of living (GIZ 2013). Education is a secondary consideration when it comes to household expenditure, and the majority of men are transient construction workers, with women taking various jobs such as cleaning, sewing bed sheets, making pickles or sweets and so on, to contribute to family income (GIZ 2013).

To explore the extent to which incremental building and mixed uses were successful in the area, 500 questionnaires were administered by 10 young male volunteers living in the neighbourhood. It was important to employ local volunteers for this project, as inhabitants would distrust outsiders exploring their area. Female volunteers, who would have had better access to female inhabitants due to social/cultural constraints, unfortunately could not participate in this data-collection process.

The questionnaire comprised four sections, covering aspects of living, working, mobility and accessibility, and perception of mixed uses, as follows:

- The first section asked about the general characteristics of the respondents.
- The second explored the living environment with regard to the different uses of space in their units.
- The third investigated mobility and accessibility, both within and in the vicinity of their housing unit/apartment block.
- Finally, the fourth was concerned with the inhabitants' perception of the mixed uses in the block they lived in and/or in their vicinity.

The questions were mainly closed ended, followed by a section asking respondents to 'please specify/explain', in order to allow the capture of complimentary qualitative data. A 91 per cent response rate was achieved.

9.6.1   General Characteristics of the Respondents

The majority of respondents were male (71 per cent), which may be because the volunteers administering the questionnaires were men. This was counterbalanced, however, through the verification of results during follow-up visits by the research team, when females were asked their opinions. Additionally, 49 per cent of respondents had lived in the area for more than 10 years, and 47 per cent for less than 10 years, which may indicate balanced responses.

9.6.1.1   Age of Respondents

Respondents were mainly young or middle-aged:
- 18 aged or less than 35 years (50 per cent)
- 35 aged or less than 55 years (41 per cent)
- 55 years and above (6 per cent).

9.6.1.2   *Education*

Educational levels varied, with the majority having only received a school education:
- Secondary school education (29 per cent)
- Preparatory (14 per cent)
- Primary (9 per cent)
- No formal education of any kind (19 per cent)
- University undergraduates (23 per cent) and postgraduates (4 per cent).

9.6.1.3   *Family Size*

With regard to family composition, respondents' family members consisted of:
- 5 members (28 per cent)
- 4 members (25 per cent)
- 3 members (21 per cent)
- 6 members (14 per cent)
- 2 members (8 per cent).

9.6.1.4   *Tenancy Type*

The types of tenancy broke down as follows:
- 48 per cent were owners of their residential units
- 40 per cent were renters
- And 9 per cent were apartment-block owners.

9.6.1.5   *Work and Its Proximity*

From the work perspective, respondents were:
- Self-employed (40 per cent)
- Employees (16 per cent)
- Students (21 per cent), unemployed (18 per cent) or retired (2 per cent).

The majority of respondents' work was in close proximity to where they lived (77 per cent). The results were as follows:
- Workplace within walking distance (44 per cent)
- Workplace in the same apartment block where the respondent lived (11 per cent)
- Or the respondent used one means of transport to go to work (22 per cent).

9.6.1.6   Apartment-Block Plot Sizes and Size of Families Therein

These were relatively small, accommodating either one residential unit (34 per cent) or two per floor (33 per cent). Around a quarter of blocks had three units per floor and only a few blocks (9 per cent) had four units per floor, which would indicate greater plot areas. Residential unit areas were generally smaller than 70 m^2 (60 per cent).

These were further broken down as follows
- Between 50 and 70 m^2 (32 per cent)
- Between 30 and 50 m^2 (24 per cent)
- Less than 30 m^2 (4 per cent).

Only 20 per cent of inhabitants lived in larger unit areas of 70–90 m^2, fewer still in 90–110 m^2 (15 per cent), and only a very few (5 per cent) lived in units greater than 110 m^2.

As for the number of family members living in different-sized units, these broke down as follows:
- Areas smaller than 30 m^2 were mainly occupied by families of three or four members – however, there were some families of six members living in an area smaller than 30 m^2
- Families living in 30–50 m^2 consisted of three, four or five family members
- Those households living in larger unit areas such as 50–70 m^2, 70–90 m^2, 90–110 m^2 or more than 110 m^2 had four, five or six family members.

9.6.1.7   Number of Rooms

With regard to the number of rooms in the residential units, 55 per cent of respondents lived in units with two bedrooms. Thus, an overcrowding rate (Eurostat 2017) was recorded of 3 members/room for a family of 6 members, which is greater than the official rate of 1.12 in Giza Governorate (CAPMAS 2006).

9.6.1.8   Living Expenses and Affordability

In terms of living expenses and the affordability of housing units, it was found that:
- The majority of residents (66 per cent) spent 15–35 per cent of their income on rent
- 24 per cent spent less than 15 per cent
- And only 10 per cent spent more than 35 per cent

With regard to transportation expenses, the majority (74 per cent) spent up to 10 per cent of their income on this, whereas 26 per cent spent more than 10 per cent. This shows the affordability of the units (when applying the affordability index) and the proximity between work and home.

9.6.2   Suitability of the Residential Unit Area

Spaces within the residential units usually served multiple functions to compensate for the relatively small size of the unit areas.

For example, irrespective of the unit area, reception rooms were generally used for:
• Receiving guests (76 per cent)
• Studying (32 per cent)
• Eating (30 per cent)
• A sleeping area for boys at night (13 per cent)
• Cooking (6 per cent).

Similarly, bedrooms were largely used for:
• Studying (61 per cent)
• Extended family gathering and watching TV (43 per cent)
• Eating (15 per cent).

Furthermore, corridors were used for:
• Storage (33 per cent)
• Placing the fridge (41 per cent)
• Laundry (39 per cent).

9.6.2.1   Suitability and Satisfaction

Sixty-six per cent of residents found their residential unit area suitable for most of their needs, as opposed to 25 per cent, who found it unsuitable. Families of six members were in general the least satisfied with the unit area they lived in, followed by families of five and four.

Still, irrespective of the number of family members and their satisfaction vis-à-vis the unit area, i.e. suitable or unsuitable (see Figure 9.1), residents have made the following adaptations:
• 46 per cent of respondents who found their unit area unsuitable added an extra room to their unit, 27 per cent added an extra floor and 18 per cent turned balconies into an extra room;
• 48 per cent of those who found their unit area suitable for most of their needs still added an extra room to their unit, 19 per cent added an extra floor, and 24 per cent turned balconies into an extra room;
• And 18 per cent of those who found their unit area suitable for all their needs also added an extra room to their unit, 18 per cent added an extra floor, and 20 per cent turned balconies into an extra room.

a   b

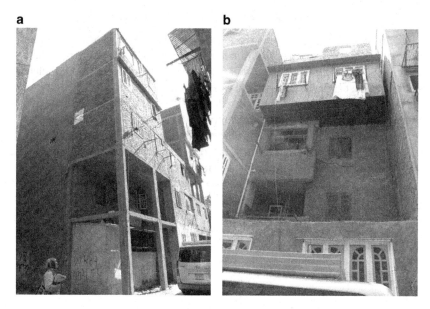

Figure 9.1 Despite the general satisfaction with the housing unit, extra rooms are still added horizontally and vertically

As noted above, and despite respondents' satisfaction with their unit areas, they still made alterations, suggesting that the area was not entirely suitable for their needs. Therefore, the fact that they could add to their unit and expand it may explain their recorded satisfaction.

9.6.2.2   Quality of Living

It was found that certain spaces within the residential units had no natural ventilation or natural lighting, with respondents reporting that this was the case of:
• Reception rooms (48 per cent)
• Followed by bathrooms (40 per cent)
• Kitchens (27 per cent)
• And even bedrooms (23 per cent).
Note that the Egyptian building code requires bathrooms and kitchens in residential units be naturally ventilated. The majority of respondents (66 per cent) used a ceiling fan for ventilation, followed by standing fans (42 per cent), and a few used air conditioning (14 per cent).

9.6.3   Structure and Quality of Apartment Blocks

Different construction systems were used in the area; buildings were either skeletal concrete structures or brick load-bearing walls with concrete slabs. In general, 33 per cent were load-bearing walls, and 64 per cent were skeletal structures. In cases where a vertical extension to a skeletal construction took place, load-bearing walls were used for the extension to reduce cost. Furthermore, additional structural support was added to load-bearing structures (Figure 9.2). The major problems relating to buildings were largely cracks (56 per cent), deteriorated façades (20 per cent) and differential settlement (18 per cent). Generally, 45 per cent of inhabitants never carried out maintenance, 25 per cent did so rarely, and 21 per cent did so only when necessary. Only 4 per cent carried out maintenance more frequently.

Maintenance, when carried out, included painting façades (39 per cent of respondents had done this), plumbing (41 per cent) and providing additional structural support (24 per cent), mainly for load-bearing structures (Figure 9.2). This maintenance work was usually carried out by a contractor (62 per cent) or by a family member (34 per cent).

Figure 9.2 Additional steel or concrete structural support added to load-bearing structures (left and middle) and for future horizontal extensions (right)

9.6.4   Mobility and Accessibility within Buildings and around Apartment Blocks

Mobility and accessibility within and around the apartment blocks were explored in the case study in order to find the extent to which informal interventions catered for and accommodated the elderly and people with impairment challenges.

9.6.4.1   Mode of Transport

The respondents used the following modes of transport:
- Walking (66 per cent)
- Microbus (62 per cent)
- The metro (40 per cent)
- Tuk-tuks (39 per cent)
- Public buses (30 per cent)
- Taxis (15 per cent).

Pedestrians mainly walk on the streets, as pavements are usually occupied by street vendors; but even if pavements are available, they are generally found to be 'too high' by those older than 35 (74 per cent).

9.6.4.2   Building Entrances

It was found that building entrances were either situated above, below or at street level. Elevated entrances, intended to protect buildings from sewage overflow, were mainly found in newly built buildings. Entrances lower than street level were largely found in older buildings and had come about as a result of the continuous over-paving of streets over the years, which had raised street levels above the entrance level (Figure 9.3). In general, inhabitants found entrance levels suitable even if they were above street level or below street level, with approval rates of 71 and 59 per cent respectively for these two types of entrance. This general satisfaction may be largely attributable to the fact that the majority of respondents (80 per cent) were younger than thirty-five. Moreover, although the majority of men found entrance levels suitable (76 per cent), only a minority of women agreed (20 per cent of women found them suitable). The elderly, however, reported the need for more handrails to enable them to access entrances.

9.6.4.3   Stairwell Accessibility

Vertical accessibility within buildings (i.e. the width of stairwells), was generally perceived as adequate by 57 per cent of respondents. Those who found stairwell widths inadequate (39 per cent) were mainly older than thirty-five. Similarly, stairwell slopes were largely considered adequate by younger respondents, but not by those older than 35. Stairwells had either

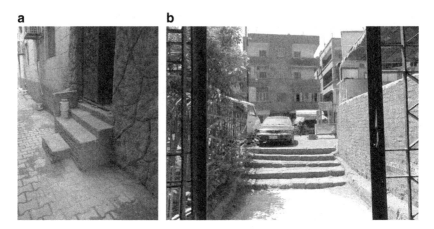

Figure 9.3 Entrance above street level not complying with code (left). Entrance below street level (right)

no natural light source (26 per cent) or only a partial one (64 per cent), rendering them dark during daytime.

9.6.4.4 Accessibility within Residential Units

As 88 per cent of respondents did not have their grandparents living with them and did not have a family member with any kind of impaired mobility, it was not possible to record accessibility challenges in this regard. But during a focus group meeting with elderly respondents (Nadim 2016b), they stressed the need to have bathrooms nearer to bedrooms (particularly for diabetics) and to have seating space available in the kitchen whilst they were cooking. One respondent with severe leg and hip problems re-arranged the bathroom by removing the bathtub and elevating the toilet seat to meet her mobility requirements.

9.6.4.5 Roofs

Roofs were also investigated for their accessibility and function suitability. Forty-two per cent of respondents had no access to their roof; this was mainly the case for those renting. Those who did have access to the roof (55 per cent) were typically extended families who all lived in the same apartment block. Roofs were largely used for storing unwanted objects/ scraps (by 43 per cent) or for raising livestock (by 37 per cent). Only 6 per cent reported using roofs for growing plants. In general, 43 per cent of the respondents found their roof not suitable for planting at all, 44 per cent found it suitable for only certain plants and only 3 per cent found it suitable for all plants. Still, 59 per cent of respondents, mainly those below the age of thirty-five, agreed that rooftops could be used more efficiently, e.g. by integrating photovoltaic cells into them (PV). Conversely, 36 per cent of respondents, mainly those older than thirty-five, did not think it likely that rooftops would be used more efficiently. This suggests, perhaps not surprisingly, that younger generations in the area were more open to change in general, and to new technologies in particular.

9.6.5   Mixed-Use Activities

Mixed uses are relatively common in the case study; 53 per cent of respondents reported that their apartment block's ground floor hosted non-residential activities, whilst 43 per cent of respondents advised that their ground floors were only residential. Non-residential activities were mainly commercial (58 per cent) or industrial in nature, e.g. car work-shops, carpentry, etc. (18 per cent).

Major problems associated with mixed uses were:
- Noise (reported by 63 per cent)
- Lack of parking space (18 per cent) for tenants and their guests
- Bad odours (20 per cent)
- Waste and refuse (8 per cent)
- Other problems recorded included disrespect on the part of commercial traders and/or their customers, and a lack of consideration shown by them towards tenants.

Generally, respondents either agreed in principle (18 per cent), or agreed conditionally (46 per cent) to mixed use, as opposed to 36 per cent who did not favour mixed use. Conditional agreement was subject to the proposition that mixed use should increase income for both tenant and owner.

9.6.5.1   Commercial-Activity Respondents

Of those working in or owning a shop in the area, 35 per cent had received secondary education, 20 per cent primary education and 20 per cent were illiterate, although around 20 per cent had attended a higher-education institution. The majority of commercial-activity respondents (77 per cent) agreed that their shop area was sufficient for their activity, whilst 22 per cent either agreed conditionally or disagreed with the statement that their shop area was sufficient. Despite the recorded levels of satisfaction with the shop area, respondents still identified the main functions missing in their shops as toilet facilities (60 per cent), storage (27 per cent) and sufficient working space (17 per cent). It was observed that non-residential activities largely extended beyond the shop's area, i.e. occupying the pavement in front of the shops and, in some cases, even parts of the street. This flexibility in terms of extending commercial activity beyond the shop's area may explain the respondents' satisfaction with their shop areas (Figure 9.4). It was not clear whether or not they realized the disruption and annoyance such extensions may cause to residents in the area. One shop owner explicitly expressed the view that shops do have the legal right to take up pavement space for their non-residential activities.

It may be concluded that the introduction of mixed uses may compensate for a lack of services in the area, create job opportunities and even lead to the desirable outcome of occupancy for ground-floor properties that are considered less suitable as living spaces for safety/security reasons (Nadim 2016b). That said, the unplanned and informal inclusion of such activities could also negatively affect residents' quality of life, and may also represent a poor working environment for those working in these non-residential spaces.

a   b

Figure 9.4 Non-residential activities extending beyond the shop area to pavements and even onto streets

9.7   A Mainstream Mixed-Use Incremental Housing Model for Egypt

Building on these challenges to government housing provision and the unplanned and informal mixing of residential and non-residential activities in informal areas, a holistic approach will be crucial in order to ensure the success and acceptance of future formal mainstream mixed-use housing models.

This section stresses and substantiates the need for mixed-use incremental housing provision, with the argument that this concept has already, and to a large extent, been successfully embraced in informal areas in Egypt. However, all of these informal interventions are lacking major characteristics, which negatively affect the quality of living and working in those neighbourhoods. In order to achieve successful and affordable mixed-use mainstream housing provision, the most significant factors for success in mixing non-residential with residential activities are discussed in the following sub-sections, with a conceptual model presented in the conclusion.

9.7.1   The Need to Integrate 'Work' into the Housing Model

The concept of life–work integration is not only important here because it arguably fits the requirements of the communities in question; it is also necessary within the Egyptian context. With 65 per cent of Egypt's population below the age of thirty (CAPMAS 2017), and a national unemployment rate of 13.7 per cent, significant challenges must be overcome in order to create the minimum 560,000 new jobs that are needed annually for the unemployed and new entrants into the labour market (World Bank 2007). Other estimates for the number of annual new jobs that need to be created annually reported a figure in excess of 640,000 (Egypt Independent 2013). In addition, 75 per cent of the unemployed are aged between fifteen and twenty-nine (CAPMAS 2017). The government's inability to provide job opportunities has further created a suitable environment for the emergence and expansion of the informal sector, and by extension, the informal mixing of non-residential with residential uses.

From a logistics perspective, the separation of uses in housing typologies places additional demands on commuting. The transport system in Egypt has long been near breaking point, with average travel speeds on a business day reported to be 15 km/h or less, due to serious traffic congestion, poor public-transport systems and high accident rates. The annual direct cost of this traffic congestion of 13–14 billion LE in 2010 (ECORYS 2010 and El-Kouedi and Madbouly 2007) amounting to 50 billion LE total cost (World Bank 2012), i.e. around $2 billion at current exchange rates is expected to reach 260 billion LE ($15 billion) by

2030 (Ahram Online 2014). Therefore, the mixed-use concept becomes an even more compelling proposition if it also helps to reduce the need for commuting.

A 'zero-commute housing' scheme is defined as one that combines residential units with workplaces in a single building or in a group of buildings (Khallash and Kruse 2012; Dolan 2012; Hoppenbrouwer and Louw 2005). This concept has arguably evolved into a recognized land-use and building type over the past four decades, in addition to becoming a marketable real-estate product (Dolan 2012). The benefits of this type of 'live–work' development include the elimination of commuting time, thereby allowing time to be spent more efficiently. In addition, being place-centred allows for greater community involvement, better connection and interaction (Dolan 2012).

The three main live–work use types have been identified as home occupation, live–work and work–live, according to the dominance of the different activities/functions. Home occupation refers to work that takes place within a residence; 'live–work' refers to work that takes place within a residence, a building, or on the same property where the dominant use is residential; and work–live refers to residences within or adjacent to a commercial space, where the work function is therefore dominant (Bailyn et al. 2001; Dolan 2012). But, irrespective of the mixing type, attention should be paid to the suitability and compatibility of non-residential activities (Dolan 2012).

9.7.2   The Success Factors for Affordable 'Living' in the Housing Model

The government's inability to meet housing demand in a manner that takes into consideration the associated socio-economic dynamics (JICA 2008; Maisel 2006) has manifested in the informal adaptation of government-provided housing (Habraken 1998; Kardash 1993; Tipple 1996), as well as the unprecedented expansion of informal interventions (Sims 2010). This has been documented by various scholars since the early 1980s; the research attributed these effects to the so-called 'mismatch' between what is provided and what end users actually need (Habraken 1998; Kardash 1993; Tipple 1996; Sims 2010). The researchers argued that the greater the mismatch, the stronger the user's urge to change their environment, and the more difficult it then becomes to manage and/or control the process. This transformation often takes the form of internal alterations, and horizontal and/or vertical expansion. In this context, end users can increase their living space by up to 60 per cent (Habraken 1998; Kardash 1993; Tipple 1996).

From a functional perspective, people tend to change their floor layouts over time for several reasons, such as to accommodate more people, initiate new businesses, and/or to reflect a change in household composition (Fulwood 1987; Dhar, Hossain and Rahman 2013). This, however, often requires a certain level of flexibility. Gijsbers and Lichtenberg (2014) defined the three different types of flexibility required: flexibility-in-use, process flexibility and organizational flexibility. Process flexibility allows change and freedom of choice during the design and construction of a building, whereas organizational flexibility refers to the ability of the organization to oversee changes. Flexibility-in-use refers to the ability to effect changes, whether spatial or functional, that are tailored to the end user's needs during their occupancy of the building. This may also be closely associated with the concept of 'extendability', whereby users start with occupying a small space for dwelling, with an intention to later extend it in response to changing needs (Fulwood 1987). This has also been considered as a means of achieving housing affordability (Kuang and Li 2012).

Adaptability is another term closely intertwined with flexibility in the extant literature. Groak (1992) defined 'adaptability' as the ability to accommodate different social needs, and 'flexibility' as the ability to achieve a different physical arrangement. But Blok and Herwijnen (2006) referred to 'adaptability' as the technical ability to continuously undergo physical changes, which contradicts Groak's definition. Furthermore, Douglas (2006) defined adaptation as including any work on a building above and beyond regular maintenance and which changes its capacity, function and performance. This may include code compliance, environmental enhancement, spatial modification and/or structure/fabric upgrading. Thus, as it appears there is no clear distinction between the terms 'adaptability' and 'flexibility' (Manewa et al. 2016), they may be used interchangeably (Mansour 2017). There are, however, two more distinctive concepts that may be used: namely, 'active' and 'passive' flexibility. Where the former refers to the ability to actively respond by changing, reacting or adapting, the latter does not require active interference in the building's structure and layout due to sufficient tolerance and capacity of space (Blok and Herwijnen 2006).

Accessibility is yet another crucial aspect of the living environment (Nadim 2016a). This is especially so in light of the UNFPA demographic report (Sayed 2018) advising that Egypt should prepare for an ageing population and a consequent increase in the dependency ratio. This is largely due to 7.5 per cent of Egypt's population is over 60 years old, and this is anticipated to reach 12 per cent by 2055 (UN 2015; CAPMAS 2017). In addition, 7 per cent of the population was estimated to have some type of physical impairment in 2006 (CAPMAS 2006), and again, this has risen to 10.5 per cent in 2017 (CAPMAS 2017). The Law of Persons with Disability in Egypt (Chapter Five, Clauses 27 & 28) requires that all new buildings and open spaces, in addition to the existing built environment, be adjusted to cater for people with all types of mobility challenges. Also, 5 per cent of subsidized housing is reserved for those with some kind of impairment. These reserved units are mainly on ground floors, but despite this their internal design often fails to consider the user's internal mobility needs. And of course, it should be noted that making homes and the environment in general safe for the elderly and the physically challenged arguably also makes them safer for younger people (Mace, Hardie and Place 1991; Cisneros et al. 2012). So in this context, the 'universal design' concept may help make daily functioning easier for the general population, whilst also addressing accessibility, visitability, functionality, and movement in a space (Mace et al. 1991; Nadim 2016a).

Another crucial term associated with 'universal design' is 'visitability' (Maisel, Smith and Steinfeld 2008). This is concerned with investigating the minimum features and standards required to make all buildings accessible to people with any kind of restricted mobility, e.g. such features as zero-step entrances and wider doorways (Mace et al. 1991; Maisel et al. 2008; Cisneros et al. 2012).

9.7.3   The Mixed-Use Incremental Housing Model

Building on lessons learned from the case study vis-à-vis mixed-use, affordable and accessible housing, and in order to allow housing to respond to individual households' changing socio-economic and demographic needs, a proactive dynamic model for housing provision in Egypt is suggested. This model is multi-faceted to adopt the mixed-use/live–work concept, and would help achieve a holistic solution to three major challenges in Egypt (Nadim et al. 2014; Nadim 2016b). Firstly, it would help respond to households' changing socio-economic needs. Secondly, it would help create jobs, which increases household income. And thirdly, it would reduce commuting, which both ameliorates traffic congestion and permits a more efficient use of time.

The suggested model identifies the main success factors for both the residential/living and the working component of future housing (Figure 9.5). It calls for the residential unit to be

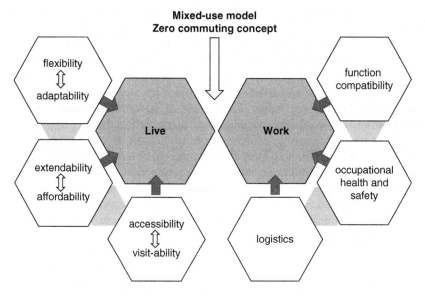

Figure 9.5 The proposed proactive mixed-use housing model (adapted from Nadim 2016b)

a. Flexible/adaptable, in order to cater for the changing social and demographic needs of households (Nadim 2016b)
b. Extendable, to allow incremental building that meets the residents' financial capabilities, thereby creating affordability
c. Accessible, in order to allow autonomous living, irrespective of mobility challenges and age.

As for the non-residential activity, in order to maintain the quality of life and work in the mixed-use development, consideration of the following should be made to alleviate hazards and disturbance to residents

a. Function compatibility
b. Occupational health and safety measures
c. Logistics.

9.8   Discussion and Conclusion

Egypt faces the dual challenges of a rising population and its increasing urbanization rate. This is compounded by its consistent inability to meet housing demand since the 1950s. The consequence of this failure has led to the expansion of informal housing interventions to date. With an estimated annual demand for more than 500,000 housing units, in addition to an estimated 2.4 million shortfall in housing supply, it will arguably be impossible to prevent the unprecedented expansion of informal interventions, unless unorthodox, innovative solutions are offered.

The various governments' initiatives to provide affordable housing since the 1970s have generally proven unsuccessful, whereas informal interventions have been on the rise since that time and have become ever more popular over the years. The failure of government initiatives to address housing shortages may largely be attributed to the fact that such schemes were, arguably, a mere application/transfer of international initiatives, and were not accompanied by the closer supervision, enforcement of building codes/regulation, or training that would have been necessary to ensure successful implementation. This might suggest that the lessons learned from international comparative interventions were not taken into consideration when these initiatives were transferred into the Egyptian context.

This chapter has highlighted the various government initiatives for affordable housing in Egypt that have been implemented since the 1970s, and explored the success factors in comparable international cases. These were contrasted with the current informal intervention model, which has seemingly been popular with Egyptians, in comparison to government-supplied housing, which arguably does not have the inherent flexibility to respond to the changing socio-economic needs of its resident householders.

A case study in one of the GCR informal areas was investigated to gauge the extent to which informal interventions had succeeded in responding to the changing socio-economic needs of the area's inhabitants. The case study demonstrated that informal areas, to a large extent, cater for diverse households with a wide spectrum of educational backgrounds, ranging from no formal education to postgraduate studies. They also offer a wide selection of residential unit areas, and allows incremental expansions and extensions to residential units and blocks. This accommodates the different financial capacities of all its households. So it could be concluded that, in general, residential units such as this one are affordable in terms of the 30 per cent affordability index.

In the informal intervention model, the mixing of residential and non-residential activities is common. Whilst this mixing helps create job opportunities and, in some cases, serves households' needs, it also has negative impacts, such as noise, bad odour and waste generation, amongst others. The results showed that inhabitants were largely satisfied with their living environment, despite their recorded dissatisfaction in terms of factors such as relatively small residential units' areas, unhealthy living spaces in some cases, poor accessibility to units and the challenges arising from the non-residential activities, etc. This contradiction between the recorded satisfaction and simultaneous dissatisfaction may be attributed to the fact that quality of living may not be a priority for inhabitants, just as long as they have a shelter or 'roof over their heads'.

The fact that the life–work/mixed-use concept is, arguably, applied in informal areas makes these areas more attractive than formal developments. But it is important to note that a clear border-line between living and working is crucial for the successful realization of the quality and dynamics of living and working in mixed-use housing provision.

The mixed-use model presented and discussed in this chapter identified major factors that will be of importance for the successful implementation of future mixed-use housing provisions. The residential/living area should allow flexibility/adaptability, extendability/affordability, and accessibility/visitability, all of which allow responsiveness to households' changing socio-economic needs whilst also considering their physical and mobile abilities (Nadim 2016a, 2016b). The non-residential part should ensure compatibility of its functions with residential activity. In this respect, non-residential activities should take occupational health and safety measures and the logistics required for the function into account. These requirements are necessary to ensure that the mixed use is acceptable to residents, and are therefore essential to the successful implementation of future mixed-use developments. Further research is currently taking place to investigate scenarios for building/construction systems that would facilitate the successful implementation of mainstream, proactive mixed-use housing provision that is incremental and affordable.

Acknowledgement

The work is part of an ongoing two-year research project funded by the Science and Technology Research Fund (STDF 5095) as part of the German Egyptian Research Fund (GERF) collaborative project investigating the future of housing in Egypt.

References

Abelson, P. (2009). Affordable housing: Concepts and policies. *Economic Papers* 28(1), 27–38.

Ahmed, M. N., Moussa, M. A. and Gaeiss, A. M. (2014). An analytical study for New Assiut City in the provision of suitable housing for low income – Evaluating 'Ibny Baytak project' – one of the national housing projects. *Journal of Engineering Sciences Assiut University Faculty of Engineering, 42*(6): 1462–1491.

Ahram Online. (2014). Cairo traffic costs Egypt LE47 bn a year: World Bank. *Ahram Online.* http://english.ahram.org.eg/News/103075.aspx

AlSayyad, N. (2011). *Cairo: Histories of a city.* Cambridge, MA: Belknap Press of Harvard University Press.

Bailyn, L., Drago, R., and Kochan, T. A. (2001). *Integrating work and family life: A holistic approach.* Massachusetts, MA: MIT, Sloan School of Management.

Blok, R., and Herwijnen, F. (2006). Quantifying structural flexibility for performance based life cycle design of buildings. Adaptables2006, TU/e, International Conference on Adaptable Building Structures, 3–5 July 2006, Eindhoven (The Netherlands).

Bredenoord, J., and Lindert, P. van (2010). Pro-poor housing policies: Rethinking the potential of assisted self-help housing. *Habitat International,* *34*(2010): 278–287.

CAPMAS. (2006). *Census of population, housing and establishments.* Cairo: CAPMAS.

CAPMAS. (2016). *Study for upgrading and developing informal areas in Egypt.* (In Arabic). Cairo: CAPMAS.

CAPMAS. (2017). Home. Central Agency for Public Mobilization and Statistics. www.capmas.gov.eg/

Casey, S. (2005). *Establishing standards for social infrastructure.* Queensland, Australia: The University of Queensland.

Chen, M. (2012). *The informal economy: Definitions, theories and policies.* Women in Informal Employment Globalisation and Organising, Working paper no 1. Retrieved from www.wiego.org/sites/default/files/publications/files/Chen_WIE GO_WP1.pdf

CIA. (2017). *The world factbook.* www.cia.gov/library/publications/the-world-factbook/fields/2212.html

Cisneros, H., Dyer Chamberlain, M. and Hickie, J. (2012). *Independent for life: Homes and neighbourhoods for an aging America.* 1st ed. Stanford, CA: Stanford Center on Longevity.

Colliers. (2015). Greater Cairo real estate market overview. Colliers International. Retrieved www2.colliers.com/en-EG

Demographia. (2019). 15th annual Demographia international housing affordability survey. 2019 Media Release.

Dhar, T. K., Hossain, M. and Rahman, K. R. (2013). How does flexible design promote resource efficiency for housing? A study of Khulna, Bangladesh. *Smart and Sustainable Built Environment,* 2(2), 140–157.

Dolan, T. (2012). *Live-work planning and design: Zero commute housing.* Hoboken, NJ: John Wiley & Sons Inc.

Douglas, J. (2006). *Building adaptation.* 2nd ed. Oxford: Butterworth-Heinemann.

ECORYS. (2010). *Cairo traffic congestion study.* Edited by ECORYS Nederland BV and SETS Lebanon. Cairo: World Bank and Government of Egypt.

Egypt Independent. (2013). Final issue: Problem of unemployment likely to worsen in Egypt. *Egypt Independent.* Retrieved from www.egyptindependent.com/final-issue-problem-unemployment-likely-worsen-egypt/

El-Batran, M., and Arandel, C. (1998). A shelter of their own: Informal settlement expansion in Greater Cairo and government responses. *Environment and Urbanization,* 10(1), 217–232.

El-Kouedi, H. and Madbouly, M. (2007). Tackling the shelter challenge of cities: Thinking it through together. World Bank. Retrieved http://siteresources .worldbank.org/INTHOUSINGLAND/Resources/339552-1180637750307/ Cairo.pdf

El-Mahdi, A. (2002). *Towards decent work in the informal sector: The case of Egypt.* Geneva: Employment Sector, International Labour Office.

Eurostat. (2017). Overcrowding rate. Eurostat. http://ec.europa.eu/eurostat/web/ gdp-and-beyond/quality-of-life/overcrowding-rate

Evans, G. (2003). The built environment and mental health. *Journal Urban Health*, 80(4) 536–555.

Fahmy, N. (2004). A culture of poverty or the poverty of a culture? Informal settlements and the debate over the state–society relationships in Egypt. *Middle East Journal*, 58(4): 597–611.

Fathy, H. (1962). Rural self-help housing. *Ekistics*, 13(80), 398–401. Retrieved from http://www.jstor.org/stable/43613693

Fulwood, B. M. (1987). Extendable houses: Process as alternative. *Housing and Society*, 14(1), 30–39.

Gijsbers, R. and Lichtenberg, J. (2014). Demand-driven selection of adaptable building technologies for flexibility-in-use. *Smart and Sustainable Built Environment*, 3(3): 237–260.

GIZ. (2013). *Participatory needs assessment in informal areas – Giza Governorate.* Bonn: GIZ.

Guran, N. and Whitehead, C. (2011). Planning and affordable housing in Australia and the UK: A comparative perspective. *Housing Studies*, 26(7–8): 1193–1214.

GOPP. (2017). *Land and urban planning: Issues and challenges for a new urban agenda.* Cairo, Egypt: GOPP. http://gopp.gov.eg/wp-content/uploads/2017/07/ Chapter-2.pdf

Groak, S. (1992). *The idea of building: Thought and action in the design and production of buildings.* 1st ed. London: E&FN Spon, an imprint of Chapman & Hall.

Habraken, N. (1998). Form and control in the built environment. In J. Teicher (Ed.), *The structure of the ordinary.* Cambridge, MA: MIT Press.

Harris, R. (1999). Slipping through the cracks: The origins of aided self-help housing 1918–53. *Housing Studies*, 14(3): 281–309.

Hoppenbrouwer, E., and Louw, E. (2005). Mixed-use development: Theory and practice in Amsterdam's eastern docklands. *European Planning Studies*, 13(7): 967–983.

HUD User. (2019). Defining housing affordability. *Hud User.* Retrieved from www.huduser.gov/portal/pdredge/pdr-edge-featd-article-081417.html

ILO. (2005). *Measurement of the informal economy.* Geneva: International Labour Office.

JICA. (2008). *The strategic urban development master plan study for sustainable development of the Greater Cairo Region in the Arab Republic of Egypt.* Cairo: Ministry of Housing, Utilities & Urban Development (MOHUUD); General Organization for Physical Planning (GOPP).

Kardash, H. S. (1983). The transformation of public housing provision in Egypt and the role of self help. Phd thesis. Newcastle-upon-Tyne, UK: Newcastle University.

Kaur, I. (2010). Government of Egypt, Japan, and the World Bank Jointly address unemployment challenges facing marginalised youth. *World Bank*. Retrieved from https://openknowledge.worldbank.org/bitstream/handle/10986/10924/5 54660BRI0Quic10Box349454B01PUBLIC1.pdf?sequence=1&isAllowed=y

Khallash, S., and Kruse, M. (2012). The future of work and work–life balance 2025. *Futures*, 44(7): 678–686.

Kipper, R. and Fischer, M. (2009). Cairo's informal areas: Between urban challenges and hidden potentials; Facts. Voices. Visions. Bonn: GIZ. Retrieved from www.egypt-urban.net/publication-cairos-informal-areas-between-urban-challenges-and-hidden-potentials-facts-voices-visions/

Kowaltowski,D. (1998). Aesthetics and self-built houses: An analysis of a brazilian setting. *Habitat International*, 22(3): 299–3112.

Kuang, W., and Li, X. (2012). Does China face a housing affordability issue? Evidence from 35 cities in China. *International Journal of Housing Markets and Analysis*, 5(3): 272–288.

Li, W. K. (2012). Does China face a housing affordability issue? Evidence from 35 cities in China. *International Journal of Housing Markets and Analysis*, 5(3): 272–288.

Mace, R., Hardie, G. and Place, J. (1991). Accessible environments: Toward universal design. In W. Preiser, J. Vischer and E. White (Eds.), *Design interventions: Toward a more humane architecture*. New York: Van Nostrand Reinhold.

Maisel, J. L. (2006). Toward inclusive housing and neighbourhood design: a look at visitability. *Community Development*, 37(3): 26–34.

Maisel, J., Smith, E. and Steinfeld, E. (2008). *Increasing home access: Designing for visitability*. Washington, DC: AARP Public Policy Institute.

Majale, M. (2008). Employment creation through participatory urban planning and slum upgrading: The case of Kitale, Kenya. *Habitat International*, 32(2): 270–282.

Manewa, A., Siriwardena, M., Ross, A. and Madanayake, U. (2016). Adaptable buildings for sustainable built environment. *Built Environment Project and Asset Management*, 6(2): 139–158.

Mansour, D. (2017). Dimensions of flexibility in housing: Synergies between informal housing in Egypt and Japanese housing. MSc thesis (unpublished). New Cairo: The German University in Cairo.

Mukhija, V. (2014). The value of incremental development and design in affordable housing. *Cityscape: A Journal of Policy Development & Research*, 16(2), 11–20.

Nadim, W. (2016a). A smart future housing in Egypt for all – a challenge or an opportunity? Proceedings of the CIB World Building Congress 2016. In K. Kähkönen and M. Keinänen (Eds.), *Proceedings of the CIB World Building Congress 2016: Volume I; Creating built environments of new opportunities*. Tampere University of Technology, Department of Civil Engineering. Construction Management and Economics. Report Vol. 18. Tampere: Tampere University of Technology.

Nadim, W. (2016b). Live-work and adaptable housing in Egypt: A zero commuting concept, lessons learnt from informal developments. *Smart and Sustainable Built Environment*, 5(3), 289–302.

Nadim, W., Bock, T. and Linner, T. (2014). Technological implants for sustainable autonomous upgrading of informal settlements in Cairo-Egypt. Presented at SB14 World Conference, Barcelona, Spain.

Nazmy, N. (2011). Ibny Baytak evaluative perspective. In M. K. El-Sayed and A. Arafat, *Land and housing in Egypt* (in Arabic). Development Partners for Research and Training, pp. 269–323.

Nientied, P., and Linden, J.-V.-D. (1988). The 'new' policy approach to housing: A review of the literature. *Public Administration and Development*, 8, 233–240.

Rakodi, C. (1989). Self-help housing: The debate and examples. *Habitat International*, 13(4), 5–13.

Rivzi, A. (1966). Self-help housing: An examination of the effectiveness of this policy in selected developing countries, MSc thesis. Vancouver: The University of British Columbia.

Rowley, A. (1996). Mixed-use development: Ambiguous concept, simplistic analysis and wishful thinking? *Planning Practice and Research*, 11(1), 85–97.

Sabry, S. (2010). How poverty is underestimated in Greater Cairo, Egypt. *Environment & Urbanization*, 22(2), 523–541.

Salama, R. (1995). User transformation of government housing projects: Case study, Egypt. PhD Thesis. McGill University Montreal, Canada.

Sayed, H. (2018). Egypt's demographic opportunity. Preliminary assessment based on 2017 census. UNFPA Egypt.

Sims, D. (2010). *Understanding Cairo: The logic of a city out of control*. Cairo: The American University Press.

Tipple, G. (1996). Housing extensions as sustainable development. *Habitat International*, 20(3), 367–376.

Trading Economics. (2015). Egypt unemployment rate. *Trading Economics*. Retrieved from https://tradingeconomics.com/egypt/unemployment-rate

Turner, J. F. (1980). Housing: Its part in another development. In *Housing: Process and Physical Form*. Philadelphia, PA: Aga Khan Award for Architecture.

UN. (1964). Manual on self-help housing. *Ekistics*, 17(103): 375–384.

UN. (2015). *World Population Prospects*. United Nations. Retrieved from www.un.org/en/development/desa/publications/world-population-prospects-2015-revision.html

UNESCO. (2017). Poverty. UNESCO. Retrieved from *Social and Human Sciences*. www.unesco.org/new/en/social-and-human-sciences/themes/international-migration/glossary/poverty/

Whitehead, C. M. (2007). Planning policies and affordable housing: England as a successful case study? *Housing Studies*, 22(1): 25–44.

World Bank. (2007). *Analysis of housing supply mechanisms – Final note*. World Bank.

World Bank. (2012, 21 August). Cairo traffic is much more than a nuisance. *World Bank*. Retrieved from www.worldbank.org/en/news/feature/2012/08/21/cairo-traffic-much-more-than-nuisance.

10 Collective Action under the Shadow of Contractual Governance: The Case of a Participatory Approach to Upgrade Cairo's 'Garbage Cities'

Nuno Gil and Samuel C. MacAulay

Abstract

The upgrading of informal urban areas is a pressing challenge for meeting the UN's goal to make cities a pathway to sustainable development. Complicating co-ordinated collective action is the diffusion of decision-making authority and control over critical resources in a context where there is a shortfall of institutions. Tackling this grand challenge thus requires designing inter-organisational contexts capable of navigating many institutional voids, including ill-defined property rights, weak regulation and inefficient markets. In this chapter, we draw on a case study of a development project that granted decision rights to the poor to upgrade Cairo's 'garbage cities' to further our understanding of this organisational challenge. Our aim is to illuminate a form of organising that is neglected in management scholarship. Its main attribute is the way by which contractual governance is supplemented with a consensus-oriented collective-action structure. Our main contribution is to theorise a trade-off central to this form of organising: collective action, under the shadow of contractual governance, economises on the high transaction costs that would otherwise be incurred to resolve ill-defined property rights. However, enfranchising the poor brings into the organisational boundaries the costs of collective action and risk of a tragedy of the commons.

10.1 Introduction

This empirical study theorises a form of organising with the following property: it supplements a nexus of legal contracts agreed upon to govern a set of resource exchanges with a collective-action structure by which decision rights are shared with other autonomous actors not governed by contracts. Motivating this choice is the recognition that the whole system is better off if its architecture allows some, but not all, resource exchanges to occur within an institutional regime of ill-defined property rights and inefficient markets. The main attribute of this form of organising is therefore the way in which it allows for collective-action governance (Hardin 1968; Ostrom 1990; Libecap 1989a) under the shadow of contractual governance (Williamson 1979).

Underlying this organisational design choice is a fundamental trade-off: incur the costs of consensus building, and the risk of a tragedy of the commons (Hardin 1968), to economise on the transaction costs that would otherwise be incurred to change the regime of ill-defined property rights and inefficient markets (Libecap 1989a, 1989b). Property rights are generally understood as a bundle of rights within a hierarchy of possible rights, including rights of ownership, access, withdrawal, management, exclusion and alienation (Schlager and Ostrom 1992; Libecap 1989a). Ill-defined property rights and inefficient markets create institutional voids that make it hard to mediate efficient and effective resource exchanges (Khanna and Palepu 1997; Xin and Pearce 1996). Institutional voids are a common characteristic of developing countries – environments where the capital, labour and product markets, legal systems, and other institutions are still transitioning towards economic liberalisation (Khanna and Palepu 1997).

In this study, we claim that the choice to supplement contractual governance with collective-action governance within a single organisational context flows from the recognition that some of the much-needed resources to achieve the higher-order goal are too costly and time-consuming to acquire through markets or regulation. Hence, contracts are employed to govern resource exchanges that are measurable, involve well-defined property rights, efficient markets and low degrees of reciprocal interdependence. But if the resources are hard to measure, markets are inefficient, property rights are ill-defined and there is high reciprocal interdependence, then consensus-oriented collective action is used instead to encourage cooperation and voluntary contributions of resources. In other words, what is distinctive in this form of organising, both in the relationships between its components and with the environment and in the principles guiding organisational design and evolution (Fjeldstad et al. 2012; Simon 1962), is the way collective action occurs under the shadow of contractual governance. Prior to entering this field, theory suggested this organisational design was unnecessarily complicated and impractical, so we were curious to understand its logic. Our analysis suggests an alternative interpretation: this form of organising is a useful social artefact for tackling socio-economic problems enmeshed in institutionally underdeveloped environments. So, like any 'contraption', though this form of organising is seemingly complex and inefficient, it is useful for a particular purpose.

We ground our insights on an organisational system formed to tackle one of the grand challenges of our time – the inhumane and undignified living and working conditions in informal settlements. The inhabitants of these urban areas lack access to basic services and infrastructure; lack property rights and are constantly exposed to the threat of eviction; and their housing rarely complies with planning and building regulations.[1] Urban informality fuels poverty, social exclusion, radicalisation, hunger, gender inequality and mass migratory pressures; all of which threaten the global order (UN-Habitat 2003, 2015). And yet, one-quarter of the world's urban population – and almost two-thirds of Africa's population – live in slums, the most deprived form of informal settlements (UN-Habitat 2003). With 90 per cent of urban growth happening in the developing world the magnitude of this grand challenge is alarming: by 2023 alone, the number of slum dwellers is projected to reach 2 billion, about a quarter of the world's population (UN-Habitat 2008). So tackling urban informality is a pressing challenge to meeting the UN's sustainable development goals.

To further our understanding of innovative organisational designs, we chose to study development projects to upgrade the informal settlements of Cairo – the world's fastest-growing city, where urban informality already affects more than 15 million people (AUC 2014). As a gateway for migratory flows into Europe, Cairo has been at the forefront of efforts from the international community to upgrade the city's informal areas. The notion of upgrading informal settlements encompasses a wide range of intertwined activities to integrate an informal area in the urban fabric along physical, social and legal dimensions. For example, improving access to basic infrastructure and public services, tackling community needs, and resolving land tenure issues. We illustrate our argument with evidence from a development project to upgrade two of the 'garbage cities' of Cairo – informal areas occupied by the Zabbaleen ('garbage people' in Arabic), a large community of informal waste pickers, the 'poorest

---

[1] 'Slums' is the technical term for the most deprived form of informal settlements (UN-Habitat 2003).

of the poor', who manage more than a third of the solid waste produced daily in Cairo.

We show, at the heart of the organisational context set up to upgrade the garbage cities, a nexus of legal contracts governing exchanges of formal resources (finance, certification, human capital and technology) between the Egyptian state, local authorities, suppliers and international actors. We also show how a collective-action structure was then added to enfranchise the poor, and let the ultimate beneficiaries directly influence capital allocation. By sharing decision rights with the poor *under the shadow of contractual governance*, it became costly for the organisational designers to exclude the poor and violate the bargain when conflict emerged due to rivalrous preferences. So there was a real risk of common losses if the participants behaved unco-operatively and chose to free-ride by ruling out compromise. And yet, this organisational design encouraged the poor to co-operate and volunteer informal resources ('know-how', networks of trust) needed to identify real problems and formulate sustainable solutions. All of which reveal a fundamental trade-off underlying this organisational choice: incur the costs of consensus building to economise on the transaction costs and delays that would otherwise be incurred to change *ex ante* the institutional regime surrounding the poor.

We organise the remainder of this chapter as follows. We first discuss organisational design for tackling grand challenges. Then we explain our methods and data set, and examine the organisational design and performance of the participatory development project set up to upgrade two of the garbage cities in Cairo. Finally, we conclude with a discussion of new forms of organising in institutionally underdeveloped environments.

10.2   Designing Organisations to Tackle Grand Challenges

Grand challenges relate to socio-economic problems that are so complex, uncertain and difficult to resolve that they seem intractable. Examples of these include ending global hunger and urban poverty, or curing cancer (Colquitt and George 2011; Ferraro, Etzion and Gehman 2015; Grodal and O'Mahony 2017). While there are no easy managerial solutions for grand challenges, management scholars agree that their underlying characteristics change extant boundary conditions in management research (Eisenhardt, Graebner and Sonenshein 2016). A recurring pattern that explains the complexity and uncertainty of the task structure for tackling grand challenges is the need to orchestrate many complementary resources controlled by multiple autonomous actors. Hence, from an organisational perspective, grand challenges require both a high degree of differentiation among the participants to attend to the different facets of the task structure, and a high degree of integration in order to achieve desirable outcomes (Knudsen and Srikanth 2014).

Organising for tackling grand challenges is particularly complex in institutional environments lacking market-supporting infrastructure, specialised intermediaries, contract-enforcing mechanisms and the codified, enacted and enforced rule of law (Khanna and Palepu 1997; George, McGahan and Prabhu 2012). To navigate these institutional voids, organisations use 'intermediaries' to broker relationships and bring about activities that could not readily happen otherwise (McDermott, Corredoira and Kruse 2009; Mair, Marti and Ventresca 2012). For example, intermediaries such as business incubators (Dutt et al. 2016) and development organisations (Mair et al. 2012) help private firms build infrastructure to support private transactions; likewise, science parks help entrepreneurs access public resources for capability and certification-building (Armanios et al. 2017). So far, the focus of this literature has been in furthering our understanding of how intermediaries help the private firm navigate institutional voids to enter and succeed in emerging markets. As a result, we still know little about how intermediaries help governments access private resources to build public goods and fill the institutional voids.

This is an important gap, because there are intermediaries whose role is precisely to help governments orchestrate the resources necessary for building public goods. In the development aid sector, donors such as private foundations, e.g. the Ford Foundation, the Bill and Melinda Gates Foundation, and multilateral organisations, such as the EU and World Bank, operate under mandates to aid struggling governments. But donors cannot provide aid unless the recipient state asks for aid and agrees to be aided (Tan-Mullins, Mohan and Power 2010). Facilitating resource exchanges between the donor and the recipient of funds are the implementation agencies. These agencies can either be fully owned by advanced economies, e.g. Germany's Gesellschaft für Internationale Zusammenarbeit (GIZ), or be part of a multilateral organisation, e.g. UN-Habitat. Their role is to support the state to develop the capabilities necessary to obtain private resources from donors, and certifying to the donors that their money will be well used. So the involvement of the implementation agency is beneficial to the donor and recipient of funds, in a role akin to intermediaries of private enterprises (Mair et al. 2012; Dutt et al. 2016).

Another task of the implementation agency is to design the inter-organisational context for implementing aid. Organisational design choices mandate interactions for exchanging and mobilising resources in the pursuit of collective goals (Gulati and Puranam 2009). As the systems architect, the implementation agency must assemble a vast network of autonomous actors that agree to colla-borate under an identifiable system goal. To succeed, the partici-pants must integrate effort, and thus resolve the problems of co-ordination and cooperation that are fundamental to any form of organising (Puranam, Alexy and Reitzig 2014); this co-ordinated and sustained collective action must also navigate the absence and weakness of institutions in the environment (George, McGahan and Prabhu 2012). To be effective, the organisation needs to mobilise both formal resources, such as finance, human capital and certifica-tion, as well as informal resources, such as 'know-how', networks of trust and traditional technologies (George et al. 2016). The complexity of this task structure asks important questions of organisational designers, such as:

- Which actors should be enfranchised and which should stay outside the organisational boundaries?
- When should legal contracts and markets be used to govern resource exchanges?
- How can norms of cooperation, mutual trust and a shared identity flourish in the absence of a centralised hierarchy and robust institutions?

We turn now to discuss how we tackled these questions through our case study of the organisational system set up to upgrade Cairo's garbage cities.

10.3   Methods and Data

Our study follows the tradition of inductive research through 'extreme cases' as a means to generate fresh evidence and yield new theoretical insights into novel forms of organising and managing (Siggelkow 2007; Eisenhardt and Graebner 2007). Our extreme case is a project-based organisational context set up to upgrade two informal settle-ments of Cairo – the world's fastest-growing city, with a population projected to grow from 2 million in 1950 to an estimated 21 million by 2020, and 29 million by 2030 (UN 2018). The lead architect was GIZ, an implementation agency fully owned by the German govern-ment, who chose to enfranchise the poor, the ultimate beneficiaries. And though multiple social dilemmas ensued after this choice, the organisational system was effective. In roughly three years, it delivered basic infrastructure to improve the welfare of two waste-picking communities living and working in the garbage cities, while changing intertwined institutions to ensure a sustainable solution. This outcome led to them winning a competitive international award,[2] making the case particularly suitable for building new insights into organising to tackle grand challenges in environments with a shortfall of institutions.

We gained access to the research site in 2016, after GIZ agreed to endorse our independent study on new forms of organising to tackle grand societal changes. Beginning in 2016, members of the research team visited Cairo three times to gain a sense of the challenge and meet international actors. At the time of writing, we were still awaiting security clearance to meet with government officials. Still, up to spring 2018, we conducted forty-three semi-structured interviews (face to face or via Skype), which were restricted to staff from implementation agencies, donors, international NGOs and consultants, using a snowball approach to identify relevant respondents. We recorded and transcribed all interviews, with a commitment to the interviewees that all quotes would be anonymised, which enabled them to be candid about politically sensitive issues. Some consultants acted as a proxy for the perspectives of the state and local governments as they had previously worked in or for public administration. We complemented interview data with the analysis of 127 archival documents, e.g. policy documents, project proposals, funding agreements, technical reports and videos, and articles in the mainstream press. A student proficient in Arabic helped with the translation of some archival documents and press articles.[3]

10.4   Analysis

10.4.1   Garbage Cities: Between a Failure of the State and the Market

Urban informality has long been a major challenge facing Egypt due to fast population growth, urban migration, lack of an affordable housing market and the successive failures of rehousing policies by the state. In Greater Cairo, this conflation of factors has forced the urban poor to settle informally in agricultural and desert lands, historic districts and even

---

[2] 2016 Guangzhou International Award for Urban Innovation.
[3] The number of interviews and archival documents refers to the totality of our data set, which includes other development projects in our sample, not just the GIZ project discussed at length in this chapter.

cemeteries (Khalifa 2015; Hegazy 2016). As the growth rate of informal areas reached 3.4 per cent per year (compared to 0.3 per cent for legal areas), millions of Cairenes were trapped in alarming life conditions in informal areas: limited access to basic utilities and social services, ram-shackle houses, and threat of forced evictions (Sims 2010). Under pressure from the international community,[4] the Egyptian state recog-nised the need to see the informal areas not as illegal settlements, but as outcomes of policies of negligence and laissez-faire (Harders 2003). To tackle the problem, in 2008 the state set up an agency, the Informal Settlement Development Facility (ISDF), but it was hamstrung by lack of resources. As Cairo's population continued to grow, alarm bells rang in Europe. As the most populous country in North Africa and the Arab world, and a transiting country for migrants, concerns about the informal areas becoming hotbeds for radicalisation and terrorism mounted.

Entwined with the grand challenge of tackling urban informality is the informal economy. For example, an estimated 10 per cent of dwellers in informal areas globally work as informal waste pickers, collecting, sorting and recycling waste in makeshift workshops and households (Walker 2013; Wilson, Velis and Cheeseman 2006). Poor solid-waste manage-ment leads to hazardous garbage piles in the streets and illegal dumping, and is a major source of public-health, sanitation and environmental problems. Responsibility for solid-waste management tends to be muddled between central and local governments, but in rapidly develop-ing cities, the local authorities rarely have the resources to carry out their tasks. Complicating matters are a number of obstacles to using the private-sector, including contractual breaches by the underfunded local authorities; sabotage by the informal sector; corruption; and the lack of local knowledge of the international firms (Wilson et al. 2006). So infor-mal waste pickers represent considerable savings for the state; both because they pick up the waste left uncollected by the public and private sectors, and because they recycle large volumes of waste, reducing the need for landfills.

And Cairo's case is telling. At the turn of the twenty-first century, Egypt's capital was embroiled in a major garbage crisis. Of over 20,000 tonnes of waste generated daily by the megacity, less than half was picked up for processing and disposal by the private contractors (Fahmi and Sutton 2006). Only the work of the

---

[4] In December 2005, Egypt hosted the meeting 'Cairo Declaration on Sustainable Arab Cities: Security of Tenure and Good Governance', where the participants committed to the UN Millennium Development Goals.

Zabbaleen averted a major public health catastrophe. The Zabbaleen are a community of 60,000–70,000 families who live in the garbage cities spread across Cairo (NSWMP 2011). The men collect garbage manually, or use donkey and motorised carts; the women and children sort waste manually for their families, or against a low daily wage for others, separating paper, plastic, glass and food into bags ready to be sold for recycling.

Living in the garbage cities, the Zabbaleen are surrounded by potentially infectious, disease-ridden garbage. There is also a generalised lack of sanitary services and healthcare and low life expectancy, and child labour is the rule. Yet the Zabbaleen economic model has proved resilient. The first major blow had been the state's decision, in the early 2000s, to privatise solid-waste management collection. This action restricted the role of local governments ('municipalities'[5]) to that of monitoring solid-waste management and excluded the Zabbaleen from collection. Facing a potential loss of three-quarters of their earnings, the Zabbaleen put even more emphasis on recycling, creating one of the world's most efficient solid-waste management systems – recycling up to 85 per cent of the collected waste; by contrast, the contractors were required to recycle only 20 per cent of the waste collected (Fahmi and Sutton 2010; Iskander 2000). Another blow came in 2009, when the state ordered the slaughter of around 300,000 pigs kept by the Zabbaleen.[6] Before the cull, the Zabbaleen would bring the waste into their households to sort the organic waste to feed the pigs, which were then sold to meat processors. After the cull, the Zabbaleen started to perform preliminary sorting near the waste bins and illegal dump sites, leaving the organic waste to decompose on the streets:

We do it [waste collection] now very quickly not to be caught. The district officer breaks our donkey carts if they see us scavenging on the street . . . they [authorities] are getting what they are paying for . . . everything was going as easy as pie during the donkey cart days. But they prevented us from work . . . we used to earn several times our current income. (Zabbaleen; EcoConServ 2010)

They [the Zabbaleen] are a backward, unorganized and illegalized community. The way they operate is unhygienic and they do not know how to benefit from the collected garbage. They are generally incompatible with a modern waste management system. (Private Contractor; EcoConServ 2010)

---

[5] Greater Cairo is administratively organised in three governorates (Giza, Cairo and Qalyubera), which collectively oversee thirty-five municipalities, or town governments.
[6] The government insisted the cull was a precaution due to the outbreak of swine flu epidemic in Mexico and the United States. But many Zabbaleen, who were predominantly Coptic Christian, complained that the order was based on religious bias since the World Health Organization had suggested that the cull was unnecessary.

By the 2010s, with the Zabbaleen still playing a critical role in avoiding a catastrophe, the state recognised that privatisation had failed. Due to a lack of local know-how, the contractors overlooked the difficulties of serving Cairo's narrow streets and alleys with their modern trucks; they also struggled to recruit staff because of the social stigma attached to garbage collectors. Complicating matters further, the municipalities struggled to pay the contractors and meet their contractual obligations. This made it hard for the contractors to reach their performance targets, triggering fees which the contractors subsequently refused to pay. Exhausted by the inefficiency of public administration, one contractor left Cairo (Scheinberg et al. 2010). In turn, the residents continued to prefer paying the Zabbaleen to collect their garbage from their doorstep, as opposed to taking the garbage out and putting it into the contractors' large bins. But the residents were frustrated that they also had to pay a 'cleaning' fee for the contractors' services. Attempts by the contractors to hire the Zabbaleen also fell flat since most of them found it more lucrative to stay in the informal sector. Occasionally, the Zabbaleen sought to sabotage the contractors' work by collecting waste before the contractors could come to collect it.

When the state asked multilateral organisations for advice, the response was clear: there was an urgent need to upgrade the garbage cities and integrate them in the formal economy (EcoConServ 2010). Seeing a funding opportunity, the German implementation agency GIZ proposed a pilot project to the Egyptian state as part of its Participatory Development Programme (PDP). This was a bilateral collaboration, initiated in 2004 to attract international funds, and GIZ's participatory approach aligned with the advice from the multilaterals. As one GIZ official said, 'experience suggests you really have to start with an integrated approach involving all stakeholders'. We turn now to discuss the organizational ideas behind the participatory approach.

10.4.2 Participatory Development: A Choice to Share Decision Rights

Participatory approaches are a response of aid development policy to a widely felt need for a power reversal between the implementation agencies and beneficiaries (Chambers 1983). The basic idea is to see the poor as development partners, or as Chambers (1983) says, 'to put the last first'. A participatory approach recognises the poor lack well-defined property rights, but control critical informal resources, e.g. know-how, networks of trust and informal economic activity. The participatory development approach was first institutionalised in the review of the UN 1986–90 Programme for African Economic Recovery and Development. It stated:

The empowerment of the people to effectively involve themselves in creating the structures and in designing policies and programmes that serve the interests of all as well as to effectively contribute to the development process and share equitably in its benefits. (Arusha 1990)

As with any decision to locate decision rights, a participatory approach is an organisational design choice (Aghion and Tirole 1997; Gambardella, Panico and Valentini 2015). It recognises that the poor are not a monolithic entity, but rather a collection of like-situated people. And since informal resources are hard to acquire through market transactions (Kogut and Zander 1996), a participatory approach does not seek a legal framework to govern resource exchanges with the poor. Instead, the idea is to enfranchise them with the help of an intermediary such as a local NGO, and so build a temporary informal organisation similar to those set up to tackle emergency situations (Majchrzak, Jarvenpaa and Hollingshead 2007). This informality belies the goal to resolve ill-defined property rights and formalise informal economic activity. But a participatory approach recognises that changes to the institutional regime surrounding the poor would be unaffordable due to the high transaction costs of bargaining, delays, information measurement, supervision, enforcement and political action (Williamson 1979).

Numerous accounts suggest that a participatory approach works better than a top-down one at encouraging the poor to voluntarily contribute informal resources and attracting good maintenance for the outcomes (Baiocchi 2003; Osmani 2008). Yet creating conditions for effective participation of the poor is not easy. Poor people tend to mistrust the authorities, lack the skills to participate in collaborative exercises and may not see how the benefits outweigh the opportunity costs (Osmani 2008). Other issues include the risks of local elites capturing the participatory activities to solidify previous inequalities, and of the poor feeling incentivised to distort information (Rigon 2014; Platteau and Abraham 2002). Relatedly, there is a risk that a participatory approach becomes a rhetorical discourse, masquerading for what is effectively a consultation process. Warnings against the 'tyranny' of the participatory approach (Cooke and Kothari 2001; Kumar and Corbridge 2002) notwithstanding, development policy claims its benefits outweigh the costs. But before we examine the implementation of the participatory approach, we must examine the contracts that enabled this approach in the first place.

10.4.3 Developing a 'Nexus' of Contracts

A 'nexus' of formal contracts governing resource exchanges was at the core of the organisational context set up by GIZ to upgrade the garbage cities of the Zabbaleen. First, there was the 2004 bilateral cooperation agreement that governed GIZ's activities in Cairo. It constituted recognition and endorsement by the Egyptian state of GIZ's participatory approach. In a country characterised by an authoritarian state, this agreement let GIZ engage with local governments, civil-society actors and the Cairenes. State endorsement also gave GIZ the opportunity to influence national policy; as one GIZ official said, 'we've a contract with the Ministry of Planning, they own the program, they're the national anchor'. As part of this agreement, GIZ co-located an operational team in the Ministry facilities, and committed to a schedule of monthly meetings and reports of its plans and activities.

One level down, GIZ formalised cooperation with the governorates, the administrative entities that represented the state locally and had delegated authority to implement the national solid-waste policy and oversee the municipalities. The latter were the administrative bodies responsible for paying the waste contractors, monitoring the activities of both the contractors and the Zabbaleen, and levying and collecting fees. For the pilot project, GIZ chose to work with the Qalyubera governorate, an entity overseeing over 5 million Cairenes spread across eleven municipalities. With the endorsement of the state, the governor entered into a contract with GIZ: in exchange for cost-free capital investment and capability building, the governorate would contribute public land to build waste-management facilities and give GIZ access to two municipalities which hosted garbage cities. As part of this contract, GIZ took governorate officials into visits abroad to show them participatory approaches in action; GIZ also set up local units in the governorates – the urban upgrading units (UUUs) – and trained UUU staff in conducting inclusive workshops with the poor:

The co-operation with GIZ and the Ministry of Planning is based on a scientific basis and a clear strategy ... the Qalyubeya governorate faced a lot of challenges related to solid waste management ... this project stands as a model for cooperation between the Governorate and civil society as it supports the desired development. (Governor of Qalyubeya[7])

Agreements with the authorities notwithstanding, GIZ lacked funds to finance the development project and was constrained by rules requiring organising costly international tenders to select suppliers. A solution emerged in 2010 when the Bill and Melinda Gates Foundation announced plans to fund five projects to fight urban poverty in Africa. For the Gates Foundation, this was an experiment to find out if there was a 'silver bullet ... something that could be transformative', as one consultant noted. In alignment with the goal of GIZ, the donor's main aim was to fund projects to improve the lives of the urban poor, and with the potential to create a model that could apply to all developing-world cities:

As the world undergoes the largest wave of urban growth in history, we believe there is an opportunity for city governments and the urban poor to work together to find solutions that will address their common problems. (Senior Programme Officer of the Gates initiative[8])

The relationship between GIZ and the Gates Foundation rapidly became symbiotic. The reputation of the GIZ–PDP programme in Egypt, the oldest GIZ programme worldwide, reassured the donor that their money would be put to good use. There was also full alignment between GIZ's participatory approach and the donor's interests in finding ways to 'engage with the poor ... turn them from being beneficiaries into partners', and let the poor be, as Melinda Gates said, 'serious actors' in the development process.[9] In turn, GIZ welcomed aid from the Gates Foundation, as it was unclear when aid from the EU, another potential donor, would arrive. Leveraging a shift of the Egyptian state towards more democratic forms of governance after the Egyptian revolution of 2011, the $5million grant from the Gates Foundation came with a commitment to a participatory approach, cost and schedule targets, and clear reporting and monitoring requirements. But unexpectedly, in 2012, the Gates Foundation decided not to further engage with urban development and delegated the management of their urban projects portfolio to Cities Alliance, a leading NGO in the sector. They made it

[7] GIZ, 'Integrated community based solid waste management in Qalyubeya: A challenge in Greater Cairo Region.' Video interview, 2014. Participatory Development Programme in Urban Areas.

[8] 'Gates Foundation awards $27.2 million to fight urban poverty in Africa', *Philanthropy News Digest*, 30 September 2010: http://philanthropynewsdigest.org/news/gates-foundation-awards-27.2-million-to-fight-urban-poverty-in-africa.

[9] Melanie Walker, '"Voices of change": A trip through Dharavi'. *Impatient Optimists*, January 2012. Bill and Melinda Gates Foundation.

known that grant amendments and no-cost extensions would be ruled out, but any outcome that met the charitable purpose using anything above 75 per cent of the funds by December 2013 would be fine; one respondent from Cities Alliance said:

> They [Gates Foundation] like to eradicate things, things you can measure and quantify. Bill Gates would ask us questions like, 'Can I buy all the slums? What's the difference between a good slum and a bad slum?' They wanted something simple, we were offering complexity ... urban development is one step forward, two steps backwards.

The nexus of contracts between GIZ, the state, the governorates, the donor and Cities Alliance established the core structure of the organisational context set up to upgrade the garbage cities. This structure evolved step by step as GIZ orchestrated the necessary formal resources, e.g. certification, finance and human capital. These resources were measurable and benefited from clear property rights, making the exchanges amenable to contractual governance. Also facilitating the conversion of these resource exchanges into transactions was low reciprocal interdependency: the idea was to pool the resources in the hands of GIZ to allow the implementation agency to get on with the job. Still, in exchange for the resources, GIZ had to negotiate a new layer of constraints. And so, contractual governance left the organisational system constrained by subgoals, a budget, deadlines, procedures and a commitment to a participatory approach. Yet, without acquiring the local expertise and trust of the Zabbaleen, this system would struggle to identify real problems and produce sustainable solutions. We turn now to examine how, for this purpose, collective action was added under the shadow of this contractual governance.

10.4.3   The Participation of the Poor in Development

The basic idea of a participatory approach is that the beneficiaries should be in a position to directly influence and share control over the processes, strategic choices and resource allocation. Put simply, the aim is to let the poor directly influence the decisions that affect their lives. Of course, to enfranchise the poor is risky. The poor are a large group with heterogeneous interests; mutual trust between the poor and local authorities tends to be low; the separate interests of the poor, donor, implementation agency and authorities may be difficult to align; and a history of co-operation and collective search for consensus is lacking. Furthermore, if conflict emerges, the shadow of contractual governance makes it costly to renege on the bargain offered to the poor – excluding the poor would then require renegotiating the nexus of contracts. This does not mean that, merely by sharing decision rights, the organisational context is open. On the contrary, the system remains closed. GIZ was the gatekeeper, with power to select new participants based upon the resources they could bring in. Which is why, in addition to the Zabbaleen, GIZ chose to enfranchise the cash-strapped municipalities and the local popular councils elected by the residents of the municipalities.

To get consensus, GIZ planned one year of regular face-to-face meetings with the poor, employing a local NGO to assemble a representative sample of attendants and facilitate the meetings. The emphasis of the meetings was to search for common ground on the underlying problems standing in the way of an effective and sustainable integration of the garbage cities in the formal city. As one GIZ official said, 'It takes a very long dialogue, lots of workshops and community meetings to understand the role of the community, the informal jobs.' The risk of common losses was high because the budget was rigid and, at any point, any one party could make demands disproportional to what it was willing to offer and refuse to make concessions, or rule out sharing private information critical to co-producing an equitable solution. In other words, a collective-action arena was created where the capital available worked as a de facto common-pool resource, juxtaposing low excludability from capital allocation decisions with high rivalry on those decisions.

Predictably, GIZ, as the systems leader, found it hard to encourage information sharing and co-operation. The Zabbaleen worried about the authorities coming to evict them and sell their land to real-estate projects. And, wary of fines, the waste pickers were also reluctant to reveal their revenues, and the places where they were picking up, recycling and dumping waste, as well as collection routes. The residents, too, were concerned about being punished by the authorities if they complained too much. In turn, the governorates did not want to make premium land available to build infrastructure to support the Zabbaleen activities. And neither did they disclose their budget for solid-waste management, because they worried the Zabbaleen could use this information opportunistically if they were to bid for contracts in the future. The municipalities did not want to reveal how much money was collected in fines either, as bribes were likely to be involved, and so were pushing instead for stricter regulation.[10] As one GIZ official said:

---

[10] While outside the scope of this study, the mistrust between the participants was not helped by the fact that the Zabbaleen belong to the minority Coptic Christian community in a country with Islam as the state religion.

We find welcoming conditions and understanding in the highest level of government and with residents . . . but to connect these two levels requires a lot of effort
from all involved . . . there were people who wanted to keep the status quo, it was
competitive . . . it was a long process to get the municipality to accept the role of
the Zabbaleen.

To encourage the parties to volunteer private information, GIZ
presented itself as a facilitator without private interest: 'There
wasn't a sense that GIZ was leading, they were supporting but
never branding it as a western donor pushing their agenda', said
one respondent. For each workshop, which could last several hours,
the Zabbaleen were free to choose the venue and the people to
represent them. In total, around 1,000 Zabbaleen participated in
the workshops; 7 committees of 10–12 residents also met weekly. In
addition, if one party was reluctant to share information in
a multilateral meeting, GIZ would meet first with that party separately to allay fears of harming their own interests by sharing private
information. As GIZ said:

We've procedures to get to consensus: When we say to community groups,
'you've to pay more' that is a financial loss for them. But if they don't pay more
they don't get proper waste management; the same for the informal sector: If you
formalise, you've more scrutiny, pay taxes, but also get a contract, more security.
For the municipality, if you improve waste management you get less anger, even if
in the short term you've to pay a bit more.

Over time, mutual trust and a sense of shared identity emerged
between the participants, enabling them to openly discuss alternative
solutions. As one GIZ official noted, 'we don't need to have the same
opinions. But if you've everyone involved, the voices that seek
a solution speak higher . . . it's about looking at solutions where
everybody is winning.' The nexus of contracts gave GIZ the authority
to offer inducements for co-operation, in that GIZ had money to
implement whatever solution was agreed upon by all the parties. Yet
GIZ was not in a position to force a solution upon the others, even if
it tried to use the money to 'buy' collaboration, because of the ill-
defined property rights and the contractual commitment to
a participatory approach. Rather, the inducements that GIZ could
offer were there to facilitate consensus building.

10.4.4 *Organisational Performance*

To examine the performance of this organisational context, we investigated three entwined dimensions central to tackling the growth of urban

informality. The extent to which the context succeeded in: (i) building basic infrastructure; (ii) changing the institutions to ensure a sustainable solution; and (iii) the elapsed time in achieving these subgoals. The evidence suggests this system succeeded in dignifying the living and working conditions in the garbage cities, while formalizing the informal activities in a sustainable fashion – and did so in a relatively short period of time. Clearly, the solutions agreed upon could not be achieved unless all parties co-operated and came to develop a sense of shared identity.

First, the activities of 200 waste pickers were formalised into four legal entities. These entities were awarded contracts from the municipalities through competitive tendering for 80 per cent of the waste produced daily; in exchange, the Zabbaleen received motorised carts and saw their workshops upgraded, at no cost to them. The municipalities were equipped, also at no cost to them, with technology to monitor the Zabbaleen, including motorcycles, GPS tracking and a Geographic Information System to map and improve waste collection routes. Second, the Zabbaleen women were organised into a legal entity. They were trained to separate material that could not be sold for recycling, but was highly combustible. In exchange, this entity was awarded a contract with Lafarge, a cement manufacturer, by which Lafarge committed to collect and transport the material to their plants to use as additional fuel.[11] And finally, the governorate received a $1.5 million investment on a waste-recovery centre and a transfer station, at no cost for them but in exchange for land. By the end of 2013, the project was almost concluded, a remarkable achievement in a sector where people perceive no-cost extensions as the norm.

Importantly, the contracts proved flexible enough to cope with the costs of collective action. For example: GIZ was allowed to retender the capital projects after bids from an international tender turned out to be unaffordable; the donor allowed money reallocations to avoid no-cost extensions, enabling GIZ to invest in units at the local hospitals to deal with the occupational issues of the Zabbaleen; the governorate agreed to make land near the garbage cities available to build the waste facilities after the Zabbaleen complained the initial land on offer was too far away, and the bilateral agreement of cooperation with the Egyptian state proved resilient enough to cope with a shift towards further centralisation by the state. This shift was

---

[11] D. Perilli, 'Lafarge tackles hurdles to refuse-derived fuels production in Egypt', *Global Cement*, 3 June 2015.

significant enough by 2015 that the new governor feared any publicity that could shine a light on the participatory approach; as one
respondent said:

China connected from LinkedIn, and we got an email to invite us to apply to the
award. We talked to the governorate . . . we had big discussions with the governor,
a new military guy; we got to convince him . . . in the end the project was
nominated and the governor got relaxed.

More challenging, though, was leveraging local outcomes to affect
the broader environment. The initial official reaction was good, and
a test run was started to create more Zabbaleen-run companies.[12]
In addition, the government the Zabbaleen to discuss a new
national solid-waste management policy (NSWMP 2014). This
warm reaction was linked to the arrival in government of Laila
Iskander, a civil-society actor passionate about helping the
Zabbaleen:

I saw the informal enterprises of garbage collecting and recycling turning from
donkey carts to trucks, from mere sorting to processing . . . competing in the true
world of private enterprise. I have no fear for the Zabbaleen. They are unbeatable.
In 2000, when the multinationals were coming in, I used to worry, I couldn't even
sleep. But now, try it, you can't beat them. You just can't. They will do anything to
access the resources.

Yet implementing the new policy was complicated. The government
initially asked GIZ to train other public agencies, but the two parties
failed to agree on how to do it – 'I can be flexible, but if it's just one action
for political reasons, I cannot do it; we had big fights', said a GIZ official.
As time moved on, the Egyptian state became more centralised and Laila
left government. Without a political sponsor, an application by the
Egyptian state to the World Bank for a $150 million loan to integrate
more Zabbaleen was dropped.[13] In sum, this organisational 'contraption'
enabled achievement of the system goal. But institutional shifts at field
level have, at least for now, constrained its diffusion within Egypt.

10.5   Discussion

As stand-alone governance structures, both contractual governance
(Macneil 1978; Williamson 1979, 1985) and collective-action governance (Olson 1965; Hardin 1968; Ostrom 1990) have been subject to

[12] S. El Wardany, 'Why Cairo recycles better than NYC in waste-picking tale: Cities,'
Bloomberg, 20 January 2015.
[13] World Bank, *Cairo Municipal Solid Waste Management Project* (P152961). Project
Information Document: Concept Stage. The World Bank, 2014.

attention by theorists in organisation design. The high transaction costs of transforming collective action into contractual governance – the costs of 'contracting for property rights' (Libecap 1989a, 1989b) – have also been extensively theorised. And the idea that simple contracts can be used in conjunction with complex governance structures reserved for complex relations is itself also not new (Williamson 1979). Yet the combination of contractual *and* collective-action governance – the idea of contracting 'for' collective action if we will – remains under-explored, both empirically and theoretically. In this study, our analysis suggests that this seemingly unwieldy form of organising can be advantageous when some of the much-needed resources exist within a regime of ill-defined property rights and inefficient markets – a frequent situation facing enterprises in developing economies.

10.5.1 The Nexus of Contracts

Economising on transaction costs is a major driver for the choice of one form of governance over another (Williamson 1979, 1985). When transaction costs are negligible, organisations lack incentives to bring activities in-house, as it is more attractive, instead, to acquire the resources they need on the market. In our focal case, the nexus of contracts governing the resource exchanges between the authorities, donor and the implementation agency is in agreement with these ideas. Exchanges of finance, land, human capital and certification were not difficult to define in terms of amount, purpose, recipient, timescale and monitoring rules; they were amenable to contractual governance (Williamson 1985). Also, these exchanges did not involve high degrees of reciprocal interdependence, and so were not difficult to decompose into contractible transactions (Baldwin 2007). Rather, orchestrating these formal resources was more about pooling them in the hands of GIZ in order to enable the implementation agency to get on with their job and implement the project.

Of course, building a nexus of contracts in an institutionally underdeveloped environment involves high transaction costs because of the structure of the political arena. But the analysis shows there was no need to write complete contracts, and indeed the nexus of contracts turned out to be flexible enough to adapt to changes in requirements over time. These findings are consistent with the idea that contractual governance assumes that, through political negotiations with reasonable costs, parties can reach sufficient alignment of interests *ex ante* of the contract agreement, and safeguards can be devised to deter opportunistic behaviour *ex post* (Macneil 1978; Williamson 1985). Hence, the nexus of contracts succeeded in unifying a group of resourceful actors towards a system goal by leveraging the advantages of a legal framework that supports and enforces resource exchanges.

The same idea applies to the contracts governing the buyer–supplier relationships. As an implementation agency, GIZ were prevented by regulation from building vast technical capabilities in-house. It would also be inefficient to do so, since the work that GIZ outsourced to contractors, e.g. design and build the waste-management facilities, was not complicated to define, required limited idiosyncratic investments and the outputs were measurable – attributes that create opportunity to economise on transaction costs by using the market mechanisms (Williamson 1979, 1991). Furthermore, the local contractors doing business on a continuing basis were in a better position to take advantage of scale economies and aggregation of collective demands than an implementation agency.

Yet this vast nexus of contracts remains insufficient to tackle a grand challenge enmeshed within a context with a shortfall in institutions. The crux of the problem is the interdependency with the poor, the ultimate beneficiaries, and with the institutional voids in which the poor are embedded. This interdependency creates uncertainty around what can be done, how to achieve this, and the extent to which the outcomes create value for the poor. If the poor are excluded from the decision-making process, this uncertainty becomes a major risk to organisational performance. First, the outcomes can fail to gain legitimacy and popularity since consultation processes with poor people struggle to harness their local knowledge (Chambers 1983; Baiocchi 2003; World Bank 2004; Osmani 2008). At the limit, if the poor perceive that they have little to gain from being consulted, they may even opt to sabotage the organisation's actions – the Zabbaleen attempts to undermine the privatisation of solid-waste management are a case in point. Second, if the poor are excluded, there is a risk later on of them asking for legitimate changes to what was agreed upon by the core participants. This risk increases the costs *ex ante* of agreeing to buyer–supplier contracts, as well as costs *ex post* since buyer–supplier contracts are seldom complete, and so adjustments in price and scope require costly and time-consuming negotiations (Williamson 1979). In other words, uncertainty associated with the lack of participation of the poor can lead to costly changes with a zero-sum quality.

And yet, forging a contract with the poor before letting them participate in the decision-making process would also be very costly. Attempts to change institutional regimes are expensive whenever the number of participants is high, information asymmetries are sharp, the interests are competing and redistribution of economic benefits is involved (Libecap 1989a, 1989b). This is exactly the case here. Hence, the only alternative left is to enfranchise the poor and embed them into the decision-making process. This choice is not easy, though, because of the costs of collective action that will ensue; there is also a real risk of a tragedy of the commons if norms of cooperation struggle to flourish (Libecap 1989a; Ostrom 1990).

In the face of this dilemma, our findings suggest the implementation agency makes a judgement that, nonetheless, it is more advantageous to enfranchise the poor than to keep them outside the organisational boundaries. But let us be clear: the endgame is still to contract *for* property rights, and this organisational 'contraption' is merely an intermediary social device for getting to that stage. We turn now to discuss how collective action under the shadow of contractual governance actually works.

10.5.2   Collective Action under the Shadow of Contractual Governance

The choice to share decision rights is an organisational design choice. By enfranchising the poor, a structure emerges, under the shadow of contractual governance, with the core attributes of collective action (Ostrom 2010):

1. Large n: The number of beneficiaries sharing decision rights is large, and the beneficiaries are costly to exclude once they are included, because the shadow of contractual governance makes it hard to renege on the promise to share decision rights.
2. Legal uncertainty: The beneficiaries and others claim rights to directly influence capital allocation because of ill-defined property rights and promises made.
3. Rivalrous interests: Donor and implementation agencies are constrained by good governance ideals and institutional pressures to deliver on time and within budget; local authorities may have an interest in preserving the status quo or adopt radical policies, e.g. slum evictions; and the poor may be wary of cooperating because of mistrust, opportunity costs and lack of skill.

By adding a large collective-action structure, a participatory approach necessarily brings advantages and disadvantages. The main advantage is to avoid the costly political negotiations necessary to clarify the ill-defined property rights *ex ante*. These costs derive from distributional concerns that any change to the institutional regime would leave some of the beneficiaries worse off, which could then trigger opposition and claims for unacceptable side payments – the failed attempt to privatise solid-waste management is a case in point. Libecap (1989a), for example, also documents the high transaction costs needed to concentrate the exploration of shared oil and gas reserves in the United States into the hands of one actor. As Libecap documents, the best way to maximise the economic value of a shared reservoir is to unitise the exploration of oil reserves. But this rarely occurs because information asymmetries, incompatible interests and equity concerns make it costly to contract for property rights. So, though oil producers struggle to contain common losses, it is not because they are not aware of those losses. They are. But contracting for property rights is more costly.

A second advantage of adding a participatory approach to contractual governance is the potential of collective action to incentivise norms of cooperation and voluntary contributions of resources (Ostrom 1990, 2005). In the case of a participatory approach to upgrade informal settlements, the idea is to ask the poor what their problems are and what they want to do to resolve those problems, as opposed to telling them what needs doing. Further, the poor are made aware that there are resources in the system to implement a solution, which is an inducement to reward cooperation. These circumstances work as an incentive for the poor to attend meetings and share private resources, e.g. know-how, networks of trust that are needed to identify the real problems and develop equitable solutions.

Of course, by bringing collective action into the organisational boundaries, the organisational designer is also bringing into the system conflict and social dilemmas. Collective action recognises that consumption of a shared resource by one user reduces the availability of that resource for others. In our focal system, *de jure*, the direct control of capital allocation remains with the implementation agency, and the finance available is constrained by the budget. But, as the poor and other stakeholders, e.g. municipalities, gain decision rights, rivalrous preferences emerge on the exact problems to solve and how to allocate capital. Rivalry yields conflict. And yet, excluding the poor after the conflict emerges is not easy because of the costs of not maintaining the bargain – excluding the poor would require renegotiating the contracts. So capital becomes a common-pool resource that is rivalrous in consumption by many actors, all of which are costly to exclude (Ostrom 1990; Gil and Baldwin 2013; Gil, Biesek, and Freeman 2015; Gil and Pinto 2018).

Importantly, the shadow of contractual governance attenuates the risk of a tragedy of the commons. First, the ability of the core actors to free-ride and abuse their power is restricted by the legal commitment to a consensus-oriented approach. If the core actors behave uncooperatively, the poor could defect and stop contributing their informal resources to the organisation, which could cause the collapse of the whole system. Second, contractual governance gives the implementation agency resources it can leverage to further induce the beneficiaries to co-operate. So if all the beneficiaries agree a mutually satisfactory solution, there are resources to implement that solution. Unlike commons governance, though, the organisational designer is not allowing for self-governance at the inner levels of action (Ostrom 1990, 2005). Instead, the implementation agency create a bargaining structure inside the organisational boundaries, while continuing to participate in the inner decision-making process side by side with the poor.

Still, a cost of supplementing contractual governance with collective action is the risk of under-provision of collective goods, under-utilisation of shared resources and organisation failure (Hardin 1968; Olson 1965). By diffusing decision-making authority with the poor, a risk emerges that the claimants will wastefully compete for shared resources. Furthermore, our evidence shows that a participatory approach is not about creating small, homogeneous groups – situations that make it more likely that individual gains from cooperating exceed individual costs (Olson 1965). Instead, a participatory approach brings together a large number of poor claimants with a smaller number of resourceful actors. This asymmetry creates an incentive for the poor to participate, as they can see there are formal resources that can be mobilised to solve their problems. But this very same asymmetry also creates a risk of 'exploitation of the larger by the smaller' (Olson 1965), as the poor may not perceive as credible any threat of the more resourceful actors to defect.

Collective-action costs notwithstanding, our study suggests that collective action under the shadow of contractual governance is a viable form of organising in an institutionally underdeveloped context. This choice creates a complex form of organising work. But this 'contraption' is attractive because of the opportunity it creates to orchestrate a vast array of complementary resources while navigating the institutional voids. Rather than taking great pains to eliminate these voids, this organisational design leverages a nexus of contracts to allow for co-ordinated collective action, despite the lack of well-defined property rights and efficient markets. And though this nexus of contracts works as a constraint on the structure of participation and solution space, it is also an enabler in that it makes resources available to induce cooperation – as long as a consensus is reached on resolving shared problems. This type of multi-actor search process is under-studied in the organisational design literature (Olsen, Sofka and Grimpe 2016; MacAulay et al., 2017). But our findings suggest that designing innovative organisational forms for collective search is key to tackling grand challenges.

10.6   Final Considerations

In this chapter, we introduce an organisational design by which a collective-action structure is added to contractual governance to navigate institutional voids. We illustrate this complex form of organising with the case of a successful project to upgrade informal settlements, a grand challenge of our times. Still, further research is needed to better understand how this complex form of organising tackles the problems of co-ordination and cooperation, and boundary conditions. We identify three areas.

First, designing a nexus of contracts to allow for collective action with other actors is a major challenge on its own (Rivkin and Siggelkow 2003). This nexus of contracts needs to unify the resourceful actors, and yet be flexible enough to cope with the vagaries and costs of collective action. Indeed, there are instances of projects to upgrade informal areas where the organisational designer chose to engage with the poor, but fell short of enfranchising them. Studying the processes involved in searching for suitable forms of organising would provide much-needed insight into how actors determine when gains from economising on the costs of changing institutional regimes outweigh the costs of collective action.

Second, more research is needed on integrating effort across organisational boundaries when one participant is much more resourceful than all the others, but has a vested interest in building consensus. In our case, the poor control critical informal resources, but the formal resources to implement the solutions are controlled by the organisational designer. Resource asymmetries are a source of fragility in collective action due to the risk of exploitation of the larger by the smaller (Olson 1965). But in our setting, the resourceful claimant is driven by a charitable purpose. This claimant is constrained by rules in its context, but has an interest in mobilising resources to enable a consensus. So we need to investigate micro-processes to avoid common losses under these boundary conditions.

Finally, scholars of collective action show that a shared identity can be forged in the absence of a centralised authority (Ostrom 1990). High levels of intrinsic motivation can even encourage a shared identity to flourish among strangers and foster a high level of trust (Majchrzak et al. 2007). But we cannot claim high levels of intrinsic motivation here, as some participants had vested interests in preserving the status quo. Rather, our findings suggest a shared identity is painstakingly built by zigzagging between bilateral and multilateral meetings. So more research is needed about the mechanisms that can encourage norms of cooperation and a shared identity to flourish when there is such a sharp heterogeneity of interests. The organisational and sociological literature on boundary organisations, with its focus on the micro-processes driving the formation of collaboration and consensus across diverse stakeholders, provides a promising avenue for generating such insights (O'Mahoney and Bechky 2008; Perkmann and Schildt 2015).

In conclusion, we reveal a complex form of organising that has been neglected, both empirically and theoretically, in management scholarship. Yet this very same form of organising is central to a debate in the development sector about how to tackle urban informality problems. Research on this organisational contraption creates an opportunity to further management scholarship relevant to the grand challenges of our time in institutionally underdeveloped contexts.

References

Aghion, P. and Tirole, J. (1997). Formal and real authority in organisations. *The Journal of Political Economy*, 105(1); 1–29.

Armanios, D. E., Eesley, C. E., Li, J. and Eisenhardt, K .M. (2017). How entrepreneurs leverage institutional intermediaries in emerging economies to acquire public resources. *Strategic Management Journal*, 38: 1373–1390.

Arusha. (1990). African charter on popular participation in development and transformation. International Conference on Popular Participation in the Recovery and Development Process in Africa. 12–16 February, Arusha, the United Republic of Tanzania.

AUC. (2014). *Egypt's strategy for dealing with slums*. New Cairo: Center for Sustainable Development, the American University in Cairo.

Baiocchi, G. (2003). Participation, activism and politics: The Porto Alegre Experiment. In Fung, A., and Wright, E. O. (Eds.), *Deepening democracy: Institutional innovations in empowered participatory governance*. London and New York: Verso Books.

Baldwin, C. Y. (2007). Where do transactions come from? Modularity, transactions, and the boundaries of firms. *Industrial and Corporate Change*, 17:155–195.

Chambers, R. (1983). *Rural development: Putting the last first*. London: Longman.

Colquitt, J. A. and George, G. (2011). Publishing in AMJ: Topic choice. *Academy of Management Journal*, 54: 432–435.

Cooke, B. and Kothari, U. (2001). *Participation: The new tyranny?* London and New York: Zed Books.

Dutt, N., Hawn, O., Vidal, E., Chatterji, A., McGahan, A. and Mitchell, W. (2016). How open system intermediaries fill voids in market-based institutions: The case of business incubators in emerging markets. *Academy of Management Journal*, 59(3): 818–840.

EcoConServ. (2010). *Consultancy for upstream poverty and social impact analysis for Egypt's solid waste management reform: Final report, December*. Cairo, Egypt: The Ministry of Local Development, United Nations Development Programme, and the World Bank.

Eisenhardt K. and Graebner, M. (2007). Theory building from cases: Opportunities and challenges. *Academy Management Journal*, 50(1): 25–32.

Eisenhardt, K. M., Graebner, M. E. and Sonenshein, S. (2016). Grand challenges and inductive methods: Rigor without rigor mortis. *Academy of Management Journal*, 59 (4): 1113–23.

Fahmi, W. S. and Sutton, K. (2006). Cairo's Zabbaleen garbage recyclers: Multinationals' takeover and state relocation plans. *Habitat International*, 30: 812–815.

Fahmi, W. S. and Sutton, K. (2010). Cairo's contested garbage: Sustainable solid waste management and the Zabbaleen's right to the city. *Sustainability*, 2: 1765–83.

Ferraro, F., Etzion, D. and Gehman, J. (2015). Tackling grand challenges pragmatically: Robust action revisited. *Organisation Studies*, 36: 363–390.

Fjeldstad, Ø. D., Snow, C. C., Miles, R. E. and Lettl, C. (2012). The architecture of collaboration. *Strategic Management Journal*, 33(6): 734–750.

Gambardella, A., Panico, C. and Valentini, G. (2015). Strategic incentives to human capital. *Strategic Management Journal*, 36(1): 37–52.

George, G., Corbishley, C., Khayesi, J. N. O., Haas, M. R. and Tihanyi, L. (2016). Bringing Africa in: Promising directions for management research. *Academy of Management Journal*, 59(2): 377–393.

George, G., McGahan, A. M. and Prabhu, J. (2012). Innovation for inclusive growth: Towards a theoretical framework and a research agenda. *Journal of Management Studies*, 49: 661–683.

Gil, N., and Baldwin, C. (2013, September). *Creating a design commons: Lessons from teachers' participation in school design*. Harvard Business School Working Paper, No. 14–025.

Gil, N., Biesek, G. and Freeman, J. (2015). Inter-organisational development of flexible capital designs: The case of future-proofing infrastructure. *IEEE Transactions in Engineering Management*, 62(3): 335–350

Gil, N. and Pinto, J. (2018). Polycentric organising and performance: A contingency model and evidence from megaproject planning in the UK. *Research Policy*, 47 (4): 717–734.

Grodal, S. and O'Mahony, S. (2017). How does a grand challenge become displaced? Explaining the duality of field mobilisation. *Academy of Management Journal*, 60 (5): 1801–1827.

Gulati, R. and Puranam, P. (2009). Renewal through reorganization: The value of inconsistencies between formal and informal organization. *Organization Science*, 20(2): 422–440.

Gulati, R., Puranam, P. and Tushman, M. (2012). Meta-organisation design: Rethinking design in inter-organisational and community contexts. *Strategic Management Journal*, 33 (6): 571–86.

Harders, C. (2003). The informal social pact: The state and the urban poor in Cairo. In E. Kienle (Ed.), *Politics from above, politics from below: The Middle East in the age of economic reform.* London: Saqi.

Hardin, G. (1968). The tragedy of the commons. *Science*, New Series, 162 (3859):1243–1248.

Hegazy, I. R. (2016). Informal settlement upgrading policies in Egypt: Towards improvement in the upgrading process. *Journal of Urbanism*, 9(3): 254–275.

Iskander, L. (2000). Urban governance: Informal sector and municipal solid waste in Cairo. 'Voices for Change – Partners for Prosperity' for the MENA region. World Bank Conference.15th March, Washington.

Khalifa, M. A. (2015). Evolution of informal settlements upgrading policies in Egypt: From negligence to participatory development. *Ain Shams Engineering Journal*, 6: 1151–1159.

Khanna, T. and Palepu, K. G. (1997). Why focused strategies may be wrong for emerging markets. *Harvard Business Review*, 75(4): 41–51.

Kumar, S. and Corbridge, S. (2002). Programmed to fail? Development projects and the politics of participation. *Journal of Development Studies*, 39(2): 73–103.

Libecap, G. D. (1989a). *Contracting for property rights: Political economy of institutions and decisions.* Cambridge: Cambridge University Press.

Libecap, G. D. (1989b). Distributional issues in contracting for property rights. *Journal of Institutional and Theoretical Economics*, 145(1): 6–24.

Macneil, R. (1978) Contracts: Adjustments of long-term economic relations under classical, neoclassical, and relational contract law. *Northwestern University Law Review*, 72: 854–906.

Mair, J., Marti, I. and Ventresca, M. J. (2012). Building inclusive markets in rural Bangladesh: how intermediaries work institutional voids. *Academy of Management Journal*, 55(4): 819–850.

Majchrzak, A., Jarvenpaa, S. L., Hollingshead, A. B. (2007). Coordinating expertise among emergent groups responding to disasters. *Organisation Science*, 18:147–61

McDermott, G. A., Corredoira, R. A. and Kruse, G. (2009). Public–private institutions as catalysts of upgrading in emerging market societies. *Academy of Management Journal*, 52(6): 1270–1296.

NSWMP (2011). *National solid waste management programme Egypt – Main report.* Cairo, Egypt: Ministry of the Environment.

NSWMP. (2014). *National strategic directives for solid waste management in Egypt.* National Solid Waste Management Programme, November. Cairo, Egypt: Ministry of the Environment.

O'Mahony, S. and Bechky, B. A. (2008). Boundary organisations: Enabling collaboration among unexpected allies. *Administrative Science Quarterly*, 53(3): 422–459.

Olsen, A. Ø., Sofka, W. and Grimpe, C. (2016). Coordinated exploration for grand challenges: The role of advocacy groups in search consortia. *Academy of Management Journal*, 59(6): 2232–55.

Olson, M. (1965). *The logic of collective action: Public goods and the theory of groups.* Cambridge, MA: Harvard University Press.

Osmani, S. (2008). *Participatory governance: An overview of issues and evidence. Participatory governance and the Millennium Development Goals.* New York: United Nations.

Ostrom, E. (1990). *Governing the commons: The evolution of institutions for collective action.* Cambridge, UK: Cambridge University Press.

Ostrom, E. (2005). *Understanding institutional diversity.* Princeton, NJ: Princeton University Press.

Ostrom, E. (2010). A long polycentric journey. *Annual Review of Political Science*, 13, 1–23.

Perkmann, M. and Schildt, H. (2015). Open-data partnerships between firms and universities: The role of boundary organisations. *Research Policy*, 44(5): 1133–1143.

Platteau, J. P. and Abraham, A. (2002). Participatory development in the presence of endogenous community imperfections. *Journal of Development Studies*, 39(2): 104–136.

Puranam, P., Alexy, O., and Reitzig, M. (2014). What's 'new' about new forms of organizing? *Academy of Management Review*, 39(2): 162–180.

Reetz, D. K. and MacAulay, S. C. (2017). Finding novelty through co-evolutionary search. *Academy of Management Proceedings*, 1: 12807.

Rigon, A. (2014). Building local governance: Participation and elite capture in slum-upgrading in Kenya. *Development and Change*, 45: 257–283.

Rivkin, J. W. and Siggelkow, N. 2003. Balancing search and stability: Interdependencies among elements of organisational design. *Management Science*, 49(3): 290–311.

Scheinberg, A., Simpson, M. H., Gupt, Y. et al. (2010). *Economic aspects of the informal sector in solid waste.* Eschborn, Germany: GTZ.

Schlager E. and Ostrom, E. (1992). Property-rights regimes and natural resources: A conceptual analysis. *Land Economics*, 68(3): 249–62.

Siggelkow, N. (2007). Persuasion with case studies. *Academy of Management Journal*, 50(1): 20–24.

Simon, H. A. (1962). The architecture of complexity. *Proceedings of the American Philosophical Society*, 156: 467–482.

Sims, D.(2010). *Understanding Cairo: The logic of a city out of control.* Cairo, Egypt: American University in Cairo Press.

Tan-Mullins, M., Mohan, G. and Power, M. (2010). Redefining 'aid' in the China–Africa context. *Development and Change*, 41: 857–881.

UN. (2018). *World urbanization prospects: The 2018 revision, online edition.* Department of Economic and Social Affairs, Population Division. New York: United Nations.

UN-Habitat. (2003). *The challenge of slums: Global report on human settlements.* United Nations Human Settlements Programme, UN Habitat. London: Earthscan.

UN-Habitat. (2008). *State of the world's cities 2008/2009: Harmonious cities.*

UN-Habitat. (2015). Habitat III issue papers. 22 – Informal settlements. United Nations Conference on Housing and Sustainable Urban Development, New York, 31 May.

Walker, M. (2013). Why is waste a dirty word? In G. Madhavan et al. (Eds.), *Practicing sustainability.* New York: Springer Science Business Media.

Wilson, D. C., Velis, C. and Cheeseman, C. (2006). Role of informal sector recycling in waste management in developing countries. *Habitat International,* 30: 797–808.

Williamson, O. E. (1979). Transaction-cost economics: The governance of contractual relations. *Journal of Law and Economics,* 22(2): 233–261.

Williamson, O. E. (1985). *The economic institutions of capitalism.* New York: Free Press.

Williamson, O. E. (1991). Comparative economic organisation: The analysis of discrete structural alternatives. *Administrative Science Quarterly,* 36 (June): 269–296.

World Bank. (2004). *World development report 2004: Making services work for poor people.* Washington, DC: World Bank.

Xin, K. R. and Pearce, J. L. (1996). Guanxi: Connections as substitutes for formal institutional support. *Academy of Management Journal,* 39(6): 1641–1658.

Part II

Exploiting Institutional Voids by Design

11 Kenya's Madaraka Express: An Example of the Decisive Chinese Impulse for African Mega-Infrastructure Projects

Uwe Wissenbach

Abstract

This chapter illustrates how the impulse of Chinese financing and contractors on the delivery of infrastructure megaprojects has given a different development option to African governments. I ground the findings on a detailed study of the Standard Gauge Railway (SGR) built by Kenya, with Chinese assistance, between 2014 and 2017. The project was originally turned down by traditional lenders (the World Bank) based on a narrow cost–benefit analysis. I trace the ability of the Kenyan–Chinese project organisation to navigate the institutional voids in the environment, and rivalry between neighbouring countries, through a powerful and centralised organisation structure. I also show, though, that the detachment of this hierarchical authority from the institutional environment comes with a real cost that imperils the potential of the project organisation to catalyse broader socio-economic growth. Still, the case suggests that a centralised approach delivers outcomes for a reasonable cost. It effectively builds an option for further future development. This, I argue, makes the Chinese approach a viable alternative to the inclusive institutional approach espoused by traditional lenders.

The author writes in his private capacity. This chapter does not reflect EU policy or views.

11.1 Introduction

Infrastructure megaprojects mobilise resources and competencies to bring about strategic change, create competitive advantage and other sources of value (Turner, Anbari and Bredillet 2013). They also drive societal change (Misic and Radujkovic 2015). The development of capital-intensive infrastructure in Africa is both a major development opportunity and a challenge, especially cross-border projects. This is mainly due to 'institutional voids' making it difficult for African countries to orchestrate the multiple resources, in particular finance, land, capabilities, regulation and local skills, necessary to carry out megaprojects (Gil and Pinto 2017). Resource orchestration is particularly challenging due to the lack of robust institutions at national and regional levels, while corruption and other governance challenges in multi-ethnic countries further complicate projects. Developing countries, therefore, need institutional intermediaries to provide capital and capacity to realise megaprojects (Gil and Pinto 2017). Access to funding has become easier through the decisive impulse of the engagement of Chinese companies and financial institutions willing to lend the funds for such projects (Bach 2016: 117), but they also – I argue – fill the institutional capacity void with a temporary project organisation to deliver change (Turner, Anbari and Bredillet 2013). With the growing involvement of Chinese banks and companies in African infrastructure projects there are opportunities and risks in addressing these challenges differently from traditional donor prescriptions. So, research on the complex tasks of project planning, design, co-ordination, implementation and regulation to ensure projects meet their objectives in the China–Africa context are highly relevant (Gil and Pinto 2017). My chapter advances this debate with a case study – the 475-km-long Nairobi to Mombasa Kenyan Standard Gauge Railway (SGR),[1] built with Chinese assistance. We show that organisational fast-tracking, with planning-implementation overlaps and improvisation that characterises the Chinese approach, has delivered a megaproject, and avoided some of the setbacks shown by Gil and Pinto (2017) for two other cases in Nigeria and Uganda.

Kenya, with its 'Look East' policy, under which it engaged China, India and other Asian countries for a large number of infrastructure projects and investment for a decade,[2] has embraced the 'lessons learnt' from Asian development states[3] – reminiscent of Hirschman's (1967)

---

[1] This chapter builds on research conducted by the author for SAIS-CARI, Wissenbach and Wang (2017), and the author is grateful to SAIS-CARI for permission to use the research data for this chapter.

[2] 'Kenya: Want growth? Look east.' *African Business Magazine*, 18 December 2011, http://africanbusinessmagazine.com/uncategorised/kenya-want-growth-look-east/.

[3] Fourie (2014) compares how Ethiopia and Kenya have learnt from East Asian models of development, and argues that both pursued 'models of modernist developmentalism that are a far cry from the grassroots, participatory and institutionalist agendas that traditional donors often promote in Africa'. Fourie's key point is that African policymakers have the agency to 'seek out and domesticate policies that are seen to have "worked" abroad, particularly in an era in which they have a greater choice in development partners'. See also Wissenbach and Kim (2013).

technique of imitating projects from elsewhere. When African leaders visit Beijing, Shanghai or Shenzhen – China's flagship special economic zone (SEZ), visited by President Kenyatta in 2013 – they find gleaming modern metropolises with top-notch infrastructure. These, arguably, are exactly what many African leaders – and citizens cursing the pot-holed roads and frequent blackouts – aspire to.[4] But their attractiveness seems to lessen in the light of insistence from traditional donors for planning prerequisites that focus on first establishing institutional capacity, regional institutions and sustainability criteria. These requirements, if not met, resulted in refusal to finance 'flagship projects' or delivered 'too little, too late' (Gil and Pinto 2017; Kaplinsky and Morris 2009).

So how has Kenya – in partnership with Chinese lenders and contractors – managed to complete the SGR and addressed the scarcity and orchestration of resources, notably finance, land and capacity? Firstly, that the SGR partnership worked, despite governance challenges such as corruption, ethnic tensions and institutional weaknesses, and a change of leadership between planning and implementation, is a fascinating story. But it has not all been plain sailing: particularly problematic and opaque seems to have been the high cost of the contract – most likely due to rent seeking – and ballooning cost of land acquisition. High compensation costs and legal challenges for compulsory land acquisition are a known obstacle to investment in Kenya (Mwangi 2017), and re-confirmed during construction of the SGR. Still, Kenya's new train, the Madaraka Express, began service as scheduled in the contracting and financing agreements on 1 June, Madaraka Day 2017.[5] The new railway has a symbolic and political value,

---

[4] Conversation with a Chinese official who guided the Kenyan president in Shenzhen (February 2014).

[5] Madaraka Day commemorates the beginning of Kenya's autonomous rule in 1963 (before full independence on 12 December 1963). Kenya's president put the SGR into the context of Kenya's anti-colonial struggle: 'It was a century and 22 years ago today when a white colonial master stood under the skies of the picturesque island of Mombasa to launch what was called the lunatic express, the railway line that linked the Kenyan coast to the shores of Lake Victoria. Kenya gained independence from the colonial regime 68 years after that date and despite the growth of population as well as economy, the country has been stuck with the old railway line, which the lunatic express train rolled on into the interior of the country. The inadequacy of the old railway system resulted in pressure on the highway from Mombasa to Nairobi, leading to delays and exorbitant costs of commuting and movement of cargo. When President Uhuru Kenyatta came into office, three Presidents and 50 years after Kenya became independent, he pledged to replace the colonial railway. He promised to construct a Standard Gauge Railway line to replace the inadequate one.' 'President Kenyatta commissions Mombasa–Nairobi SGR, rides on historic inaugural passenger train', *Republic of Kenya Presidency*, 31 May 2017, www.president.go.ke/2017/05/31/president-kenyatta-commissions-mombasa-nairobi-sgr-rides-on-historic-inaugural-passenger-train/.

and its inauguration, just two months ahead of a crucial national election, was no coincidence.

Secondly, the SGR's overall contribution to national and regional development is much harder to establish. It is, of course, a long-term issue, but it has been hotly debated in the Kenyan media. The Kenyan government, without giving a methodology, has projected that the Madaraka Express will contribute 1.5 per cent annual GDP growth.[6] There are many projections about infrastructure bottlenecks and potential, but in many cases it is not clear how realistic they are. There is, though, consensus that a lack of infrastructure is hampering Kenya's growth.[7] The underdeveloped infrastructure, and the time it takes to transport goods between Nairobi and the port of Mombasa, is a major reason for lack of investment in Kenyan manufacturing (Berger 2011; Sanghi and Johnson 2016: 3–4). So the SGR is at least a strategic step forward in terms of changing that situation. It will certainly attract passengers and freight, which is the system goal and main justification for the project. Attracting more foreign trade and investment is a wider development goal underlying Kenya's national development strategy (Vision 2030) and its 'Look East' policy. And here Kenya's interests also converge with China's holistic approach: to engage in infrastructure financing that may benefit Chinese companies in the long run through increased trade and investment in Africa's emerging markets (Kaplinsky and Morris 2009).[8] So Kenya is now another addition to China's 'Belt and Road Initiative'.[9]

Thirdly, and of particular interest in this context, the original rationale for the SGR to promote regional integration has evolved, with shifting coalitions and political priorities compounded by the lack of a regional institution to effectively co-ordinate national governments. Kenya's new Madaraka Express supplants the Kenya–Uganda metre-gauge railway from Mombasa to Kampala built more than 100 years ago by the British. Known as the 'Lunatic Express' because of its high cost in financial and human terms,[10] for critics, the SGR is a repeat of that story; an expensive

---

[6] 'New railway to boost Mombasa container capacity, says CS', *Daily Nation*, 28 March 2016, p. 29; the report quotes Cabinet Secretary for Transport James Macharia.

[7] Economist Intelligence Unit Country Report Kenya, generated 15 January 2018: http://country.eiu.com/FileHandler.ashx?issue_id=1766237560&mode=pdf.

[8] See O. M. Otele, 'Understanding Kenyan agency in the acquisition and utilization of Chinese development finance in the transport infrastructure, 2003–2017.' Unpublished PhD thesis, Shandong University, 2018: 124, 134, 149.

[9] 'Where Africa fits into China's massive Belt and Road Initiative', *The Conversation*, 28 May 2017: http://theconversation.com/where-africa-fits-into-chinas-massive-belt-and-road-initiative-78016.

[10] The term 'Lunatic Express' was coined by Charles Miller in his 1971 *The Lunatic Express: An Entertainment in Imperialism*. On the story of the Lunatic Express, see: www.theeast african.co.ke/magazine/-/434746/660876/-/view/printVersion/-/32dc3d/-/index.html.

Chinese folly with doubtful benefits.[11] Studies by the World Bank (WB) in 2013 and regional institutions (Berger 2011; CPCS 2014) support that view, as they concluded that the SGR had no business case and the Kenya government should have simply rehabilitated the existing metre-gauge railway. So this chapter will build a baseline for future research on whether the Madaraka Express is another lunacy or a genuine contribution to both Kenya's and East Africa's development.

11.2   Research Questions and Hypotheses

The thesis advanced in this chapter is that the Chinese approach provides a complete package – feasibility study, design, financing, engineering, procurement and construction – for infrastructure megaprojects (without direct money transfers to African governments).[12] It is suited to those African countries where government leaders look at promoting growth and development, as well as enhancing power, competitiveness and prestige through megaprojects, thus emulating Asian development states in the region (Fourie 2014). Here development 'is not principally a global good, but remains essentially defined as something – wealth and power – a nation wants to achieve within its boundaries' (Wissenbach 2011).

Differing from traditional donors, China can deliver a 'package deal' (Kaplinsky and Morris 2009) that provides both capital and project delivery know-how acquired through China's own infrastructure megaproject-driven developments of the last few decades. Critically, though, this is not enough (as Gil and Pinto 2017 show) if their African counterparts cannot solve some of the key challenges, such as land acquisition, ethnic tensions, vested interests and bureaucratic obstacles. Another challenge for African countries is the lack of genuine commitment to regional integration and infrastructure planning processes to make the projects work for socio-economic development beyond national boundaries.

This chapter aims to provide answers to two major questions:

1. How did Kenya and its Chinese partners manage to overcome many of the megaproject management challenges and succeed in finishing the project?

    i. Key success factors that project management literature (reviewed below) has identified for planning and implementing the project were not in place. And yet, despite Kenya's, and the region's,

---

For an interesting, illustrated comparative history of the two railways see Chao, 'A tale of two railways', *Thee Agora*, 6 October 2015:www.theeagora.com/a-tale-of-two-railways/.

[11] J. Kaiman, '"China has conquered Kenya": Inside Beijing's new strategy to win African hearts and minds', *LA Times*, 7 August 2017: http://beta.latimes.com/world/asia/la-fg-china-africa-kenya-20170807-htmlstory.html.

[12] See Otele, 'Understanding Kenyan agency', 171.

institutional voids – such as finance, government planning and implementing capacity, local skills base, further compounded by obstacles such as Kenya's neo-patrimonial political culture, local politics in a multi-ethnic state and politicised land issues – the project was completed.

2. Why has the regional system goal of the SGR unravelled? Cross-border infrastructure – its original objective – is generally believed to be a driver of integration, but why in the East African community does rail and other infrastructure remain fragmented and national?

On the one hand, I show at the project-organisation level of analysis that a tight-knit partnership between the Government of Kenya (GoK) – and especially the Presidential Delivery Unit – and Chinese actors, insulated from normal accountability processes and occasionally defying court orders,[13] enabled project completion – to the schedule agreed in the financing agreement – in spite of incomplete planning and opaque cost calculations. And, on the other hand, I show how such an opaque structure amplified some externalities in the environment and led to cost overshoots, how those were hedged for and improvisation. There has been a trade-off between opacity and efficiency: the speedy completion of development projects has made the Kenyan government 'disregard its own governance principles on public participation, accountability, transparency and integrity'.[14]

Finally, I also show how other countries that were supposed to support the scheme defected, forcing Kenya to rethink the whole system goal. However, in this respect, evolutions in the regional goals are not found in the SGR project itself, or in the involvement of Chinese contractors, but in political competition and differences between presidents, and the overall lack of regional institutions and frameworks for coordinating cross-border infrastructure megaprojects in East Africa.

To disentangle the two stories, I first analyse the planning and implementation of the railway project as such. Secondly, I analyse the wider goal of national and regional development.

11.2.1 *Planning and Implementation*

Kenya did manage the delivery challenges; an important success factor was an efficient hierarchical centralisation of project management and supervision through the office of Kenya's president. How this approach

---

[13] 'Anger as rail construction begins in Nairobi National Park', *The East African*, 1 March 2018, www.theeastafrican.co.ke/news/Rail-construction-begins-in-Nairobi-National-Park/2558-4325068-ksd9xq/index.html.

[14] Otele, 'Understanding Kenyan agency', 137.

performed in the Kenya context is the main focus of this chapter. The other focus is on the related challenges, such as land acquisition and the wider rationale of the project.

I borrowed the meta-organisation concept from Lundrigan, Gil and Puranam (2014), who use it to improve the understanding of whole planning and delivery through a network structure of legally autonomous actors collaborating to achieve a system-level goal, i.e. a complex megaproject. I argue that the SGR meta-organisation, characterised by centralised decision making and the political prior-ity of a national (and elite) flagship project focused on on-time delivery of the project, was a major factor in success. And all this despite planning problems (land acquisition) and (probably) inflated cost due to rent seeking and lack of competitive bidding. Its closed and hierarchical organisational design somewhat resembles the suc-cessful arrangements of US national prestige projects of the 1950s and 1960s – also characterised by opacity and disregard for cost and other issues (Lenfle and Loch 2017). The Madaraka Express was elevated to a top-level symbolic national priority – like Kennedy's project to put a man on the moon at any cost – which an upgrade of the colonial railway line, as proposed by the WB, could not have achieved.

11.2.2 Rationale and Development Goals

The SGR's original rationale was much more prosaic: to relieve road congestion, accelerate freight transport and improve connectivity with landlocked countries such as Uganda and Rwanda (Berger 2011). However, the regional goal of connectivity with the East African Community (EAC) countries[15] was compromised by defections and rea-lignments of political leaders, and the absence of any planning and imple-mentational authority to promote or co-ordinate regional infrastructure 'master plans'. So, the orchestration of the resources challenge beyond national boundaries has been a major problem for the system–goal and cost–benefit scenarios. Kenya's SGR is, so far, the only completed railway

---

[15] The EAC is a regional integration agreement between Kenya, Uganda, Tanzania, Rwanda, Burundi and South Sudan. It is one of the more integrated Regional Economic Communities in Africa (Bach 2016: 97–99) and has, in recent years, improved the soft infrastructure for regional and transit trade, by means such as common tariffs (customs union) and the introduction of the Electronic Single Window System at Mombasa, which has already cut the time needed to import cargo from Mombasa to Uganda from 18 to 3 days. See also Otieno et al. (2013).

megaproject in the EAC region,[16] at least for its first phase.[17] A preliminary assessment is that regional integration through infrastructure megaprojects has become a race to build competing parallel railway lines (Cooksey 2016) and parallel oil pipelines.[18] And the market size of the region is crucial for any megaproject to realise its potential. Still, while Kenya has arguably realised a megaproject that should bolster its standing in an increasingly competitive region, a Kenya-only railway distorts the cost–benefit ratio, Kenya's debt burden and the connectivity in the region. Meaning, long-term benefits will have to be re-assessed.

Unreliable data and projections will, though, be a thing of the past once the Madaraka Express has been operating for some years and its wider impacts become measurable. So this chapter will not add to speculation, but review some of the projections and questions that, at the time of planning and start of operations, were used to promote or criticise the project in order to establish a baseline for future research. Time will, in due course, provide more answers, but until then, while pessimists see a 'white elephant', political leaders believe in the transformative power of rail infrastructure, as evidenced by China's example.

11.3   Literature Review

The Kenyan SGR story contributes to the academic debate about mega-project (under)performance, which for a long time has been limited to project management's 'iron triangle' (finishing projects on time, on

[16] Ethiopia, which is not part of the EAC, in October 2016 opened a 756 km electrified railway built by Chinese companies to connect Addis Ababa with the port of Djibouti, which handles 90 per cent of Ethiopia's external trade (V. Defait, 'Un train chinois pour booster l'économie éthiopienne', *Le Temps*, 4 October 2016: www.letemps.ch/monde/2 016/10/04/un-train-chinois-booster-leconomie-ethiopienne). The new railway was built between 2011 and 2016 with a total investment of $4 billion, according to the *Railway Gazette*. The Ethiopian section of the line cost $3.4 billion, 70 per cent of which was provided by the China Exim Bank and 30 per cent by the Ethiopian government. The Djibouti government contributed $878 m to the project. ('Special report: How five major African projects are supported by China', *Smartrail World*, 10 November 2016: www .smartrailworld.com/five-major-african-projects-supported-by-china). This railway is often used as a per-km cost comparator to the Kenyan SGR.

[17] Phase 2 covers 490 km linking Nairobi and Malaba (Ugandan border), for which the government approved the conclusion of commercial contracts between Kenya Railways and the China Communications Construction Company Ltd (CCCC) in March 2016. Phase 2A to Naivasha is under construction for which the government has obtained a loan from China (US$1.5 billion). Phases 2B to Kisumu and 2C to Malaba are only in preliminary planning. 'Kenya launched Phase 2 of SGR project', *Railway Pro*, 20 October 2016: www.railwaypro.com/wp/kenya-launched-phase-2-of-sgr-rail-pro ject/.

[18] Cannon (2017) and author's interviews with managers from Tullow Oil and Toyota Tsusho, August 2016.

Table 11.1 *SGR Phase 1 (Mombasa–Nairobi) project overview*

Construction contract amount	3.804 billion
Funded by	The government of the Republic of Kenya (15%) and the Export-Import Bank of China (85%)
Contracting agency	Kenya Railway Corporation
Engineering procurement and construction contractor	China Road and Bridge Corporation
Date of construction commencement	12 December 2014 (Kenya Independence Day)
Planned date of commission	31 May 2017
Planned date for start of operations	1 June 2017 (Kenya Madaraka Day)
Operator	China Communications Construction Company

Source: Adapted from 2015 China Road and Bridge Corporation Social Responsibility Report 2015 on Mombasa–Nairobi SGR Project

budget and within specifications; Dimitriou 2014: 389), and a self-defeating finding that most projects overshoot budgets and encounter delays (Flyvbjerg and Sunstein 2015), or, as Mir and Pinnington (2014) put it: 'In spite of many researches done so far, it is still not clear what are the causes of megaproject success and failures.'

I turn now to these 'many researches' and review some of the relevant literature.

Mega-infrastructure projects 'play a pivotal role in the socio-economic development and sustainability of modern societies' (Lundrigan et al. 2014: 2) and are usually defined as large scale, significant and complex in nature, transforming the landscape rapidly and profoundly, and contributing to economic and social development (Eyiah-Botwe, Aigbavboa and Thwala 2016: 81).

Dimitriou (2014: 391) defines mega-transport projects as 'land-based transport infrastructure investments in the form of bridges, tunnels, road and rail links or combinations of these, that entail a construction cost of over US$1 billion, which are frequently perceived as critical to the "success" of major urban, metropolitan, regional, national developments and even transnational developments'. Misic and Radujkovic (2015: 72) simply and poetically characterise them as 'colossal, captivating, costly, controversial and complex'. All this applies to the SGR, which included railways, bridges and adjacent facilities such as stations and container depots.

Infrastructure megaprojects have increased their share of global GDP in recent years, with a particularly high percentage of project-based capital formation in emerging countries such as China and India (Turner et al. 2013). Despite this trend, most literature on megaprojects and related project management still examines mainly Western cases (Turner et al. 2013; Dimitriou 2014; Misic and Radujkovic 2015; Cooke-Davies 2002; Lundrigan et al. 2014). These are largely implemented on models of orderly growth in pluralistic settings (Gil and Pinto 2017: 16–17, 25). Literature on Chinese megaproject management in Africa is limited and nascent, tends to characterise Chinese approaches as opaque and undercutting good governance (Gil and Pinto 2017), and has largely been driven by the WB (Foster et al. 2009) and by Western researchers who fear that China would undermine Western aid; meanwhile, Chinese scholars have defended China's policies and rejected Western criticism (He 2007; Li 2009). Yet, an independent study found that Chinese contractors used by the WB did not perform any worse than Western ones (Farrell 2016). While the literature on China's involvement in African infrastructure is growing, it has hardly been examined from a planning and implementation point of view, and often framed as a political issue with comparisons to colonial exploitation of Africa (Alden 2007; Davies 2011). More sober analysis shows that Chinese aid should not be seen as undermining Western aid, but complementing it and offering choices to African countries (Wissenbach 2007, 2011; Bräutigam 2011). Little African scholarship, especially on megaprojects, exists (Corkin, Burke and Davies 2008; Schiere and Rugamba 2011)[19] but should be encouraged to better reflect the perspective of the main stakeholders and build up knowledge.[20]

At the same time, a consensus seems to be emerging that success and failure of megaprojects – at least for the largely Western case studies – are difficult to define in generic ways (Dimitriou 2014; Cooke-Davies 2002). The main reasons for this are complexity and the power of context (Dimitriou 2014). So qualitative case studies taking account of models within context, and their complexity, such as the one offered in this chapter, make an important contribution to this nascent field of study by further illuminating policy and organisational processes.

Interestingly, a large amount of literature examines the reasons for megaproject failure, positing that most projects face major challenges in one way or another on cost, delays or criticism by key stakeholders (Flyvbjerg and Sunstein 2015). Misic and Radujkovic (2015: 72) find 'Megaprojects are united by their extreme complexity – both in technical

---

[19] Otele, 'Understanding Kenyan agency.'

[20] Kenyan businesses and universities have created a pressure group – the Regional Megaprojects Coordination Council, RMPCC – to enhance local content and skills transfer while trying to upgrade their own capacity to deliver and build up knowledge through research (Interview, K. Desai, 3 January 2018). This is a remarkable development.

and human terms – and by a long record of poor delivery.' Flyvbjerg and Sunstein (2015) even postulate a malevolent hiding hand that ensures the vast majority of infrastructure projects across the world are 'impeded by a double whammy of higher-than-estimated costs and lower-than-estimated benefits' and that this 'undermines project viability in a majority of cases, instead of saving projects by the creative benefit-generation claimed by the Benevolent Hiding Hand'. This logic is some-what flawed, as it suggests abandoning any infrastructure projects except those in an almost ideal world absent of any systematic bias, with high technical competence and a high degree of insulation from politics and public accountability.

In fact, the principle of the benevolent hiding hand, as formulated by Hirschman (1967), suggests that, especially in developing countries, hiding uncertainties about project challenges or overestimating project benefits is a key factor in actually getting challenging projects off the ground. This encourages risk averters with limited resources and skills to take risks (Hirschman 1967: 19) and, in some cases, make them successful through their approaches to creativity and improvisation when unexpected problems occur. So the approach of Gil and Pinto (2017) to work with the grain and find ways to deal with inevitable institutional voids and governance challenges – such as lack of capacity, corruption, etc. – seems more relevant. And arguably, this is the case for Kenya's SGR, where economic benefits were exaggerated – ignoring several studies – and then wrapped in patriotic rhetoric to get the job done, while challenges such as cost and land acquisition were hidden or underestimated. While the jury is still out on the wider development benefits, and whether they justify the high cost, the fact is that the train is operating, against the odds and apparently successfully.

Hirschman (1967: 17–18) identified one way the hiding hand supports the 'pseudo-imitation' technique that makes believe that projects can be based on successful experiences elsewhere. This arguably rhymes with the Chinese and other Asian development states' rhetoric about the transfer-ability of their own successful development story to African countries (Wissenbach and Kim 2013). Essentially, Hirschman encourages project planning and implementation while escaping the many requirements and preconditions to development (Hirschman 1967: 19), such as the policy and institutional prescriptions of the WB and Western donors that later came to be known as the Washington Consensus. This learning-by-doing, trial-and-error approach underlying the African projects with Chinese intermediaries inverts the Western mainstream approach to, first, solve governance and institutional capacity problems before embarking on megaprojects (Gil and Pinto 2017). Ironically, fifty years after his essay, with the completion of Kenya's SGR, African leaders and their Chinese partners may well have vindicated Hirschman.

11.4   Research Method and Fieldwork

Data collection started in 2014 and ended in March 2018. In order to evaluate the planning, contracting and financing process, I used official documents and media reports, as well as focused interviews with stakeholders such as the managing director of Kenya Railways (KR), business association members and politicians. Media in Kenya are competitive, and so provided diverse opinions from commentators, civil society and interest groups, as well as investigative reports. To understand Chinese–Kenyan interactions during the construction phase, I, together with a Chinese colleague,[21] conducted field research along the SGR track to obtain primary information on local impacts that allowed checking claims about the project by both proponents and opponents. We visited three construction sites and interviewed three Chinese and local managers and employees, as well as the governors of Mombasa and Taita Taveta counties. Interviews focused on implementation schedule, local employment, local content, community involvement, technology transfer and environmental governance (Wissenbach and Wang 2017).

During construction, the project was divided into nine sections, varying in length from 5 to 135 kilometres. We visited Section 1 (Mombasa), Section 2 (Voi) and Section 7 (Emali) in August 2015. On separate occasions, I met with Kenyan business representatives and, after the Madaraka Express started operations, I interviewed a European journalist based in Nairobi and the chair of the Regional Mega Projects Coordination Council (RMPCC[22]) and read through dozens of user comments on Kenya Rail's Facebook posts on the train.

The contractor – China Road and Bridge Corporation (CRBC) – was not available for interviews but the company has made a considerable public relations effort, providing information to local media and a corporate social responsibility report on the SGR project in 2015. This indicates that the company was keen to not only provide, but also control information, confirming the typical opacity of arrangements between African and Chinese governments and contractors (Gil and Pinto 2017).[23]

---

[21] Yuan Wang, PhD candidate at Oxford University. This research was supported by SAIS-CARI and resulted in a policy brief and a working paper. I thank SAIS-CARI for allowing me to draw on this research.

[22] Mr Kevit Desai, 3 January 2018.

[23] Opacity is common in other deals as well, as they are essentially business deals with non-disclosure requirements.

11.5   Analysis: Planning and Financing of the SGR

In this section, I review the project rationales: how they evolved, and the planning, financing and contracting of the SGR, as far as information is available to shed light on the meta-organisation and the project cost. The National Assembly's Public Investment Committee special report on the procurement and financing of the construction of the SGR Phase I of 29 April 2014 (PIC 2014) provides a certain number of details, but contracts, feasibility studies and financing agreements themselves are not publicly available.

11.5.1   Rationale and Regional Plans: The Embryonic Phase[24]

The SGR project was initially crafted under the Northern Corridor Initiative (2008)[25] by the presidents of Kenya and Uganda. It was meant to give a boost to regional economic integration, development and growth. The regional SGR plan goes hand in hand with the trend, since the early 2000s, of mega-infrastructure projects 'to link more efficiently land-locked and coastal states' in Africa (Bach 2016: 115). Overcoming the drawbacks of their landlocked position was the key motivation for Uganda and Rwanda, while for Kenya – in competition with Tanzania – the key was the national interest in sustaining the country's economic dominance in East Africa by revamping its infrastructure.[26] This, so the rationale suggested, should produce both regional and global connectivity, as the involvement of and explicit connection with the Chinese 'Belt and Road' initiative show.[27]

A 2013 Tripartite Agreement provided that the SGR would be extended from Nairobi to Malaba on the border with Uganda, while the final phase was supposed to run from Malaba to Uganda's capital

---

[24] I follow the classification of phases proposed by Lundrigan et al. (2014: 11). The embryonic phase is where project founders craft a system goal, scope and budget and consider design with outside help.

[25] A former minister of transport told the Kenyan Parliament that an SGR had been discussed several times since 2003 as an integral part of Vision 2030 and of the modernisation of the Northern Corridor, which was officially launched by Presidents Kibaki of Kenya and Museveni of Uganda in October 2008 (PIC 2014: 65). The Northern Corridor Transit Transport Coordination Authority was created in the mid-1980s following the signing of the Northern Corridor Transit Agreement by Burundi, Kenya, Rwanda and Uganda.

For the 2013 summit communiqué on the SGR and oil pipeline: 'About us', *Northern Corridor Integration Projects*: www.nciprojects.org/about/about-us 2018.

[26] Otele, 'Understanding Kenyan agency', 132.

[27] Cobus van Staden, 'One belt one road and East Africa: Beyond Chinese influence', *The Jamestown Foundation*, 10 November 2017: https://jamestown.org/program/one-belt-one-road-east-africa-beyond-chinese-influence/.

Kampala – like the colonial railway – and on to Kigali (Rwanda) by 2018 (PIC 2014: 59), with a link to South Sudan. Vanheukelom et al. (2016: 19) describe the situation at the time of that agreement: 'the interests of Rwanda, Uganda and Kenya are closely aligned around the Northern Corridor in what the regional newspapers have called the "Coalition of the Willing". This sub-set of EAC member states is prepared to intensify its co-operation in the face of explicit resistance from Tanzania, reflecting the priority Uganda and Rwanda give to lowering transport costs, and the market opportunity seen by interest groups in Kenya vying for bigger market shares for their ports and transport industries.'

However, the GoK also referred to the SGR as one of the national flagship projects in the second medium-term plan (2013–2017) under its Vision 2030 development plan, originally adopted in 2008 under President Kibaki (2002–2012).[28] It built on Kibaki's Economic Recovery Strategy (ERS), which identified poor infrastructure as a major obstacle to development. Efficient modern infrastructure was 'seen as one of the most critical factors to lowering the costs of doing business and opening up income-generating opportunities for poor households'. And investment in transport was meant 'to position Kenya as the most efficient and effective transport hub of the East and Central African region and promote national aspirations for socio-economic reconstruction and development. It will also facilitate improvement and expansion of transport infrastructure in a manner that will reduce transport costs and also open new frontiers for economic development.'[29] The ERS foresaw the rehabilitation of the existing metre-gauge Kenya–Uganda railway from colonial times, and, in November 2006, the governments of Kenya and Uganda contracted the running of their railways to Rift Valley Railways (RVR) for twenty-five years with 'the goal of making export, import and domestic freight-handling more efficient'.[30] This privatisation of the colonial railway was already considered as having been unsuccessful in 2011 'because of the financial and technical weaknesses of RVR' (Berger 2011).[31] It was around this time that the idea of

---

[28] 'Second medium term plan 2013–2017 transforming Kenya', *SDG Funders*: http://sdgf unders.org/reports/second-medium-term-plan-2013-2017-transforming-kenya-pathway-to-devolution-socio-economic-development-equity-and-national-unity/.

[29] Office of the Prime Minister Sessional Paper No. 10 of 2012, pp. 12 and 24, https://espas .secure.europarl.europa.eu/orbis/sites/default/files/generated/document/en/KENY A2030.pdf.

[30] Office of the Prime Minister Sessional Paper No. 10 of 2012, p. 13.

[31] Rift Valley Railways (RVR) which is 85 per cent owned by an Egyptian equity fund, Qalaa Holdings, that increased its share in freight carried from Mombasa to Uganda to 1.883 million tons in 2015 (*Business Daily*, 2 October 2015, p. 7 and interview with Karim Sadek of Qalaa, *Business Daily*, 9 September 2015, pp. 16–17). However, RVR has made huge losses and its concessions to exploit the metre-gauge railway were revoked by

a totally new SGR gained traction, supported by CRBC and vigorously pursued by President Kenyatta as soon as he assumed office in 2013.[32]

But an independent consultancy report on the Northern Corridor Infrastructure Masterplan (Berger 2011), commissioned by the Northern Corridor secretariat, estimated that an SGR was unlikely to materialise before 2020 at the earliest – so the fact that Phase 1 of the SGR was completed in 2017 is noteworthy. That report assigned a high priority in the regional master plan to the repair and rehabilitation of the existing metre-gauge railway (Berger 2011: 17). The old railway carried only 0.9 million tonnes of cargo annually from the Indian Ocean into Kenya and Uganda – compared to Mombasa's throughput of 22 million tonnes in 2013 (PIC 2014: 23) – and at a snail's pace at that.

The WB came to a similar conclusion: its Africa Transport Unit carried out a cost–benefit analysis of four alternatives to the SGR in August 2013 that compared the estimated investment cost per kilometre (2009 prices) with the expected benefits in terms of freight volume and estimated revenue (World Bank 2013). The four options were:

1. Rehabilitating the existing metre-gauge network, which would hit capacity constraints by 2030.
2. Upgrading the existing network to a higher standard with the same gauge, which would be justified if an additional 6.2 million tonnes (mt) per year of freight could be added.
3. Upgrading the existing network to standard gauge on the same alignment.
4. Constructing a standard gauge (1,435 mm) track on a new right-of-way.[33]

The WB (World Bank 2013) concluded that there was no case for an SGR – Options 3 and 4 – and found Option 2 most appropriate. This was based on a demand forecast estimate that rail freight traffic would reach 14.4 mt per year by 2030 for the entire EAC rail network, while building the SGR would require a volume of 55.2 mt per year to be economically viable.

A study commissioned by the EAC secretariat came to a similar conclusion (CPCS 2014). Moreover, with a Tanzanian–Rwandan SGR railway project also planned, it appeared that there might be two new SGRs

both the Kenyan and Ugandan governments ('Uganda rethinks Kenya SGR over funding gaps', *East African*, 6–12 January 2018). RVR defaulted on its loans and is thus effectively out of business: 'Lenders stare at $234.2m loss from Qalaa's RVR loans default', *East African*, 22 January 2018: www.theeastafrican.co.ke/business/Lender-loss-from-Qalaa-RVR-loans-default-/2560-4273360-ljr3vfz/index.html.

[32] Otele, 'Understanding Kenyan agency', 157–160.

[33] Options 1–3 would not have required land acquisition.

built for the EAC area, casting further doubts on the economic case.[34]
This meant that the business case chosen by Kenya was not really con-
vincing – if one goes by the WB's summary assessment, which does not
calculate wider potential socio-economic benefits; it only focuses on
freight revenue. Still, the presidents of Uganda, Kenya and Rwanda
decided at the summit in 2013, when they launched the Northern
Corridor Initiative that addressed the long delays of cargo from
Mombasa to the final destination, to include 'the construction of a new
Standard Gauge Railway (SGR) from Mombasa to Kampala, Kigali and
Juba'.[35] So, leaders ignored the institutional advice and studies they had
themselves commissioned (Berger 2011; CPCS 2014) and those from the
WB (World Bank 2013).

Which is why the controversy about the cost and the economic case of
the SGR reflects the debate raised by Flyvbjerg and Sunstein (2015); the
GoK seemingly embarked on a megaproject based on an assumption of
a benevolent hiding hand (Hirschman 1967) that would ensure high
development benefits without substantiating the case, as opposed to
a more cautious WB approach. It is important to contrast the narrow
cost–benefit calculation – construction and capital cost versus revenue
from freight and passengers – which can be calculated or estimated with
a certain amount of precision, as in the WB and CPCS studies, with the
announced wider impacts on development, which are far more challenging to estimate over the long run. These differences in evaluation are also
mirrored in scholarly debates; Flyvbjerg and Sunstein (2015: 7) use just
first-year user benefits in order to measure cost–benefit, whereas
Hirschman's work (1967) looks at capital-intensive investment as a long-
term process.

The WB's (World Bank, 2013) business case similarly focused only on
freight volume and cost, and did not take account of wider non-user
benefits such as potential to catalyse private or public investment, job

---

[34] According to the *East African* (21 May 2017), Tanzania was struggling to finance its
SGR, in particular as the new president, Magufuli, cancelled an earlier agreement with
a Chinese firm reached by his predecessor. In this case, the WB did not support an SGR
solution but was ready to invest US$200 m to rehabilitate the existing central railway,
which is dysfunctional (CPCS 2014).

[35] 'About us', *Northern Corridor Integration Projects*, www.nciprojects.org/about/about-us.
They signed the Tripartite Agreement for the development and operation of a Standard
Gauge Railway linking Mombasa, Kampala and Kigali with branch lines to Kisumu
(Kenya) and Pakwach/Gul-Nimule (Uganda), between the Republics of Kenya, Rwanda
and Uganda, in August 2013. The Republic of South Sudan acceded to the agreement in
May 2014, extending the line to Juba. The protocol for the development and operations
of the Standard Gauge Railways was signed by Kenya, Uganda, South Sudan and
Rwanda in May 2014. 'Standard gauge railway', *Northern Corridor Integration Projects*,
www.nciprojects.org/project/standard-gauge-railway.

creation or savings of costs, e.g. for road maintenance, air pollution and road safety. The CPCS study (2014) did provide more detail on the rail-versus-road business case (see below), but also remained limited to trade and traffic volumes. Railways, even when operating at a loss, are still considered essential public services, with environmental and safety advantages over road transport (and in most cases, users do not cover the cost for either) that, for a long time, were not taken into account financially in any way.

11.5.2   The Business Case: Rail versus Road?

The lack of a strong rail infrastructure puts brakes on growth. Transport costs in East Africa can, as reported locally, 'account for up to 30 to 50 percent of export value and up to 75 percent for landlocked countries. Delays add additional costs of $400 to $500 per trip for freight forwarders crossing borders.'[36] Existing roads cannot cope with the increasing volume of freight hauled from Mombasa to places as far as the DRC and Rwanda. Hundreds of thousands of trucks move back and forth on a single 520 km track road between, and through, Mombasa and Nairobi. From my own observations, thousands of trucks are often stalled for hours in traffic at the entrance of Mombasa to reach the port. Accidents are frequent, and road maintenance is costly. Truckers I interviewed are also subject to rogue 'road tolls' extorted by traffic police, a practice organised to such an extent that drivers are given cash budgets for this purpose by their employers. So the SGR intends to alleviate this record of congestion and cost of road haulage.

However, increasing the rail market share of freight will be problematic as pricing and times are more complex calculations; it is generally accepted within the industry that railways require distances of over 600 km to be competitive against trucking (CPCS 2014: 40). Vested interests, such as trucking and logistics companies based mainly in Mombasa, are working against the SGR and the government's compulsory measures to redirect freight to the SGR.[37] In this context, it is important to remember that trucks will still be needed to service the vast hinterland and landlocked countries not reached by the railway, and those needs are increasing with regional development – population growth, income growth and local road construction. Container and bulk freight is the most suitable to be shipped by rail, and price and reliability

[36] *The East African*, 22–28 August 2015, p. 34.
[37] 'Long on promise, short on delivery: SGR makes little impact on the counties it traverses', *The East African*, 4 March 2018. www.theeastafrican.co.ke/business/SGR-makes-little-impact-on-the-counties-it-traverses/2560-4327632-m5ll1fz/index.html.

will be essential factors; CPCS (2014) estimated that the SGR had to charge 20–25 per cent less than truck companies to be competitive. Cargo services started on 1 January 2018, and the freight rates announced by Kenya Rail correspond to that range: to transport a 20' container costs $500 and a 40' (30 t and below) container costs $700. This excludes last-mile transportation costs, but the rates are inclusive of terminal placement charges and all loaded containers are charged at gross weight. A 16 per cent VAT charge is only levied for domestic freight.

Finally, there is the challenge of maintenance and operation management of the railway – a key challenge, given that the existing metre-gauge railway became largely defunct because of lack of investment and management capacity (Berger 2011).

11.5.3 The Wider and Non-User Benefits

There are many other possible benefits that were not considered in the studies, such as generation of business activities directly or indirectly related to the railway and the stations (Otieno et al. 2013; Sanghi and Johnson 2016), but these seem to form part of the government's hopes for the SGR's contribution to Kenya's GDP. The overall Chinese foreign economic policy strategy – the Belt and Road Initiative – suggests that there may well be follow-up investments, business and standard-setting by Chinese actors.[38]

In fact, the Kenyan president's vision extends beyond the simple calculations of freight volumes and cost: he argued that 'the establishment of special economic zones, modelled on China and built close to new, mostly Chinese-built, transport links was critical for job creation in Kenya'.[39] Here Kenyatta voices what Hirschman (1967) described as pseudo-imitation, i.e. the direct transfer of another country's development experience to his own, underestimating the difficulties, such as what it takes to actually set up a SEZ like Shenzhen and make it work successfully (Woolfrey 2013). It should be noted that Export Processing Zones (EPZs) in Kenya (Sanghi and Johnson 2016: 6) and SEZs in general there have rarely been successful, and even in China, where they arguably have been, it was a challenging, long-drawn-out process (Farole and Akinci 2011; Zeng 2015). This presents both opportunities and threats to Kenya's private sector, 'which has to overcome its sense of entitlement and raise its competitiveness'.[40] Sanghi and Johnson (2016: 2) also warn

---

[38] Van Staden, 'One belt one road.'

[39] 'Kenya president urges rebalance of China-Africa trade', *Financial Times*, 15 May 2017.

[40] Interview, K. Desai, 3 January 2018.

that 'without a strategy for knowledge sharing, local firms will miss out on the spill-over effects from investment, a crucial part of increasing competitiveness of the domestic economy'. The latter – as we have seen above – was one of the rationales for Kenya's infrastructure projects.

Some wider socio-economic benefits already became visible during implementation: the SGR construction has provided thousands of local jobs, and helped the local economy, if only temporarily. SGR workers' patronage of local businesses drove up demand for daily consumption. Their extra cash prompted several banks to open new branches to provide services to these employees, some of whom were starting their own small businesses[41] – one of the stated system goals of Kenya's infrastructure strategy. Some of the short-term benefits during construction were contested. Due to the project organisation giving EPC to the Chinese contractor, Kenyan businesses felt excluded from promising opportunities. Pressure by Kenyan cement manufacturers directed at the president successfully resulted in the reversal of the initial agreement with CRBC to import cement from China. So all the cement used for the project was then purchased from Kenyan cement industries. Some of the construction services – slope protection, drainage works, supplies, vehicle hire – as well as the telecom, banking and other services to the contractors and their camps, were also sourced locally (Wissenbach and Wang 2017). Since the SGR started passenger services, more tourists have taken the train to Emali or Voi to do safaris in Amboseli and Tsavo national parks, prompting hotels to buy more vehicles to shuttle passengers from the train stations.[42] Interestingly, Kenyan business, government and academia have started to coalesce to better organise such processes for accessing megaproject markets, creating leverage for local infrastructure and economic regulation sparked by the SGR project.[43]

11.5.4 *Kenyan Planning and Costing: Gestation Phase*

In the gestation phase of a project, the core members select suppliers that operate through formal contracts (Lundrigan et al. 2014: 13). Although the business case for the SGR was weak and the wider benefits remained vague, the Kenyan government made it a national flagship project that had to be finished during President Kenyatta's first term in office. Despite the Northern Corridor summit of 2013, the embryonic phase of a regional conception diverged from the 'hard' gestation phase as contracting

---

[41] Interviews with community representatives in Voi, August 2015, and Wissenbach and Wang (2017).
[42] Interview with European journalist based in Nairobi, 3 January 2018.
[43] Interview K. Desai, 3 January 2018.

became a purely national matter with weak regional co-ordination and the ensuing risk of diverging plans, operators and standards. In the railway sector – unlike the reformed road-sector-governance set-up – Kenya had an institutional void, lacking a sound institutional and regulatory framework and local capacity: no railway had been built in a hundred years, and the management had been poor, and so was outsourced by KR, and its Ugandan counterpart, to a foreign holding – RVR. Chinese financing and capacity were, thus, indispensable given the reluctance of other lenders to engage in the sector beyond rehabilitation of existing old infrastructure.[44]

A memorandum of understanding (MoU) between the GoK and the CRBC was signed in August 2009 to carry out the feasibility study and preliminary design of the SGR. There was no cost to the GoK, provided the study was only used by KR and the CRBC. This was accepted as part of 'a standard requirement for Chinese-funded projects to establish the feasibility themselves before involving their treasury and banks' (PIC 2014: 26, 74). After some discussion with the CRBC, Kenya opted for a diesel-powered train with a possibility to upgrade to electric, given that Kenya's power supply is still plagued by frequent blackouts. This decision to proceed without making the SGR dependent on other infrastructure projects for power generation avoids a potential critical resource bottleneck, unlike the situation in some neighbouring countries, where electric railway plans could face problems if contingent power projects were delayed.[45]

A competitive tender initiated by KR for an independent feasibility study was cancelled by the Transport Ministry in 2008, and direct negotiations with the CRBC, based on the MoU, began (PIC 2014: 26–31). The CRBC presented the feasibility study to the Transport Ministry in January 2012 with an estimated cost of $3.4–$3.8 billion, while in 2010 the Ministry of Finance had requested a concessional loan for the construction of a new SGR at a cost of $2.5 billion from the government of China (PIC 2014: 27). According to the testimony of the director of Kenya's Public Procurement Oversight Authority (PPOA), upon completion of the feasibility study (January 2012) and review by KR, the CRBC was awarded a tender in July 2012 to construct the SGR at a cost of $1.15 billion. But KR withdrew the award, citing that the procurement was government-to-government, and therefore not subject to the Public Procurement and Disposal Act 2005. The director testified that the PPOA had advised against the use of such direct procurement

---

[44] Otele, 'Understanding Kenyan agency', 145, 165, 206–207.
[45] A. Olingo, 'Ethiopia, Tanzania electric trains to speed up cargo movement, lower costs of transport', *The East African* no. 1210, 6–12 January 2018, p. 9.

and had requested additional information, which was not forthcoming, while KR argued that section 6(1) of the Act, which exempts government-to-government funding from competitive tendering, should apply (PIC 2014: 30). The solicitor general endorsed this view in October 2012 (PIC 2014: 31). The testimony of the acting managing director of KR to the PIC confirmed the sequence of events and gave details about the scope of work – 609 km of single track[46] – and that KR had entered into a commercial agreement on the construction of the SGR at a total cost of $3.804 billion, subject to the contractor securing financiers for the project. KR pointed out that the government was seeking a loan of $3.233 billion to cover 85 per cent of the project cost, while Kenya's direct contribution would be 15 per cent of the cost – $571 million (PIC 2014: 34–35). The variations of the cost were not explained.

KR also informed the National Assembly Committee that it was nego-tiating with the CRBC commercial turnkey contracts for civil works, and for the supply and installation of facilities, locomotives and rolling stock focusing on project conditions, payment schedules, bills of quantities, requirements, specifications and price, as well as aiming at achieving a maximum capacity of 22 mt of cargo per annum. KR claimed to have reduced the price for the civil works from an estimated $2.64 billion to $2.21 billion (PIC 2014, 37–38).

The Cabinet Secretary for national treasury also testified to the Committee, confirming that Cabinet had approved the SGR project in August 2012, followed by the signing of a bilateral agreement with Uganda, which was later converted into the above-mentioned tripartite agreement with Rwanda at the Northern Corridor Initiative summit in early 2013.

Treasury provided further details of the financing requested from China, in October 2012, for a loan of $3.23 billion from EXIM Bank of China. This comprised a concessional loan of $1.6 billion over 20 years, with a grace period of 7 years and an interest rate of 2 per cent p.a., and a commercial loan of $1.63 billion for 10 years, with a grace period of 5 years and insurance cover of 6.93 per cent of the commercial loan and interest of six months LIBOR +360 basis points. The concessional loan has a grant element of 35 per cent (PIC 2014: 47–48). The treasury Cabinet Secretary also gave a breakdown – different from KR's – of the major elements of the cost: $2.657 billion for civil works; $1.146 billion for facilities, locomotives and rolling stock; $80 million for compulsory

---

[46] Note that Phase 1 between Mombasa and Nairobi is only 473 km, suggesting that the costing of the feasibility study covered a longer track. This is what the PIC understood (PIC 2014, 36).

acquisition of 2,253 hectares of land for the railway corridor; $10 million for the Embakasi Inland Container Depot near Nairobi – which required another million for land acquisition; and $3 million for project supervision (PIC 2014: 48). Overall, the process has been less than clear and the different cost indications emerging from these testimonies merely add to the confusion about 'real cost'.

11.5.5 *Financing and Delivery Phase under a New President*

The SGR planning and contracting process concluded, apart from the financing agreement, prior to the 2013 elections, which brought in a new president, Uhuru Kenyatta – he was involved in the planning as a member of the previous Cabinet. The new president went on a state visit to China in August 2013, where he secured financing for the SGR.[47] In May 2014, during his visit to Kenya, Chinese Premier Li Keqiang and Uhuru Kenyatta signed a $3.8 billion financing agreement to build the SGR with the CRBC, a company that had previously carried out mainly road projects in Kenya. And so, after about six years of gestation, the SGR project meta-organisation had acquired all the critical resources needed to begin construction (Lundrigan et al. 2014: 16) – except some of the land, as we will see below. The overriding role of the president and the Chinese government was evident in this process. Interestingly, there was no disruption, despite a change of leadership – presidents, ministers and even a new constitution.

Construction started on 12 December 2014 – Kenya's Independence Day, emphasising the patriotic importance of the SGR. And it was only one year before the planned completion, in 2016, that Kenya's Ministry of Transport acquired another critical resource – an operator for the SGR. The contract was directly awarded to China Communications Construction Company (CCCC), the parent company of the CRBC.[48] This indicates that KR had made no plans for the operation.[49] To defend this choice, the government argued that building and operating within the same company would ensure that the contractors remedy possible construction defaults.[50] But it is fair to say that the Kenyan government did not have a choice, as the railway without a company to operate

---

[47] 'President Kenyatta commissions Mombasa–Nairobi SGR', Republic of Kenya Presidency.

[48] Kiarie Njoroge, 'Why Chinese bank imposed SGR line operator on Kenya', *Business Daily*, 18 May 2016, p. 6, www.ipsos.co.ke/NEWBASE_EXPORTS/Banking/160518_Business%20Daily_6_b49af.pdf .

[49] Presentation by Kenya Railways to KEPSA, Nairobi, 12 April 2016.

[50] 'RVR loses deal to run standard gauge railway to Chinese contractor', *The East African*, 7–13 May 2016, and confidential source, 15 May 2016.

and maintain it would have been useless, and an international tender may not have been possible in such a short time period. This does, though, show a lack of planning beyond the construction of the railway itself by the GoK. More worryingly, there is no clarity either about how railway maintenance has been planned for.[51]

The railway opened passenger services on 1 June 2017, and passengers have adopted the railway enthusiastically – 2 million passengers between June 2017 and November 2018 – which is understandable, since tickets are priced more cheaply than the bus fares between Nairobi and Mombasa, and the journey is several hours shorter than by road – and certainly safer. According to passenger interviews and social media comments, the passenger trains are usually fully booked, but the siting of the terminals, which are outside city centres, creates additional travel time and expenses.

After this review of the progress of the megaproject from its embryonic phase to operation, I review the meta-organisation that accomplished this.

11.6   Discussion

11.6.1   How Did Kenya Manage to Overcome the Many Obstacles to Completing the SGR?

After securing financing and technical assistance from China, the project organisation was crucial for Kenya to overcome the many obstacles to completing the SGR. A first key characteristic of the project organisation was the central role of the Office of the President, the project founder and pinnacle of the central government. The pre-eminence of the presidency in the Chinese-funded project is not unique to Kenya.[52] The primary stakeholders forming a steering committee (SC)[53] consisted of the Presidential Delivery Unit; the Ministry of Transport; Kenya Rail; National Treasury; National Land Commission; Ministry of Industrialisation; Kenya Bureau of Standards; Ministry of Environment, etc. The president regularly met with the contractors and stakeholders in the field.[54] They built a highly hierarchical network

---

[51] Interview, K. Desai, 3 January 2018.   [52] Otele, 'Understanding Kenyan agency', 162.

[53] By contrast, Uganda's SGR SC is described as characterised by bureaucratic in-fighting that paralyses its planning (J. Barigaba, 'Uganda refocuses on metre gauge rail as Kenya delays SGR', *The East African*, 6–12 January 2018, p. 8.). This may also explain the dysfunctionality of the Ugandan expressway project, cited by Gil and Pinto (2017).

[54] 'President Kenyatta commissions Mombasa–Nairobi SGR', Republic of Kenya Presidency.

of organisations, where the president was the top authority with power to settle disputes or to override other government levels to ensure implementation. A quote from President Kenyatta explains why: 'I have a problem with bureaucrats. We frustrate our partners when we take years to approve infrastructure projects they are interested in funding.'[55] It was a centralised, bureaucratic system designed to resolve disputes, to avoid infighting between ministries and agencies, to allocate resources, but it was vulnerable to the private interests of the people at the top, given that other institutions in the environment were not sufficiently strong to challenge. Interviews with Chinese and Kenyan SGR managers and RMPCC officials confirmed the central role of the president and his office for solving local disputes and overcoming bureaucratic obstacles. Due to Kenya's devolution in 2013, though, there has been conflict with other powerful levels of government – especially the elected governor of Mombasa, an opposition leader – about the ownership, revenue division and management of critical infrastructure at Mombasa, as well as land issues (see below).

A second key characteristic was the particular feature of Africa–China projects: the whole process was outsourced to Chinese contractors who were responsible for on-time, on-budget project delivery under a system of incentives and penalties, with the company paid via the lending institution, not the Kenyan Treasury.[56] Hence, the capacity of the contractor was very important. Due diligence was exercised in a rather casual way through a short study visit to China (PIC 2014: 38–40). Otherwise, the CRBC's established presence in Kenya was a factor in the contract award (PIC 2014: 73).

These two characteristics made the completion of the SGR by Kenya and its Chinese partners quick and on time, despite obstacles, which defied predictions in Berger's (2011) study that an SGR would not be available before the 2020s. The challenges to the project organisation were compensation for land acquisition, corruption and debt sustainability, and they were all the responsibility of the Kenyan government.

11.6.1.1   The Challenges from Local Politics and Land Issues

Relocation, land expropriation and compensation are major issues for any infrastructure project (Gil and Pinto 2016; Mwangi 2017). For the SGR, the budget planned in 2014 for land acquisition – $8 million for

---

[55] 'EAC presidents back $78billion mega projects, but who will foot the bill?', *The East African*, www.theeastafrican.co.ke/business/East-African-Community-78-billion-megaprojects/2560-4317838-df9f12/index.html.
[56] Interview with CRBC manager, August 2015.

compulsory acquisition of 2,253 hectares of land for the railway corridor, plus $1 million for the Embakasi Inland Container Depot near Nairobi (PIC 2014: 48) – was far below the real expenditure of around $325 million.[57] On 12 April 2016, Mr Maina, the managing director of KR, a parastatal organisation, which in the SGR case managed some of the compensation funds on behalf of the National Land Commission (NLC),[58] complained that 'dealing with land acquisition issues and the legal rights of owners was a nightmare'. Maina raised the question of whether the country could afford such a generous land compensation scheme, and argued that further extensions of the railway would be even more costly.[59]

Land acquisition largely took place during implementation – except for the land already owned by KR, along the existing metre-gauge railway, or by the government, e.g. national parks. Land ownership in Kenya is complex, with both private and community ownership in place. Land transactions are often subject to speculation, corruption and elite manipulation in a neo-patrimonial political culture. Kenya's legislation on land has, despite important reforms in 2009/10, significant gaps and weaknesses (Mwangi 2017: 5). Compulsory acquisition, as defined by the Land Act, gives the state power to acquire any title for a public purpose, subject to compensation payment. The high level of legal protection of private property and absence of valuation criteria, plus overlapping competencies and undefined processes of different agencies, makes compulsory acquisition an expensive affair and marred by technical issues and litigation 'to a point where the government feels the cost of compensation is making projects untenable' (Mwangi 2017: 11). Landowners can appeal against the compensation offered by the NLC in courts, but normally construction can continue while appeals are in process. As a result, the budget earmarked for these purposes ballooned, yet in our focal case substantive delays usually associated with land acquisition were almost only observed in Mombasa – the shortest construction section – due to the strong opposition of the governor.

[57] Neville Otuki, 'Compensation for SGR land exceeds budget by Sh2.8bn', *Business Daily*, 14 November 2016: www.businessdailyafrica.com/economy/Compensation-for-SGR-land-exceeds-budget-by-Sh2-8billion/3946234-3452294-22gh77/index.html, and James Wanzala, 'Sh8 million set aside to compensate landowners displaced by rail project', *Standard Media*, 7 April 2014, www.standardmedia.co.ke/business/article/2000108808/sh8-billion-set-aside-to-compensate-landowners-displaced-by-rail-project.

[58] John Njagi, 'Sh11billion already paid to railway beneficiaries, land records show', *Daily Nation*, 28 March 2016, p. 13.

[59] Presentation by KR to KEPSA, Nairobi, 12 April 2016. See also: 'Audit report reveals Sh500m lost in SGR land compensation scheme', *The Standard*, 27 June, 2016, p. 6.

Influence of local politics on land issues   Kenya has a long history of ethnic violence and disputes over land ownership (Hornsby 2013; Oloo 2015).[60] The politicisation of land issues in Kenya also resurfaced and affected the SGR construction. CRBC employees occasionally faced hostility from the local community, who were often not informed about the SGR; this is a recurrent problem of Kenyan governance,[61] despite devolution and an active civil society. To deal with this, CRBC hired local advisors and implemented CSR projects (Wissenbach and Wang 2017). Some land disputes were related to cultural aspects, for instance, the relocation of burial grounds during construction, which required rites to be held and paid for. In Mombasa, the land compensation claims, backed by opposition politicians such as the governor, posed significant obstacles to the railway's construction.[62] Mombasa also wanted to avoid negative consequences for the truck and logistics companies based there.[63] The governor of Mombasa, Hassan Ali Joho, argued that resettlement and compensation issues should be viewed in a historical context, and that 'ancestral interest'[64] should be included in the valuation by the NLC and KR. Complicating land acquisition in some cases were disputes over who owned the land – the traditional local community, who had no title deeds, or the migrants from other parts of Kenya who had been issued with them. This is a long-standing source of political grievance on the Kenyan coast.[65]

[60] For instance, in Naivasha, Maasai herders prevented CRBC workers from accessing their land before compensation was paid by the government: Antony Gitonga and Robert Kiplagat, 'Swazuri: Dispute over SGR land resolved', *Standard Digital*, 12 January 2018; www.standardmedia.co.ke/business/article/2001265656/land-commission-moves-to-resolve-land-dispute).

[61] Liz Mahiri, 'Community's anxiety about LAPSSET fueled by lack of information', *Rift Valley Institute*, 6 January 2017; http://riftvalley.net/news/community%E2%80%99s-anxiety-about-lapsset-fueled-lack-information#.WZQ3NaoUmUk.

[62] Daniel Tsuma Nyassy, 'Hands off railway project, firm tells county officials', *Daily Nation*, 22 June 2015. Retrieved from www.nation.co.ke/counties/mombasa/Mombasa-Standard-Gauge-Railway-CRBC/-/1954178/2761446/-/ymg5ooz/-/index.html, and 'Swazuri tells off politicians on railway project', *Daily Nation*, 2 July 2015. Retrieved from www.nation.co.ke/news/Swazuri-tells-off-politicians-on-rail-project/-/1056/27734 34/-/nt5k5uz/-/index.html.

[63] Brian Ocharo, 'Stalled SGR section costing taxpayers dearly', *Daily Nation*, 4 November 2016, www.nation.co.ke/news/Stalled-SGR-section-costing-taxpayers/105 6-3440586-6ago23z/index.html.

[64] Interview with Hassan Ali Joho, 8 August 2015.

[65] See for instance: *Redress for Historical Land Injustices in Kenya*, Kenya Human Rights Commission: www.khrc.or.ke/publications/114-redress-for-historical-land-injustices-in-kenya/file.html; International Crisis Group, Kenya's Coast: *Devolution Disappointed*, Crisis Group Africa Briefing No.121 Nairobi/Brussels, 13 July 2016: https://d2071and vip0wj.cloudfront.net/kenya-s-coast-devolution-disappointed.pdf. In May 2014 the governor proposed devolution of the port to the county government and in December 2015 the County Assembly passed the Mombasa County Port Authority Bill aimed at

In a somewhat similar case in Embakasi, the Nairobi County government obtained a court order to prevent residents on the construction site from claiming compensation, as the owner of the land was the county government. And though the squatters had settled on it illegally, no one had objected to the informal settlements for decades. But, unlike the fear that the SGR would harm local trucking businesses, which caused delays in Mombasa, the Embakasi Inland Container Terminal and train stations were welcomed by the Nairobi governor.

In conclusion, the land disputes largely reflected the inchoate legal ownership framework, historic and political grievances. Those aspects were not addressed in the national government's contract with the Chinese company, but were left for the Kenyan government to plan and manage. These issues resulted in a significant cost overshoot, but few delays.

Corruption   The SGR project was criticised for its non-competitive contracting arrangements. Critics and the Kenyan media have suspected large-scale corruption, but not much evidence has been produced for those claims. [66] The opacity of the costing itself and a simple comparison with the per-kilometre cost of the Ethiopia–Djibouti railway, and the confusion over varying costs (see above) has, for many observers, been enough to conclude that national elites – notorious for corruption scandals (Wrong 2009) – illicitly benefited from the process. And indeed, in August 2018 the managing director of KR, the chairman of the NLC and several other officials were arrested for corruption charges in the process of land acquisition for the SGR. This corruption is thus very likely another factor inflating the SGR cost.

The rent-seeking aspect of the project is an issue that project management literature has not focused on, but it is a recurrent problem, and not only in the Africa–China context. Flyvbjerg and Sunstein (2015: 5) have included power play as a deliberate activation of the malevolent hiding hand underestimating difficulties or cost, and overestimating benefits in order to make the project look good on paper to secure project approval

managing the port and collecting revenue. However, the port is exempt from devolution under the Kenyan constitution: www.theeastafrican.co.ke/business/East-Africa-traders-protest-Bill-on-port-of-Mombasa–/–/2560/3010162/-/dg3crsz/-/index.html.
[66] Such as David Ndii, managing director of Africa Economics: 'Are megaprojects worth billions spent?', *Daily Nation*, 10 February 2017, www.nation.co.ke/oped/Opinion/are-megaprojects-worth-billions-spent/440808-3808440-modebj/index.html; https://www.theelephant.info/sgr/2017/06/13/david-ndiis-take-on-the-sgr/, or John Githongo, anti-corruption activist and former anti-corruption official of President Kibaki: 'An open letter on the state of the nation and corruption', *JamiiForums*, www.jamiiforums.com/t hreads/an-open-letter-on-the-state-of-the-nation-and-corruption.593826/

and funding. This would, in the SGR case, have to be nuanced by taking account of the neo-patrimonial political culture (Bach 2013; Wrong 2009), which makes infrastructure projects subject to elite capture for rent seeking. Interestingly, though, the collusion of officials and road contractors had been one reason why Kenya's government, in 2003 under President Kibaki, blacklisted local road contractors and, instead, preferred to work with Chinese contractors, such as CRBC (Hornsby 2013: 709). Significantly, corruption is singled out as the most important obstacle to doing business in Kenya by the 75 Chinese companies surveyed by the Sino-African Centre of Excellence in 2014, with 53 per cent calling it a very significant obstacle and another 15 per cent a significant one (Sanghi and Johnson 2016: 26).[67] So, while evidence for corruption is notoriously difficult to produce, it can be inferred from the above that it has at least been a factor in the excessive cost and, possibly, a factor even in the decision for the SGR option.

11.6.1.2   *Mitigating Financial and Debt Risks*

Unlike some other developing countries where access to capital is a major challenge (Gil and Pinto 2017), Kenya has access to international capital markets – it launched a successful 2 billion Eurobond in 2014 and again in 2018, and has a good fiscal outlook (World Bank 2017).[68] More interestingly, Kenya – under pressure from the Chinese lenders – also devised a dedicated financial hedging strategy for the railway construction, which makes the railway operation less dependent on revenue. To secure the Kenyan share of project funding – mainly dedicated to land acquisition and compensation – and the repayment of the Chinese loans, the GoK introduced, in 2013, a new levy of 1.5 per cent of the customs value on goods imported into Kenya for the Railway Development Fund (RDF; PIC 2014: 53). EXIM Bank allegedly also insisted on the GoK taking measures to guarantee business to the SGR.[69]

Some critics are, though, concerned about Kenya's ability to sustain the debt from the costs of the project and exchange rate risks to the economy and future trade opportunities.[70] And Kenya has an enormous trade deficit with China (Sanghi and Johnson 2016). This is also

---

[67] Transparency International ranks Kenya 145/176, with a score of 26/100 on its Corruption Perception Index 2016. www.transparency.org/country/KEN.
[68] Economist Intelligence Unit Country Report Kenya, generated 15 January 2018: http://country.eiu.com/FileHandler.ashx?issue_id=1766237560&mode=pdf.
[69] Otele, 'Understanding Kenyan agency', 180–181.
[70] Jaindi Kisero, 'Are the Chinese-funded projects worth debts we are sinking in?', *Daily Nation*, 30 March 2016, p. 14.

a concern voiced by President Kenyatta who 'wants to emulate Ethiopia by inviting Chinese manufacturers to the country [...] attracting jobs in labour-intensive industries such as textiles, shoes and agro-processing as one way of tackling the trade imbalance'.[71] The WB (World Bank 2017), though, notes that Kenya is losing competitiveness in the East Africa market vis-à-vis China and its neighbours due to cheaper imports from China and very low labour productivity in Kenya.[72] The imports of railway construction-related equipment and supplies led to a temporary import surge from China in 2015, due to imports of steel materials, locomotives and wagons worth around $2 billion,[73] deteriorating further the bilateral trade imbalance.

The Economist expects 'Kenya's public-sector debt stock to rise from 56.6% of GDP in 2017/18 to 61.7% of GDP in 2021/22, which is sustainable, barring macroeconomic instability, although debt-servicing costs will continue rising'.[74] But though Kenya does not fall in the category of developing countries lacking access to capital (Hirschman 1967; Gil and Pinto 2016), and so was in a stronger position to negotiate with its Chinese partners, it still has to enhance its overall economic competitiveness and consolidate its fiscal position in view of subsequent infrastructure investments.[75]

11.6.2   Why Have Cross-Border Rail Infrastructure Plans Been Derailed?

When the four presidents of Kenya, Uganda, Rwanda and South Sudan gathered in Mombasa on 28 November 2013 to launch the works for the SGR, they seemed to lay the foundations of a truly regional infrastructure project. But, on Madaraka Day 2017, when the Kenyan president commissioned the new railway, the other African leaders were conspicuously absent. Indeed, the regional dimension proved particularly volatile: in December 2013, South Sudan plunged into civil war; in 2016, reports – subsequently denied[76] – suggested that Rwanda would rather join

---

[71] 'Kenya president urges rebalance of China-Africa trade', *Financial Times*, 15 May 2017: www.ft.com/content/947ea960-38b2-11e7-821a-6027b8a20f23.

[72] World Bank Kenya Economic Update, April 2017, No. 15 Box B.1.

[73] 'China's exports to Kenya reach Sh295billion on railway construction', *Business Daily*, 5 February 2016, p. 7.

[74] Economist Intelligence Unit Country Report Kenya, generated 15 January 2018: http://country.eiu.com/FileHandler.ashx?issue_id=1766237560&mode=pdf.

[75] 'The World Bank in Kenya: Overview', *The World Bank*, www.worldbank.org/en/country/kenya/overview.

[76] 'Rwanda wants the best of both SGR worlds, North and Central', *The East African*, 13 June 2016.

Tanzania's Central Corridor linking up with a refurbished TAZARA railway to be built by another Chinese company. This blow to Kenya's SGR project came on the heels of a decision by Uganda to build an oil pipeline through Tanzania instead of Kenya, while Kenya indicated the SGR might end up in Kisumu rather than go to Uganda.[77] And so, instead of a regional network, the SGR looks like a truncated replica of the colonial stand-alone railway. If confirmed, this abandonment of regional infrastructure plans would mark a major shift in the politics of regional integration, with the national interests of the three countries no longer in alignment (Vanheukelom et al. 2016: 19). Kenya would find itself on its own with two megaprojects – the SGR and the oil pipeline – having to compete with planned alternatives to upgrade the Central Corridor led by Tanzania. Still, by the beginning of 2018 it seemed that Uganda and Kenya were once again in alignment on the railway.[78]

The possible emergence of an alternative SGR between Rwanda and Tanzania significantly affects the economic rationale of the EAC transport plans, given that freight volumes would be divided between two lines in East Africa, reducing the overall market size – crucial for viability calculations – and increasing competitive pressures (CPCS 2014). On the one hand, having two ports and two railways reduces potential bottlenecks in each port, but on the other reduces carrying capacity limits of both. But for Chinese companies, a second SGR from Dar es Salaam to Kigali presents a golden opportunity. Competition will be good for business, but reduces profitability of the railway(s), with government investment likely to face more serious debt repayment challenges. The realignments, in fact, follow current traffic flows – most cargo destined for Rwanda is handled by Dar es Salaam, while the much bigger volume destined for Uganda mostly transits through Mombasa. The EAC has not been able to reconcile the competition between Tanzania and Kenya, whose ports compete for business of the landlocked countries of central Africa through Tanzania's 'Central Corridor' and Kenya's 'Northern Corridor', and the landlocked countries try to play on those two options to extract concessions. The cost of the SGR all the way to Kampala will have to be secured by Uganda, unless this landlocked country continues to rely on road transport for its increasing needs. But at least it can draw on Kenya's experience.

---

[77] 'Kenya to terminate railway at Kisumu after Rwanda exit', *Business Daily*, 18 May 2016, p. 15; James Anyanzwa, 'East Africa's joint mega railway project at the crossroads', *The East African*, 29 January 2019: https://allafrica.com/stories/201901280552.html.

[78] J. Barigaba, 'Uganda refocuses on metre gauge rail as Kenya delays SGR', *The East African*, 6–12 January 2018, p. 8.

When Kenya introduced the railway development levy (RDL), mentioned above, as a financing model for its budget contribution and repayment of the loans to China, the move sparked controversy in the region. A unilateral tax that not only increased the cost of doing business, it was also in violation of the EAC Customs Union protocol. This stipulates in Part D, Article 10 that 'the Partner States shall, upon the coming into force of this Protocol, eliminate all internal tariffs and other charges of equivalent effect on trade among them'. Kenya was duly forced to suspend its 1.5 per cent RDL on imports to Kenya from other EAC member states in March 2014, after the East African Business Council – a private-sector organisation – filed a complaint with the EAC Council of Ministers arguing the levy was equivalent to internal tariffs and other charges. The levy still applies to goods entering Kenya and shipped on to the other countries. In June 2014, the EAC decided to introduce a 1.5 per cent infrastructure development levy (IDL) EAC-wide to replace national RDLs. Kenya, though, persisted with its own RDL, while Uganda and Rwanda adopted the EAC IDL. Tanzania also introduced a national RDL in 2015, also at 1.5 per cent.[79] So political negotiations on ways to reconcile funding for investments and competitiveness and integration concerns are likely to continue.

The disintegration of the coalition of the willing, and the lack of involvement of existing regional institutions such as the EAC in the SGR or other regional megaprojects, and a regional fiscal mechanism like the RDL, reveal the challenges for cross-border infrastructure in Africa. They also confirm that regional integration remains hostage to leadership interests, and is limited to trade facilitation and aspirational rhetoric. Incidentally, Otieno et al. (2013) show regional integration per se does not attract more foreign direct investment (FDI).

The SGR demonstrates that regional infrastructure plans cannot rely on regional institutional arrangements such as the EAC.[80] In fact, the EAC was never the locus of regional infrastructure planning and financing, as the sidelining of its studies (CPCS 2014) showed. Instead, the railway plan relied on very limited networks of political leaders and elites, and not on institutional co-operation between national agencies. The Northern Corridor infrastructure initiative was pursued by presidents meeting outside the EAC framework, which proved ineffective. EAC

---

[79] 'Press Center: Freight Shipping Logistics News', *AeroMarine Capital*, 21 May 2014: http://aeromarine.co.ke/news/1166/76/Rail-levy-collection-exceeds-target-despite-EAC-deal/; 'Long way to go in curbing trade barriers within EAC', *Business Daily*, 14 June 2016, p. 9.

[80] Another example is the successful Trademark East Africa initiative, which was a bottom-up private-sector and donor-driven project.

leaders have very different fundamental approaches to infrastructure construction, and as long as the EAC secretariat has no power and funds to fill regional planning voids, then national agencies and outside intermediaries – Chinese or others – will need to realise the leaders' dreams.[81] Which is why one of the main rationales for the SGR – regional connectivity – evolved into a national prestige definition of development through modern infrastructure, and the old cross-border railway was abandoned. And infrastructure plans, albeit part of proclaimed regional schemes, were largely decided in national political settings with outside – Chinese – partners. It is thus, somewhat disingenuous to 'blame' China for preferring bilateral deals (Schiere and Rugamba 2011). There is simply no regional contracting authority that external financiers, such as the Chinese companies and China EXIM Bank, can engage with, hence one of the key challenges of cross-border infrastructure megaprojects in Africa is overcoming fragmentation and closed national systems between countries. RMPCC is lobbying for such regional co-ordination, and Ugandan and Kenyan steel makers have apparently agreed to cooperate when pushing for contracts during further SGR construction.[82]

11.7   Conclusion

The thesis advanced in this chapter was that the Chinese approach to infrastructure megaproject financing and construction is suited to those countries in Africa where government leaders look at promoting growth and development, while simultaneously enhancing power, competitiveness and prestige, through megaprojects. I showed that China's 'package deal' successfully provided capital and project delivery know-how. I also showed that, as predicted by Hirschman (1967) and Gil and Pinto (2017), implementation required improvisation. Furthermore, I trace the success in delivering the project on time to a very hierarchical project meta-organisation that could be mobilised to solve key challenges, such as land acquisition, local and ethnic tensions and bureaucratic obstacles. It is also likely that the SGR was very costly,[83] possibly due to rent seeking[84] and land-acquisition cost. It may never recoup cost through usage alone.

---

[81] 'EAC presidents back $78billion mega projects, but who will foot the bill?', *The East African*, www.theeastafrican.co.ke/business/East-African-Community-78-billion-megaprojects/2560-4317838-df9f12/index.html.

[82] Interview with RMPCC chair Mr Kevit Desai, 3 January 2018.

[83] However, Flyvbjerg and Sunstein (2015: 7) note that for all railway projects in their extensive database there is an average cost overrun of 40 per cent and a benefit shortfall of 34 per cent, implying that Kenya's experience is not out of the global 'normal'.

[84] Absence of competitive bidding forecloses an in-depth assessment of the adequacy of the cost or of cheaper alternatives, and it might hide corruption. The absence of competitive

Still, a narrow cost–benefit analysis may miss the point that railways can be catalysts of economic growth and create non-user benefits, and, in that respect, they can be sensible public investments. In the SGR case, the risk of debt sustainability associated with the cost side of the calculation is mitigated through the RDL. It is a fiscal safeguard ensuring the GoK can repay its debt – and it is dynamic; more trade due to the SGR means the more the RDL will yield to the treasury. Kenya has the fiscal space to shoulder the SGR cost. I looked at the relative success of the SGR at two levels – that of the megaproject organisation and at the level of the wider and regional socio-economic benefits the project was supposed to facilitate and my findings allow the following conclusions.

Firstly, the prioritisation of the SGR as a presidential prestige project helped brush aside common challenges of managing uncertainty, stakeholders and accountability, which is reminiscent of past Western prestige projects. The business case for the SGR was not made convincingly, and advice from the WB and EAC to instead upgrade the existing metre-gauge network was ignored. The role for Chinese actors as both the capital intermediary and supplier enabled government to orchestrate the resources in a way that has worked in Kenya to build a megaproject vindicating Hirschman's thesis of the benevolent hiding hand. Through imitation to some extent, and less through improvisation during implementation and through providing 'know-how', which Kenya lacked, the Chinese partners filled many of Kenya's institutional voids.

Secondly, the involvement of the Kenyan president allowed the setting up of the hierarchical and largely closed and opaque meta-organisation. Leadership by the president and his office, plus the Chinese partners, overrode most opposition and ensured completion of the SGR project. But, on the Kenyan side, land acquisition was insufficiently planned and prepared for, and had to be improvised, resulting in higher than expected compensation cost – but few delays. The only other solution to this, which is politically difficult, is legal reforms. During implementation, the organisation opened up somewhat to strike deals with landowners who had to be compensated, and some private sector organisations and local politicians that lobbied hard for getting a share of the subcontracting of inputs – notably labour and cement (Wissenbach and Wang 2017).

Thirdly, at the wider level, only time will tell whether the SGR is socio-economically beneficial beyond narrow cost–benefit calculations of passenger and freight volumes. The government may take regulatory measures encouraging rail transport, or make it more compelling, or even

bidding is part of the 'normal' Chinese practice, which protects the contractor and the state bank loans, but it was also legal under Kenya's law.

further levy road tolls on trucks to level the playing field. This is politically contested by vested interests. An *ex post* assessment of the business case, which should be completed in a few years, will also have to take account of the general notion that public infrastructure has other criteria for success, other than profit or even payback of investment – to which the RDL contributes. These could include public service provision; safer alternatives to road transport; environmentally friendly alternatives to road transport of both cargo and passengers; avoidance of police corruption; and experiences and skills gained from first-mover advantage, with which to increase the share of local content in future infrastructure projects. Concrete measures to promote investment, skills transfer and job creation that underlie Kenya's development vision will have to be implemented, and done in co-operation with the private sector, whose involvement brings with it funding and business acumen to make up for lack of government capacity.[85] These wider benefits will have to be negotiated as part of the normal Kenyan institutional set-up, which is different from the temporary fast-tracking of a project through the centralised meta-organisation.

Optimistically, train stations could lead to the establishment of economic clusters (SEZs or business parks), although there is currently little evidence that zoning for such parks has started, let alone construction. Optimists can also point to the fact that even the colonial 'Lunatic Express' led to Kenya's urbanisation and development (Kenyan cities such as Nairobi, Voi, Mitto-Andei, Kitale and others were initially railway construction camps) and to economic growth along its track, although the railway itself was never profitable. The key for Kenya's state and private sector will be to actively manage the wider economic and social dynamics effectively, beyond waiting for traffic to come to the railway. For instance, creating successful SEZ clusters along the SGR requires higher labour productivity, local infrastructure, energy and close co-operation with the private sector, and better regional co-operation (Woolfrey 2013).

This chapter acknowledges the complexity of various factors – notably on the Kenyan side of the project – which is characteristic of megaprojects, and which makes it impossible to define generic factors and criteria for success once one moves beyond a narrow evaluation of project management – the iron triangle. Kenya's SGR belies Flyvbjerg and Sunstein's (2015) claim that difficulties and costs are optimistically underestimated, whereas creativity and benefits are optimistically overestimated and that this 'will haunt the project during delivery as a double whammy of cost overruns, delays, and other unanticipated hardships compounded by

---

[85] Interview, K. Desai, 3 January 2018.

benefit shortfalls'. The Kenyan case shows that context matters and that there is a specific combination of institutional factors that determine project and wider system outcomes. The SGR operational success is an open question, but at least the project shows that capital-intensive technology can indeed be developed in contexts characterised by institutional voids.

Sadly, the regional rationale for the SGR unravelled as, at least for the time being, its cross-border dimension is far from being realised, while the existing metre-gauge Kenya–Uganda Railway has been decommissioned. Regional integration plans exist on paper, but the reality is fragmented and national. Leaders, who took the relevant decisions in summits, ignored studies and their own commitments, and differed fundamentally on whether and how to involve the private sector and donors. This resulted in political and economic competition and, in an even less beneficial balance of costs and benefits for the SGR, without its regional dimension. Regional extension is still possible, provided Uganda can access funding and address its land and planning challenges, and perhaps draw lessons from Kenya's experience.

In sum, the Kenyan case suggests that the partnership of an African government with a constellation of Chinese actors is a viable alternative to fill critical infrastructure voids – a known bottleneck for economic development. Unlike Western prescriptions, this pragmatic approach can navigate institutional voids, notably in design, planning, land acquisition and inter-organisation co-operation. Still, this approach is not cost-free – its detachment from the institutional context impairs the potential of the outcomes to catalyse broader social and economic benefits. And yet, development projects are ultimately about building options for further economic growth. The partnership with China leaves the option open for the East African governments and the local private sector to seize the opportunities the SGR presents for national development and, perhaps, ultimately for regional connectivity.

References

Alden, C. (2007). *Emerging countries as new players in LDCs: The case of China and Africa.* www.iddri.org/Publications/Emerging-countries-as-new-ODA-players-in-LDCs-The-case-of-China-and-Africa.

Bach, D. (2013). Régimes politiques, pratiques systémiques et dynamiques de l'émergence dans les états africains et post-soviétiques. *Revue internationale de politique compare,* 20(3) (2013): 153–169.

Bach, D. (2016). *Regionalism in Africa: Genealogies, institutions and trans-state networks.* London: Routledge.

Berger, L. (2011). *Northern Corridor infrastructure masterplan: Final report executive summary*. Paris: Louis Berger. www.ttcanc.org/documents/The%20Northern %20Corridor%20Infrastructure%20Master%20Plan.pdf.

Bräutigam, D. (2011). Aid 'with Chinese characteristics': Chinese foreign aid and development finance meet the OECD-DAC aid regime. *Journal of International Development* 23: 752–764. DOI:10.1002/jid.1798.

Cannon, B. J. (2017). Opinion: The struggle for East Africa's oil. *Anadolu Agency*. http://aa.com.tr/en/analysis-news/opinion-the-struggle-for-east-africa-s-oil/ 742397.

China Road and Bridge Corporation. (2016). *The social responsibility report 2015 on Mombasa-Nairobi SGR project*. Beijing: CRBC.

Cooke-Davies, T. (2002). The 'real' success factors on projects. *International Journal of Project Management*, 20(2002): 185–190.

Corkin, L., Burke, C., and Davies, M. (2008). *China's role in the development of Africa's infrastructure*. Working Papers in African Studies. Washington, DC: Johns Hopkins School of Advanced International Studies.

Cooksey, B. (2016). Railway rivalry in the East African Community. GREAT Insights Magazine, 5(4) July/August. http://ecdpm.org/great-insights/regional-integration-dynamics-africa/railway-rivalry-east-african-community/

CPCS Transcon International Ltd. (2014). *EAC Railway Sector Enhancement Project*. Working Paper: Policy Matrix. CPCS Ref/13062. St. Michael, Barbados: CPCS.

Davies, M. (2011). How China is influencing Africa's development. In J. Men and B. Barton (Eds.), *China and the European Union in Africa: Partners or competitors?* Belgium: College of Europe, pp. 187–205.

Dimitriou, H. T. (2014). What constitutes a 'successful' mega transport project? *Planning Theory & Practice*, 15(3): 389–430.

Eyiah-Botwe, E., Aigbavboa, C. and Thwala, WD (2016). Mega construction projects: Using stakeholder management for enhanced sustainable construction. *American Journal of Engineering Research (AJER)*, 5 (5):80–86.

Farole, T. and Akinci, G. (eds.) (2011). *Special Economic Zones: Progress, emerging challenges, and future directions*. Washington, DC: The International Bank for Reconstruction and Development/ The World Bank. http://documents .worldbank.org/curated/en/752011468203980987/pdf/638440PUB0Exto00B 0x0361527B0PUBLIC0.pdf.

Farrell, J. (2016). *How do Chinese contractors perform in Africa? Evidence from World Bank projects*. Washington SAIS-CARI Working Paper 3. Washington, DC: SAIS-CARI. https://static1.squarespace.com/static/5652847de4b033f56d2bd c29/t/573c970bf8baf3591b05253f/1463588620386/Working+Paper_Jamie+ Farrell.pdf

Flyvbjerg, B. and Sunstein, C. R. (2015). The principle of the malevolent hiding hand; or, the planning fallacy writ large. Preliminary draft 4.3. https://arxiv.org /ftp/arxiv/papers/1509/1509.01526.pdf

Foster, V., Butterfield, W., Chen, C. and Pushak, N. (2009). Building bridges: China's growing role as infrastructure financier for Sub-Saharan Africa. Trends and Policy Options Vol. 5. Washington, DC: World Bank Publications.

Fourie, E. (2014). East Asian lessons for Ethiopia's Hailemariam and Kenya's Kenyatta? *ECPDM: GREAT Insights Magazine*, 3(4): 20–21.

Gil, N. and Pinto, J. (2016). *Structure-performance relationships in complex system developments: The case of infrastructure projects in developing economies*. Working Paper 18 June 2016. The University of Manchester.

Gil, N. and Pinto, J. (2017). *Between accountability and ambition: Organizational duality in public goods provision in emerging markets*. Working Paper 15 December 2017. The University of Manchester.

He, W. (2007). The balancing act of China's Africa policy. *China Security*, 3(3) (2007): 23–40.

Hirschman, A. O. (1967). The principle of the hiding hand. The Public Interest. *National Affairs*, Winter 1967. www.nationalaffairs.com/public_interest/detail/the-principle-of-the-hiding-hand.

Hornsby, C. (2013). *Kenya: A history since independence*. London: Tauris.

Kaplinsky, R. and Morris, M. (2009). Chinese FDI in sub-Saharan Africa: Engaging with large dragons. *European Journal of Development Research*, 21 (2009): 551–569. https://link.springer.com/content/pdf/10.1057%2Fejdr.2009.24.pdf.

Lenfle, S. and Loch, C. (2017). Has megaproject management lost its way? Lessons from history. In B. Flyvbjerg (Ed.), *The Oxford handbook of megaproject management*. DOI:10.1093/oxfordhb/9780198732242.013.2. www.oxfordhandbooks.com/view/10.1093/oxfordhb/9780198732242.001.0001/oxfordhb-9780198732242-e-2

Li, R. (2009). Xifang dui Zhong Fei hezuo de waiqu ji qi zhengwei [Distorted China-Africa Cooperation and the Refutation], *World Economics and Politics*, 4 (2009): 16–25.

Lundrigan, C., Gil, N. and Puranam, P. (2014). *The (under)performance of megaprojects: A meta-organizational perspective*. Working Paper December 2014. The University of Manchester. www.researchgate.net/publication/291374272_The_Under_Performance_of_Megaprojects_A_Meta-Organizational_Perspective.

Mir, F. A. and Pinnington, A. H. (2014). Exploring the value of project management: Linking project management performance and project success. *International Journal of Project Management*, 32 (2014): 202–217.

Misic, S. and Radujkovic, M. (2015). Critical drivers of megaprojects success and failure. *Procedia Engineering*, 122(2015): 71–80.

Mwangi, P. M. (2017). Challenges of land issues to investment in Kenya. N.p.

Oloo, A. (2015). The triumph of ethnic identity over ideology in the 2013 general election in Kenya. In Kimani Njogu and Peter Wafula Wekesa (Eds.), *Kenya's 2013 general elections: Stakes, practices and outcomes*. Nairobi: Twaweza Communications, pp. 48–63.

Otieno, M., Moyi, E., Khainga, D. and Biwott, P. (2013). Regional integration and foreign direct investment in east African countries. *Journal of World Economic Research*, 2(4): 67–74.

(PIC) The Public Investments Committee. (2014, 29 April). National Assembly (PIC 2014): Special report on the procurement and financing of the construction of Standard Gauge Railway from Mombasa to Nairobi (Phase 1).

Sanghi, A. and Johnson, D. (2016, March). Deal or no deal: Strictly business for China in Kenya? Policy Research Paper 7614. Washington, DC: The World Bank Group.

Schiere, R. and Rugamba, A. (2011). Chinese infrastructure investments and African integration. African Development Bank Group. Working Paper Series, 127. www.afdb.org/fileadmin/uploads/afdb/Documents/Publications/WPS%2 0No%20127%20Chinese%20Infrastructure%20Investments%20.pdf.

Turner, R., Anbari, F. and Bredillet, C. (2013). Perspectives on research in project management: the nine schools. *Global Business Perspectives*, 1(1): 3–28.

Vanheukelom, J., Byiers, B., Bilal, S. and Woolfrey, S. (2016). *Political economy of regional integration in Africa: What drives and constrains regional organizations?* Synthesis Report. The European Centre for Development Policy Management. http://ecdpm.org/wp-content/uploads/ECDPM-2016-Political-Economy-Regional-Integration-Africa-Synthesis-Report.pdf.

Wissenbach, U. (2007). China, Africa and Europe: Africa's attractions. *The World Today*, 63 (4):7–9.

Wissenbach, U. (2011). China–Africa relations and the European Union: Ideology, conditionality, realpolitik and what is new in South–South co-operation. In C. M. Dent (Ed.), *China and Africa development relations*. London: Routledge.

Wissenbach, U. and Kim, E.-M. (2013). From polarisation towards a consensus on development? The EU and Asian approaches to development and ODA. In T. Christiansen, E. Kirchner and P. Murray (Eds.), *The Palgrave handbook of EU–Asia relations*. London: Palgrave Macmillan.

Wissenbach, U. and Wang, Y. (2017). *African politics meets Chinese engineers: The Chinese-built Standard Gauge Railway Project in Kenya and East Africa. SAIS-Cari Working Paper No. 13*. Washington, DC: Johns Hopkins University School of Advanced International Studies. https://static1.squarespace.com/static/565 2847de4b033f56d2bdc29/t/594d739f3e00bed37482d4fe/1498248096443/S GR+v4.pdf.

Woolfrey, S. (2013). *Special Economic Zones and regional integration in Africa*. Trade Law Centre Working Paper N° S13WP10/2013. www.tralac.org/files/2013/07/S 13WP102013-Woolfrey-Special-economic-zones-regional-integration-in-Africa-20130710-fin.pdf.

World Bank (2013). *The economics of rail gauge in the East Africa community*. World Bank-Africa Transportation Unit. Available at http://bodmastec.com/sgr1/wp-content/uploads/2014/06/World_bank_Report_on_the_Standard_Gauge_Rail way.pdf.

World Bank. (2017). *Kenya economic update*. April 2017 Edition No. 15. https:// openknowledge.worldbank.org/handle/10986/26392.

Wrong, M. (2009). *It's our turn to eat: The story of a Kenyan whistleblower*. London: Fourth Estate.

Zeng, D. Z. (2015). *Global experiences with Special Economic Zones: With a focus on China and Africa*. Washington, DC: World Bank. http://documents.worldbank .org/curated/en/810281468186872492/Global-experiences-with-special-eco nomic-zones-focus-on-China-and-Africa.

12 No One-Size-Fits-All Organisational Solution: Learning from Railway Developments in South Africa and Ethiopia

Innocent Musonda, Trynos Gumbo, Boniface Bwanyire, Walter Musakwa, Chioma Okoro and Nuno Gil

Abstract

Against the backdrop of an increasing demand for efficient, effective and sustainable new infrastructure developments in Africa, this study examines two rapid railway transportation projects to explore alternative ways of organising. The analysis focuses on the Gautrain railway system in South Africa and the Addis Ababa City Light Rail Transit (AA-LRT) system in Ethiopia. Adopting a comparative approach, we investigate how the two capital-intensive project organisations succeeded in overcoming system bottlenecks, and in dealing with complex interfaces with the institutional environment. Our focus is on the structures designed by the project promoter to acquire the necessary formal resources – finance, human capital, certification and land – and to manage the interdependency with the environment. We also investigate the extent to which the developments succeeded in creating broad value beyond the private value appropriated by the private firms involved in design, construction and operations. In agreement with organisation design literature, our analysis suggests the design of the governance structures is directly influenced by the political and sociocultural environment. Therefore, we argue, designing project organisations to deliver infrastructure in Africa is not a problem with a one-size-fits-all solution.

12.1 Introduction

There is a large body of scholarly literature on the governance of new infrastructure development projects in advanced economies, but less so on project governance in developing countries – environments with a shortfall of institutions – and in African countries in particular. Governance is generally understood as the set of designed structures and procedures that enable and constrain collective action. Extant literature, grounded in advanced economies, reveals alternative forms of governance that vary from highly centralised to more decentralised approaches to managing the project participants and the interfaces between the project organisation and environmental stakeholders (see Gil and Pinto 2018 for a review). The idea that one particular approach might be 'superior', and so should be adopted in a prescriptive way as a regulatory device, has, in general, been criticised as an effort to promote a normative and mimetic isomorphism that may lead to a misfit between project governance and context (Biesenthal et al. 2018). Yet, this leaves unclear how the choices to design a governance structure and procedures can respond effectively to an institutionally under-developed environment. In this chapter we further our empirical understanding of how Africa as a context impacts project governance through a study of two contemporaneous railway projects in sub-Saharan Africa.

Importantly, both railway projects aimed to address a major transport infrastructure gap, a typical challenge of sub-Saharan African countries (World Bank 2010). Indeed, in Africa, inefficient regional links and limited household access to public transport are the norm, and the density of transport networks relative to population and land is consistently lower than in middle-income countries (Bogetic and Fedderke 2005). Complicating matters, the price of services such as road transport is much higher, with the tariffs paid often many times over those paid in developing countries (World Bank 2010). Yet, if closing the transport infrastructure gap is an imperative for Africa, and especially for sub-Saharan Africa, the question of how to achieve this higher-order goal is not trivial. Infrastructure delivery is directly affected by the institutions, or lack of, in the environment, including regulation, contract enforcement mechanisms, independent judiciary, and the availability or existence of efficient markets for products, labour and capital. So, the interdependences with institutions, and corresponding structures designed to cope with these interdependences, matter as much as technical factors to determine performance (Biesenthal et al. 2018; Miller and Hobbs 2005).

In this study we illustrate how the two railway systems, the Gautrain in South Africa and the Addis Ababa City Light Rail Transit (AA-LRT) in Ethiopia, were organised to deliver on their intended goals, and how the respective project organisations dealt with complex interdependency with the environment. For each case study we examined how the railway development was financed and organised, the institutional framework, and whether organisational design choices enable broader value creation. Our findings reveal a fundamental variation in the way the political and sociocultural environment directly influenced governance design choices. And so, we argue, there is no one-size-fits-all organisational solution for large infrastructure projects in Africa.

We organise the remainder of this chapter as follows: we first discuss the need for investment in new infrastructure development in Africa, and various system bottlenecks that may stymie progress. Then, we carry on an analysis of the governance structures that were adopted in the two focal cases. We conclude with a discussion on how organisational design choices sought to relate to the context and value creation.

12.1.1 Background

African cities will experience, for decades to come, massive pressure to develop new infrastructure stemming from fast urbanisation and population growth (Stren 2014). Indeed, one of the reasons why African countries are seen to be not as competitive as their counterparts in other developing countries is because of poor infrastructure (AfDB 2013a; Moghalu 2014; World Bank 2017). The growing demand for urban infrastructure, particularly transport, means Africa's railway infrastructure should receive increased consideration (AfDB 2015). From this perspective, the development of South Africa's Gautrain and Ethiopia's AA-LRT are both welcome efforts to tackle the problem of lack of transport infrastructure in Africa. The Gautrain was planned to meet projections for increased demand because of economic and population growth in South Africa's Gauteng Province, an urbanised area containing the country's largest city, Johannesburg, and its administrative capital, Pretoria (GMA 2011). Equally, AA-LRT was a response to the mounting transport challenges facing Addis Ababa, Ethiopia's fast-growing city and capital (Sabatino 2017; UN-Habitat 2017).

Needs for transport infrastructure notwithstanding, new developments need careful planning, organisation, implementation and management to be effective, efficient and sustainable. Furthermore, the system-level goals informing new schemes should be clear, well defined and not only be driven by the political interests of powerful actors text (Flyvberg 2014). But putting these recommendations into action is not easy. Infrastructure development is affected by many system bottlenecks and challenging interfaces with external stakeholders; project organisations may collapse or fail to deliver value if they do not tackle these challenges effectively and fend off pressure from private interests (Allport et al. 2008;

Othman 2013). For a sub-Saharan-African context in particular, the extant literature suggests a number of challenging issues that project promoters need to tackle:

- **Financing:** Finance can be hard to acquire because many African governments are not in a position to borrow on capital markets, or because they fail to convince lenders that the projects are value for money (AfDB 2013b; DOT South Africa 2017).
- **Central government as promoter:** The role of the central government as a promoter of infrastructure projects is a contentious one. Some argue the central government should not assume an active role, but rather be concerned with policy formulation, outsourcing as much work as possible to private firms (Williams and Samset 2010). But other authors contend that a lack of, or inadequate level of institutional, professional and political support from central government is a frequent cause of project failure (Allport et al. 2008).
- **Land acquisition:** Many infrastructure projects, notably those in the realm of transport, involve land acquisition, forced displacement of people and businesses and the acquisition of rights of way; unsurprisingly, many of these projects are significantly delayed or even abandoned due to difficulties in dealing with land issues (ESI Africa 2017; PwC 2014).
- **Public buy-in:** Public resistance has frequently been cited as a reason for the collapse of project organisations (Han et al. 2009). It is the job of project organisations to try to gain as much legitimacy as possible for their endeavours, in order to undercut opposition in the environment. In view of the risks associated with lack of public buy-in – e-toll roads, for example, are highly controversial – project promoters should proactively seek to gain public acceptance and support for the grand idea (Naidoo 2013; PwC 2014).
- **Planning capabilities:** Planning capabilities can be difficult to acquire in an African context. But they are necessary to reduce uncertainty, mitigate the risks of things going wrong and increase the chances of delivering within the initial targets, and so raise perceptions of positive performance (Allport et al. 2008). Planning capabilities are also important in attracting funding and ensuring the project is a source of broad value creation.
- **Procurement:** Increasingly more infrastructure assets, notably transport, are delivered through strategic alliances between the public and the private sector, the so-called public–private partnerships (PPPs). This is so to the extent that some multilateral organisations have come to see PPPs as the preferred model of financing infrastructure (Asian Development Bank 2016; OECD 2012; Wentworth and

Makokera 2015). Yet ensuring equitable value appropriation through PPPs is challenging, as there are often major asymmetries in contractual capabilities between the public and private actors.

- **Allocation of risk:** Improper allocation of commercial and technological risks in buyer–supplier relationships often results in disputes and slippages of project targets that can trigger generalised perceptions of project failure. For example, Han et al. (2009) identify conflicts between buyers and suppliers rooted in asymmetrical risk allocation as one of the major causes of delay in railway-network development projects.
- **Transport integration:** Integrating public transport systems is about seeking ways in which different systems can complement one another, as opposed to compete, in order to create value for passengers and users in general. A successful transport system is one that offers convenience to the public by integrating one mode with other modes, so that the public is more willing to switch from private to public transport (PWC 2014).
- **Operations:** The feasibility of large projects, such as railway systems, depends on plans for operations, and schemes often become unviable if planning fails to capture the real user needs (Winch 2013). A lot of attention in planning must, then, focus on the post-commissioning period and corresponding contractual arrangements.

The fact that the two railways schemes at the heart of this study are now both operational and perceived as sources of broad value creation suggests their project governance structures must have found effective ways to deal with the aforementioned challenging issues, and so both cases merit research. However, before we turn to discuss our methods and examine our data, we first briefly review what we know about the way institutions affect the governance of infrastructure projects.

12.1.2 Project Governance and Institutional Environment

Large infrastructure projects are socio-technical undertakings embedded in institutional frameworks (Biesenthal et al. 2018; Miller and Hobbs 2005). Hence, the adoption and retention of many organisational practices are often more dependent on social pressures for conformity and legitimacy than on technical and/or economic pressures. And although there is a lot of emphasis on the technical aspect of project delivery, designing the institutional arrangements often precedes the technical work in large infrastructure projects (Chi, Chen and Shi 2014; Dille and Soderhund 2011).

Alone, the technical and economic inputs and outputs cannot define the design of the project organisations, except in functional terms (Biesenthal et al. 2005). To the contrary, project organisations are social constructions defined by those who fund them, those who contest them and those who use them (Biesenthal et al. 2005, 2018; Morris and Geraldi 2011). Indeed, the extent to which the context supports the project organisation is a major factor to determine whether the organisation is efficient and effective, and whether the output creates long-term value.

12.2   Methods

This empirical study focused on two project organisations set up to develop railway infrastructure in sub-Saharan Africa: the light rail transport system in Addis Ababa, the capital city of Ethiopia, and the Gautrain high-speed train in the Gauteng province of South Africa. Our focus was on the governance design choices that arguably contributed to make these two investments broad sources of value creation, despite the many bottlenecks they encountered along the way. Our sources of archival information included project reports, third-party reports and other project documents, e.g. strategic plans, strategic visions and other information available on governmental websites and those of private operators. We triangulated this information with interviews with key project participants.

For the Gautrain project, we interviewed five top managers in different departments of the Gautrain Management Agency (GMA): these were the Transport Integration and Planning unit; Technical Services; Operations and Performance; Assets and Maintenance Assurance; and Portfolio Management. The participants were selected because of their managerial capacity and by virtue of being involved in the Gautrain project from its inception. For the Addis Ababa project, we conducted an equivalent set of interviews, and also leveraged informal access to other participants, as one of our informants had been directly involved in this project.

In both cases, we focused the analysis around three areas of interest: acquisition of formal resources, organisational structure and value creation. In addition to the information obtained through interviews and archival documents, we also sieved through press articles published in the local media; we used Gautrain, AA-LRT, rapid rail transport in Africa, and the names of top project managers as key words in internet search engines.

12.3   Analysis

12.3.1 *The Gautrain Rapid Rail*

The Gautrain is Africa's first rapid rail system and is located in the Gauteng province of South Africa. The Gautrain is widely perceived as a symbol of pride for Gauteng in particular and South Africa as a whole. The railway was a strategic initiative of the Gauteng provincial government, and was planned in order to meet future transport demands anticipated as a result of local economic and population growth. At the time of planning, Gauteng Province, which is the country's economic hub, was already struggling with traffic congestion on most of its major routes connecting the three metropolitan municipalities of Johannesburg, Pretoria and Ekurhuleni. Connections between these three metros were mostly road-based. In addition, there was a car culture, in which people mostly commuted by car to work.

Gautrain was developed in order to change the way people travelled and to ease traffic congestion, as well as to advance the higher-order goal of creating a 'smart' metropolitan area based on mixed land uses and industrial corridors, and to promote the rejuvenation of central Johannesburg and Pretoria (GMA 2011). According to the Gauteng's twenty-five-year Integrated Transport Master Plan, designed to improve public transport systems within the province, the Gautrain was planned to be the backbone of all public transit in Gauteng. So it was envisaged the Gautrain would promote mobility and accessibility, redirection of urban growth, economic development and rural development beyond the urban edge.

The initial planning and pre-feasibility investigations for Gautrain were undertaken in 1997/98. Driven by these initial studies, the local government decided to develop an 80-kilometre rapid rail system with two major corridors: the north–south spine between Tshwane and Johannesburg, and the east–west spine between OR Tambo International Airport and Sandton (GMA 2011). The east–west route, designated Phase 1, would start from Sandton station via Marlboro, to Rhodesfield station in Kempton Park, and then connect at the OR Tambo International Airport. The north–south route, Phase 2, was designed to start from Park Station precinct in central Johannesburg and proceed north underground for six kilometres beneath the Parktown ridge to Hatfield. Station locations were evaluated using socio-economic criteria. Indeed, several economic appraisals suggested the Gautrain could considerably contribute to socio-economic development, efficient land use and a reduction in traffic congestion and air pollution.

Specifically, an independent project review showed that the project had the potential to:

- Lower traffic congestion, resulting in substantive travel cost savings
- Save costs associated with accidents of about R475 million per annum (2003 Rand prices)
- Save R3,845 million per year in vehicle operating costs by the year 2030 (2003 prices)
- Save R7,114 million per year in time costs for passengers travelling in the corridor by 2030 (2003 prices)
- Contribute about 1 per cent to the Gross Geographic Product of Gauteng, with approximately 74 per cent of that impact in the Gautrain Province itself (GMA 2011).

In 2000, a couple of years after the initial studies were published, the Premier of Gauteng announced the project as one of the strategic initiatives of the provincial government to promote long-term growth (GMA 2014, 2015). The news provoked many criticisms from environmental actors, including politicians, academics, media and affected residents, who were not convinced of the value proposition. The project was criticised for its impact on the environment, its poor socio-economic benefits and its optimistic timelines as well as an overly optimistic ridership estimate – some observers called it 'the train for the rich'. Local communities, who saw their property values reduced by the plans, contested the route, and other stakeholders took legal action, for example the Muckleneuk/Lukasrand property owners and residents association (Case No. 28192/04, 2004). In the face of criticism, the Premier of Gauteng at that time, Mbazima Shilowa, put on a show of force in parliament in 2005:

Nothing has changed. The train is being built to ease congestion, stimulate economic activity and create jobs. That was our plan in 2000 and it still is. We are expecting financial closure in December and the sod-turning ceremony has been planned for January. (Cited in Cox 2005)

Retrospectively, when reflecting on how the provincial government had succeeded in undercutting opposition to the scheme, one top manager at GMA highlighted two factors – the elected leaders' political commitment and their clarity of purpose. Another respondent said:

if it was not for the provincial involvement, the project may not even have proceeded ... because of the vested interest they had in making sure this thing happened, they made it a priority; it was not a national government priority ... political will was on the provincial level, the lobbying and getting the necessary funds and guarantees and so on ...

A major challenge to implement the railway plans was finding ways to overcome the financial bottleneck. Gautrain aimed to be the first high-speed rail link in South Africa and, for that matter, in Africa. So it was clearly perceived as a high-risk enterprise. Furthermore, as it was a development championed at a regional level, the provincial government struggled to persuade the national government to finance the project in its totality. And the Gauteng government lacked the wherewithal to finance the project too; as one respondent said:

This project belongs with the Department of Gauteng Roads and Transport ... If I have to take this project and go to the national government, PRASA (National rail authority), they would say, 'I've got all these projects that I have to look at.'

We turn now to discuss how this bottleneck was overcome through an alliance with a private actor, and thus through the choice to set up a PPP.

12.3.1.1   The Governance Structure

The decision to develop the project as a PPP was informed by the fact that Gauteng Province could not afford to fund the scheme – which, in 2005, it was forecast would cost over R20 billion – on its own. Neither was there any political will in central government to fully finance the railway development. Indeed, according to the Gautrain Chief Operating Officer there was little fiscal space at national level to finance Gautrain because the state was facing multiple pressure in all spheres of governance; the national budget for infrastructure alone was, at that time, around R235 billion (in 2010 terms), most of which was borrowed money with explicitly guaranteed terms. The state-owned entities (SOE) themselves had borrowed about R100 billion to finance their own capital projects.

The arrangement to enter into a concession with a private actor was led by the Province Support Team (PST), who had also undertaken the planning and feasibility studies. The PST were retained during the development stage as contract managers, and thus made responsible for managing the design and construction processes, as well as the legal and environmental compliance processes. An independent certifier was appointed to check procurement and economic elements. It is worth noting that socio-economic development obligations were included in the concession agreement. Figure 12.1 illustrates the contractual structure during operations, which was designed before the PPP was signed off and was instrumental in order for the state to go to the market and find a private partner (a so-called concessionaire).

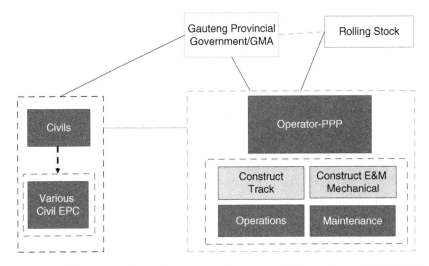

Figure 12.1 Gautrain contractual structure (Adapted from GMA 2015)

As Figure 12.1 shows, a private entity was appointed to deliver the project on a design, build and operate basis. In turn, the GMA was made contractually responsible for providing the capabilities to oversee and manage the infrastructure asset during the operational period. The GMA was tasked with ensuring the private partner maintained and looked after the asset until March 2026, after which, full ownership of the asset was set to return to Gauteng Province. A penalty system was attached to the monthly performance measurement, whereby if the concessionaire fell short in respect of any performance measures, their payment would be reduced for that month. We turn now to examine the governance of the acquisition of two critical resources – finance and land – in more detail.

12.3.1.2   *Acquiring the Finance*

One key element highlighted by respondents as critical to the sustainability of the project organisation were the governance choices to handle the financial risks. First, to mitigate cost escalation during implementation, the promoter chose to invest in performance-based specifications as part of the tender documents. One respondent said:

They [potential concessionaires] submitted proposals based on output specifications, for instance, a train that can run from the Airport to Sandton in 15 minutes ... We did not say, 'this is how the trains should look like' ... they had to go and say, 'Okay, to get that we have to do this'. So the whole design specs in terms of what happens on the track level, what happens on the trains, the nose, speed profile, they had to come up with and say, 'I propose this rolling stock; it's available in the market and can comply and give you what you want . . . how you do it, what materials you use, what management systems you need.'

Other financial risks related to the bankability of the project, which was important to ensure private-sector competition in the tender process and interest in constructing, operating and maintaining the railway. Some financial risks were rooted in uncertainty around cost escalation, currency fluctuation, changes in employment rates and country taxes. Yet the greatest financial risk was around the ridership forecast, since financial viability partially depended on a dedicated feeder and distribution system. As this was the first public transport initiative to rely on the diversion of commuters from private-car use to the rail system in South Africa, uncertainty was high in terms of usage and revenue. Consequently, a patronage guarantee, to cover missed revenues in case of a shortfall in demand, was determined by the provincial government to make the project more attractive to the concessionaire. In addition, the provincial government also agreed to make a contribution to the capital costs. The provincial government then determined to select the bidder with the lowest cost combination of provincial contribution and patronage guarantee on the basis of net present value.

The negotiations were informed by two models: one to demonstrate viability – the provincial model – and the other to govern the contractual relationship – a base-case financial model. The first model determined the minimum required total revenue (MRTR) that was needed to operate and maintain the system, taking into account corporate tax, loan stock servicing, debt servicing, overheads, operator's fee, renewals and maintenance. The second model, developed by the concessionaire, captured the operating costs and revenues during the concession period. The latter model was based on contractually committed costs as influenced by economic variables, such as inflation, interest and foreign exchange rates. Both models were necessary to give the winning concessionaire confidence in the financial solution proposed in the first model, which was inclusive of costs and revenue assumptions.

In the end, the Gautrain project organisation succeeded in accessing five sources of finance, including a national grant (44.2 per cent); a local grant from the provincial government (26.1 per cent); provincial borrowing (18.4 per cent); private-sector borrowing (9.5 per cent); and private-sector equity (1.8%). But as one respondent said of the public funds, 'strictly speaking we report to the provincial legislature ... provincial funding actually comes from the national treasury'.

12.3.1.3   *Acquiring the Land*

To tackle the challenge of land acquisition, the Gautrain project organisation counted on the central government's support. In addition, Bombela, the winning concessionaire, and the provincial government set up a stakeholder relationship and communication structure to update and interact with all affected local communities, public relevant authorities and other third parties. Although we lack details of how the compulsory land acquisition process unfolded, this task was assigned to the provincial government.

Specifically, the Gautrain directly affected 1,100 properties. The provincial government was made responsible for expropriation of the required land, and for acquiring land-use rights, including payment of compensation to owners in compliance with the law. In view of the time constraints, and the complications associated with land acquisition in a country that is founded on constitutional democracy, land acquisition was planned in tranches in order to match the construction access requirements. Still, the delivery of land in time instalments proved problematic and involved land disputes that ended up in court; inevitably, the land-related problems brought about by conflicts of interest with local communities impacted on the timescale, but it is unclear whether the provincial government had to compensate the private partner, or the amounts involved. Challenges notwithstanding, the provincial government succeeded in settling all court cases.

12.3.1.4   *Value Creation*

The Gautrain railway began operations in 2010. A variety of reports have suggested that, since its opening day, the Gautrain has successfully built a positive perception of its impact on public transport, and, as envisaged, it has to some extent reduced traffic congestion on the roads. Gautrain passenger numbers have also increased since the opening day. For example, KPMG reports that in 2015, the Gautrain transported 60,000 passengers per day, and 77 per cent of these passengers owned cars; a GMA indicated that passenger numbers, estimated at 300,000 on inception had increased to 800,000 in January 2015. One respondent said:

The increase in passenger numbers as a result of the Gautrain infrastructure has managed to change public perceptions about public transport positively ... It was evident in 2012 that we were going to run out of capacity with the passenger levels we were getting.

Whilst cost slippages during project delivery led to disputes between the provincial government and the private partner, the formal arrangements between the public and private actors turned out to be sustainable. This outcome was attributed in part to the popularity of the system, and to robust revenue collection enabled by an automatic fare-collection system. The success of Gautrain in creating value beyond the private value appropriated by the concessionaire has encouraged the provincial government to propose seven more rail routes (measuring a total of 140 km) along identified 'high-mobility corridors' as part of the province's twenty-five-year Integrated Transport Master Plan. One respondent described this new development:

The prefeasibility and feasibility studies have been done. We submitted to National Treasury in November 2017, so we're awaiting Tier 1 approval. We are in the process of procuring the services of a service provider to do the preliminary route alignment study . . . .Gautrain 2 is proposed to be implemented in phases . . . we hope construction will soon be underway.

12.3.2 The Addis Ababa Light Rail Transit (AA-LRT)

The grand idea for the AA-LRT system can be traced to 2000, when the Lyon Urbanism Agency and the municipality of Addis Ababa entered into a long-term co-operation on urban planning mobility, financed by the French government. As part of this Ethiopian–French co-operation, planners concluded that there was a need to develop a mass transport system along the two main axes of the city: east–west and north–south. But the actual development of the railway project would only gain traction several years later in 2009, when a group of Chinese actors expressed formal interest in developing a detailed design, building and operating the railway system, which they estimated would cost $475 million (cash prices); construction would then start in 2012, and the railway would open three years later.

The project was a response to the mounting public transport challenges of Addis Ababa – Ethiopia's capital, which was responsible for around half of the country's GDP. Addis Ababa was one of Africa's fast-growing cities with a population of circa 4 million in 2008, and growing at 3.9 per cent annually, forecasted to reach over 10 million inhabitants by 2037. Unsurprisingly, the public transport system was failing to meet demand, and also falling short of the expectations of the local authorities. In Addis Ababa, the movement of commuter minibuses was chaotic and hazardous, and there were hundreds of fatal traffic accidents every year. Environmental pollution was also a concern, with a high risk of anthropogenic greenhouse-gas emissions from an aged hydrocarbon-powered fleet. In response to all these issues, the central government agreed to endorse the recommendations of the Lyon–Addis Ababa co-operation to develop an urban railway (Nallet 2018). The plan was to build two lines connecting 44 stations, one east–west (17.35 km) and another north–south (16.9 km), to reach a passenger capacity of 60,000 people per day, with a design speed of 80 km/hr.

12.3.2.1   *The Governance Structure*

The AA-LRT organisation was structured as a so-called turnkey project commissioned by the Addis Ababa government with the oversight of the Ministry of Transport (MOT) in central government. Under this arrangement, the MOT appointed a steering committee to work with the Addis Ababa City Roads Authority, which had already established an AA-LRT working unit in 2007 (Jemere 2012). The central government further entrusted the Ethiopian Railway Corporation (ERC), a state-owned company, to develop the AA-LRT lines (Nallet 2018). One year later, in 2008, the ERC assumed management responsibility for the AA-LRT project and floated a turnkey project tender. There is limited information publicly available about the supplier selection process; whilst three tenderers submitted proposals, it is known that pre-contract negotiations failed because of high costs and vague cost-breakdown estimates. Things would only take a turn for the better in July 2009, when the China Railway Engineering Company (CREC) took the initiative to offer a conceptual design and a corresponding cost estimate. A deal was then cut behind closed doors, which resulted in CREC securing a turnkey contract starting in September 2009, with financing to be provided by a Chinese lender (more on that later). In addition, the ERC, which was also entrusted with the responsibility for railway operations and maintenance, chose to outsource this job to Shenzhen Metro Corporation until 2020 – and again, this was done through an opaque process (Nallet 2018).

12.3.2.2   *Acquiring the Finance*

Acquiring the finance to build the AA-LRT was a bottleneck which delayed the start of the project. To overcome this hold-up, Ethiopia turned to Chinese lenders. The AA-LRT had been quoted by CREC at $475 million (cash prices), excluding land acquisition costs. The

Export-Import Bank of China – a state-owned bank – then proposed financing 85 per cent of this cost through external debt; local authorities were charged with raising equity on the open market for the remaining 15 per cent of the cost forecast by the Ethiopian government; cost figures for land acquisition are not in the public domain. A memorandum of understanding (MoU) was signed between CREC and the Government of Ethiopia, paving the way for the signing of a loan agreement in June 2011, with 15 per cent of equity raised (*Mail Online* 2017; Mohapatra 2015). As the railway neared completion in 2014, the Shenzhen Metro Group received operating and maintenance rights with a contract worth $100 million for three years, starting in the first quarter of 2015 and terminating in August 2018. The contract included provisions regarding the training of local personnel to build capacity to take over the management of the system after August 2018 (Sabatino 2017; Tarrosy and Vörös 2018). Under this contract, the Shenzhen Metro Group receives the income from ticket purchases. Lack of transparency also characterised the negotiations with the Chinese operator.

By delegating the entire development to a Chinese contractor, the local authorities succeeded in overcoming the lack of skilled labour in Ethiopia, another system bottleneck. The railway opened in November 2015, against an initial public expectation that it would only open in 2016 (Grey 2016; World Folio 2016). But these facts, per se, tell us little about organisational efficiency because the lack of information available makes it unclear whether the cost and schedule targets were ambitious or highly conservative. But it is fair to say that the AA-LRT project rode on the strength of the political will and commitment of Ethiopia's government, visible through many initiatives geared towards reducing bureaucratic red tape (Nallet 2018). And the central government insists that Ethiopia got a good deal based on the feasibility study, and on the environmental and social impact assessment (Jemere 2012).

12.3.2.3   Acquiring the Land

Perhaps the most daunting issue facing the project promoters was acquiring the necessary land whilst avoiding tribal issues, and keeping the corresponding land acquisition costs under control. The railway lines run through an already built-up area, and compensation payments for land were unavoidable; landowners were unhappy, however, with the compensation amounts and procedures. Furthermore, Addis Ababa is home to multiple ethnic groups, including the Omoro, the largest single ethnic group within Ethiopia, as well as much smaller but powerful ethnic groups, including the Amhara and the Tigrayans. Symptomatic of the lack of transparency characterising the governance structure, there is hardly any information publicly available as to how the state resolved the land issues, and the exact amounts that were spent. Detailed information about land disputes is also limited, although there is evidence that these disputes occurred. For example, the AA-LRT had to deal with heritage issues, as the route crossed areas that reflected the history and cultural heritage of, not only Addis Ababa, but Ethiopia at large. For example, the line passed through two squares with statues of Emperor Menelik II and of St Abune Paulos, a former archbishop of the Ethiopian Christian Orthodox Church, both erected in 1941. The authorities had to assure the public that the statues, and what they stood for, would not be defiled. But we struggled to acquire more data about how these land disputes were resolved.

12.3.2.4   *Value Creation*

For the Ethiopian government, the AA-LRT is a story of success and broad value creation. In 2017, an AA-LRT spokesperson claimed the train service had carried more than 50 million passengers and made a positive impact on Addis Ababa. The system goal was to alleviate the shortage of transport for lower-income people, which officials claimed had been met, after recording that 60,000 people used the railway daily (News24 2017; online). Other figures suggest the railway is financially viable in operations. During the Ethiopian fiscal year 2016/17, the state-owned ERC earned $5 million in revenue from the AA-LRT, under the management of the Chinese operator. The money was earned through fare collection from an estimated 35 million passengers, which produced a daily income of about $14,000 (Tarrosy and Vörös 2018; Xinhua 2017). Furthermore, operational records suggest there has been a significant reduction in traffic congestion and in journey time – by two-thirds for those travelling from the periphery of the city; there was also an improved average transport speed from 10 km/h (by road travel) to 22 km/h (by AA-LRT) (C40 Cities Climate Leadership Group 2018).

Experts have also lauded the system's low pollution levels with regard to reductions in emissions and gases. Although full emission-reduction data is not available, the cumulative emission-reduction potential of the system is projected to be equivalent to 1.8 million tonnes of carbon dioxide (tCO_2e) by 2030 (C40 Cities Climate Leadership Group 2018). In terms of environmental sustainability, the AA-LRT system is rated to be environmentally friendly because it is powered by low-carbon electricity from geothermal, hydropower and wind-power sources, in addition to the Ethiopian electric grid (Sabatino 2017).

Additionally, the project is reported to have created 13,000 jobs during construction; the railway also employs around 1,100 people in operations (C40 Cities Climate Leadership Group 2018; Xinhua 2017). And at its construction peak, the AA-LRT project organisation employed over 4,500 workers. Aware of the large scale of these figures, the ERC sought to use the project as a catalyst to develop capabilities, and to retool and up-skill local enterprises – 'for each and every discipline in the contract, there is a clause that enforces [*sic*] the contractor to arrange capacity building program training', said one manager. Capability-building efforts are estimated to have added approximately $3 million per kilometre to the project. But some accounts suggest that the results have been somewhat disappointing, because in some grades the training and skills transfer did not happen. This partial non-compliance with the contract terms, coupled with the prevalence of short-term contracts, highlights the issues of lack of opportunity for local firms in infrastructure developments funded by Chinese actors.

Another area where value-creation opportunities seem to have been missed relates to poor integration of the railway with the existing transport network (Nallet 2018). Whilst the Chinese firm built on the existing master plan to produce a concept design for the AA-LRT, planners complain that there was limited dialogue and co-operation with relevant public agencies and other stakeholders (Nallet 2018; Tarrosy and Vörös 2018). This centralised approach thus produced a railway that many observers feel is disconnected from the city's transport network, creating numerous safety issues due to poor design at intersections with roads. As one observer commented:

We have the issues of integration. . . . We are planning to make an agreement with minibuses. Now we know that there is no harmony and that we have to organize an infrastructure for integration . . . .We don't have direct relations with the other transport agencies but we are planning to coordinate the transport in the city. For now, we don't cooperate. (Nallet 2018)

In particular, observers have highlighted the poor integration between AA-LRT and the rapid bus transit systems. As a result, commuters have to walk long distances to get to the stations and cross streets cluttered with vehicles to walk between the tram and bus stations. The lack of dedicated parking at the tram stations has created an additional safety risk, as motorists and contract taxis have taken over the outer lanes of the roads running adjacent to the railway lines (Endeshaw 2013). Commuters also complain the trains are frequently overcrowded. But as one of them said, 'It's better than nothing' (Nazret 2017).

All in all, it seems fair to say that a broad group of stakeholders succeeded in appropriating value from the AA-LRT, and that the railway is contributing to the city's socio-economic growth. This is to the extent that the project, the first urban railway in sub-Saharan Africa, has been praised for elevating the status of Addis Ababa to that of an international city (Nallet 2018). Still, the fast growth of Ethiopia's population and its economy means that the AA-LRT is already unable to meet demand during most of the hours of operation, and that therefore the trains are running at full capacity. Aware of this, the local authorities are planning an expansion to cover other parts of the city and create more opportunities for value creation.

12.4   Discussion

Our analysis illustrates that the governance of new infrastructure developments in Africa does not have a one-size-fits-all organisational solution. Rather, we observe two fundamentally different designs, which were the outcome of choices made by the respective governments. We turn now to discuss how the organisational choices were contingent on the choice of the intermediary in charge of mobilising much-needed finance, and thus relate the governance structure to the institutional environment.

12.4.1 *Organisational Choice and the Institutional Environment*

From a national institutional perspective, South Africa and Ethiopia could not be more different. South Africa is an established constitutional democracy with numerous institutional checks and balances scrutinising public investment decisions. In contrast, Ethiopia, despite its federal political system, is led by an authoritarian government that maintains a firm grip over public investment decisions – to the extent that some observers controversially call Ethiopia the 'China of Africa'.[1] It was, then, not surprising that the Ethiopian state had latitude to forge ahead with a capital-intensive PPP without subjecting the deal to scrutiny from other stakeholders in the environment. Through bilateral agreements, the Ethiopian government borrowed from China, and thereafter appointed a Chinese contractor for the project. But contrary to Western standards of transparency, accountability and good governance in public investment, there was no competitive bidding. And it was the secrecy cloaking the

---

[1] 'Ethiopia needs to change its authoritarian course', *Financial Times*, 9 January 2018.

contractual arrangements, together with an authoritarian approach to land acquisition, which enabled the project to be completed in just four years – a remarkable achievement by any standard.

In marked contrast, the Gautrain scheme suggests an approach to organising much more in line with recommendations from Western development agencies. The elapsed time between formulating the grand idea and getting the project off the drawing table was actually not radically different albeit institutional pressures for accountability and transparency. The difference in the Gautrain case is that the local authorities succeeded in finding a private partner through the market – an effort that failed for Addis Ababa. To go to the market, the Gautrain had to be registered with the central treasury department for approval; and the premier of the provincial government had to appear before a national parliamentary committee to give evidence. The province's management agency also had to testify before the national parliamentary portfolio committee on transportation to satisfy the lawmakers on the project's feasibility and socio-economic impact. We turn now to discuss in more detail how organisational choices across the two cases were contingent on their institutional contexts.

12.4.2 Designing Governance

In a project organisational context, governance is broadly about the structures and the processes that need to be put in place to manage relationships with the project participants and other stakeholders, and support decision making. In the Gautrain project organisation, the central government had no direct oversight on internal decision making. Rather, this was a scheme promoted by a regional government in partnership with a private actor, a structure in line with Western recommendations to put local governments in charge of local development (Allport et al. 2008; UNCDF 2018; Williams and Samset 2010). But this was possible because South Africa's institutional framework gave local authorities the autonomy to do so, and there were efficient markets for the provision of railway systems.

Still, the Gautrain scheme was fully aligned with the government's national development plans. And the national government's stake, by way of funding, gave the project the necessary legitimacy without which the project organisation could have collapsed (Han et al. 2009). The involvement of the state also meant that the investment was intensely scrutinised by the public and media. It was the job of the provincial government to manage this interdependence with the environment. And indeed, through the office of the premier, the provincial government addressed public concerns, which ranged from ridership estimates and costs to impact on land use. The provincial government also set up working units to manage the planning process before the concession agreement was signed, and later to manage the interface with the concessionaire during operations. We found no evidence of direct influence by central government on the design and staffing of these structures. And indeed, evidence of the strength of South Africa's polycentric governance can be seen in the refusal by the then Premier of Gauteng, Mr Shilowa, to comply with the national parliamentary transport portfolio committee, which recommended that the province drop the idea of building a new railway and, instead, upgrade the existing metro rail.

In marked contrast, there was limited effort from the AA-LRT project organisation to enfranchise other stakeholders in the environment. Admittedly, the grand idea was rooted in a transparent collaboration between the Addis Ababa government and French organisational actors. And there were efforts to invest in capability building through an Institute of Technology, which suggests centralisation and stakeholder engagement are not mutually exclusive. Still, to quickly overcome the financial bottleneck, the national government chose to centralise decision making, and enter into a partnership with Chinese actors that bulldozed its way to implement the AA-LRT – an approach that was showcased as part of the government's renewal agenda (Nallet 2018). The limited influence on decision making of the local authorities goes against Western policy – which suggests this approach makes it hard to acquire know-how relating to local needs and so maximise opportunities for creating local value. And though our evidence does not suggest the AA-LRT failed to meet local needs, it did miss opportunities for better integration with the city master plan. Still, AA-LRT gained legitimacy because it actually responded to local demands for better public transport in Addis Ababa. The fact that the railway is running frequently overcrowded trains, with low-income passengers, evinces its success in addressing a major transportation gap.

Of course, from the perspective of Western agencies, the design choices of the Ethiopian government – rooted in a narrow, bilateral and transactional deal-based order – violate good governance standards for the sake of getting things built quickly. Public budgeting and land acquisition need to be handled carefully in a rules-based order built on individual freedom, free markets, democracy and property rights – and thus, under this Western social construction, development is a slow process. Admittedly, the Ethiopian state first tried to go to the market to find a concessionaire before hammering out a deal with the Chinese actors. And, the state reportedly compensated landowners who had to be evicted to make way for the AA-LRT. Furthermore, in Ethiopia, all land belongs to the state and landowners are only deemed leaseholders; so the Ethiopian state had regulation on its side when it mobilised imminent domain laws to acquire land. Still, we could not find any publicly available information on land disputes – a 'highly political topic', as one respondent said. Presumably, though, land acquisition must have been a highly contested process, given the variety of ethnic groups that populate Addis Ababa, and the fact that government was under the control of a powerful, but minority, ethnic group.

It is clear, though, that the governance choices of the Ethiopian state could never have worked in South Africa, a democratic state where any efforts to go ahead with a centralised and opaque approach would create a major public backlash. This is exactly what happened when a public protest against toll roads forced the central government to drop a plan for a much-needed road in Gauteng. In contrast, in Ethiopia, the local stakeholders have limited capacity to voice their opposition to initiatives from the central government. And the visibility of how much actual opposition there is on the ground is itself limited because of restricted information flows in the public media.

In sum, our analysis reveals two fundamentally different sets of organisational design choices by which the system architects sought to adapt the architecture of the project organisations to the institutional context. What worked for Ethiopia would not work for South Africa, and vice versa. Yet both partnerships represent efforts by public authorities to address critical transport infrastructure gaps, and seem to have created broad public value. The speed with which Ethiopia obtained a much-needed railway shows the attractiveness of 'looking east' for African governments. Further, Gautrain is an important reminder that some organisational choices for development only available to more institutionally developed countries.

12.5   Conclusion

In this chapter we argue that there is no one-size-fits-all organisational solution to developing large infrastructure in institutionally under-developed countries. We ground our argument on two cases, one in a democratic state and another in an authoritarian state. Both developments succeeded in producing public goods that are sources of broad value creation. Enabled by fundamentally different institutional environments, and seeking to relate to them, the two forms of organising in the pursuit of similar higher-order goals differed radically.

Of course, our work has limitations. We lacked detailed data on how both project organisations went about acquiring the necessary land. For the Gautrain, land acquisition was regulated by the laws on land-use rights, but more work is required to understand how exactly the eminent domain laws were mobilised, and how contestation and opposition were handled. We know even less about how land was acquired for the Addis Ababa railway. However, it is reasonable to assume the authoritarian state may have resorted to forceful forms of action to evict people. This important issue merits further investigation. We also lack data required to evaluate organisational efficiency. Gautrain's concessionaire was chosen through a competitive bidding process, but it is unclear how they were compensated for delays in providing land, for example, and thus the extent to which there was equitable distribution in value. In turn, it is very unlikely we will ever be able to evaluate whether the AA-LRT development was or was not efficient. What we know is that, in both cases, the promoters did not rush into capital-intensive construction until they had secured finance – an important decision in terms of reducing uncertainty and ensuring organisational survival (Allport et al. 2008).

Limitations notwithstanding, our findings are important. Development of basic infrastructure is a key enabler of socio-economic growth. But the African countries are not all alike. Different states are at different stages of institutional development, and have chosen divergent development paths. It is not our job here to discuss whether one path is superior to another – a complex discussion that has been made even more challenging, as Western democracies are increasingly hobbled by fiscal pressures and populism. Rather, our job here has been to show that different institutional environments can be leveraged to enable different forms of organising. Africa's population is growing rapidly. So we do not have the luxury of ruling out effective solutions on the basis that they fail to conform to a particular normative framework.

References

African Development Bank (AfDB). (2013a). Improved infrastructure to support Africa's competitiveness. *AfDB Group*. www.afdb.org/en/blogs/afdb-championing-inclusive-growth-across-africa/post/improved-infrastructure-to-support-africas-competitiveness-11755/.

African Development Bank (AfDB). (2013b). Structured finance: Conditions for infrastructure project bonds in African markets. *AfDB Group*. www.afdb.org

/fileadmin/uploads/afdb/Documents/Project-and-Operations/Structured_Fina nce_-_Conditions_for_Infrastructue_Project_Bonds_in_Markets.pdf.
African Development Bank (AfDB). (2015). Rail infrastructure in Africa financing policy options. *AfDB Group*. www.tralac.org/news/article/8609-rail-infrastructure-in-africa-financing-policy-options.html.
Allport, R., Brown, R., Glaister, S. and Travers, T. (2008). *Success and failure in urban transport infrastructure projects*. London: The London School of Economics. www.imperial.ac.uk/media/imperial-college/researc h-centres-and-groups/centre-for-transport-studies/Success-and-Failure-in -Urban-Transport-Infrastructure-Projects.pdf.
Asian Development Bank (AsDB). (2016). Closing infrastructure gap. *AsDB*. w ww.adb.org/news/op-ed/closing-infrastructure-gap-bambang-susantono
Biesenthal, C., Clegg, S., Mahalingam, A. and Sankaran, S. (2018). Applying institutional theories to managing megaprojects. *International Journal of Project Management*, 36: 43–54.
Bogetic, Z. and Fedderke, J. (2005). Infrastructure and growth in South Africa: Benchmarking, productivity and investment needs. *Proceedings of the Economic Society of South Africa Conference*. 7–9 September. Durban, South Africa.
C40 Cities Climate Leadership Group. (2018). Addis Ababa – Light Rail Transit Project. *C40.org*. www.c40.org/awards/2016-awards/profiles/107.
Chi, C.S.F., Chen, Y. and Shi, W. (2014). Managing institutional change in international infrastructure projects. *Proceedings of the Engineering Project Organisation Conference*. 29–31 July. Colorado, United States of America.
Cox, A. (2005, 24 November). Gautrain criticism dismissed by Shilowa. *IOL*.
DOT South Africa (Department of Transport South Africa DOT). (2017). Financing, funding and charging. *DOT*. www.transport.gov.za/documents/11 623/39906/12_FinancingFundingCharging2017.pdf/c0f27c6d-8a93-4109-ac 70-f4d882ff6dc4
Dille, T. and Söderlund, J. (2011). Managing inter-institutional projects: The significance of isochronisms, timing norms and temporal misfits. *International Journal of Project Management*, 29(4): 480–490.
Endeshaw, Y. (2013). Harmonization of light rail transit and principal arterial streets: A case study on the Addis Ababa East-West AA-LRT line and principal arterial streets. Unpublished thesis. Addis Ababa University, p. 100.
ESI Africa. (2017, 8 June). Uganda: Land acquisition disputes cause project delays. Spintelligent (PTY) Ltd. www.esi-africa.com/uganda-land-acquisition-delay-projects/.
Flyvberg, B. (2014). What you should know about megaprojects and why: An overview. *Project Management Journal*, 45(2): 6–19.
GMA (Gautrain Management Agency GMA). (2011). *From dreams to reality*. Gauteng, South Africa: GMA.
GMA (Gautrain Management Agency GMA). (2014). *Gautrain: Our journey to a better Gauteng. Economic impact of the Gautrain system and future expansion on the province. Main Report*. Gauteng, South Africa: GMA.
GMA (Gautrain Management Agency GMA). (2015). *Case studies*. Gauteng, South Africa: GMA.

Gil, N. and Pinto, J. (2018). Polycentric organizing and performance: A contingency model and evidence from megaproject planning in the UK. *Research Policy*, 47 (4) 717–34.

Grey, E. (2016). Improved access for Ethiopia: Opening the Addis Ababa-Djibouti line. *Railway Technology*. www.railway-technology.com/features/fea tureimproved-access-for-ethiopia-opening-the-addis-ababa-djibouti-line-483 6968/ .

Han, S.H., Yun, S., Kim, H., Kwak, Y.H., Park, H.K. and Lee, S.H. (2009). Analysing schedule delay of mega project: Lessons learned from Korea train express. *IEEE Transactions on Engineering Management*, 56(2): 243–256.

Mail Online. (2017, 12 March). Light rail fails to fix Ethiopia's traffic troubles. *Daily Mail*. www.dailymail.co.uk/wires/afp/article-4305404/Light-rail-fails-fix -Ethiopias-traffic-troubles.html

Miller, R. and Hobbs, B. (2005). Governance regimes for large complex projects. *Project Management Journal*, 36(3): 42–50.

Moghalu, K. C. (2014). Competitiveness and economic transformation: Africa's imperative. Tralac Trade Law Centre .www.tralac.org/news/article/5647-competitiveness-and-economic-transformation-africa-s-imperative.html.

Mohapatra, D. R. (2015). An economic analysis of light rail transit in Addis Ababa, Ethiopia. *European Academic Research*, 3(3): 3114–3144.

Morris, P. W. G. and Geraldi, J. (2011). Managing the institutional context for projects. *Project Management Journal*, 42(6): 20–32.

Naidoo, R. (2013). E-toll roads: Analysing a case of collective moral disengagement in an e-government project. *The African Journal of Information and Communication*, 2013: 108–122. https://repository.up.ac.za/bitstream/han dle/2263/37015/Naidoo_E-toll_2013.pdf?

Nallet, C. (2018, February). The challenge of urban mobility: A case of Addis Ababa Light Rail, Ethiopia. *Notes de l'Ifri*. Paris: Institut Francais des Relations Internationales (Ifri).

Nazret. (2017). Addis Ababa Light rail fails to fix Ethiopia's traffic troubles. *Na zret.com*. www.nazret.com/2017/03/14/addis-ababa-light-rail-fails-to-fix-ethiopias-traffic-troubles/.

News24 (online). (2017, 12 March). Light rail fails to fix Ethiopia's traffic troubles. News24.com. www.news24.com/Africa/News/light-rail-fails-to-fix-ethiopias-traffic-troubles-20170312.

OECD. (2012). *Strategic transport infrastructure needs to 2030*. Paris: OECD Publishing.

Othman, A. A. E. (2013). Challenges of mega construction projects in developing countries. *Organisation, Technology and Management in Construction*, 5(1): 730–746.

PwC. (2014). Trends, challenges and future outlook: Capital projects and infrastructure in East Africa, Southern Africa and West Africa. PwC. www .pwc.co.za/en/assets/pdf/capital-projects-and-infrastructure.pdf.

Sabatino, C. (2017). Light rail transportation systems are built in Ethiopia. *Global Delivery Initiative*. Delivery Note, Centre for Public Impact. A BCG Foundation, June. Assessed 28 February 2019: www.globaldeliveryinitiative.org/library/case-studies/light-rail-transportation-systems-are-built-ethiopia

Stren, R. (2014). Urban service delivery in Africa and the role of international assistance. *Development Policy Review*, 2014, 32 (S1): s19–s37.

Tarrosy, I. and Vörös, Z. (2018, 13 February). China and Ethiopia, Part 1: The light railway system. The Diplomat. https://thediplomat.com/2018/02/china-and-ethiopia-part-1-the-light-railway-system/.

UN-Habitat (United Nations Human Settlements Programme). (2017). *The state of Addis Ababa 2017: The Addis Ababa we want*. Nairobi, Kenya: UN-Habitat.

UNCDF (United Nations Capital Development Fund UNCDF) (2018). *UNCDF local financial initiative – case study no. 2: Mpale Village 50Kw solar micro grid unlocking public finance*. New York: UNCDF.

Wentworth, L. and Makokera, C. G. (2015). Private sector participation in infrastructure for development. *South African Journal of International Affairs*, 22(3): 325–341.

Williams, T. and Samset, K. (2010). Issues in front-end decision making on projects. *Project Management Journal*, 41(2): 38–49.

Winch, G. M. (2013). Escalation in major projects: Lessons from the Channel Fixed Link. *International Journal of Project Management*, 31(5): 724–734.

World Bank. (2010). *Africa's infrastructure: A time for transformation*. Edited by V. Foster and C. Briceño-Garmendia. Washington, DC: World Bank. https://siteresources.worldbank.org.

World Bank. (2017, 9 February). Improving conditions for people and businesses in Africa's cities is key to growth. Press Release February 9. Washington, DC: World Bank. www.worldbank.org/en/news/press-release/2017/02/09/world-bank-report-improving-conditions-for-people-and-businesses-in-africas-cities-is-key-to-growth.

World Folio. (2016). Game-changing railway hallmarks the 'African Renaissance'. Worldfolio.com. www.theworldfolio.com/interviews/gamechanging-railway-hallmarks-the-african-renaissance/3874/.

Xinhua. (2017). Ethiopia earns 5 million USD from Addis Ababa Light Rail Transit in 2016/17 fiscal year. Xinhuanet.com. www.xinhuanet.com/english/2017–08/29/c_136563136.htm.

13 Building Institutions or Capital Investment? Organisational Duality in the Pursuit of Socio-Economic Development

Nuno Gil, Jeff Pinto and Rehema Msulwa

This inductive study proposes a duality in the design of organisations set up to pursue socio-economic development. Dualities exist when organisations pursue objectives that are jointly desirable, but difficult to reconcile. We ground the research on a sample of inter-organisational contexts set up to pursue development by way of improving basic transport infrastructure in two of Africa's fast-growing cities, Lagos (Nigeria) and Kampala (Uganda). Our findings reveal sharp variation in the way two desirable objectives are prioritised: to build capital public goods and build the local institutions. When the institutional intermediary that brokers resource exchanges is a 'traditional' development agency, e.g. the World Bank, the focus is on building institutions. But when the intermediary is an 'emerging' agency, e.g. the China Eximbank, the focus is on quick capital investment. Our analysis reveals underlying design attributes that make the two objectives organisationally incompatible. Building institutions requires orderliness and transparency to reduce the uncertainty caused by interdependence with the environment; quick capital investment requires adaptability and opaqueness to cope with the high uncertainty associated with exploiting institutional voids. And it is this incompatibility that encourages a focus on either mitigating or exploiting the shortfall of institutions. We conclude by building on this design duality to lay down the rudiments of a theory of organisational design and performance in the context.

13.1 Introduction

'Institutional voids' refer to prevailing features of emerging economies, including the lack or malfunction of basic infrastructure, inefficient markets, poor regulation, and a weak judiciary and contract-enforcement mechanisms that hinder resource exchanges (Khanna and Palepu 1997, 2010; Delios and Henisz 2000; George, McGahan and Prabhu 2012; Eesley 2016). To navigate this shortfall of institutions, firms use 'institutional intermediaries': agents that broker resource exchanges between two or more parties that otherwise could not occur, and help to create and develop institutions (Dutt et al. 2015). Extant studies suggest that organisations have agency to choose which intermediaries to work with and the corresponding approach to navigate institutional voids (van der Vegt et al. 2015). Hence, some organisations see institutional shortcomings as constraints that the intermediaries can help to fill to attenuate uncertainty and mitigate risks (Meyer et al. 2009; Regner and Edman 2014; McDermott, Corredoira and Kruse 2009). Others see the institutional voids as 'opportunity spaces', which the intermediaries can help exploit to create and appropriate value (Wood and Frynas 2006; Khanna and Palepu 2010).

This literature is instructive in illuminating who the intermediaries are, and what they do (Khanna and Palepu 1997, 2010; Maguire, Hardy and Lawrence 2004; McDermott et al. 2009; Mair, Marti and Ventresca 2012; Dutt et al. 2015; Armanios et al. 2017; McDermott et al. 2009). But research has yet to address how the choice of intermediary impacts organisational design choice (Dahan et al. 2010). We know that organisational design is contingent on the institutional environment to which the organisation must relate (Lawrence and Lorsch 1967; Thompson 1967; Scott 1981). Hence, we can expect a choice between intermediaries to also be a choice between different organisational designs. In other words, a choice to mitigate or exploit institutional voids can be expected to be a choice in terms of the system components, the relationships between components and between the system and the environment, and the principles guiding organisation design and evolution (Simon 1981; Fjeldstad et al. 2012). Yet we still know little, empirically and conceptually, of the linkages between the two sets of choices. This logic leads to our core research question: how does choice in the selection of an institutional intermediary relate to choice in the organisational design to navigate institutional voids?

To address this question, we undertook an empirical study on the international development sector – a multinational industry which contributes to around 10 per cent of the GDPs of emerging economies (OECD 2014). Two main factors make this sector suitable for exploring links between choice in institutional intermediary and organisation design. First, the development agencies are critical intermediaries in helping struggling states access capital and other resources, e.g. human capital and technology, that are necessary to pursue socio-economic development. And secondly, with the economic rise of China, borrowers have gained the agency to choose between two fundamentally different forms of institutional intermediation.

About two-thirds of development assistance is provided by the 'traditional' development agencies, including multilateral organisations such as the World Bank (WB) and development agencies owned by advanced economies (OECD 2014). Traditional agencies make assistance conditional on the recipients conforming to Western ideals of 'good governance' as defined by the agencies on behalf of their principals, the taxpayers – transparency, accountability, equity, stakeholder engagement and rule of law (Burnside and Dollar 2000; Hermes and Lensink 2001). Recipients that fail to meet these standards cannot qualify for assistance. In other words, traditional intermediaries act as 'open-system intermediaries' that seek to improve the general institutional environment and to create benefits for parties that go beyond a restricted set of participants (Dutt et al. 2015).

The other third of development assistance comes from the 'emerging' intermediaries – development agencies owned by countries that lie outside of the OECD Development Assistance Committee; China, unsurprisingly, bears by far the greatest weight in this group. Assessing assistance disbursed by China is difficult because the Chinese authorities are traditionally discreet. Still, in Africa alone, reliable figures suggest that Chinese financial assistance equals that disbursed by the WB (Hwang and Bral 2016), and dwarfs that of the Western agencies.[1] Crucially, Chinese assistance is not tied to governance ideals (Henderson 2008; Henderson, Appelbaum and Ho 2013). Which is not to say the Chinese actors act as closed-system intermediaries, only seeking to create benefits for the participants in systems enabled by Chinese credit. This is not the case. But Chinese assistance does tend to replicate the Japanese model of assistance to China decades earlier. Thus, it tends to be only tied to procuring as much Chinese technology and services as possible and to changing the institutions only so far as is strictly necessary to ensure the capital goods can function and are sustainable.

To explore logic between choice in intermediation and organisational design, we conducted a multiple case study. This inductive approach is particularly useful for building new arguments with which to explain an underexplored general phenomenon and address the 'how' questions (Eisenhardt 1989). This method allowed us to delve deeply into a small number of inter-organisational contexts, or 'meta-organisations' (Gulati, Puranam and Tushman 2012), set up to pursue development, and study

---

[1] For example, from 2000 to 2015, $63 billion was disbursed by the China Eximbank against $1.7 billion by the USA Eximbank (Eom et al. 2017).

them over time. We controlled for extraneous variation by restricting our sample to organisational cases pursuing similar objectives – filling gaps in basic transport infrastructure, a widely accepted prerequisite for socio-economic development (WEF 2018). Hence our sample includes contexts enabled by traditional agencies, and others enabled by Chinese credits. In other words, we assembled a sample of contexts 'racing' (Gehman et al. 2017) to pursue development. For this chapter, we illustrate our claims with the cases grounded in sub-Saharan Africa.

Our main contribution is to theorise a duality of building institutions and quick capital investment. Design dualities exist when organisations wish to pursue objectives that are jointly desirable, but find it hard to reconcile them because the attributes that underlie one pole of the duality tend to be incompatible with those underlying the other pole (Lawrence and Lorsch 1967; Evans and Doz 1989; March 1991). These difficulties explain why organisations often choose to focus on only one of the poles of the duality, as opposed to both, for example, to exploit or explore; to integrate or differentiate (Evans and Doz 1989; Gulati and Puranam 2009). There are examples of organisations pursuing jointly desirable objectives successfully (Gulati and Puranam 2009). But more commonly, organisations choose 'gains from focus' over 'gains from ambidexterity' (Birkinshaw and Gibson 2004; Smith and Tushman 2005).

In this study we link variation in organisational design to the difficulties in reconciling two desirable objectives: building institutions and building infrastructure. We find that organising for building institutions is guided by the principles of orderliness and transparency. In contrast, organising for attracting *quick* capital investment requires adaptability and opaqueness. As these two sets of design attributes are organisationally incompatible, organisational designers choose to focus on one of the two poles of the duality: Either developing the institutions first and then building capital goods, or attract capital investment first, and then build the institutions. Crucially, the more the choice shifts towards building the institutions first to reduce environmental uncertainty, the more capital investment is pushed back – to the extent that delays can compromise any chances of building the infrastructure. But focusing on quick capital investment offers no guarantees, either, that the infrastructure will be built because of a real risk of organisational collapse stemming from the high level of uncertainty associated with exploiting institutional voids. These insights suggest that one form of organising cannot be regarded as superior to the other.

We structure the remainder of this chapter as follows. We first discuss organisational design choice as a means of navigating institutional voids. We then describe our methods, setting and data. In the analysis, we examine the logic linking the choice between alternative forms of intermediation to pursue socio-economic development, and the corresponding choice in organisational design. The discussion builds on this duality to lay down the rudiments of a contingency theory of organisational performance within this context.

13.2   Organisational Design to Pursue Socio-Economic Development

Institutional voids reflect the absence or underdevelopment of the institutional conditions that enable market efficiency and resource exchanges (Khanna and Palepu 1997, 2010; George et al. 2012; Doh et al. 2017). They are a characteristic of developing countries – in which around 80 per cent of the world's population is projected to be living by 2100 (UN 2017). To enter and succeed in these vast emerging markets, those private firms which decide not to internalise functions to avoid institutional voids resort to intermediaries to help either mitigate or exploit the institutional weaknesses in the environment (Meyer et al. 2009; Mair et al. 2012; Regner and Edman 2014; Armanios et al. 2017; Doh et al. 2017).

This research, though instructive as to how firms and intermediaries jointly create and appropriate value, leaves unanswered how the governments themselves can work with intermediaries to fill the institutional voids that hamper business activity. Institutions are public goods, and the lack of public goods is the greatest challenge that businesses face in emerging markets (Khanna and Palepu 1997, 2010); public goods are necessary to improve the *business context* and increase the returns of private investments in a generalised way (Lazzarini 2015). Furthermore, hazards associated with the lack of public goods make it hard for governments to attract long-term private investment (North and Weingast 1989; Kivleniece and Quelin 2012).

Yet there is a vast array of development agencies whose role is precisely to act as intermediaries, and help struggling governments acquire private resources to build public goods: some are multilateral organisations such as the WB, others are official development agencies that are fully owned by more advanced economies. It is the role of these agencies to broker resource exchanges between the recipient country governments, the primary donors (taxpayers of donor countries) and for-profit contractors (Martens 2005). Several motives drive development agencies to offer assistance on behalf of donors: genuine aid motives, such as alleviating poverty and inequality; commercial motives around helping national suppliers gain access to developing-country markets; and political motives to enhance alliances between donors and borrowers. In all cases, development assistance cannot be disbursed unless the recipients author- ise its implementation on their sovereign territory.

From an organisational design perspective, development assistance spurs the formation of an inter-organisational context by which multiple autono- mous actors agree to collaborate under an identifiable higher-order goal. Under this form of organising there is no single designated leader with sufficient power to centralise decision-making authority. Rather, the higher-order goal and organisational design are the products of a negotiation between the development agency, donors, recipient and other powerful stakeholders in the context (Martens 2005; Mohan and Lampert 2013; McLean and Schneider 2014). These negotiations involve high transaction costs to attenuate information asymmetries; agree on contracts *ex ante*; and mitigate the risks to the development agency of adverse selection and moral hazard *ex post* contract signature (Martens 2005).

As donor and recipients operate in different political constituencies, the negotiated agreements are the result of political compromises and the bargaining power of each participant. Misalignments of interests are corrected through tied or conditional loans – restrictive conditions that reduce the decision rights of the recipient of funds in exchange for access to donor resources. Input conditionality can be procedural, to increase donor leverage over organisational inputs and activities, or geographical, to impose procurement of goods and services in the donor country; out- put conditionality ties assistance to changes in the recipient's institutions, e.g. administrative reforms and policy decisions. Still, these inter- organisational contexts are *not* open systems. In open systems, the leaders provide a democratic framework and control mechanisms under which members self-select and volunteer for tasks (Lakhani and von Hippel 2003) and membership develops with relative autonomy (Lee and Cole 2003). By contrast, in these contexts, sovereign stakeholders only gain decision rights if they are awarded them by the donor, the intermediary and the recipient. In other words, this group of core actors acts collec- tively as a gate-keeper, with the power to select new members based upon the resources that those potential members can contribute (Rothaermel and Boeker 2008).

The economic rise of China has given recipients agency to choose between traditional and emergent intermediaries; as the recipients exer- cise agency, they are presumably also choosing between different organi- sational designs. Since organisational design mandates interactions for exchanging and mobilising resources in the pursuit of collective goals (Gulati and Puranam 2009), it is fitting to explore the logic linking intermediation and organisational design choices.

13.3   Methods

This inductive research adopts a case-study approach – an approach that allows researchers to generate insights that might be obscured or absent in large-*N* comparative studies (Eisenhardt, Graebner and Sonenshein 2016). We chose to focus on organisational cases pursuing socio-economic development by way of tackling voids in basic infrastructure – a form of development assistance that gives the donors leverage over the inputs and activities (Martens 2005). These contexts have two attributes that make them suitable for case research: their organisational life spans long periods of time (many years, if not decades), and they unfold enmeshed within the environment (Hirschman 1967; Yin 1984; Eisenhardt 1989).

Specifically, all the cases in our sample pursued development by way of tackling pressing gaps in transport infrastructure. This is a widely recognised bottleneck to development (Kistruck et al. 2013), but emerging economies struggle to attract private finance for transport infrastructure due to the long payback periods; the risks of project delays and cost overruns; and the concerns of private investors about the unpopularity of compulsory land acquisitions and evictions. Development agencies are thus key intermediaries to help governments redress this void. In our sample, some cases benefited from assistance from traditional intermediaries, and others from the Chinese intermediaries. So we sought to build a sample that could reveal the influence of differing forms of intermediation in organisational design.

To increase the generalisability of our claims, we varied the institutional environment for infrastructure investment (Henisz 2002). While we are studying projects in Asia (India) and Africa, in this chapter, we illustrate our emerging claims with findings from two countries in sub-Saharan Africa: Uganda and Nigeria. Uganda represents a dominant state, with so-called 'big-man rules', where the political leadership has consolidated its grip on power, most institutions are weak and the public–private divide is blurred (Levy 2014). In Nigeria, some studies claim the institutional checks and governance are more developed than in Uganda (Levy 2014); in others, though, Uganda fares better than Nigeria with regard to control of corruption, the rule of law and government effectiveness (Kaufmann and Kraay 2017).[2]

Table 13.1 summarises the following aspects for each case: the higher-order goal, the infrastructure development objective; the core participants;

---

[2] These rankings are also consistent with the 2014 Transparency International Corruption Perception Index for 175 countries which ranks Nigeria and Uganda close (136 and 142, respectively).

Table 13.1 *Cases: System goal, capital investment, core participants and data*

Cases	Lagos first metro line (Nigeria)	Bus rapid transit corridor (Nigeria)	First highway (Uganda)	Kampala road upgrade (Uganda)
System-level goal	Reduce 6-hour commute for over 300,000 daily ridership	Reduce traffic congestion (< 2 per cent of 20 million trips/day use public transport)	Reduce average time from capital to airport to spur socio-economic growth	Reduce traffic congestion (90 per cent roads unpaved)
Infrastructure development objective	First urban metro railway line in Lagos (27.5 km long)	First bus rapid transit corridor (24 km 1st phase; 14 km 2nd phase)	First highway linking Uganda's capital (Kampala) to main airport	Upgrade 1,200 km network of colonial roads
Core participants	#3 Lagos government; Transport agency LAMATA (#)CCECC (state-owned Chinese contractor)	#3 Lagos government; Transport agency LAMATA (#) World Bank	#4 Uganda government; Roads authority UNRA ($) China Eximbank, CCCC (state-owned Chinese contractor)	#3 Uganda government; Kampala government World Bank
Development assistance	2009, ~$1.2billion supplier's credit w/ conditions not in public domain	2002 $150 m loan 2011, $190 m loan (10-year grace period, 40-year maturity)	2009, $350 m; with 5-year grace period and 25-year maturity	2007, US$30 m, 2013, US$200 m (with 10-year grace period; 40-year maturity)
No. of interviews	18	19	24	20
No. of actors interviewed and their designations	9 Lagos government, LAMATA, CCECC, consultants (#4), Nigeria Railways, World Bank	7 Lagos government, LAMATA, bus operator, Ekobank, World Bank, consultants (#2)	12 Uganda government (#3); UNRA, CCCC, World Bank, consultants (#3); development agencies (#2)	8 Uganda gov't (#2); Kampala government, World Bank; consultant; UNRA; development agencies (#2)
Archival data	17	44	23	40
No. of documents by category	6 presentations 9 technical and financial reports 2 external communication reports	7 presentations 32 technical and financial reports 5 external communication reports	1 presentation 6 technical and financial reports 16 external communication reports	1 presentation 8 external communications 31 technical and financial reports

the development assistance; and data sources. All cases were seeking to develop transport infrastructure that was the first of its kind in the local context. In Lagos, Nigeria's capital – and the sixth largest city in the world – we studied two cases: the developments of the city's first metro line with Chinese credit, and the first network of bus rapid transit (BRT[3]) corridors with WB credit. In Uganda, we also studied two cases: one project to develop the country's first motorway to link the capital, Kampala, to the country's main international airport, and the other, enabled by WB credit, to upgrade the capital's decrepit network of colonial-era roads.

13.4   Data Collection and Analysis

The bulk of the data collection started in mid-2013 and lasted three years. We spent one week in each country conducting face-to-face interviews with the leading participants of the cases. We also carried out site visits to get a better sense of the work on the ground, and did Skype interviews with participants who were not available when we visited the country. Each visit required months of preparation to select the research sites, gain authorisation to conduct fieldwork and agree a schedule of interviews. To identify and gain access to research sites, we worked with civil servants who were postgraduate students at our university. These key informants leveraged their professional networks to facilitate access to representatives of public agencies and permit privileged access to data sources.

Using a 'snowball approach' (Biernacki and Waldorf 1981) we managed to interview public agencies, private contractors and consultants, and the development agencies; we tape-recorded and transcribed all semi-structured interviews (see Appendix for the interview protocol). We offered anonymity, but were not asked to sign non-disclosure agreements; occasionally, though, we were asked not to use particular quotes. We also produced hand-recorded verbatim notes of our informal chats with the project managers who took us on site visits. Our key informants helped us move around the cities, and occasionally attended the interviews and leveraged their local know-how to also ask questions. When gaps in the data emerged in the analysis, we conducted follow-up interviews by phone and/or e-mail.

To improve data accuracy and the robustness of the insights (Jick 1979), we triangulated the verbal accounts against archival data (Miles

---

[3] A BRT corridor consists of a roadway dedicated to buses in order to combine the capacity and speed of a metro railway with the lower costs and flexibility of a bus system.

and Huberman 1984). The leading public agencies in each case shared with us technical reports, presentations and articles published in official publications. We supplemented this data with information that we found online. The documents made available by the WB included feasibility studies, progress reports and technical studies; information publicly available on the cases involving Chinese credit is more limited. But because the focal infrastructure gaps were so critical to local development, the projects were closely monitored by local media (in English). To access relevant articles, we googled the names of top management and elected leaders involved in development projects. Another data source was Skys craperCity.com, the world's largest online forum on urban development.

Our core motivation was to establish logic between intermediation and organisational design. Relatedly, we wanted to explore how this logic impacted progress towards the system-level goal. To this purpose, we first produced chronological and factual accounts of each case to guard against account bias (Miles and Huberman 1984; Langley 1999). We shared these accounts with our respondents to gather extra data and allow for member checks. Our data analysis started by building longitudinal maps based on these accounts. In each map we charted the organisational evolution along three attributes: structure of participation, resource acquisition and progress towards the system-level goal. We complemented this analysis with coding and tabular displays of our data (Strauss and Corbin 1990). We drew initial codes from the institutional voids literature to explore each system's approach to navigating the institutional voids; then we interrogated data, drawing codes from the basic definition of system architecture in terms of organisational components, relationships between components and the environment, and principles guiding organisation design and evolution. As we cycled between data and theory, we gradually established logic linking choices in intermediary, organisational design and progress towards the system goal.

13.5 Analysis

We start the analysis by examining first how differing approaches to navigate institutional voids impacted two organisational attributes: the structure of participation in decision making and the focus agreed upon by the participants. We then analyse the underlying principles that guided organisational design and evolution towards the system-level goal.

13.5.1 Organisational Design to Navigate Institutional Voids

When the goal is to promote socio-economic development by way of developing basic infrastructure, there is a need to acquire many complementary resources, such as finance, land, permits, human capital and technology. Complicating resource acquisition is the distribution of the direct control of these resources across many autonomous actors. Further complicating this task is the lack of developed institutions. This raises the question for the development agency, the intermediary in control of the finance as to what the organisational priorities should be.

13.5.1.1   From Local Ambition towards Building Institutions

Traditional intermediaries, such as the WB, operate constrained by the principle that development assistance cannot be effective unless the institutions in the context evolve (Gupta et al. 2014). Hence, although developing basic infrastructure is an objective for these intermediaries, and, indeed, a precondition for development, building institutions is also both of these (Stokke 1995; Knack 2003). Faced with a dilemma over which objective to prioritise, the choice goes to building institutions.

One example involved the WB and the Lagos government. At the turn of the last century, the dearth of public transport was choking the development of Lagos, a city with a population of 7 million and rapidly growing. The WB insisted that steps needed to be taken to first build institutional capacity – 'we felt a need to create an agency that was appropriately structured to drive the level of transportation in Lagos', said one WB official. This public agency, LAMATA, was established one year later in 2002, with the help of a $100 million loan. In addition to allowing for urgent repairs to the existing roads, the finance enabled LAMATA to offer remuneration packages capable of attracting managerial talent – and also to create an incentive for staff not to succumb to illegal activities. Officials from LAMATA and the WB explained:

We had a clear, bold vision from the onset and everybody knew what that vision was all about . . . [the] aim and purpose are to make a difference to Lagos, to the institutions, as well as to civilization. (LAMATA official)

In Nigeria even good guys can become bad guys . . . [But] LAMATA has the money, the independence, and they are doing good work . . . LAMATA is a beacon of good public management in a dark place. (WB official)

Four years later, in 2006, with Lagos' population surpassing 9 million, LAMATA published an ambitious transport master plan. It included a network of nine BRT corridors and seven metro lines, to be delivered by 2020. But the WB committed finance to develop only one of the BRT corridors – 'a question of being prudent, of capturing the low-hanging fruit', said one official. And, much to the disappointment of LAMATA, the WB ruled out assistance for the metro lines, as it felt the institutions were not ready yet.

The context involving the WB and the government of Kampala, Uganda's capital, offers a second example of this emphasis on building institutions. This context could be traced to the mid-2000s, when both parties recognised that the lack of basic transport infrastructure was a bottleneck to the development of Kampala – a city of 1 million, growing by 5 per cent per year, still relying on a network of unpaved colonial roads, and where 40 per cent of the population lived in slums.[4] Coming to the rescue, the WB committed assistance in 2007 through the KIIDIP-Kampala Institutional and Infrastructure Development Project. But the focus rapidly shifted to reforming institutions, this is transform the bankrupted local government into a leaner organisation, clear of corruption, and capable of applying for loans and collecting local taxes effectively. As the WB stated:

The Government of Uganda had originally requested support for a project of about US$98 million, mainly focusing on infrastructure, to be implemented over a five year period. Given the need for institutional reform ... a three phased 10-year adaptable program loan is proposed.[5]

Reforming local government to the liking of the WB, a 'positive step in the right direction', as one WB official put it, turned out to be a seven-year effort. And it would be 2014 before the WB would agree to mobilise finance for transport infrastructure. We turn now to analyse how the focus changed in the projects enabled by Chinese credit.

13.5.1.2   When Meeting Local Ambition Becomes the 'Main' Objective

Development assistance from China is rooted in the non-interference policy stipulated in the 'Eight Principles of Foreign Economic and

---

[4] World Bank, *Implementation Completion and Results Report*. Kampala Institutional and Infrastructure Development Adaptable Program Loan Project. 27 June, Report No. ICR00002916, 2014; also the World Bank, *Growth Challenge: Can Ugandan Cities Get to Work?* Uganda Economic Update, 5th edition. Report No. 94622, February 2015, Washington, DC.

[5] World Bank, *Project Appraisal Document*. Kampala Institutional and Infrastructure Development Adaptable Program Loan Project. Report No. 35847-UG, 12 September 2007.

Technological Assistance' (Brautigam 2009). This policy, reaffirmed in a 2010 White Paper on Foreign Aid, makes the allocation of assistance independent of regime type or governance quality in the borrower state (Tan-Mullins, Mohan and Power 2010). Coupled with the non-interference policy is institutional pressure to act quickly – 'We should hasten the implementation of our "going out" strategy', said China's Premier Wen Jiabao (*The Economist* 2009). Hence the focus is to exploit institutional voids in order to address local needs for infrastructure.

One example is the inter-organisational context formed to develop Uganda's first highway. The lack of a highway connecting the international airport to Kampala was a major bottleneck to local development – the situation was so dire that a 51 km journey could easily take up to three hours. The local ambition to fill this gap was central to the master plan published by the Uganda National Roads Authority (UNRA) in 2008. The idea gained traction when the China Eximbank committed assistance on the back of a visit from China's Premier to Uganda – 'people who want to be rich should build a road first', said the Chinese ambassador to Uganda, when the two states signed a Memorandum of Understanding (MoU). A year later, and by exploiting weaknesses in procurement laws, the Ugandan state directly awarded the construction contract to CCCC, a state-owned Chinese firm. As one local official explained – 'there's no way to stop any government from approving whatever is needed to put up infrastructure that was needed yesterday'.

A similar pattern was observed in the case of Lagos' first metro-line (so-called blue line). This line was a priority in the 2006 master plan produced by LAMATA, the agency endorsed by the WB – 'we're going to have congestion no matter how much road we build. So we need mass movers,' said one local official. Still, the WB ruled out assistance on the grounds that the institutions were not ready and noted that another line (the red line) would do more for poverty alleviation. LAMATA explained it was prioritising the blue line because federal government was not making land available for the red line – a lack of co-operation rooted in national politics. Still, the WB was not convinced – 'the national interests are often subjugated to personal interests', said one WB official. Unmoved, LAMATA turned to Chinese credits and forged a deal in 2009 with CCECC, a Chinese state-owned contractor, to build the blue line by 2012.

We turn now to examine the underlying organisational design attributes of the two objectives, and the difficulties of reconciling them.

13.5.2 *Organisational Design and Evolution towards the Goal*

The interdependence of organisations with their environment creates a source of uncertainty that threatens the survival of those organisations (Cyert and March 1963). To avoid collapse, organisational designers manipulate organisational boundaries and share decision rights – trading off fewer externalities for a loss in decision-making autonomy. This is also what a sovereign state does when it enters into an arrangement with an intermediary. In terms of membership, the participants of these organisational contexts are the same – donor, intermediary, recipient and contractors; the contractual mechanisms that govern the relationships are also similar. But we find substantive variation in the principles guiding further choice in organisational design and evolution, as a function of how the participants agreed to navigate institutional voids.

13.5.2.1   *When Orderliness and Transparency Rule*

The cases enabled by WB credit suggest two intertwined principles guiding organisational choice – orderliness and transparency. Orderliness is about ensuring that the resources that are necessary to achieve the goal are orchestrated step by step to reduce uncertainty in the organisation's ability to meet the results to which it commits in exchange for funds. Transparency is about ensuring that the organisational actions are scrupulous enough to bear scrutiny from third parties. The two principles reinforce one another, and both cascade down from the view that both the intermediary and the recipient of funds need to be accountable to their respective citizens and taxpayers (World Bank 2011).

The WB's arrangements with the Kampala government are telling. As has been said, the WB agreed in 2007 that it was necessary to upgrade the city's road network. But assistance was made conditional on meeting the donors' governance ideals – only possible if resource exchanges were transparent and orderly, to reduce uncertainty caused by interdependences with external stakeholders. Hence, the focus for the first seven years (enabled by a $33 million loan) was on reforming the Kampala government step by step, by interfacing with central government and the legislative environment: ultimately, most local staff were asked to reapply for their jobs; the pay scales of top officials were boosted to levels that the WB officials themselves were uncomfortable with; all management were put on three-year contracts; and a policy of 'zero' tolerance to corruption was adopted. After seven years, the WB officials claimed that Kampala was 'a city on the rise'. But little had been done to address the transport infrastructure gap: only 40 km of the 1,200 km colonial-era road network had been upgraded, and 75 per cent remained unpaved;[6] one WB official said:

> We encourage transparency and accountability. That is number one for everybody working on the project . . . Then two, we also encourage people to report any forms of corruption. Then three, there is vigilance. We do close monitoring . . . that alone is one way of curbing corruption . . . every step has to be reviewed by us.

It was only in 2014, pleased with the institutional reform, that the WB deemed that the context was ready to evolve into the next stage, and the intermediary agreed to KIIDP2, a $175 million second assistance package that allocated 90 per cent to infrastructure building, notably roads. Still, the WB again ruled out any quick capital investment. Rather, the recipient was asked to set new procurement procedures before awarding supplier contracts – 'the beauty is . . . we're transforming; we don't have systems set, we're setting systems', said one local official. The recipient was also asked to turn down offers for feasibility studies by Chinese firms in exchange for building contracts – the 'carrot', as one local official put it. And to further reduce uncertainty, road upgrades were not permitted to start on the ground until most land had first been acquired transparently in order to increase cost-forecast reliability. As one official explained:

> The difficult part is the determining the land values . . . [and] whether certain people are eligible or not . . . For the WB, whoever is being deprived of a livelihood should benefit. Yet, the Ugandan state thinks that if you settled in the road reserve you should not get compensated. We settled for the latter because the money would [otherwise] be prohibitive.

Accepting that it would take a long time to relieve the transport infrastructure bottleneck, the participants reset the targets to upgrade just a *fifth* of Kampala's road network by 2020 – by which time, the city's population is projected to reach 10 million.

The analysis of the arrangements between the WB and the Lagos government reveals similar underlying design attributes. Lagos was Africa's fastest-growing city. But it took five years (2002–07) to build the institutions to the point where the WB regarded LAMATA as an honest, law-abiding public agency – 'we call it the ugly victory of LAMATA', said one official. During this period, the WB helped

---

[6] World Bank, *International Development Association Project Appraisal Document*. Second Kampala Institutional and Infrastructure Development Project, Report No. PAD800, 2014.

LAMATA design procurement procedures based on WB standards, and to set up a governance board involving powerful local stakeholders. The intermediary insisted that their job was to first help build 'competent' institutions. But this orderly, transparent approach meant forgoing any chances of effectively tackling the transport infrastructure gap. Hence, of the nine BRT corridors identified as critical, the WB helped to finance just one (completed in 2008), and then, additionally, a 13 km extension of that same corridor – completed in 2015. Further, the WB ruled out financing rail schemes – 'the WB say bigger projects are opportunities for corruption', complained one official. By 2015, with Lagos' population nearing 20 million, a six-hour commute had become the norm for millions of Lagosians relying on a fleet of 75,000 Danfos, an informal network of old minibuses. The frustration of the local officials was clear; one said – 'we can't afford a 15–20 year planning process … the problems are evident and the solutions are there … don't see anything happening'. And, struggling to build consensuses, LAMATA did away with the governance board – a key institution that had taken a long time to build.

We turn now to examine the attributes underlying the contexts enabled by the Chinese credit.

13.5.2.2   When Adaptability and Opaqueness Rule

In the contexts enabled by Chinese credit, our findings reveal that the principles of opaqueness and adaptability ruled organisational design choice. Opaqueness relates to a deliberate decision to keep information flows covert, and to centralise, in a tight-knit coalition between the recipient and intermediary, the decision-making process for determining which stakeholders join the system and the corresponding resource exchanges. Adaptability refers to the capacity to rework organisational choices in order to overcome institutional voids that threaten to stall progress. Our findings suggest the two principles are mutually reinforcing: opaqueness enables reworking organisational choices that would be politically costly had the institutions forced more visibility on the decision-making process. Both principles can be traced to Chinese policy governing intermediation which calls for urgency and secretiveness; as the China Eximbank president said – 'If the water is too clear, you don't catch any fish' (Brautigam 2009, 296).

The case of the Uganda's first motorway is telling. Once the China and Uganda heads of state signed an MoU in 2009, it took less than two years for the Uganda Parliament to approve a $350 million loan. In exchange, a \$476 million design-and-build contract was awarded to CCCC, a Chinese state-owned contractor that had been blacklisted by the WB for fraudulent practices.[7] Another Chinese firm was directly awarded a contract to supervise the works, and a commitment was made to give the road management contract of the future toll road to a Chinese firm too. All the deals were wrapped in secrecy; one WB official observed:

China does not want to participate in the development partner groups … we heard about the highway for the first time almost when the contracts had been done … if I'm not mistaken that is the most expensive project that Uganda has had up to now … the issue is, how are their loans negotiated?

These deals exploited weakness in the Uganda's Public Procurement and Disposal Act that was supposed to enforce competitive bidding. The claims from UNRA, the roads authority, that the contract price had been independently scrutinised failed to fend off public allegations of inflated prices and bribes. But calls in the media to annul the contract were pushed back by press sympathetic to the government, who reported this criticism as 'an astonishing tale of how foreign mafia gangs are exploiting the whistle-blowing privileges in Uganda to sabotage government projects'.[8]

After signing off the contracts, the Chinese firms were quick to mobilise technology and human capital to get the project off the ground even before land had been acquired. But then, delays with the land acquisition process slowed down progress. In Uganda, a 1998 Land Act vested all land in its citizens through formal and informal land-tenure systems; in case of disputes, the Land Act prohibited the government from seizing land until the compensation value had been agreed by the public courts.[9] As it happened, the secrecy that enabled the fast-track arrival of the contractors could not eliminate three related problems: (i) the government lacked funds to acquire private land at court-determined fair value; (ii) the public courts lacked human capacity to settle land disputes; and (iii) powerful stakeholders – notably the Buganda kingdom, a subnational landowner with much autonomy from the state – blocked changes to the Land Law.[10]

---

[7] 'World Bank applies 2009 debarment to China Communications Construction Company Ltd for fraud in Philippines road project', *World Bank*, 29 July 2011, www.worldbank.org/en/news/press-release/2011/07/29/world-bank-applies-2009-debarment-to-china-communications-construction-company-limited-for-fraud-in-philippines-roads-project.

[8] http://s3.amazonaws.com/china_resources/14881/2013–06-08_02_37_03_-0400_5133-investigation-unra-resists-sabotage-museveni-clears-entebbe-expressway.html#sthash.2xF1gFNd.dpuf.

[9] Uganda Land Act 1998, Chapter No. 227.

[10] J. Kabengwa, 'Kabaka opposes land amendment bill', *Daily Monitor*, 7 August 2017.

To get around these issues, the participants sought adaptation. Where an alternative alignment was feasible, the route was moved in order to cut deals with less powerful landowners. In other instances, construction progressed to the right and left of the land yet to be acquired, while a solution for the missing parcel was being sought. Of course, these changes threw the initial targets into disarray. But the leaders tried to keep the slippages hidden from the public eye. In 2010, when the contracts were signed off, the opening date was set at 2016, where it remained until 2016, when the state announced a new date, 2019. The state has also not shared any extra information on costs, but press reports suggest the land acquisition costs alone have increased fivefold. Still, while the focus is on quick capital investment, there is evidence of real efforts to reform institutions. The lawmakers in Parliament have not only proposed an amendment to change the Land Law, but have also been working on changing Ugandan laws to allow for tolled roads – 'we'll be taking away people's right to move', said one local official about the fact current law does not allow toll roads unless there is an equivalent alternative.[11] In a demonstration of optimism that the laws will change, the Ugandan President symbolically commissioned the highway in 2018: 'we're grateful for this principled and decisive economic support from our friends in China', he said.[12]

Our second example is the Lagos first metro rail. After the WB ruled out assistance for this project, the local actors embarked on an international junket to seek finance. This quickly led to a contract with a state-owned Chinese firm backed by a Chinese bank. The contractors committed to open the line in 2012, but it is wholly unclear how the two parties managed to cut a deal, given that LAMATA had yet to acquire most of the necessary land and the state was cash-strapped. Uncertainties notwithstanding, the Chinese contractors were quick to start construction – 'they [Chinese contractors] just want to sort out our problems and do the work', said one respondent, while suggesting that bribes might have been involved – 'they don't mind getting their hands dirty'.

As it happened, the system ran foul of the very same institutional voids it exploited. The Lagos government had legal power to seize private land, but this power was circumscribed to situations where the landowner lacked a Certificate of Occupancy. Because the administrative process to issue these certificates was riddled with corruption, LAMATA

---

[11] F. Musisi, 'Proposed new land law sparks public outrage', *Daily Monitor*, 26 August 2016.
[12] President Musevini officially opens the Kampala-Entebbe Express highway: www .youtube.com/watch?v=p22bLFaEA7w, visited 27 February 2019.

struggled to exercise its power. Complicating matters, the Lagos government lacked the capacity to evict illegal occupants and prevent them from returning – 'we put the cart before the horse', said a LAMATA official. To enable progress, the participants turned to adaptation. First, the route was changed after the military refused to part with their land. Next, the route was shortened to a third of its planned length. Amidst this uncertainty, the participants also invested in building institutions, rushing a twenty-five-year concession to a private firm to supply and run trains.[13] Construction then occurred in fits and starts until it stopped in 2013, when the Lagos government ran out of money – 'that's the mentality here, pay as you go', said one respondent. The concessionaire contract was then terminated, and LAMATA entered into negotiations with a potential Chinese concessionaire.[14] In the meantime, the opening date has been constantly put back, even if 'we've achieved 95 per cent completion' has become the standard laconic statement. And there is no visibility in terms of cost escalation; still, the local actors remain supportive of their Chinese partners. As one official said:

> Let me give you a good thing about CCECC ... they're really ready to deliver and satisfy their clients. When you award them a particular contract it takes less time for them to start construction and mobilisation ... They won't say, 'the government isn't paying, I won't work.'

In sum, our analysis reveals how differing approaches to the navigation of institutional voids translate into differing organisational designs in the pursuit of similar system-level goals. This variation reflects a duality of two desirable objectives. The core participants in both organizational contexts are the same. But the design attributes that underlie organising for building institutions are incompatible with those underlying organising for quick capital investment. When the focus is on the former, orderliness and transparency are paramount. If the focus shifts to capital investment, adaptiveness and opaqueness rule. Importantly, by choosing to focus on either pole of the duality, both organisational designs struggle to achieve the higher-order goal, albeit for different reasons.

13.6   Discussion

Institutional voids relate to the scarcity of public goods in emergent economies. These voids hinder the mechanisms that allow resource

---

[13] 'Eko Rail wins Lagos Blue Line concession', *Metro Report International*, March 2012.
[14] C. Gabriel, 'Lagos: We are building a new Nigeria through the rail project – LAMATA boss', *Vanguard*, 27 August 2014.

exchanges, goal alignment and co-ordinated collective action (Khanna and Palepu 1997, 2010). To navigate these voids in the pursuit of their goals, organisations work with intermediaries (McDermott et al. 2009; Meyer et al. 2009; van der Vegt et al. 2015). Thus, institutional weakness promotes new forms of (meta-) organising. Yet the intermediaries are not all alike (Doh et al. 2017). Since organisational design is contingent on the environment that the organisation needs to relate to, this study set off to explore how the choice in intermediaries relates to organisational design choice.

We grounded our study in the international development sector – a context where the development agencies act as the intermediary to help the state acquire private resources. In contexts with a shortfall in institutions, the actors with the capability to mobilise resources gain decision-making power (George et al. 2016). In agreement organizational design choice once the borrowers settle on the choice of intermediary, the intermediary gains decision rights on system architecture. Because traditional and emergent intermediaries have differing architectural preferences, differing forms of organizing ensue.

13.6.1 From Choice of Intermediary to Design Duality

Our study reveals substantive variation in organizational design choice. This variation belies the fact that all the contexts in our sample were set up to tackle a similar challenge – socio-economic development. The forms of organizing were similar in terms of key participants. But as the approach agreed upon to navigate institutional voids varies, the organisational focus varies too: either capital investment or building institutions. And since the two objectives are organisationally incompatible, the participants choose to focus on one objective to the detriment of the other.

Importantly, all sampled cases reveal a need to engage in a degree of institution building. Institutions are more than just background conditions: they directly influence strategic choices available to an organisation, and organisations are known to achieve and sustain competitive advantage through strategies that overcome, shape and capitalise on the nature of their institutional environments (Khanna and Palepu 1997, 2010; Henisz, Dorobantu and Nartey 2014). For example, at the very least, there is a need to resolve property rights for new capital goods, e.g. write concessionaire agreements; there is also a need to handle resource exchanges with sovereign stakeholders, some of which are hard to carry out without changes to the institutions, e.g. land laws. But the more the focus shifts towards building institutions, the more complex issues emerge at the interface with different levels in public administration and the legislative environment, and thus delays ensue. Still, even when the participants agree to exploit institutional weakness and restrict organising to the 'project' level, the inter-organisational context remains interdependent with the environment because many critical resources are controlled by external stakeholders.

Underlying this choice of focus is the organisational incompatibility of the two desirable objectives, which suggests a duality (Evans and Doz 1989; Birkinshaw and Gibson 2004; Smith and Tushman 2005; Gulati and Puranam 2009). In organisational studies, one known duality is associated with the differing incentive and co-ordination mechanisms needed to support exploration and exploitation projects (Burns and Stalker 1961; Brown and Eisenhardt 1997). Other dualities relate to integration–differentiation, or cost reduction–product differentiation (Lawrence and Lorsch 1967, March 1991). Organising to pursue dualities and to balance conflicting demands is recognisably difficult. Which is why many organisations choose to focus on only one pole – the one they perceive offers better opportunities for institutional success or profitability. In agreement, the organisations in our sample, too, chose 'gains from focus' (Porter 1985) instead of 'gains from ambidexterity' (Tushman and O'Reilly 1996; Brown and Eisenhardt 1997; Birkinshaw and Gibson 2004).

13.6.1.1   *Organising to Mitigate Institutional Voids*

The traditional intermediaries chose to act as institutional entrepreneurs by insisting on the refinement and development of the local commercial and administrative environment before disbursing assistance (Mair et al. 2012; Acemoglu and Robinson 2012). This choice is consistent with the interest of open-system intermediaries in creating common goods in order to support broader resource exchanges (Dutt et al. 2015). Underlying this choice are two specific design attributes: orderliness and transparency. Orderliness allows time to negotiate institutional changes with multiple stakeholders (Libecap 1990). In turn, transparency in the way the system acquires key resources, e.g. land and supplier capabilities, is necessary to ensure that the system plays by the rules that it espouses and seeks to build. The two principles are mutually reinforcing. Demands for orderly growth allow for transparency in decision making, e.g. supplier selection through competitive bidding. Moreover, calls for transparency slow down resource exchanges, which allows more time to grow the organization step by step.

Both principles are rooted in the notion that progress in capital-intensive developments should flow 'downwards' like a waterfall, an idea that became enshrined in the West from the 1970s onwards (Cleland and King 1968; Boehm 1981). These principles gained further traction with the popularity of stage-gate development models (Cooper 1990; Morris 1994; Brooks 1995). So it is not an option for the traditional intermediaries to violate these principles; were they to do so, they would fail to attain external validation in terms of what the norms deem appropriate.

13.6.1.2   Organising to Exploit Institutional Voids

The contrast with the contexts enabled by Chinese credit could not be greater. The deals with the Chinese lenders are subjected to limited public scrutiny, so it is hard to say whether their structures are imposed upon the borrowers, or are the outcome of a mutual preference. Irrespectively, our findings reveal that opaqueness and adaptability enable quick capital investment; these two principles are also mutually reinforcing. Opaqueness leaves the external stakeholders in the dark as to what exactly is going on. This reduces the political costs from late changes if efforts to exploit weak institutions backfire. In turn, adaptability reduces incentives to increase visibility in decision making, in the knowledge that some late changes could otherwise trigger a public outcry.

Specifically, to achieve quick capital investment, the suppliers need to be brought on board early on, which is not compatible with orderly growth. Rather, by letting suppliers join in before acquiring other complementary resources, the participants are accepting high uncertainty about what can actually be done and how much it will cost. It is thus likely that things will change along the way, which requires adaptability. This flexible form of organising is not new. Indeed, it resonates with insights on organising in high-speed environments where improvisation, iterations, real-time experience and flexibility rule at the expense of cost efficiency (Eisenhardt and Tabrizi 1995; Iansiti 1995). The basic idea is that the gains from reducing the development life-cycle outweigh the adaptation costs incurred to cope with late information and externalities (Thomke 1997; Gil and Tether 2011). What is different here, though, is to see adaptability as a guiding principle applied in an environment with a shortfall of institutions. This is where adaptability becomes entwined with restricted information flows that keep external stakeholders at arm's length. Together, the two principles enable to capitalise on poor institutions to accelerate capital acquisition, e.g. selecting suppliers without using market mechanisms.

13.6.2   *Towards a Theory of Organising to Navigate Institutional Voids*

Our insights suggest a duality in the design of inter-organisational contexts set up to pursue socio-economic development. Seeing this duality enables the debate on the performance of this population of organisations to shift away from the search for a superior design towards the challenges of designing alternative forms of organising. And crucially, this duality gives us a basis on which to develop the rudiments of a theory of designing organisations to navigate institutional voids. Institutions are a source of value in that they put pressure on organisations to credibly commit to follow promised and/or reasonable procedures (Freeland and Sivan 2018). Hence, institutions enable development. But capital investment for basic public goods, too, is a key enabler of development. So, if we accept this duality, we need to see performance differently.

Our study suggests that intermediaries are constrained by their surrounding institutional environment. Traditional intermediaries are constrained by Western governance ideals (Burnside and Dollar 2000; Hermes and Lensink 2001) and the project's 'golden triangle' of cost-schedule-scope (Cleland and King 1968; Morris 1994; Flyvbjerg, Bruzelius and Rothengatter 2003; Oliveira and Lumineau 2017). And so, in contexts enabled by traditional credit, neglecting the building of institutions is not an option. In turn, Chinese lenders must respond to the donors' ambition to accelerate outward economic expansion (Henderson, Appelbaum and Ho 2013), and win the political favour and economic benefits of the recipient states (Tull 2006; Brewer 2008). This makes it mandatory to fast-track capital investment. As the two objectives are incompatible, the only alternative left is to focus on one of the two.

However, our analysis suggests that gains from focus are insufficient to achieve the ultimate goal. Orderliness and transparency build institutions, but compromise the organisation's capacity to eliminate infrastructure gaps. Furthermore, there are also limits to the extent, under these guiding principles, that the organisation can be effective. Enfranchising powerful stakeholders can be insufficient to encourage norms of collaboration (Dorobantu, Kaul, and Zelner 2017) – the failure of LAMATA's governance board to build consensus is a case in point.

Yet, a general disregard for transparency, inclusiveness, and institutional checks and balances cannot also eliminate interdependences with the environment. And as the organisation seeks quick capital investment, this focus leads to bottlenecks – problems that need resolving to achieve the objective, but for which no easy remedies exist (Baldwin 2014). A case in point is the time-consuming land disputes that ensue after a decision to exploit ill-defined property rights. At the limit, systems that seek to grow in an opaque, adaptable way can collapse, as the Lagos metro line case shows – riddled by cash-flow problems, this system is yet to convince another intermediary to render assistance, and its future therefore remains wholly uncertain.

With gains from either focus alone insufficient to achieve the system goal, it has been hard to move forward the debate on performance. On the one hand, some development scholars have argued that a 'superior' form of organising should see building institutions as the end result, not a means to an end (Hirschman 1967, 1984; Moyo 2009). This choice would attenuate the propensity of the recipients to underestimate their ability to tackle all the difficulties and troubles that future events may bring. Hirschman encapsulated this bias for hope in his so-called 'hiding hand principle', defined as 'essentially a way of inducing action through error' (Hirschman 1967, 28). However, other scholars argue that Hirschman's claims ignore the difficulties and obstacles on the ground (Alacevich 2014); in other words, organising for building institutions needs to be first, and that development, per necessity, is a 'slow process' (Baum 1978; Burnside and Dollar 2000). With the debate unresolved, the recipients turned to Chinese credit. For its harsher critics, Chinese intermediation is nothing more than a 'narrow elite business dialogue' and 'rogue aid' (Naim 2007) that induces the borrowers to build up unsustainable levels of debt (Dreher and Fuchs 2011; Naim 2007; Vines and Campos 2008; Dreher and Fuchs 2011; Henderson, Appelbaum and Ho 2013). But there are those who see here a 'golden opportunity' (Moyo 2009) for recipients to build basic public goods without tiresome strings attached (Hernandez 2017).

In this study, we propose a design duality as a new conceptual foundation to reset this debate. In complex task environments, the assessment of alternative choices happens under conditions of uncertainty (Perrow 1984; Gavetti and Levinthal 2000). When the institutions are robust, uncertainty puts emphasis on cognitive processes and forward-looking models about the future outcome of various alternatives, while limiting the value of experience and feedback (Gavetti and Levinthal 2000). However, in environments with a shortfall in institutions, the individual preferences of powerful actors hold sway (George et al. 2012). It is thus important to make this duality explicit in order to enable cash-strapped governments to make informed decisions. Related to this, this duality points to a need to rethink how we define and measure performance. It is rarely documented how much time elapses between starting to pursue development and the time it takes to achieve *both* objectives – capital investment and building institutions. But if we accept that there is a duality, this elapsed time is a crucial measure of organisational performance.

13.6.2.1   *Designing Ambidextrous Organisations*

We know of organisations pursuing jointly desirable dualities successfully (Gulati and Puranam 2009). We tend to assume complementarities exist between the informal and formal organisations in terms of supplementary fit, where both push in the same direction (Milgrom and Roberts 1990; Kogut and Zander 1996; Siggelkow 2002). Nevertheless, it is not unusual for activity in complex organisations to go on 'in permitted violation of the rules' (Perrow 1984), and, indeed, informal interactions among groups can shape the rules of the game (North 1991). In other words, the formal and informal organisation can support different poles of a duality, but if they 'compensate' for each other, this duality can be leveraged into an effective hybrid arrangement (Brown and Eisenhardt 1997; Gibson and Birkinshaw 2004; Gulati and Puranam 2009; Doh et al. 2017).

The idea of a compensatory fit between the formal and informal organisation in the pursuit of socio-economic development is thus not to be dismissed. In institutionally advanced settings, practitioners often recognise the need for orderly growth in capital investment is a 'planning fallacy', and the formal organisation is known to give practitioners latitude to compensate through the informal organisation (Brooks 1995; Porter 1995). Things are different when there is a shortfall of institutions. In these settings, private firms are known to rely on informal institutions (Mair et al. 2012), interpersonal trust (Narayanan and Fahey 2005), and social networks (Dieleman and Boddewyn 2012). But the traditional intermediaries act constrained by good governance ideals. Hence, even if they recognise that private firms may resort to dubious means to influence governments to obtain preferential treatment and deter competition (Fligstein 1996), traditional intermediaries cannot endorse informal ways to speed up capital investment to compensate for the formal emphasis on building institutions.

In contrast, the Chinese intermediaries are not constrained by these institutional pressures. Hence, in the contexts enabled by Chinese credit, informal private gains are an enabler to speed up capital allocation. In other words, the informal organisation supplements the focus of the formal organisation in quick capital acquisition. Yet, this supplementary fit also compromises the organisation's capacity to achieve the system-level goal – socio-economic development.

13.7 Conclusion

In this study, we propose the rudiments of a contingency theory of designing organisations to navigate institutional voids. We do so by deploying an organisational design lens to make sense of variation in inter-organisational contexts set up to pursue socio-economic development – a grand challenge of our times (Tihanyi, Graffin and George 2014). Our central claim is that participants in this context face a duality of building institutions and acquiring capital – two objectives that are organisationally incompatible. This incompatibility forces organisational designers to choose either one or the other pole of the duality, but we find that the gains from focus insufficient to meet the unifying system goal. This insight gives us a new conceptual foundation to further our understanding of organisation design and performance in this context.

The choice to focus on either pole of the duality is contingent on the institutional environment that surrounds the intermediary. Rushing capital acquisition while neglecting the building of institutions is a high-stakes gamble. Still, this choice is permissible for Chinese intermediaries. Of course, developing countries vary in terms of state fragility – the degree to which the state is unable and/or unwilling to deliver basic public services (Chauvet and Collier 2004). We conjecture that governments in less fragile states have more limited agency to choose between intermediaries. But this in no way reduces the urgency of further research into how to design inter-organizational contexts to pursue socio-economic development.

Appendix – Protocol for the Formal Research Interviews

- Where did the idea for the transport development project come from?
- How are major decisions on who the project participants are?
- Who are the most influential project stakeholders?

- What is the role of the development agency?
- What were the major challenges faced by the projects?
- How is decision-making authority distributed?
- Who has decision rights to influence the targets of the development projects?
- When were the performance targets announced publicly?
- Who announced the performance targets? Have they stayed stable?
- What makes your approach to new infrastructure development unique?
- Do the public agencies have authority to set up robust contingencies?
- Who resolves the disputes with landowners and other stakeholders?
- Who monitors the progress and outcomes of the development projects?

References

Acemoglu, D. and Robinson, J. A. (2012). *Why nations fail: The origins of power, prosperity, and poverty.* London and New York: Crown Publishers.

Alacevich, M. (2014). Visualizing uncertainties, or how Albert Hirschman and the World Bank disagreed on project appraisal and what this says about the end of 'high development theory'. *Journal of the History of Economic Thought*, 36, 137–168.

Armanios, D. E., Eesley, C. E., Li, J. and Eisenhardt, K. M. (2017). How entrepreneurs leverage institutional intermediaries in emerging economies to acquire public resources. *Strategic Management Journal*, 1373–1390.

Baldwin, C. Y. (2014). Bottlenecks, modules and dynamic capabilities. Harvard Business School Working Paper, No. 15–028, October 2014. (Revised May 2015.)

Baum, W. C. (1978). The World Bank project cycle. *Finance and Development* 15 (4): 10–17.

Biernacki, P. and Waldorf, D. (1981). Snowball sampling: Problems and techniques of chain referral sampling. *Sociological Methods & Research, 10*: 141–163.

Birkinshaw, J., and Gibson, C. (2004). Building ambidexterity into an organisation. *MIT Sloan Management Review*, 45(4): 47–55.

Boehm, B. W. (1981). *Software engineering economics.* Englewood Cliffs, NJ: Prentice-Hall.

Brautigam, D. (2009. *The dragon's gift: The real story of China in Africa.* Oxford: Oxford University Press.

Brewer, N. (2008). *The new Great Walls: A guide to China's overseas dam industry.* Berkeley, CA: International Rivers.

Brown, S. L. and Eisenhardt, K. M. (1997). The art of continuous change: Linking complexity theory. *Administrative Science Quarterly*, 42(1): 1–34.

Brooks, F. P., Jr. (1995). The mythical man-month: *Essays on software engineering.* Anniversary Edition. Indiana: Addison-Wesley Longman.

Burns, T. and Stalker, G. M. (1961). *The management of innovation*. London: Tavistock.

Burnside, C. and Dollar, D. (2000). Aid, policies, and growth. *American Economic Review*, 90 (4) (September): 847–68.

Chauvet, L. and Collier, P. (2004, January). *Development effectiveness in fragile states: Spillovers and turnarounds*. Oxford: Centre for the Study of African Economies, Department of Economics, Oxford University.

Cleland, D. I. and King, W. R. (1968). *Systems analysis and project management*. New York, NY: McGraw-Hill.

Cooper, R. (1990). Stage-gate systems: A new tool for managing new products. *Business Horizons*, *33*(3): 44–55.

Cyert, M. D. and March, J. G. (1963). *A behavioral theory of the firm*. Englewood Cliffs, NJ: Prentice-Hall.

Dahan, N., Doh, J. P., Oetzel, J. and Yaziji, M. (2010). Corporate-NGO collaboration: Creating new business models for developing markets. *Long Range Planning*, 43: 326–342.

Delios, A. and Henisz, W. J. (2000). Japanese firms' investment strategies in emerging economies. *Academy of Management Journal*, 43(3): 305–323.

Dieleman, M., and Boddewyn, J. (2012). Using organisation structure to buffer political ties in emerging markets: A case study. *Organisation Studies*, 33: 71–95.

Doh, J., Rodrigues, S., Saka-Helmhout, A. and Makhija, M. (2017). International business responses to institutional voids. *Journal of International Business Studies*, 48(3): 293–307.

Dorobantu, S., Kaul, A. and Zelner, B. (2017). Nonmarket strategy research through the lens of new institutional economics: An integrative review and future directions. *Strategic Management Journal*, 38(1): 114–140.

Dreher, A. and Fuchs, A. (2011). Rogue aid? The determinants of China's aid allocation. Courant Research Centre, 'Poverty, Equity and Growth'. Discussion Paper 93, University of Goettingen.

Dutt, N., Hawn, O., Vidal, E., Chatterji, A., McGahan, A. and Mitchell, W. (2015). How open system intermediaries address institutional failures: The case of business incubators in emerging-market countries. *Academy of Management Journal*, 59, 818–840.

Eesley, C. (2016). Institutional barriers to growth: Entrepreneurship, human capital and institutional change. *Organisation Science*, 27 (5): 1290–1306.

Eisenhardt, K. M. (1989). Building theories from case study research. *Academy of Management Review*, *14*(4): 532–550.

Eisenhardt, K. M. and Tabrizi, B. N. (1995). Accelerating adaptive processes: Product innovation in the global computer industry. *Administrative Science Quarterly*, *40*(1): 84–110.

Eisenhardt, S., Graebner, M. E. and Sonenshein, S. (2016). Grand challenges and inductive methods: Rigor without rigor mortis. *Academy of Management Journal*, 59(4): 1113–1123.

Eom, J., Hwang, J., Atkins, L., Chen, Y. and Zhou, S. (2017). China Africa Research Initiative at the School of Advanced International Studies. Policy Brief No. 18. Johns Hopkins University.

Evans, P. and Doz, Y. (1989). The dualistic organisation. In A. Laurent (Ed.), *Human resource management in international firms*. Basingstoke, UK: Macmillan.

Fjeldstad, Ø. D., Snow, C. C., Miles, R. E., Lettl, C. (2012). The architecture of collaboration. *Strategic Management Journal*, 33: 734–750.

Fligstein, N. (1996). Markets as politics: A political-cultural approach to market institutions. *American Sociological Review*, 61(4): 656–673.

Flyvbjerg, B., Bruzelius, N. and Rothengatter, W. (2003). *Megaprojects and risk: An anatomy of ambition*. Cambridge, UK: Cambridge University Press.

Freeland, R. F. and Sivan, E. W. Z. (2018). The problems and promise of hierarchy: voice rights and the firm. *Sociological Science*, 5(7): 143–181.

Gavetti, G., and Levinthal, D. (2000). Looking forward and looking backward: Cognitive and experiential search. *Administrative Science Quarterly*, 45: 113–137.

Gehman J., et al. (2017). Finding theory–method fit: A comparison of three qualitative approaches to theory building. *Journal of Management Inquiry*, 27 (3): 284–300.

George, G., Corbishley, C., Khayesi, J. N. O., Haas, M. R. and Tihanyi, L. (2016). Bringing Africa in: Promising directions for management research. *Academy of Management Journal*, 59(2): 377–393.

George, G., McGahan, A. M. and Prabhu, J. (2012). Innovation for inclusive growth: Towards a theoretical framework and a research agenda. *Journal of Management Studies*, 49: 661–683.

Gibson, C. B. and Birkinshaw, J. (2004). The antecedents, consequences, and mediating role of organisational ambidexterity. *Academy of Management Journal*, 47(2): 209–226.

Gil, N. and Tether, B. (2011). Project risk management and design flexibility: Analyzing a case and conditions of complementarity. *Research Policy, 40*, 415–428.

Gulati, R. and Puranam, P. (2009). Renewal through Reorganisation. *Organisation Science*, 20(2): 422–40.

Gulati, R., Puranam, P. and Tushman, M. (2012). Meta-organisation design: Rethinking design in inter-organisational and community contexts. *Strategic Management Journal*, 33: 571–586.

Gupta, S., Kangur, A., Papageorgiou, C. and Wane, A. (2014). Efficiency-adjusted public capital and growth. *World Development*, 57, May: 164–178.

Henderson, J. (2008). China and global development: Towards a Global-Asian era? *Contemporary Politics*, 14(4): 375–392.

Henderson, J., Appelbaum, R. P. and Ho, S. Y. (2013). Globalization with Chinese characteristics: Externalization, dynamics and transformations. *Development and Change*, 44: 1221–1253.

Henisz, W. J. (2002). The institutional environment for infrastructure investment. *Industrial and Corporate Change*, 11(2): 355–389.

Henisz, W. J., Dorobantu, S. and Nartley, L. J. (2014). Spinning gold: The financial returns to stakeholder engagement. *Strategic Management Journal*, 35 (12): 1727–1748.

Hermes, N., and Lensink, R. (eds.) (2001). *Changing the conditions for development aid: A new paradigm*. London: Frank Cass.

Hernandez, D. (2017). Are 'new' donors challenging World Bank conditionality? *World Development*, 96 (August): 529–549.

Hilling, D. (1996). *Transport and developing countries*. London: Routledge.

Hirschman, A. O. (1967). *Development projects observed*. Washington, DC: Brookings Institution.

Hirschman, A. O. (1984). A dissenter's confession: The strategy of economic development revisited, in G. M. Meyer and D. Seers (Eds.), *Pioneers in development*. Oxford: Oxford University Press.

Hwang, J. and Bral, D. (2016). How Chinese money is transforming Africa: It's not what you think. Policy Brief 11/2016, China Africa Research Initiative at the School of Advanced International Studies. Baltimore, MD: Johns Hopkins University.

Iansiti, M. (1995). Shooting the rapids: Managing product development in turbulent environments. *California Management Review*, 38(1): 37–58.

Jick, T. D. (1979). Mixing qualitative and quantitative methods: Triangulation in action. *Administrative Science Quarterly*, 24(4): 602–611.

Kaufmann, D. and Kraay, A. (2017). *Worldwide governance indicators project*. The World Bank. info.worldbank.org/governance/wgi/pdf/wgidataset.xlsx.

Khanna, T. K. and Palepu, K. G. (1997). Why focused strategies may be wrong for emerging markets. *Harvard Business Review*, 75(4): 41–54.

Khanna, T. and Palepu, K. G. (2010). *Winning in emerging markets: A road map for strategy and execution*. Boston, MA: Harvard Business Press.

Kistruck, G. M., Sutter, C. J., Lount, R. B., Jr. and Smith, B. (2013). Mitigating principal-agent problems in base-of-the-pyramid markets: An identity spillover perspective. *Academy of Management Journal*, 56: 659–82.

Kivleniece, I. and Quelin, B. V. (2012). Creating and capturing value in public-private ties: A private actor's perspective. *Academy of Management Review, April*, 37(2): 272–299.

Knack, S. F. (2003). *Democracy, governance, and growth*. Ann Arbor, MI: The University of Michigan Press.

Kogut, B. and Zander, U. (1996). What firms do? Coordination, identity, and learning. *Organization Science*, 7(5): 502–518.

Lakhani, K. R. and von Hippel, E. (2003). How open source software works: 'Free' user-to-user assistance. *Research Policy*, 32(6): 923–943.

Langley, A. (1999). Strategies for theorizing from process data. *Academy of Management Review*, 24: 691–710.

Lawrence, P. R. and Lorsch, J. W. (1967). *Organisation and environment: Managing differentiation and integration*. Boston, MA: Harvard Business School.

Lazzarini, S. G. (2015). Strategizing by the government: Can industrial policy create firm-level competitive advantage? *Strategic Management Journal*, 36(1): 97–112.

Lee, G. K. and Cole, R. E. (2003). From a firm-based to a community-based model of knowledge creation: The case of the Linux kernel development. *Organisation Science*, 14(6): 633–649.

Levy, B. (2014). *Working with the grains: Integrating governance and growth in development strategies*. New York, NY: Oxford University Press.

Maguire, S., Hardy, C. and Lawrence, T. B. (2004). Institutional entrepreneurship in emerging fields: HIV/AIDS treatment advocacy in Canada. *Academy of Management Journal*, 47: 657–679.

Mair, J., Marti, I. and Ventresca, M. J. (2012). Building inclusive markets in rural Bangladesh: how intermediaries work institutional voids. *Academy of Management Journal*, 55(4): 819–850.

March, J. G. (1991). Exploration and exploitation in organisational learning. *Organisational Science*, 2(1): 71–87.

Martens, B. (2005). Why do aid agencies exist? *Development Policy Review*, 23(6): 643–663.

McDermott, G. A., Corredoira, R. A. and Kruse, G. (2009). Public–private institutions as catalysts of upgrading in emerging market societies. *Academy of Management Journal*, 52(6): 1270–1296.

McLean, E. V. and Schneider, C. J. (2014). Limits of informal governance? The scope of conditionality in the World Bank. Annual Meeting on the Political Economy of International Organisations. Princeton, NJ.

Meyer, K. E., Estrin, S., Bhaumik, S. K. and Peng, M. W. (2009). Institutions, resources, and entry strategies in emerging economies. *Strategic Management Journal*, 30(1): 61–80.

Meyer, K. E. and Peng, M. W. (2016). Theoretical foundations of emerging economy business research. *Journal of International Business Studies*, 47(1): 3–22.

Miles, M. B. and Huberman, A. M. (1984). *Qualitative data analysis: A sourcebook of new methods*. Beverly Hills, CA: Sage Publications.

Milgrom, P. and Roberts, J.(1990). The economics of modern manufacturing: Technology, strategy, and organization. *American Economic Review*, 80(3): 511–528.

Mohan, G. B. and Lampert, B. (2013). Negotiating China: Reinserting African agency into China–Africa relations. *African Affairs*, 112(446): 92–110.

Morris, P. W. (1994). *The management of projects*. London: Thomas Telford.

Moyo, D. (2009). *Dead aid: Why aid is not working and how there is a better way for Africa*. London: Allen Lane.

Naim, M. (2007). Rogue aid. *Foreign Policy*, 159: 95–96.

Narayanan, V. K., and Fahey, L. (2005). The relevance of the institutional underpinnings of Porter's five forces framework to emerging economies: An epistemological analysis. *Journal of Management Studies*, 42: 207–223.

North, D. C. (1991). Institutions. *The Journal of Economic Perspectives*, 5(1): 97–112.

North, D. C. and Weingast, B. R. (1989). Constitutions and commitment: The evolution of institutions governing public choice in seventeenth-century England. *The Journal of Economic History*, XLIX(4): 802–832.

OECD. (2014). Aid to developing countries rebounds in 2013 to reach an all-time high. Paris: OECD.

Oliveira, N. and Lumineau, F. (2017). How coordination trajectories influence the performance of interorganisational project networks. *Organisation Science*, 28 (6), 1029–1060.

Perrow, C. (1984). *Normal accidents: Living with high-risk technologies*. Princeton, NJ: Princeton University Press.

Porter, M. E. (1985). *Competitive advantage*. New York: Free Press.

Porter, T. M. (1995). *Trust in numbers: The pursuit of objectivity in science and public life*. Princeton, NJ: Princeton University Press

Regner, P. and Edman, J. (2014). MNE institutional advantage: How subunits shape, transpose and evade host country institutions. *Journal of International Business Studies*, 45: 275–301.

Rothaermel, F. T. and Boeker, W. (2008). Old technology meets new technology: Complementarities, similarities, and alliance formation. *Strategic Management Journal*, 29(1): 47–77.

Sachs, J.(2005). *The end of poverty: How we can make it happen in our lifetime*. London: Penguin Books.

Scott, W. R. (1981). *Organisations: Rational, natural, and open systems*. Englewood Cliffs NJ: Prentice Hall Inc.

Siggelkow, N. (2002). Misperceiving interactions among complements and substitutes: Organizational consequences. *Management Science*, 48(7): 900–916.

Simon, H. A. (1981). *The sciences of the artificial*. 2nd ed. Cambridge, MA: MIT Press.

Smith, W. K. and Tushman, M. L.(2005). Managing strategic contradictions: A top management model for managing innovation streams. *Organisation Science*, 16(5): 522–536.

Stokke, O. (1995). *Aid and political conditionality*. London: Frank Cass.

Strauss, A. and Corbin, J. M. (1990). *Basics of qualitative research: Grounded theory procedures and techniques*. Thousand Oaks, CA: Sage Publications.

Tan-Mullins, M., Mohan, G. and Power, M. (2010). Redefining 'aid' in the China–Africa context. *Development and Change*, 41: 857–881.

The Economist. (2009, 21 July). China's 'going out' strategy.

Thomke, S. H. (1997). The role of flexibility in the development of new products: An empirical study. *Research Policy*, 26, 105–119.

Thompson, J. D. (1967). *Organisations in action*. New York: McGraw-Hill.

Tihanyi, L., Graffin, S. and George, G. (2014). Rethinking governance in management research. *Academy of Management Journal*, 57: 1535–1543.

Tull, D. (2006). China's engagement in Africa: Scope, significance and consequences. *Journal of Modern African Studies*, 44(3): 459–79.

Tushman, M. L. and O'Reilly, C. A. (1996). Ambidextrous organisations: Managing evolutionary and revolutionary change. *California Management Review*, 38(4): 8–30.

UN. (2017). World population prospects: The 2017 revision, Department of Economic and Social Affairs, Population Division. New York: United Nations

Van der Vegt, G. S., Essens, P., Wahlström, M. and George, G. (2015). Managing risk and resilience. *Academy of Management Journal*, 58: 971–980.

Vines, A. and Campos, I. (2008). *Angola and China: A pragmatic partnership?* Washington, DC: Center for Strategic and International Studies.

WEF. (2018). *The global competitiveness report 2017–2018*. Edited by Klaus Schwab. Geneva: World Economic Forum.

Wood, G. and Frynas, J. G. (2006). The institutional basis of economic failure: Anatomy of the segmented business system. *Socio-Economic Review*, 4: 239–277.

Woods, N. (2008). Whose aid? Whose influence? China, emerging donors and the silent revolution in development assistance. *International Affairs*, 84(6): 1205–21.

World Bank. (2011). World development report 2011: Conflict, security and development. Washington, DC: World Bank.

Yin, R. (1984). *Case study research: Designs and methods*. Los Angeles, CA: Sage Publications.

Afterword

Nuno Gil

As we prepared to wrap up this book and send all the chapters to our publisher, I had the chance to travel to Africa to test, with a group of local scholars and policy makers, the central argument: that underlying the diversity of forms of organizing set up to develop basic infrastructure and in this way promote socio-economic development lies a duality of building institutions and building technology – two desirable objectives with underlying design attributes that make them organisationally incompatible. The setting was the city of Livingstone, a stone's throw from the majestic Victoria Falls – two places charged with references to a bygone Western colonial era which, for good and for ill, is part of Africa's history. But also an era from which there is little to learn in terms of designing organizations to equip Africa with the much-needed infrastructure to cope with the conflation of rapid population growth, urban migration and climate change. It was heartening that our audience bought into our core idea and related to the dilemma that we believe faces organisation designers. But pertinent questions were also raised as to where this 'duality' leaves us, and if the focus on either pole of the duality exhausts the solution space of forms of organizing that can be designed in order to tackle grand challenges when there is a shortfall of institutions in the environment.

Working on this book as lead editor for two years gave me the opportunity to think hard and long about these questions. As the body of evidence accumulated, the difficulties on the ground in designing organizations capable of reconciling the two objectives became very apparent. But we should not rush to accept that we are stuck between a high-stakes gamble – focus on building basic infrastructure despite institutional shortcomings, which amplifies the risks of corruption, bribes, kickbacks, and organisational collapse – and delaying infrastructure building until the institutions are first developed, which creates a real risk of not building the basic infrastructure at all, due to difficulties associated with first building those institutions. Indeed, accepting that there are no other choices would be remiss, considering the fast pace of Africa's population

411

growth – in the two years that it took to produce this book, Africa's population – of which 60 per cent are aged only 24 years old or younger – increased by about 65 million people, which is about the size of the UK's population!

Instead, we propose that, yes, there is an organisational duality between building institutions and building technology. But this idea enables us to lay down a new research agenda and formulate questions that were previously overlooked because they were obscured by the debate between superior versus inferior organisational designs. Specifically, we need to investigate new ways to define and measure the performance of the organizations that build infrastructure. This duality suggests that Western criteria for the evaluation of performance of organizations – which are rooted in 'good' governance ideals and the project's time-cost-scope golden triangle – are inadequate. These criteria rightly recognise the value of building institutions but wrongly ignore the elapsed time incurred in this task. And compressing this elapsed time is a desirable objective, too. But if allowing for a degree of informal private gains, opacity and lack of accountability for public spending may be necessary evils in order to fast-track infrastructure building, where do we draw the line? How can we ensure that this will not end up simply allowing predators to appropriate public resources in order to serve the private interests of a restricted few? Furthermore, at what point in the evolution of the institutions in the environment can we rule out the idea of exploiting institutional voids in order to accelerate infrastructure development? Or put differently, what contingencies determine when organisational designers should prioritise one pole of the duality over the other?

We should also not allow the idea of a design duality to force us into thinking that a search for forms of organising that are more ambidextrous is *the* answer. 'Seeing' a duality is not the same as saying this duality exhausts the space of the organisational designs that are possible. And our evidence does suggest other viable organisational designs. The self-governance structure designed by the Cairenes to improve living and working conditions in the informal settlements is a case in point. And so it is the public–private arrangement that enabled the development of South Africa's Gaultrain railway system without involving an institutional intermediary – a testament to local success in building institutions.

Allow me to advance here an analogy with how African Bushmen see the survival of prey species for carnivores. Zebras, giraffes, impalas, gnus and other species graze in mixed herds. By sharing the abundant resources of the savannah, they all gain heightened awareness of potential predators. With their long necks, giraffes see predators at greater distances, zebras have superb hearing, and impalas and gnus bring large numbers to the group. In other words, each species brings with it a set of unique complementarities that all together help to keep at bay the predators that are hidden in the bush. Of course, predators occasionally succeed. But the Bushmen believe that by grazing together and sharing the resources of the savannah, the multiple species are increasing their own individual chances of survival.

The body of evidence assembled for this book does not suggest that one single group of intermediaries holds all the cards to help the African policy makers in their struggle to bridge gaps in basic infrastructure. On the contrary, the evidence suggests that the policy makers of emerging economies have agency to make choices between differing forms of organizing. And crucially, the evidence also suggests that we should not be naïve. Lurking in any institutionally underdeveloped landscape are predators – organizations and individuals which just want to appropriate public resources in order to maximise private gains. But I conjecture that a diversified population of organisational designs better equips African countries to chase socio-economic development, while fending off attacks from the predators that are keen to exploit the continent's abundant common resources.[1]

In sum, working on this book has opened my eyes to two different ways of seeing efforts by which intermediaries seek to help the governments of emerging economies to pursue socio-economic development. This is not a story about searching for *the* superior form of organising; it is a story about complementarity between forms of organising at the two poles of a duality. I am also not arguing that espousing informal private gains is a prerequisite for socio-economic development. Or that there is, or there is not, moral equivalence at the two poles of the duality. But I am, nevertheless, convinced that we all gain more than we lose in 'seeing' this duality. This duality exists by design. This does not mean this way of looking out alone offers us solutions to equip Africa with much-needed basic infrastructure and institutions to cope with 4.5 billion people by 2100. Or for accommodating the largest cities on earth, such as Lagos, Kinshasa, Dar es Salaam, Khartoum and Niamey, all projected to exceed 55 million people by 2100. But perhaps by framing the problem in this way, we will see new organisational designs and complementarities that can be mobilised to tackle this grand societal challenge of our time; solutions that, until now, were invisible to us.

---

[1] My children call it the 'Savannah theory'. We are nowhere near there, yet. But the thought was much appreciated.

Figure A.1 A mixed herd sharing the natural resources of the savannah

One thing is clear: There is no time to waste. The evidence is in front of us for those who want to see it. As I set off to leave Africa, I left behind a long queue of trucks waiting to cross the river Zambezi at the border between Botswana and Zambia by pontoon ferry. Locals claim that the average waiting time for a truck to cross is around two weeks. A new bridge to open up trade and promote tourism is expected to open by 2019. But the stubborn fact that the nearest alternative is the Victoria Falls Bridge, completed in 1905, is cause for thought.

Equipping Africa with basic infrastructure as well as institutions is the fight of our lives. It is a global race. But not a race where there are individual winners and losers. It is a race against time. If we succeed, we all win. But if we should fail, humanity loses.

Index

Printed in the United States
by Baker & Taylor Publisher Services